10/29/93

# SCIENCE UNDER SIEGE

# SCIENCE

## UNDER

# SIEGE

## Balancing Technology and the Environment

### Michael Fumento

WILLIAM MORROW AND COMPANY, INC.
*New York*

It is the policy of William Morrow and Company, Inc., and its imprints and affiliates, recognizing the importance of preserving what has been written, to print the books we publish on acid-free paper, and we exert our best efforts to that end.

Library of Congress Cataloging-in-Publication Data

Fumento, Michael.
      Science under siege / by Michael Fumento.
        p.    cm.
      Includes index.
      ISBN 0-688-10795-8
      1. Environmental health—United States.   2. Environmental
protection—United States.   3. Errors, Scientific.   I. Title.
RA566.F86      1993
363.1—dc20                                                    92-14307
                                                                 CIP

Printed in the United States of America

First Edition

1  2  3  4  5  6  7  8  9  10

BOOK DESIGN BY PAUL CHEVANNES

For Mary, whom we almost lost

"Bright Eyes, how can you close and fail?
How can the light that burned so brightly
suddenly burn so pale?"

# Acknowledgments

My first and foremost thanks are to my able and untiring research assistant, Mary Oliver, for her efforts in making this a much better book and less tedious to write than it would otherwise have been. Matt Kaufman served as an editorial consultant and sounding board for the entire manuscript. Without the assistance and encouragement of Billy Richards, this book would probably not exist. Dr. Petr Beckmann, publisher of the Boulder, Colorado–based *Access to Energy* newsletter, has served as an able consultant on the chapters concerning electric and magnetic fields and as an inspiration by his ever-willingness to challenge the prevailing myths with a sharp tongue and an even drier sense of humor. David Rothbard and Craig Rucker of the Committee for a Constructive Tomorrow (CFACT) were of great assistance on the chapter on food irradiation, as was Dr. Edward Josephson, professor of food science and nutrition at the University of Rhode Island. Dr. Edwin Carstensen, professor of physics in the Department of Electrical Engineering at the University of Rochester, was key in helping me understand and simplify the difficult aspects of electromagnetic radiation. Dr. Bruce Ames of the Department of Biochemistry, University of California at Berkeley, has helped this project in many ways, among them his contributions to the chapters on Alar and rodent testing of carcinogens, to which his Berkeley colleague Dr. Lois Gold was also of great help. Dr. Michael Gough, program manager of Biological Applications at the congressional Office of Technology Assessment, was also invaluable to me as a phone consultant on the dioxin and Agent Orange chapters, as well as on other parts of the book. Dr. Donald Stedman, professor of chemistry at the University of Denver, was a sine qua non to the chapter on gasohol and to my understanding of clean air regulations—to the extent that clean air regulations are comprehensible. Dr. Joel Hay, chairman of the Department of Pharmaceutical Economics at the University of Southern California, has also been an able general consultant. Alan Hoffman at *Investor's Business Daily* was responsible for the book's graphics.

My friends and agents Glen Hartley and Lynn Chu have repeatedly made efforts on my behalf that go above and beyond the call of duty to a client. Liza Dawson, my editor at William Morrow and Company, has displayed, in addition to her considerable talents with a pencil, a rare courage in accepting a manuscript that resists running with what has so aptly been labeled the "herd of independent minds."

The Sarah Scaife and W. H. Brady foundations, along with the Madison Institute for Educational Affairs and the Center for Science, Technology & Media, provided generous support for this project.

I would also like to mention three persons who were a source of great inspiration to me as exemplars in their wisdom and courage. Dr. Alexander Langmuir, former chief epidemiologist at the federal Centers for Disease Control in Atlanta, brought to epidemiology the rigorous scientific methodology thanks to which the discipline came of age. All epidemiologists and all of us who do research and publish in the field of epidemiology are indebted to him. Edith Efron, whose work is cited repeatedly in this book, elevated science journalism to a new height, even as others were bringing it to new lows. Miss Efron has influenced my thinking since I was an adolescent, when I found an article of hers so eye-opening that I kept it in my wallet until it fell apart years later.

Her willingness and ability to challenge with painstaking research a status quo built on ignorance and sentimentalism will continue to inspire other writers and thinkers long after she has gone.

And gone, alas, is Warren Brookes, the hardest-working science and economics reporter in the country. Always several years ahead of the learning curve, he departed several years ahead of schedule as well. Science had no greater defender than he.

# Contents

# Introduction

There is nothing we could not do. Invisibility, levitation—anything. I could float off this floor like a soap bubble if I wished. I do not wish to, because the Party does not wish it. You must get rid of those nineteenth-century ideas about the laws of nature. We make the laws of nature.

—Party Member O'Brien in George Orwell's *1984*[1]

As the first millennium drew to a close, many a medieval man was terrorized by the notion that life on Earth would go out with it, that somehow God had decided that one thousand years was enough. As the end of the second millennium approaches, we are once again warned that the end of the world is nigh. This time, however, it is not God who threatens to pull the plug, but we. We pump death-dealing chemicals into our water, air, food, and soil. Our personal computers are as deadly as they are useful. The very energy that makes modern man's life so much easier than that of previous generations, that runs his lights, heaters, refrigerators, air conditioners, ovens, and household appliances, is pumping cancer into the bodies of his children. Notwithstanding our long life expectancies, we in the developed world are under a constant and growing assault from the products and by-products of modern living.

Or are we?

Did dioxin cause massive illness among residents of Love Canal and among Vietnam vets exposed to it through Agent Orange?

Does it still threaten persons living downstream from paper plants that release small amounts of it into waterways? Has a chemical sprayed on apples to promote growth promoted cancer in children instead? Does your video display terminal at work or home really threaten your life or that of your unborn child? Do the power lines that carry electricity to your house bring cancer as well? Do legally mandated gasoline additives really clean up the air, or do they simply line the pockets of unscrupulous businessmen and politicians?

Activists have compared the environmental health problems of today with the scourge of communicable and infectious diseases in earlier ages. As one activist put it, "Earlier generations lived in fear of polio and smallpox. Nowadays, the most deadly epidemics we face are man-made. Chemical dumpsites, radioactive wastes, acid rain, toxic shock syndrome . . . food additives and more. These are the perils that most threaten our health today."[2] In the last few years they have produced hundreds of books, countless television shows, and a spate of movies that disseminate this message to the public.

But is what they are telling us accurate? Or does the real assault on the public come not so much from chemicals, computer terminals, and electricity as it does from the media, environmental activists, government bureaucrats and politicians, and industry opportunists who warn us that modern life carries with it a multitude of new risks of death?

Are the conclusions these books and shows and movies seek to beat into our consciousness scientifically based? Or are they built on arguments that disdain science, like those of the Party in George Orwell's *1984,* which viewed science as either the enemy or a thing to be manipulated?

Finally, is it possible that by concentrating so much attention and money on preventing slight or unverifiable risks we are diverting attention and other resources away from the many real risks in life?

Current environmental issues are numerous, and often they overlap. Nonetheless, they can be broadly broken down into three categories. First, there are the macro issues: global warming, the ozone layer, and acid rain. These alleged problems spill over borders, involving potentially more than one country in the case of acid rain, and the whole planet in the case of global warming and the ozone layer. Second, there is population control, which can be considered either a local or a global problem. If man is a great threat to the planet, it seems reasonable to reduce his numbers. The bible of the population control movement is the 1968 book *The Population Bomb* and the writer of this gospel is Paul Ehrlich, whose teachings have won many a disciple. Third, there are the micro issues. These are the things that may occur all over the country—indeed, all over the planet—but are still localized in their effect.

This book will concentrate on the micro issues for two reasons. First, they are the ones for which we have the most data and for which the least speculation is required. In the case of population control and the macro issues, the argument of the doomsayers is that if we don't begin taking severe measures, something awful is *going* to happen. By contrast, in the case of the micro issues, the assertion is that something awful has, to some extent, *already* happened and that this harm foreshadows worse to come. The micro issues are thus the most susceptible to empirical analysis, and therefore the most readily proven or disproven. Second, the micro issues also have the greatest impact at this time. Ehrlich's prediction that tens of millions of Americans would have died by now has thus far proven wrong, though he continues to hold that his only mistake was in timing. Whatever havoc global warming may wreak has not yet materialized, and while skin cancer rates have been going up for some time now, there is no evidence that this results from a thinning ozone layer rather than from an increase in the number of people exposing themselves longer to the sun and to tanning beds. The death toll from any of these macro issues, if they are indeed to have a lethal effect, remains a thing of the future. In the case of the micro issues, however, we are told that deaths are occurring in the present. Death—and life—are very much the subjects of this book.

As all the major micro environmental issues are too numerous to examine in detail, this book will not be encyclopedic in its reach, but rather will function as an expedition. If that expedition is successful, it will bring back all sorts of information that apply to subjects not broached in these pages, including those that will not materialize for years to come. It will tell us what threats may be real and which of them may be exaggerated or even nonexistent; it will tell us about the people we trust to make decisions that affect our lives—the environmentalists who lobby the politicians, the politicians who pass laws and set up bureaucracies, the bureaucrats who carry out those laws and promulgate their own, and the media, who we trust to fairly and accurately report to us the impact of those decisions and the conditions that led to those decisions in the first place.

This book is a plea for rational public policy, one that says a life saved is a life saved regardless of whether the threat to that life is environmental or something else in nature. I had originally thought that this point would be made strictly through the telling of others' experiences, but that was not to be. To celebrate completion of the book, I and my research assistant, Mary Oliver, planned to drive to San Francisco from our homes in Los Angeles. We never made it. While negotiating Pacific Coast Highway, the car spun out, plunged headfirst off a cliff, rolled several times, and stopped just short of the jagged rocks at the shoreline, 350 feet down. Mary suffered massive head injuries and a broken neck, bleeding profusely for two hours while we waited for equipment that could effect a rescue from such forbidding terrain.

I was told in doctor's parlance that she probably would not live. She did, and has since fully recovered. But less fortunate were two brothers who some months earlier had gone off the cliff at the same spot, marked now with a half-hidden white wooden cross. The U.S. Environmental Protection Agency has issued regulations with price tags ranging from $6.9 million to $3.5 billion per theoretical life saved, and California supplements these regulations with the most stringent and costly environmental regulations in the nation. Yet apparently the state thought that a guard rail, which costs all of $1,000 per 100 feet, including installation, was too expensive to prevent further loss of life at what it already knew to be literally a dead man's curve.

May my readers be spared such a brutal lesson in the economics of resource allocation, but may they also realize that such casualties in suffering and in death are not merely theoretical. Nor do they just happen to "the other guy." They are very real, and they are ones with which we must all come to terms.

Michael Fumento<br>Los Angeles, California

*So long as the mother, Ignorance, lives, it is not safe for Science, the offspring, to divulge the hidden causes of things.*

—Johannes Kepler

*Ignorance is strength.*

—Party slogan, George Orwell's *1984*

# CHAPTER 1

# The Alarm over Alar

It's sweet and it doesn't have any of that stuff they spray on apples.[1]

—George Bush, on why he drinks carrot juice

"The most potent cancer-causing agent in our food supply is a substance sprayed on apples to keep them on the trees longer and make them look better." Those were the first terrifying words heard by an estimated fifty million viewers of a terrifying segment of CBS's *60 Minutes*, broadcast on February 26, 1989.[2]

And there was literally panic in the streets:

- In the Los Angeles public school district—second largest in the nation—cafeteria workers in over five hundred schools yanked apples, apple sauce, and apple pie from lunch line counters and deleted these products from their menus.[3] Across the nation and even in Asia,[4] stock boys and store managers pulled apple products off their shelves and packed them away, and threw out their fresh apples.
- Frenzied parents, scared for their children's lives, flooded their family physicians with calls.[5]
- In short order the price of apples fell to their lowest point in years—around $7 for a 420-pound box, well below the $12

19

break-even level—and remained depressed for most of 1989.[6] Industry economists have estimated immediate out-of-pocket losses for Washington State apple growers alone of $135 million for 1989. That doesn't include other expenses such as publicity campaigns to repair a damaged reputation, or costs to processors. It also doesn't include other states, although Washington is by far the largest producer of red apples. This $135 million was part of a projected revenue of $875 million, representing a 15 percent loss.[7]

- Apple shipments from warehouses in California to Maryland declined precipitously, costing orchards a fortune and throwing produce markets into chaos. In some parts of the country, the sale of apple juice came to a virtual halt.[8] Prices plunged—and in the months that followed, a number of orchards, most of them small and family-owned, collapsed and underwent foreclosure. "It was a real bloodbath for us this year," said Dennis Walsh, the manager of a seventy-eight-year-old apple cooperative that declared bankruptcy in 1989 after the alarm. The market was so bad that growers couldn't give their apples away, according to Walsh. "The Alar thing came after a couple of bad back-to-back years. It just killed the growers."[9]

This was the Great Apple Scare of 1989, the result of one of the slickest, most cynical fear campaigns in recent American history. The immediate target was Alar, the trade name for daminozide, a growth regulator used to promote uniform ripening of red apples and to improve the fruit's appearance. That chemical, which had been used for twenty-one years with no observable ill effects and which had been knowingly allowed to remain on the market by the Environmental Protection Agency (EPA), was suddenly tried, convicted, and sentenced to death by the media. In fact, the larger target of those responsible for the Alar hysteria was all chemical pesticides, which many environmental extremists believe must be banned—through legislation and regulation if possible, through a smear campaign if necessary.

## AN APPLE A DAY?

Alar is a chemical that was developed by the Uniroyal Chemical Company of Bethany, Connecticut, in the early 1960s to be sprayed over orchards growing varieties of red and Golden Delicious apples. It has also been used on grapes, cherries, peaches, pears, peanuts, and tomato transplants in greenhouses, and is still used on ornamental plants.

The chief advantage of Alar for the apple grower was that it allowed an entire orchard to be harvested just once instead of periodically over six weeks as individual fruits ripened. For marketers, the advantages lay in the production of more uniformly shaped and colored fruit, and in extending the usual six- to eight-month shelf life of apples up to a year. Alar can double the volume of fruit produced during the first seven years after planting, by prompting the tree to blossom one and one-half to two years earlier than otherwise. Even after that initial period, by keeping the fruit on the tree and off the ground, the chemical saved some apple growers as much as 25 percent of their crop a year. By preserving the fruit after it was picked, it allowed consumers to have fresh red apples all year long. Alar was not only the best chemical for the job, it was the only chemical with those abilities and as such was treated as a godsend when it was introduced.[10]

Both *60 Minutes* and the Natural Resources Defense Council (NRDC), the environmentalist group that planned the anti-Alar campaign, however, downplayed the practicality and economy of Alar, treating it as though it were little more than a food dye, "improving the cosmetic appearance of crops." The media often bought into this as well. In a prealarm story, the *Los Angeles Times* ran a lengthy piece on Alar entitled "It's About Apples, and Growers' Attempt to Make Them Redder."[11]

## A FLY IN THE APPLESAUCE

After developing Alar, in 1966 Uniroyal submitted rat-feeding studies to the U.S. Department of Agriculture, then in charge of pesticide regulation. The rats had developed no tumors and the pesticide was approved, although the test would not pass today's standards since too few rats (thirty-seven) were used.[12]

When Alar breaks down in processing for applesauce or apple juice and to some extent in the apple itself, it forms unsymmetrical 1, 1-dimethylhydrazine (UDMH), which—and this really tickled *60 Minutes* reporter Ed Bradley—is related to the chemical hydrazine that is used as a rocket fuel.[13] Of course, you would probably need to eat a few million jars of applesauce to achieve lift-off. In 1985, the EPA released a draft document looking at four rodent tests performed in the 1970s—three by one researcher, Dr. Bela Toth—and one in 1984, and found Alar "is a clear carcinogen in that it induces a highly significant increase in the incidence of blood-vascular tumors which are normally found at very low incidence in Swiss mice."[14] If you received a press packet from the NRDC, as I did in January of 1990, you would have gotten this information along with a breakdown of the results of the early studies.[15]

Scant attention (two sentences) was paid in the press packet to the findings of the Federal Insecticide, Fungicide and Rodenticide Act (FIFRA) Scientific Advisory Panel (SAP) in September 1985. In fact, after the panel finished evaluating the studies, the EPA reported: "Each of these studies, however, has been examined by the Agency and the FIFRA Scientific Advisory Panel, and has been found not to provide an adequate basis for regulatory action at this time."[16] The EPA subsequently stated that "audits and reviews of these studies have revealed that some of the studies yielded equivocal results and that the other studies have serious flaws or shortcomings in the test methodology and documentation. These facts have led EPA to conclude that the existing studies, singly or in combination, are inadequate to serve as the basis for regulatory action against daminozide."[17] One member of the panel, toxicologist Christopher Wilkinson, put it more succinctly. "The data were terrible," he said.[18] A cancer researcher who was then employed by the EPA and had done a toxicological study on Alar, told me, "There were so many problems, Toth didn't even pass the laugh track."[19]

Specifically, with the Alar studies it appears that in some cases the dose of Alar given to the animals was so large it directly killed (as opposed to giving cancer to) the animals. This is referred to as exceeding the "maximum tolerable dose," or MTD. Further, a subsequent reexamination of the slides of the test-animal tissues and organs suggested that the actual tumor incidence was less than had been reported. Further still, Toth had not used data from concurrent control animals (a control animal is one that is similar to the test animals and treated identically except that it is not given the agent being tested for carcinogenicity), but rather used control animals from an experiment conducted several years earlier. He later published the results from concurrent controls, which showed that they suffered diseases similar to those incurred in the Alar-fed animals.[20]

There were also flaws in the UDMH studies. The UDMH was allowed to remain in the water so long that most of it probably had broken down into different chemicals. The animals used were acknowledged to have suffered, prior to entry in the study, from "severe degenerative diseases." And, again, it appears that the MTD may have been exceeded.[21]

Given these problems, the EPA left Alar and UDMH in the question mark category, listing them as "possible carcinogens." It also lowered its estimate of potential cancers from UDMH from between 1,000 to 10,000 per million to instead 45 per million.[22] (If something is no more than a "possible carcinogen," assigning a death rate to it is problematic, to say the least. But more on this later.)

Now here's where the scenario gets really interesting. Apparently the EPA officials had expected the SAP to rubber-stamp its decision. When it did not, Uniroyal officials were jubilant. But after the meeting, Steven Schatzow, then director of the EPA's Office of Pesticide Programs, herded SAP members into his office. The angry Schatzow demanded, "How can you do this to us?" After a heated exchange with the scientists, he concluded, "Look, I can't tell you what to do, but you might like to think about this once again." The scientists were stunned by such flagrant interference, and all refused to back down.[23] The aforementioned former EPA researcher told me, "It was the only time I've ever seen the SAP angry. In all the years I'd been with the EPA, I never saw a directive come down like that in *that* direction." She explained that under Reagan appointee Anne Burford Gorsuch, directives had come down to give the green light to questionable chemicals, but never had she seen the EPA give the red light to a chemical no more harmful than any number of other chemicals that the EPA had not hesitated to approve. When I asked Schatzow in 1991 why he took the actions he did, he readily stated that he had already come to the conclusion that Alar or at least UDMH was a carcinogen before the SAP panel ever met. He explained that while he was not a scientist, there were scientists at the EPA who were convinced that, even though the Toth study was flawed, Alar or at least UDMH was a carcinogen, and they convinced him as well. He said he also believed the SAP panel was very "conservative" in a political sense. Of his angry reaction to the SAP panel he said, "When you've invested time in a subject you get pumped up on it."[24]

Thus, in January 1986, the agency reluctantly delayed its proposed ban. But it ordered Uniroyal to continue testing Alar for carcinogenicity and to launch new studies to check for UDMH-induced genetic damage.[25]

But now, in light of the regulatory setback, the NRDC, consumer activist Ralph Nader, and other antichemical activists sprang into action.[26] Through threats, intimidation, and their access to media outlets, they waged war against Alar. On national television in 1987, Nader boasted of how he got supermarkets to ban Alar-treated apples:

> So I decided to go direct to the supermarkets. I called up the head of Safeway one day, in Oakland, California . . . [and] I said, "We're going to start a campaign to get Alar out of apples but why don't you save us a lot of trouble and yourself by saying that you're not going to buy any apples or apple products with Alar from your growers." A week later [he] puts out a press release saying no more Alar apple products are being bought. . . . So then we called up Grand Union, Kroger, A&P and guess what, we said, "Safeway's not selling Alar-treated apples anymore." So they got them out.[27]

Those stores didn't stop selling Alar-treated apples because scientific data showed the chemical to be dangerous or because they at least thought scientific data showed it to be dangerous or because consumers demanded that they stop using it. They did so because a man with a very big stick exerted brute intimidation against them. Similar pressure has been brought to bear against stores selling irradiated food, as will be seen in Chapter 7.

Meanwhile, the results of numerous tests came in to the EPA. Three tests to see if UDMH caused genetic damage proved negative.[28] A fourth, initially fuzzy, was repeated and also turned out negative.[29]

Two more animal tests on Alar also came in prior to the 1989 scare. Later a *Reader's Digest* writer reported on what happened with those tests. "The EPA phoned Ray Cardona at Uniroyal and ordered the company to *quadruple* the UDMH maximum dose levels. Cardona hung up in disbelief. The EPA was stacking the deck" (emphasis in original).[30]

The results of a ninety-day UDMH feeding study several years earlier had indicated that the MTD for UDMH was 20 ppm per day. The EPA was ordering Uniroyal to use four times that, four times the number that could kill mice directly without necessarily causing cancer.[31]

Uniroyal tried to appeal the EPA's demand. It went to Wilkinson, who was no longer on the SAP panel, and urged him to use his credibility with the EPA to get the agency to reconsider. Wilkinson said, "We went along to tell EPA that it was crazy to do this because you'd be exceeding the maximum tolerated dose and the animals would die." But, he added, the EPA took "not one whit of notice."[32]

These two higher-dose tests were reported by the International Research and Development Corporation (IRDC) in August 1988. The studies involved feeding rats and mice at various dosage levels, and they demonstrated that Alar did not increase the incidence of cancer in either mice or rats when fed doses as high as 10,000 parts per million (ppm), or 1 percent of the entire diet, per day. Alar was completely off the hook. (This notwithstanding, *60 Minutes* specified that the "most potent cancer-causing agent in our food supply" was "this one chemical called *daminozide* [Alar], not UDMH" [emphasis in original].[33] UDMH was also negative at all doses in rats. In mice, however, while no tumors were observed at either 10 or 200 ppm/day after two years, one mouse of a group of forty-five that had been fed UDMH for one year at 40 ppm/day had a lung tumor, and blood vessel tumors (both benign and malignant). Lung tumors (benign only) were observed in eleven of fifty-two animals that had received 80 ppm of UDMH per day. As Wilkinson and Uniroyal had warned, the mice died in droves during the study. Indeed, an amazing *80* percent of the mice had died prematurely because of extreme toxicity, strongly suggesting that the MTD had again been surpassed.[34]

An independent review of all the studies to that date by Dr. Christine Chaisson of Technical Assessment Systems, a former EPA researcher and present consultant to the EPA, Uniroyal, and other organizations, found that "the weight of the evidence clearly favors classification of daminozide as non-carcinogenic."[35] Although the "Chronology for Daminozide" in the NRDC's packet ends with a date in January 1989, and although the chronology appears quite comprehensive, it omitted the 1988 studies.

No study on Alar or UDMH would *ever* demonstrate a cancer risk. The next to last study was released in September 1989, several months after the Alar scare. In it, IRDC reported the results of its two-year study of rats and UDMH, stating that "it is this writer's opinion that these results do not provide conclusive evidence for a test article related oncogenic [carcinogenic] effect in this study."[36] It is important to note that this is standard phraseology for an animal carcinogenic study. Keeping in mind that it is impossible to prove a biological negative, the studies will simply report that there is no evidence to support a positive finding.

The final UDMH study, released in February 1990, reported: "The test substance did not induce any unusual or unexpected tumors but did appear to increase the incidence rates for two common tumors of the lungs and blood vessels"; yet it further stated that indications were "the MTD was exceeded in both high and low dose animals."[37]

But the EPA decided to ignore the possibility that the MTD had been exceeded, which makes sense since it had been the agency that ordered the MTD to be exceeded in the first place. It also decided to ignore the results of the tests on rats. It also decided to ignore the non-MTD mouse-test results. Thus, on February 1, 1989, EPA Acting Administrator John Moore issued a statement finding that "there is inescapable and direct correlation" between exposure to UDMH and "the development of life-threatening tumors"[38] and that therefore the EPA would soon propose barring Alar. In the interim he urged farmers currently using the chemical to stop.[39]

Amazingly, at the same time, on February 1, 1989, the EPA released a three-page statement detailing the results of laboratory animal studies on Alar and UDMH to date. The statement reported: "[1] Although biological trends were noted in the mouse study, tests at 10,000 ppm for two years with the parent compound

[Alar, as opposed to UDMH] were statistically negative for cancer response. . . . [2] The cancer response in the current UDMH data is seen only in one species at a relatively high dose. . . . [and] [3] Mutagenicity data for UDMH are equivocal to negative."[40] This refers to, among others, a test developed by University of California, Berkeley, Department of Chemistry, researcher Dr. Bruce Ames, that analyzes a chemical to determine if it causes mutations in bacterial DNA. The ability of a chemical to cause such mutations has been shown to have a fairly high correlation with chemicals that cause cancer in lab animals.[41]

A fourth finding of the EPA in the February 1989 report was "mice in the 'high dose' study are dying early." The agency said that it believed "the death of these mice was due to the tumors, but it may nonetheless be argued that the deaths were the result of excessive toxicity, which may compromise the outcome of the study."[42]

Thus, the EPA's own findings seemed in complete contradiction with its ruling. That made the agency at least a little uneasy, and was the explanation Moore gave for why he was not using EPA's authority to immediately suspend the use of Alar.[43] It was not much consolation to Uniroyal or to apple growers—rather like Henry VIII's messenger telling Catherine Howard that she would soon lose her head but that she could console herself that it would be a private ceremony. Yet, this refusal to invoke an immediate ban, according to *The New York Times* report, provoked "outrage" on the part of some environmentalists.

But they needn't have worried. For help, in the form of the NRDC, Fenton Communications, the American media, and *60 Minutes* in particular, was fast on its way.

## NRDC AND FENTON TO THE RESCUE

The Natural Resources Defense Council was founded in 1970 and serves as the litigation arm of the environmentalist movement though it does not normally conduct scientific studies itself. With about one hundred thousand members, it is one of the most powerful and well-funded of the nation's environmental organizations and in 1985 was rated the most influential of them by congressional and EPA staff members. As the title of a *Wall Street*

*Journal* article indicated, NRDC's "Influence on U.S. Environmental Laws, Policies, Earns It a Reputation as a Shadow EPA."[44] The NRDC is politically nowhere near the mainstream. Gregg Easterbrook, a regular writer for the *Atlantic, Newsweek,* and the *New Republic,* and a self-described liberal, identifies the NRDC as "hard-left; reporters rely on it for quotes expressing outrage at anything government or industry does."[45]

In 1987, the NRDC, along with Ralph Nader and Nader's Public Citizen group, filed suit against the EPA and Uniroyal in an attempt to banish Alar, but the Alar case was one that the NRDC could not win. In late 1988, the U.S. Court of Appeals for the Ninth Circuit (Washington State) threw the case out, claiming that the NRDC lacked jurisdiction to make the challenge.[46] So the NRDC decided to shift tactics and bypass the EPA and the courts with a study called *Intolerable Risk: Pesticides in Our Children's Food.*[47]

Orchestrating the NRDC campaign was a public relations firm called Fenton Communications. Fenton, led by David Fenton, is an ideologically motivated organization, having earlier done work for the Marxist Sandinista government in Nicaragua, the Marxist Grenadan government of Maurice Bishop, and Soviet- and Cuban-backed Angola, which contracted to pay Fenton a minimum of $180,000 a year plus expenses to carry out an "information strategy," including contacts with "influential editors, reporters, producers, anchormen, columnists and news media executives in the United States."[48] David Fenton was so pleased with his handling of the Alar campaign that he developed a case of what mobsters call "diarrhea of the mouth" and released a document boasting unabashedly of how he had used practically the entire American media as if they were minions.

Fenton explained that he divided the campaign into two sections in hopes that the media would treat it as separate stories, because "more repetition of NRDC's message was guaranteed." The media took the bait, along with the hook, the line, and the sinker. Story one was the NRDC's *Intolerable Risk* study. Story two, set for release one week after the release of story one, had popular actress and longtime supporter of environmental causes Meryl Streep announcing the formation of Mothers and Others for Pesticide Limits.[49]

By agreement, CBS's *60 Minutes* was allowed to break the

*Intolerable Risk* story.[50] That agreement necessarily prevented the NRDC from submitting its report to the scientific community for "peer" review and publication in a journal of science or medicine. NRDC's decision to publish in the lay press suggested that it wished to avoid this burden. (Indeed, then-Food and Drug Administration [FDA] Commissioner Frank Young later stated, "This is one of the worst instances of where statements were made without the benefit of scientific review."[51]) Follow-up interviews were arranged months in advance with major women's magazines like *Family Circle, Woman's Day,* and *Redbook,*[52] usually bearing titles similar to *Redbook*'s "The Foods That Are Poisoning Your Child."[53] Appearance dates were scheduled for *Donahue,* ABC's *Home Show,* and double appearances on NBC's *Today Show.* Mothers and Others made separate appearances on all of those shows and in many other places as well. From here the story simply snowballed, with MacNeil/Lehrer, *The New York Times* and *The Washington Post* doing follow-up stories[54] (although the *Post* later did a critical one),[55] as did all three evening network shows.[56]

But dupery didn't account for all of the favorable media reaction. At a conference sponsored by the Smithsonian Institution in September 1989, titled "Global Environment: Are We Overreacting?" and cochaired by the CEOs of ABC, CBS, NBC, Turner Broadcasting System, Warner, Time, and *The Los Angeles Times* among others, Charles Alexander declared, "As the science editor of *Time* I would freely admit that on this issue we have crossed the boundary from news reporting to advocacy." That statement received a heavy round of applause. NBC reporter Andrea Mitchell agreed, saying, "Clearly the networks have made that decision now, where you'd have to call it advocacy." Then-executive editor of *The Washington Post* Ben Bradlee did offer a cautionary note, stating, "I don't think there's any danger in what you suggest. There's a minor danger in saying it because as soon as you say, 'To hell with the news, I'm no longer interested in news, I'm interested in causes,' you've got a whole kooky constituency to respond to." To which *Wall Street Journal* editorial writer David Brooks, who appears to present to have been the only reporter in the country who felt the public had a right to hear about the conference, sardonically noted, "Mr. Bradlee is right. Probably a lot of 'kooks' believe in objective journalism."[57]

At the height of the Alar alarm, the U.S. Senate called a special

hearing, at which Streep and others urged that Uniroyal immediately pull Alar off the market so that consumers could be sure
apples were completely safe. "What's a mother to do?" she
asked.[58] Congressman Gerry Sikorski (D-Minn.), himself vice
chairman of the House Subcommittee on Health and the Environment, also testified at the Senate hearings. Sikorski admitted
at the hearings, "I am not a scientist or researcher, a medical
doctor or oncologist, a biologist or horticulturist. I am [only] a
father."[59] But on the first *60 Minutes* Alar installment he nonetheless felt he had the expertise to charge that the EPA "is turning
American parents into the malevolent stepmother in Snow White,
handing out enticingly red but fatal apples to our children."[60]
Indeed, quite ignoring the lag time between inducement of damage to DNA that eventually results in cancer and the actual appearance of the tumor, often twenty years or more, Sikorski told
*60 Minutes* viewers, "Go to a cancer ward in any children's hospital
in this country. See these bald, wasting away kids." Even if everything NRDC claimed about Alar were true and these kids lived
on a pure applesauce and apple juice diet, they wouldn't have
had *time* to have gotten their cancer from Alar. The imagery was
stark. It was moving. It was false.

As is often the case during scares, industry helped cut its own
throat. Those companies judged "unacceptable" by *Consumer
Reports* announced immediate measures to stop using Alar-
treated apples, while those that scored well on the survey sought
to capitalize on it. For example, Beech-Nut Nutrition Corporation, fresh from its conviction and $2.2 million fine for having
sold sugar water as apple juice, was so happy with its score on
the test that it sent out two press releases alerting the media to
the survey even before *Consumer Reports* released it, with one
of them stating that the corporation's president would "be available for interviews about what the study findings mean for mothers of infants and for the safety of the nation's food supply
generally."[61]

Stores got in on the act too, even before the NRDC scare, by
selling apples they declared to be "Alar-free." Alas, surveys done
by newspapers in several metropolitan areas revealed that luxury
and health-oriented stores were not necessarily selling Alar-free
apples, even when they specifically claimed they were. Those
stores had the best of both worlds—profiting from the use of Alar

while they profited from the fear of it.[62] Even Safeway was implicated in such a practice, indicating that they had put one over on Ralph Nader—undoubtedly much to his chagrin.[63]

Fenton's memo included the words, in bold type, "Usually, it takes a significant natural disaster to create this much sustained news attention for an environmental problem. We believe this experience proves there are other ways to raise public awareness for the purpose of moving the Congress and policymakers."[64] Indeed.

Although both the EPA and the American Council on Science and Health (ACSH), an organization that frequently counters pesticide alarms, moved quickly to counter the NRDC effort, the mainstream media for the most part gave them short shrift or ignored them altogether. Thus, for example, *USA Today* gave no room to the opposition in its "cover story" on the NRDC report and but two sentences to the EPA in its cover story on Mothers and Others (which it quickly allowed to be refuted).[65] The article also put in large type right below the title, " 'She [Meryl Streep] wants safe food. We all do.' $3 call to group," followed by a 900 telephone number. In effect, it provided free advertising on the front page of the newspaper to a number that would bring in money for Mothers and Others.

Indeed, while Fenton's campaign was beautifully orchestrated, it would have failed but for the eager complicity of a media reacting, as is its wont, to the pressure for sensational stories. The titles of these articles are worth the proverbial thousand words. In addition to *Redbook*'s "Poisoning," *Time* proclaimed, "Watch Those Vegetables, Ma," titled another story, "Dining with Invisible Danger," and titled yet another story, "Do You Dare to Eat a Peach?" *Newsweek*'s offering began "WARNING!" with the letters taking up one fifth of the page, and continued "Your Food, Nutritious and Delicious, May Be Hazardous to Your Health." *USA Today* declared, "Fear: Are We Poisoning Our Children?" *People* alluded to Jimmy Stewart's stone honest Mr. Smith with "Ms. Streep Goes to Washington to Stop a Bitter Harvest," and *Woman's Day* asked "Are Pesticides Poisoning Our Children?"[66]

Clearly the media were convinced. Clearly they very much wanted to be. Indeed, even a representative of the NRDC later said that the media distorted and simplified the NRDC report, admitting that "most of the press reports" lacked "context or perspective."[67] But what was the real story?

## THE PROFITS OF DOOM

Three months after its Alar blockbuster, *60 Minutes* aired its second show on the subject. Ed Bradley began the follow-up by attacking the credibility of Elizabeth Whelan, president of the ACSH, whom it had invited onto the show to dispute the NRDC's Alar claims. Said Bradley, "Dr. Whelan readily admits her organization is subsidized by food processing companies and pesticide manufacturers, including Uniroyal, which makes Alar." Then he said to Whelan on camera, "It just seems to some people that you are supporting a chemical, Alar, and you're taking money from the people who make it; that therefore, that might influence your judgment."[68] Never mind that he could have gotten any number of experts who did not get chemical industry money to say what Whelan did, the fallacy built into the Bradley attack was that somehow those defending synthetic chemicals are always operating out of the profit motive, while the NRDC and its ilk operate out of the pure goodness of their hearts. But as an editorial by *Science* editor Daniel Koshland, Jr., written as a reaction to the Alar scare, put it:

> It's time to recognize that public interest groups have conflicts of interest, just as do business groups, even though their public positions are [straightforward]. Businesses prefer to be out of the limelight; public interest groups like to be in it. Because they are selling products in the marketplace, businesses downplay discussions of hazard. Because public interest groups acquire members by publicity, they emphasize hazards. . . . Businesses today have product liability and can incur legal damages if they place a dangerous product on the market. Public interest groups have no such constraints at the moment.[69]

While the ACSH receives most of its funding from foundations, it does also receive money from businesses that it sometimes ends up defending, including those in the chemical industry, environmental groups like to dismiss ACSH as merely an industry front, with Whelan crying, "My pesticide, right or wrong!"[70] Writes Gary Null in his book *Clearer, Cleaner, Safer, Greener:* "Contrary to what its name suggests, the council is privately funded and, more often than not, functions as a mouthpiece for the industry."[71]

Clearly, one's source of revenue can and does influence one's actions. Wrote one author:

> A detailed survey . . . confirmed that magazines which carried cigarette advertisements (which accounted for 15 to 30 percent of their total ad revenues) failed miserably in reporting about the contribution of cigarettes to environmentally induced disease. Candid reports by journalists have revealed that magazines carefully discouraged pejorative comments about their advertisers, particularly those of tobacco products.[72]

The group that conducted that study was the ACSH, and the author referred to was Elizabeth Whelan. And the point she makes is correct. When people give you money on a steady basis, there is inevitably a quid pro quo. On the other hand, it would be foolish to suggest that the ACSH are a bunch of mercenaries. No one has ever suggested that Whelan does not earnestly believe in the general causes of her organization.

Further, imagine a prosecutor telling a jury, "Pay no attention to the defense attorney; after all, he's being paid by the defendant!" Yes, in America even chemical companies deserve a fair trial. Both the ACSH and the NRDC are advocacy organizations; both make their living by promoting a set view. The responsible reporter takes both sides with a grain of salt, as would a responsible juror. The problem is, to most of the media jurors it seems the chemical companies and their lobbyists are always the bad guys, and they convict them before the trial even starts.

As for the NRDC, Fenton told the leftist magazine *Propaganda Review* his campaign was designed so that revenue would blow back to the NRDC from the public. The group sold a book about pesticides, *For Our Kids' Sake,*[73] written by a journalist who is also an active foe of food irradiation,[74] through a 900 number advertised on the *Donahue* show and within a year ninety thousand copies had been sold.[75] In a May 22, 1989, memo to his own interested parties, Fenton noted that a "modest investment by NRDC re-paid itself manyfold in tremendous media exposure (and substantial, immediate revenue . . .)."[76] If it is true that ACSH gets 10 percent of its money from pesticide companies like Uniroyal, it's also true that NRDC gets 100 percent of its money by convincing donors that chemical companies like Uniroyal are poisoning the environment.

As will be seen in future chapters as well, the last refuge of the scoundrel (to paraphrase Dr. Samuel Johnson) in the arena of science and politics is to go after motives. If someone says something you don't like and can't refute, attack his motivation. The beauty of going after motives is that it not only allows you to sidestep an argument (which won't be noticed by the reader who isn't looking out for such things), but if you can't find a motive, you can always make one up.

A favorite personal example came to light when I was perusing an article about asbestos in a small quarterly, the *Health-PAC Bulletin*, where I read: "The New York State Asbestos Advisory Committee, in its February 1990 report to Governor Mario Cuomo, accused the Safe Buildings Alliance [SBA] of having conducted 'an extensive and highly misleading disinformation campaign,' including articles placed in *Readers Digest* [*sic*] and *Forbes*."[77] That is, indeed, exactly what the Advisory Committee said, although it gave no indication of how the Safe Buildings Alliance had managed to do this and, indeed, gave no evidence at all to back up its charge.[78] As the author of the "placed" *Reader's Digest* article,[79] I found this accusation to be of interest. I had never heard of the Safe Buildings Alliance until I began work on the article. But who am I to argue with Cuomo's commission or the *Health-PAC Bulletin*? And incidentally, no, the *Health-PAC Bulletin* made no effort to refute the facts of either the *Forbes* or the *Digest* article. It didn't have to. That's the beauty of *ad hominem* attacks. If someone says something you don't want to deal with, you simply assign them an ill motive and you're done with them.

Naturally, *60 Minutes* also profits from controversies in which it becomes involved. It is not for nothing that the show has consistently been near the top in ratings since its inception in 1968. Portraying big corporations like Uniroyal as greedy ogres who think nothing of destroying people's lives is one way to keep the show's ratings high.

## CALCULATED RISK FACTOR

All the media hype aside, just what is the risk of getting cancer from Alar? It depends on who's making the estimate. Using its new data, the NRDC calculated that some 5,500 to 6,200 pre-school children will eventually get cancer from exposure to Alar and seven other pesticides or metabolites (breakdown products) in just the first six years of life. For Alar specifically, they translated that into a risk of 240 cancers in a population of one million. As it happens, the NRDC's "new data" was the EPA's *old data,* which had been gathered before 1985 and had been rejected. But NRDC attorneys Janet Hathaway and Al Meyerhoff said it was the "best data available."[80] Which it was, of course, for them. They simply ignored the two later tests that had appeared by then.[81] As the EPA's John Moore commented in the May-June 1989 issue of the *EPA Journal,* the NRDC findings were "gravely misleading" because they were based on data "rejected in scientific peer review together with food consumption data of unproven validity."[82] Moore said: "In the Alar case, the public was very prone to give credence to the selective and inappropriate use of data regarding consumer risks and to believe 'the worst' despite counter statements from EPA."[83]

In addition, the NRDC built in the most conservative "safety factors" imaginable into its calculations concerning intake and effect. Wilkinson, in fact, calculated that the NRDC had overstated childhood exposure by as much as 389 times.[84] Further, the California Department of Food and Agriculture discovered that the NRDC had arbitrarily excluded from its study food samples with *no* detectable pesticide residues. This alone exaggerated pesticide consumption estimates up to 500 times.[85] Thus, while the EPA standard, if used to estimate pedestrian deaths at a street crossing, would assume the crosser to be blind, lame, and deaf, the NRDC standard would assume him to be blind, able only to crawl, deaf, and crossing the Indianapolis Speedway on Memorial Day. The EPA's new figures had calculated a risk to infants, from exposure for just eighteen months, of nine in one million, which was one–twenty-fifth times lower than the NRDC estimate.[86]

The NRDC said that since children have lower body weights and ingest more Alar-containing products than do adults, they are at much greater risk. Indeed, said the NRDC, more than 50 percent of a person's total lifetime risk is incurred during the first five years of life.[87] Thus, the title of the *Redbook* article: "The Foods That Are Poisoning Your Child"[88] and the other titles mentioned above specifically referring to children. The NRDC's reasoning here, however, was specious. As far as the way chemicals are processed internally is concerned, there are any number of differences in the way that adults and children metabolize a given chemical; and testing on young and old animals has shown little difference in tolerance for carcinogens based on age. The best human data available, which concerns smoking and lung cancer, indicates that only a small fraction of the risk accrues during the first few years of exposure.[89] (Whether this applies to oral ingestion of a substance can be quite a different matter, of course.)

A joint statement of the FDA, the EPA, and the U.S. Department of Agriculture read: "Data used by NRDC which claims cancer risks from Alar are 100 times higher than the Environmental Protection Agency estimates were rejected in 1985 by an independent scientific advisory board created by Congress." It immediately went on to say that "it should also be noted that risk estimates for Alar and other pesticides based on animal testing are rough and are not precise predictions of human disease. Because of conservative assumptions used by EPA, actual risk may be lower or even zero." The statement concluded: "The FDA, EPA, and the U.S. Department of Agriculture believe there is not an imminent hazard posed to children in the consumption of apples at this time despite claims to the contrary."[90]

Further, Moore noted in his congressional testimony that "on March 1, 1989, the National Research Council (NRC)—a part of the National Academy of Sciences—released the most comprehensive report ever assembled on the relationship between diet and health. The NRC found that there was no evidence that residues of individual pesticides in our diet contribute significantly to the overall risk of getting cancer."[91]

## WHAT DOES AN ESTIMATED RISK MEAN?

It is not widely understood what EPA or other organizations' estimates of cancer risks really mean. When such a body says "We believe that there will be as many as twelve hundred excess cancers from product X per year," most people think that really represents twelve hundred people, as if the EPA got into a time machine, went into the future, and ticked off the bodies as they entered the morgue. In fact, there are numerous recurring problems with each such estimate the EPA and other official and unofficial bodies put out. One is that they almost always extrapolate from lab animals to humans, an assumption that may not be valid. Another is that they assume that that which kills lab animals at high doses will also kill humans at the tiniest of doses. This assumption, too, may not be valid. Both of these fallacies are discussed in the next chapter.

Still another problem is that mathematical models give a range of risk estimates. When the EPA or NRDC or whoever says "as many as," they are providing an upper-bound estimate. The upper-bound estimate is the worst-case scenario. And by worst case, just that is meant. Dr. Fred Hoerger, in a paper presented at a 1985 seminar, illustrated the upper-bound estimate and its inherent distortion.

> It can be said that the upper-bound estimate of rainfall for the United States is 15,000 inches per year. Since yearly rainfall in the United States averages from a few inches to perhaps 50 or 60 inches per year, this sounds outlandish. For a moment, let me justify my estimate on the basis of "prudent" predicting principles. The historical record shows the highest single-day rainfall was 43 inches in Alvin, Texas in 1979. Simply multiplying this number by the number of days in a year and extending it to the entire United States gives my estimate of 15,000 inches.[92]

What these estimating officials don't usually tell you (unless a reporter bothers to ask them) is that the *best-case* scenario is almost always zero. But because the statement "may cause anywhere from zero to twelve hundred deaths" can (1) make it look like the estimator really has no idea, and (2) doesn't make for a good story or a good way of attracting attention to a possible problem, the bottom range of the estimate is rarely provided by the media.

## THE END OF ALAR—AND THE BEGINNING OF WHAT?

On May 15, 1989, the apple industry, citing a sharp drop in sales, announced that representatives of the apple industry would stop using Alar by the fall. They said the move was purely financial and that they believed the use of the chemical posed no threat to health.[93] Uniroyal also tossed in the towel, first halting distribution for spraying on food plants in the United States,[94] and later doing so worldwide. This has occurred even though no other country has taken action against Alar.[95] At this writing, Alar is still used for ornamental plants, but the EPA has moved to ban that, as well.[96] According to Uniroyal, Alar at the time of the alarm accounted for less than 1 percent of the company's gross revenues.[97] In addition, congressional legislation was about to be introduced to ban the chemical.[98] Neither for the apple industry nor for Uniroyal was the fight for truth worth the losses they were taking in image and, in the case of the apple growers, in sales.

The British refused to buy into the Alar alarm of their American cousins. The Independent Advisory Committee on Pesticides in a December 1989 report stated: "When all worst case assumptions are combined . . . the intake by infants of UDMH turns out to be 150 times less than the level shown to produce no tumors in animals." The report concluded that "even for infants and children consuming the maximum quantities of apples and apple juice, subjected to the maximum treatment with daminozide, there is no risk from UDMH." The Ministry of Agriculture, Fisheries and Food accepted the advice of the Advisory Committee.[99] Yet Uniroyal felt it would no longer even continue shipping Alar overseas,[100] in part because some of that fruit might end up being imported back into the country, thus starting the melee all over again.[101]

And so, Alar is gone, but its legacy lives on. "The Alar controversy served as a sparkplug for public concern," said NRDC's Janet Hathaway a year after the scare. "Now, there is activity under way to translate that concern into lasting pesticide reform. Alar was symptomatic of the problems that permeate the whole regulatory process."[102] To be sure. But they aren't the problems that Hathaway would have us think.

In the wake of the scare, FDA Commissioner Young condemned the NRDC and its *Intolerable Risk* report, saying, "There has to be a real scientific process, and we have to be able to inform the American people where risks are real. . . . This is one of the worst instances of where statements were made without the benefit of scientific review. That's not the way to do business." Continued Young, "You cannot do risk assessment by media."[103] An ad hoc group of fourteen prominent scientific organizations representing one hundred thousand microbiologists, toxicologists, veterinarians, and food scientists also spoke up, calling the health risks from approved agricultural chemicals "negligible or nonexistent" and stating flatly that the "public's perception of pesticide residues and their effects on the safety of the food supply differs considerably from the facts." What especially concerned them, wrote *Washington Post* business reporter Malcolm Gladwell, was that industry's decision to abandon Alar only fueled the public's misperceptions. "Lurking in the back of the minds of the scientists is a fear that the environmental movement, emboldened by its success in the Alar case, will now move on to other, more economically important agricultural chemicals."[104] That also concerned some of Uniroyal's people. "We sold out on Alar," one told me.

## GETTING PERSONAL

Uniroyal's decision to drop the domestic sale of Alar rendered congressional legislation moot. But that was not enough for some members of the lofty body. Senator Joseph Lieberman (D-Conn.), a member of the EPA oversight committee, and Senator Harry Reid (D-Nev.) attacked the EPA for its waffling on Alar, saying it was riddled with proindustry bias. They decided that the best course of action was to pursue the SAP board that had unanimously rejected the early tests indicating Alar and UDMH as carcinogens, and called for an inquiry into their alleged conflicts of interest. Lieberman stated this charge on the second *60 Minutes* Alar show.[105] He singled out two members of the SAP board as having violated the ethics code; one of whom was Chris Wilkinson. Wilkinson's alleged violation was in having met with the EPA on Uniroyal's behalf, although he had already left the SAP by that time. The other charged member had done something similar on a different subject.[106] After an investigation, the Department of Justice cleared both Wilkinson and the other panelist. The United States inspector general cleared the other six panelists without investigation.[107] Whether the actions will have a chilling effect with future independent advisory boards, as was presumably the intention, remains to be seen.

It is interesting that the alleged conflicts of interest on behalf of the panelists were for having some connection to industry, even if the connection began after they had left the panel. Yet environmental activists such as Ellen Silbergeld, who will figure prominently in the section of this book on dioxin, sat on the EPA's Science Advisory Board at the same time she worked for the Environmental Defense Fund, and no one seems to think anything of it. In fact, *Science* quoted Silbergeld discussing the conflict of interest problems concerning board members and industry without even hinting that she might have had one.[108]

## THE APPLE GROWERS STRIKE BACK

On November 29, 1990, a group of apple growers representing eleven Washington growers filed suit against CBS and the NRDC. It charged that the industry lost more than $100 million following the *60 Minutes* shows. Washington State grows more than 50 percent of the apples sold in the nation's supermarkets. The suit, seeking unspecified damages running to millions of dollars, alleges tortious interference with business. In other words, it is as if butcher A is suing butcher B and a newspaper because butcher B told the newspaper that butcher A was taking deliveries from the local horse farm and the newspaper printed it. Burt Chestnut, an apple grower from Wenatchee who is a plaintiff in the suit, said, "The gain is for agriculture in general nationwide, that we stop this misleading information by the media and scare tactics by environmental groups. We want the media to be responsible." But Steven Berzon, a lawyer representing the NRDC, said the lawsuit could have a chilling effect on public activism. "Beyond Alar, this suit threatened by a small group of Washington growers raises fundamental issues of free speech, and the right of citizens to petition the government on important questions of public policy," said Berzon.[109]

But the right of free speech, whether that guaranteed in the Constitution, which pertains only to government attempts at restriction, or the more restrictive "right" against one's neighbors, has never been seen as limitless. If the head of the Washington apple growers accused Berzon of being a dues-paying member of the Aryan Nations white supremacist group and that in fact was not the case, the grower could be sued for libel and be held responsible for damage to Berzon's reputation. Does such a law have a "chilling effect" on what the apple growers may do? Certainly, but it's the kind of chill that society wants to encourage. Before you accuse someone of being a card-carrying member of a hate group, you'd better have good evidence because you can cause tremendous damage to a person if you're wrong. How strange that an organization the size and strength of the NRDC should insist that you take its word for something without waiting for all the facts to come in and then not hold it accountable for its being wrong later.

## THE WAGES OF CRYING WOLF

Clearly, NRDC's media campaign was a brilliantly executed end run around the court system, the legislature, and most importantly, scientific peer review. It scored a touchdown of terror. The first to suffer were the stores; then came the apple growers, then Uniroyal. But Uniroyal and the stores will survive, as will most of the apple growers. The ultimate victims are those for whom the NRDC claims to be an advocate, the consumers.

This is especially so for consumers making a marginal living. The poorer one is, the higher is the percentage of one's income that is spent on food. Fenton boasted to *Propaganda Review* that because of the Alar scare, "lines started forming in health food stores. The sales of organic produce soared. All of which we were very happy about."[110] It is okay for the wealthy David Fenton or the attorneys of the NRDC to pay health-food store prices for their staples. It's okay for a millionaire like Meryl Streep. But what will it do to the marginal poor who cannot qualify for food stamps or for the poor who refuse to use them? Yet the not-so-hidden agenda of the NRDC and many other environmental public interest groups is to eliminate all chemical pesticides. As the environmental writer for the *Los Angeles Times* noted: "While the NRDC has 30 lawyers and 20 scientists, it has no economist to weigh the costs of an environmental reform against its benefits."[111] In October 1989, Janet Hathaway, in response to a Bush administration pesticide-monitoring plan, stated: "Allowing the EPA to condone continued use of a chemical whenever the benefits outweigh the risks is absolutely anathema to the environmental community."[112] Even when the benefits *outweigh* the risks? Are those the words of an official for a group interested in applying science for the betterment of humanity, or perhaps of one that has gone over the deep end into fanaticism and utopianism?

Fanatics see everything in absolutes. Perspective means nothing to them. Indeed, perspective is deadly to the cause of the pesticide alarmists. So what if UDMH only causes cancer in mice and not rats? *Ban Alar.* So what if by the same or even stricter standards more than a score of natural chemicals have been found to be carcinogenic and have not been banned? *Ban Alar.* So what if, even assuming UDMH to be a human carcinogen, its health benefits outweigh its risks? *Ban Alar.*

One argument used by alarmists that will be discussed throughout this book is known as "erring on the side of caution." Actually, it is not an argument at all; in fact it's not even a nonargument. Rather, it's an antiargument. It says: Instead of debating this issue, let's just assume that I'm right, because if I'm not right, no one will die, but if I am right, lives will be saved. Erring on the side of caution would dictate the banning of all products containing Alar—and many other products, as well. Radio talk show host and journalist Gary Null, in *Clearer, Cleaner, Safer, Greener,* writes:

> One of the most often used reasons for the EPA's decision not to act on a particular pesticide is that it lacks sufficient scientific data to warrant limiting or banning the pesticide. In and of itself, this reliance on scientific certainty is a case for alarm. Many critics, for instance, wonder why the government agencies, which are supposed to be protecting the public health, do not shift the burden of proof and insist that the chemical industry prove the safety of the chemical.[113]

Simple. You can't prove a negative. You can never say a chemical is not an animal carcinogen, simply because no matter how many tests have been run, the next one may show a positive result. By this standard no chemical can ever be proven safe. One only has chemicals that have been proven unsafe, chemicals that haven't been proven unsafe, and chemicals that haven't yet been tested at all. By this standard, any time someone raises a question about a chemical, the chemical banned. That's how "erring on the side of caution" works. Yet, as we will see, regarding virtually every major issue discussed in this book, alarmists will err on the side of caution. The reason is simple: On such a basis, they can never, ever lose. They can provide the weakest arguments in the world, but they will still prevail. What will not prevail is sanity and a proper allocation of resources. The fact is that if we always erred on the side of caution, we would bankrupt the country. Yet, when each case is considered individually, the erring proposition may lull us with its siren song.

Consider the environmental referendum California passed three years before the Alar scare in November 1986, Proposition 65, which directed the governor to list chemicals "known to the state" to cause cancer or reproductive toxic effects, followed by the posting of warnings regarding those chemicals, followed still later by a prohibition against discharge of those chemicals in significant amounts into any actual or potential source of drinking water. The terminology of the act is a nightmare to figure out, the number of chemicals to be listed has already grown from twenty-six to well over two hundred,[114] and few of the enforcement provisions have yet gone into effect. Indeed, strictly speaking, the proposition would prohibit alcoholic drinks, since alcohol is one of the listed chemicals, being both a carcinogen and a cause of birth defects. According to Jeffrey Nedelman, vice president for public affairs for the Grocery Manufacturers of America: "In California, the birth-defect standard is ten times more stringent than anything any scientific organization in the world has endorsed." During hearings on Proposition 65, he says, "the state government brought in as witness top Ph.D.s from the academic community and people from Washington. They found toxicologists, food scientists, risk assessors, and to a man they all said this is crazy, this makes no sense. [Environmental activist Tom] Hayden was there. When his turn came he said, 'I've heard what you have to say, and my only reaction is that we in California want to be better.' "[115]

But better than what, and at what price? Depending on who you ask in California, the state needs more money for police, more money for fire protection, more money for the homeless, more money for AIDS hospices, or simply more money left in people's pockets where it can be spent as they see fit. Should the people of California be funneling their money into a program that essentially puts a little more polish on already sparkling chrome, or should it put its money into uses where the benefit for the dollar is much earlier on the diminishing returns curve?

Alar is gone, at least for use on food-producing plants, but the conflict continues. The issue continues to be used by extremist environmentalists and others as if the threat were as real as first presented. Moreover, the removal of Alar was a successful effort on the part of environmentalist extremists who are constantly in search of an easy new target. Quite possibly as a result of the Alar victory, their "take the pledge"-against-pesticides campaign was kicked off in September 1989, the idea being to eventually cow all grocery stores into taking part.[116] The battle against Alar was merely a small part of the war against pesticides in general, which is a small part of the war against man-made chemicals in general, which is a small part of the war against technology in general. And make no mistake, the assailants, the besiegers of science, will settle for nothing short of total victory.

# CHAPTER 2

# Of Mice (and Rats) and Men: The Politics of Cancer Testing

The World Has Cancer, and the Cancer Is Man.[1]

—The Second Report of the Club of Rome, 1974

Relying on animal testing, the government informed Americans that a fruit was contaminated with a cancer-causing chemical sprayed by farmers. Mothers panicked, stores cleared the shelves of the product, and the fruit industry lost tens of millions of dollars. But no, this wasn't Alar sprayed on apple trees and the year wasn't 1989; it was a weed killer sprayed on cranberries and the year was 1959. That was the Great Cranberry Scare, which unfortunately happened around Thanksgiving of that year. Most Americans busy pitching cranberries and cranberry sauce into the trash were not told that this allegedly dangerous chemical had replaced paint thinner as the previous weed killer of choice in cranberry bogs, at far lower cost and toxicity and dose. Nor were they told that in all probability the weed killer was utterly harmless to humans in the amounts they would be exposed to, that the only groups necessarily at risk were the lab animals who were dosed with huge amounts of the stuff.[2]

The word "carcinogen" in the Natural Resources Defense Council (NRDC) report, *Intolerable Risk,* or indeed in any ref-

45

erence to UDMH or Alar, is based exclusively on animal studies in which massive doses of a chemical are dumped into the animal's body. In the case of UDMH, the daily dose that caused tumors in mice was over 266,000 times higher than the amount ingested every day by those humans (preschool children) alleged to be most at risk. On a per apple basis, assuming the highest amount of UDMH found in a single piece of fruit, a person would have to eat 861 pounds of apples a day in order to ingest just 1 ounce of UDMH a day.[3] Such a discrepancy between what the test animals get and what humans actually consume is not unusual. In 1984, the government banned the insecticide EDB as a carcinogen, yet a person would have to eat 400 tons per day of EDB-laced foods to equal the amount fed rats.[4] In the assessment that the EPA makes to decide what dose to humans may have a hypothetical one-in-a-million chance of causing cancer, the animal receives on average 380,000 times that human dose.[5]

Such studies make a huge number of assumptions, of which two are particularly important. First, it is assumed that enough is known about the mechanism of cancer to permit lab animals to serve as stand-ins for human beings. Second, it is assumed that the results of testing animals with massive doses can be extrapolated to predict for cancer in humans ingesting comparatively tiny doses. Both of these assumptions are generally accepted by the media and by the scientists whom the media regularly tap for information. Yet they are often pooh-poohed by the general public, which seems to carry an inherent prejudice against being compared with rodentia and which has difficulty with the concept of extrapolating from, say, tens of thousands of diet colas a day to one a day. Nevertheless, such prejudices have been passed off as the musings of the ignorant masses and Ralph Nader has stated that "one thing scientists agree on, there is no safe threshold for a cancer-causing substance."[6]

That continues to be the view of the general media and of the environmental activists, but the intellectual opposition has been building force, and its bible has become a voluminous 1984 work by Edith Efron, *The Apocalyptics*. Despite initial desperate efforts to treat her as an irresponsible radical, by the time the dust had settled in 1987, Efron's thesis (and photo) was sitting on the cover of *Cancer Research*, the official scientific journal of the American Association of Cancer Research.[7]

Efron provided flesh for the intuitive belief that something is wrong with pumping a rodent full of chemicals to nearly toxic levels and seeing if any adverse reactions take place. She began by showing that even the scientific community didn't believe it, at least at first. In 1977, John Higginson, founding director of the International Agency for Research on Cancer (IARC), stated: "There is . . . no rational biological method of extrapolating from animals to man."[8] Yet, just one year later, Lorenzo Tomatis of the IARC announced: "In the presence of appropriate experimental carcinogenicity data and in the absense of adequate human data, it is reasonable to regard chemicals for which there is 'strong evidence' of carcinogenicity *as if* they were carcinogenic to humans" (emphasis added).[9] What had happened? Efron wrote: "There were no reasons given for this change in policy except the avowed desire to be 'more useful' to 'national and international authorities.' "[10]

For example, in 1976, David Rall, then-director of the National Institute of Environmental Health Sciences, told Lesley Stahl of CBS on the special "The Politics of Cancer": "Mice and rats predict very well for human cancer."[11] But how did he back up that statement? He immediately added:

If you don't accept the mouse and the rat data, you only have one alternative, and that's letting the human population be exposed for about 25 years and if in fact the compound was carcinogenic you can have a small epidemic of chemical carcinogeneses in man after that 25 years. So I think there's no alternatives. We have to view the mouse and rat data as predictive for man.[12]

The first part of Rall's statement, that mice and rats predict well for humans, is problematic, as will be seen shortly. And the second part contradicts the first part. Indeed, it has all the logic of a medicine man who, when asked how effective shaking a rattle and invoking the gods is in curing a dying man, says: It is very effective for if that doesn't work, then there is no other treatment. If that is the best Rall can do, then we may as well throw dice for each chemical, or perhaps, à la Judge Learned Hand's famous statement, merely "hang" every tenth chemical. Indeed, as will be seen, that is exactly what has happened.

\*     \*     \*

The maximum tolerated dose (MTD) theory is simple enough. Essentially, it involves two surrogates, or substitutions, for real-world exposure. First, instead of humans it uses animals. The reason for that is obvious enough. Second, instead of using vast numbers of animals and giving them doses similar to what humans would be exposed to, MTD uses only a few animals and gives them massive doses, the idea being that it maximizes the chance of finding tumors. Otherwise, according to the MTD theory, it would be prohibitively expensive to test millions of animals, not to mention the difficulty in finding enough people willing to clean their cages.

The MTD thesis, however, has two major weaknesses. First, a chemical which causes cancer in a rodent will not necessarily cause cancer in a human. Indeed, frequently, that which causes cancer in a rat won't do so in a mouse or vice versa. If one chemical has different effects on two such closely related species, clearly the effect it has on either of them is of limited usefulness in evaluating the risk to such a different species as humans which have a life span much longer than that of rats or mice. Such differences in carcinogenicity among lab animals are common. Of 427 chemicals tested in both rats and mice in the animal cancer test database of Berkeley biologist Dr. Lois Gold, almost one fourth tested positive in mice and negative in rats or vice versa. An earlier (1987) evaluation of 214 chemicals tested by the National Institutes of Health National Toxicology Program (NTP) found similar results.[13] Conversely, important human carcinogens may not be detected in standard tests on rodents, as was the case for a long time in the testing of tobacco, and is still questionable about alcohol,[14] the first of which is the largest identified cause of cancer in the United States.[15] Further, while those who rely on the rodent MTD tests accept the rationale that that which causes a specific type of tumor in an animal has a good chance of causing that same tumor in a human, that rationale does not hold up between closely related species. Knowing that a chemical is positive for carcinogenesis at any given site in a rat gives it only a 50-percent chance of causing cancer in a mouse at that same site and vice versa.[16]

As one might suppose, the accuracy of prediction between either rats and humans or mice and humans would not be as good as that between the closely related species of rats and mice. The correlations between hamsters and mice and hamsters and rats are even less than that for rats and mice. Sixty-four percent of rat carcinogens are positive in hamsters, and 61 percent of mouse carcinogens are positive in hamsters.[17] Bearing in mind that because about half of all chemicals are positive in each species, then by sheer chance one would expect a 50 percent accuracy of prediction between species. Given all this, is there any rational reason to treat a mouse or a rat as a little man or woman? Indeed, one study found that nineteen out of twenty probably human *non*-carcinogens were positive in rodent tests, implying that the true positive correlation rate might be as low as 5 percent.*[18]

Rodent MTD tests have identified as carcinogens about half of 800 chemicals tested.[19] Few scientists believe that about half of all chemicals are truly carcinogens, human or rodent.[20] Only 12 percent of chemicals were found to be positive in systematic *Salmonella* mutagenicity testing (the Ames test) of 2,205 chemicals in Japan.[21]

---

*This also has some implications for testing pharmaceutical products on animals before testing them on humans, but there are some important differences. For one, notes Bruce Ames, the doses of, say, a would-be Alzheimer's drug given to the animal is usually much closer to what humans would be receiving than the amount of a possible carcinogen with which a lab animal is dosed.[22] For another, the testing of pharmaceuticals looks at toxicology (the poisoning of an animal), rather than carcinogenicity (the induction of cancerous tumors). Toxicology is much better understood than carcinogenicity; thus, it's far easier to determine whether a rat's reaction to a pharmaceutical is similar to that of a human than it is to determine the similarity of their reactions to a possible carcinogen. Further, the rule of thumb in pharmaceuticals testing is to begin with rodents and to progress to monkeys and then to humans. Results using a monkey as a subject won't always predict findings in the case of a human, any more than a mouse will always predict for a rat, but certainly the species and, hence, the correlations are much closer. The expense of breeding and keeping apes, especially chimpanzees, which are in terribly short supply, rules them out for carcinogenicity testing. For all this, it remains true that sometimes pharmaceuticals used in complex animal-testing procedures will show different results when humans are the subjects, both in terms of side and beneficial effects. And one does wonder how many would-be effective treatments for humans have never been put into use simply because they had adverse effects on rodents that, had they been tested originally on humans, would never have posed a problem. But ethics prevents direct testing on humans for most pharmaceuticals, although sometimes exceptions are made for AIDS because it is ultimately fatal, and in the first years of AIDS research, no animal could be found that developed human AIDS.

Clearly there are real problems here. A test that very often identifies something as being there that isn't there, is no more useful than a test that identifies something that truly is there but does so only a small part of the time. For example, one could devise a test that detects breast cancer in women 100 percent of the time. All you would have to do is to say to each woman, "You've got breast cancer." You would never miss a single cancer, but the number of false positives would render your scheme useless. Similarly, a test that finds half of all chemicals tested to be carcinogenic tremendously diminishes the validity of labeling anything as such. But we want "carcinogenicity" to have meaning. We want to be able to warn people away from certain chemicals, or to regulate those chemicals, or to ban them altogether. We cannot base public policy on a test that finds half of all chemicals carcinogenic any more than we can base the decision to do breast cancer surgery on the basis of a test that finds all women positive for breast cancer. What happens under such conditions is that a secondary test becomes necessary to limit the list.

With animal carcinogens, that secondary test has proven to be a strictly arbitrary one, as would have to be the case when a ban is imposed upon one chemical that causes certain tumors in lab animals while a hundred others that cause those same problems are ignored. The principal type of arbitrary test employed is that of natural versus synthetic. With few exceptions, natural chemicals will be exempted from regulation even if they should cause several species of lab animals to explode with cancer. But a synthetic chemical whose test results may be questionable with even one species of animal—as was the case with the Alar breakdown product UDMH—is subject to being banned. The natural/synthetic double standard is a theme that will be repeated throughout this book.

## THE NO-THRESHOLD THEORY

Just as there is no great certainty that either a rat or a mouse or even both a rat and a mouse predict for human cancer, there is even less reason to believe that if massive doses of a chemical cause tumors in lab animals, comparatively tiny doses will necessarily have a similar effect on humans.

The assumption that massive doses predict carcinogenicity for even tiny doses as small, perhaps, as a single molecule is known as the linear dose-response theory. It says that a substance which is harmful at high levels will cause harm at lower levels; the risk declines but never becomes nil. This is also the rationale that is used for the "no threshold" theory, meaning that there is no level below which no harm is caused. As will be seen in subsequent chapters with other chemicals and substances, supporters of this theory have simply said that since no one knows where the threshold should be placed, none should be recognized.

There is plenty of empirical evidence that the no-threshold model is often false. As Efron writes:

> Man cannot digest . . . nutrients without saliva and digestive bacteria, both of which, according to the data, have been implicated as carcinogens or as producers of carcinogens. Man cannot function as a sexual being or reproduce his own kind without sexual hormones, and they too have been reported to be carcinogenic. Finally, man cannot seek shelter from the elements or from predatory beasts, or cook any natural foods in order to detoxify them, without fire, but combustion is said to produce [carcinogens].[23]

If, says Efron, "the 'prudence' of the no-threshold theory were to be invoked, crucial physiological functions might have to be medically prohibited. A theory which, according to the scientific literature, would kill off the human species cannot be accepted as prudent."[24] It is interesting to note that in the area of direct toxicity (that is, direct poisoning as opposed to the inducement of cancer through carcinogenicity), the no-threshold theory doesn't hold at all. The principle in toxicity, *Dosis sola facit venenum*—Only the dose makes the poison—applies. Thus, that which has no effect at one level (say, iron) may be medicinal at a higher level and a deadly poison at a higher level still. A single iron tablet has been known to kill human babies.[25] Some chemicals that we normally regard as poisonous are actually therapeutic at low levels. Arsenic, for example, is the prime ingredient in arsenical drugs such as that used to treat amebic dysentery. Other chemicals that we generally regard as therapeutic, such as the heart medicine digitalis (foxglove), are in fact poisonous not just at concentrated levels but at the levels at which they normally exist in nature.

## THE "MOVING THRESHOLD" THEORY

All of this counts for naught with the no-threshold cancer theorists. They counter suggestions of a carcinogenic threshold with
what could be termed the moving threshold principle. It says that
because different metabolisms will utilize chemicals differently,
thresholds will vary from person to person. Hence no single
threshold exists for humans, and since "a prudent policy of cancer
prevention requires protection of the most sensitive individuals
in the population,"[26] as Dr. Umberto Saffiotti* of the National
Cancer Institute's (NCI) Experimental Pathology Laboratory and
others have put it, anything proving carcinogenic in any animal
must be assumed to be carcinogenic for some human somewhere
at even the lowest level.

If that's not enough for you, there is also the synergism theory,
which states that while one chemical at one level might not be
carcinogenic, a combination of chemicals may prove to be so.
Thus, in response to the assertions of a Gold/Ames article in
*Science,* Dr. Frederica P. Perera, assistant professor at the Division of Environmental Sciences at the Columbia University School
of Public Health, declared: "In light of the uncertainty about
mechanisms and human dose-response, the assumption of low-
dose response for carcinogens continues to be a reasonable one."
This is nothing more than the "erring on the side of caution"
antiargument. But then she immediately goes on to say: "It is
consistent with the fact that humans are exposed to multiple carcinogens, capable of additive and even multiplicative effects."[28]
In other words, chemical A may not cause cancer at tiny doses,
nor may chemical B or C. But combine the three and—*voilà!*—
cancer. Thus, since it may be decades before we even know about
the carcinogenicity of B and C, let's go ahead and ban A at all
levels right now.

Both the moving threshold and the synergism theories are ap-

---

*Saffiotti was one of the founding fathers of the movement that argued that
cancer to a great extent is the result of industry and technology. In 1970, he
was chairman of the Ad Hoc Committee on the Evaluation of Low Levels of
Environmental Carcinogens," which informed the Surgeon General that "the
mass" of cancer could be prevented by legislation.[27]

pealing and carry some scientific backing. It is unquestioned that some people are sensitive to chemicals at levels that don't bother other people, and that some chemicals may prove more carcinogenic when combined with others. But there are three major problems with applying these theories. One arises when the subject of natural carcinogens comes up, which will be discussed shortly. Another is that while some chemicals may increase the carcinogenic effect of others, other chemicals appear to *decrease* carcinogenic effects. Indeed, some of those decreasers may, when acting alone, be themselves carcinogenic. Thus, while the dioxin TCDD has proven to be a potent animal carcinogen in various studies, as will be discussed in Chapter 4, one study showed that it effectively inhibited cancer formation in mice who had been dosed with two known carcinogens, benzo(*a*)pyrene and dimethylbenz(a)anthracene.[29] By banning chemical A, for all we know we'll be getting more cancers, not less.

The third counter to the moving threshold and synergism arguments is one that may send some cancer worrywarts through the roof but will make most people realize how silly this whole business is. Consider this: If it is possible that two slightly carcinogenic substances can combine to form a much more potent carcinogen, might it not be possible that noncarcinogen Y and carcinogen Z can combine to form a much more potent carcinogen than Z would normally be? Absolutely. In fact, it is even possible that two *non*carcinogens can combine to form a carcinogenic effect! This possibility, mind you, was brought to the world's attention by none other than Dr. Saffiotti.[30] So what do we do now? Start banning noncarcinogens as well because of the multiplier effect they may have on carcinogens or on other noncarcinogens? It is a regulatory nightmare. Indeed, it is simply unworkable.

In the face of all this, the EPA's position on MTD testing remains nothing but the "erring on the side of caution" argument. "When the current data do not resolve the issue," wrote eleven EPA scientists in a 1991 letter to *Science*, "EPA assessments employ the assumption basic to all toxicological evaluation that effects observed in animals may occur in humans and that effects observed at high doses may occur at low doses, albeit to a lesser extent."[31] At that point, they simply assume the worst. But note the key word, which appears twice: may. It *may* and it *may,* which is to say it may not and it may not. It may also be that when an entrail reader gives you your fortune, he is accurate. Certainly Julius Caesar learned that lesson the hard way. But this is the late twentieth century and one would like to think we can do better.

The Office of Science and Technology Policy conceded in 1979: "Extrapolation from the animal mode to the human represents something of a leap of faith."[32] That is no less true today than it was then. There is no more evidence now than there was then to support the MTD animal testing; indeed, there is hardly pressure to look for such evidence, since the testing theory has gained such widespread approval. And this is one of the saddest aspects of this whole thing. While we continue to rely on testing methodology that is terribly flawed, we are encouraged to be lax in efforts to develop a test that really works. "If it ain't broke, don't fix it," as the popular expression states. Of course, it ain't broke only because it never worked.

## THE DELANEY PARADOX

Like the EPA, The Food and Drug Administration (FDA) has a great interest in what is or is not carcinogenic; it is the FDA's job to regulate what Americans are allowed to ingest as food and medicine. The FDA's policy toward carcinogens is ostensibly guided by the Delaney Clause, a forty-seven-word statement that was included as part of the Food Additives Amendment passed in 1958 and named after Congressman James J. Delaney of New York. The clause specifies: "No additive shall be deemed to be safe if it is found to induce cancer when ingested by man or animal, or if it is found, after tests which are appropriate for the evaluation of the safety of food additives, to induce cancer in man or animal."[33] In practice—that is, under FDA regulations—the clause is applied to processed foods but not to fresh fruits and vegetables. With the latter, an "action level" is established that allows one part or less per million, also known as "negligible risk," to be carcinogenic. With processed foods, however, the rule, at least in theory, is absolute. No parts per *anything* is allowed.

And there's the rub. For when the Delaney Clause was passed, 50 parts per million (ppm) was considered the practical equivalent of zero, while today, scientists are measuring in parts per quintillion in some cases and continue to work to measure even smaller units. Thus, levels of allegedly carcinogenic chemicals that were ignored not too many years ago are now used to ban chemicals. Accordingly, we find ourselves chasing what has been called a "receding zero." The Alar alarm provides a nice example of such zero chasing. In order to paint apple producers as villains, *60 Minutes* used a 1989 Consumers Union (the publishers of *Consumer Reports*) survey showing Alar residues in two thirds of thirty-two apple juice products that ostensibly no longer contained the chemical.[34] The Consumers Union said its testing had found traces where another survey had not because it was now using a test that detected 0.01 to 0.02 parts per million, instead of the old one that could only find 0.5 to 1.0 ppm, a fiftyfold increase in sensitivity.[35] (No effort was made to test for UDMH.)[36] The problem with this apparently damning evidence is that the test was now so sensitive that quite possibly it was picking up residue from spraying that had occurred in a growing season prior to when the farmer stopped using the chemical.[37] Extended to its ultimate conclusion, increasingly sensitive testing will find molecules of virtually anything in virtually everything we ingest. This is a manifestation of the law of diffusion. As one pharmacology paper put it:

> If a pint of water is poured into the sea and allowed to mix completely with all the water on the surface of the earth, over 5,000 molecules of the original sample will be present in any pint taken subsequently. The general conclusion to be drawn from these calculations is that nothing is completely uncontaminated by anything else.[38]

John Allen Paulos makes the point more entertainingly, perhaps, when he points out in his best-selling book *Innumeracy: Mathematical Illiteracy and Its Consequences* that with each breath we take we have a 99 percent chance of inhaling a molecule that Julius Caesar exhaled in his dying breath.[39] That kind of gives you a feeling of really being a part of the bigger picture, doesn't it?

The Delaney Clause is on a collision course with the law of diffusion. If applied literally it will eventually prohibit the consumption of everything. Thus, add to the other problems of the "one-molecule/no-threshold" theory that it is physically impossible to comply with a law that mandates the removal of that molecule.

Environmentalist and population control advocate Garrett Hardin offers his own theory as to how Congress came up with such a harebrained scheme. "The Delaney Act was passed," he said, "because congressmen are old men. They are afraid of cancer. Because they're scared, they wanted zero tolerance. They did not get any scientific advice. Environmentalists who are scientists would never support a zero tolerance level for anything. There are a lot of environmentalists who have poor scientific training."[40]

The National Academy of Sciences (NAS) recommended in their 1987 report *Regulating Pesticides in Food: The Delaney Paradox* that the Delaney Clause be abolished. In its place, they suggested a new standard of "negligible risk" to be determined by the executive and legislative branches of the federal government.[41] The Bush administration proposed that the standard should include carcinogens falling into the range of one in one hundred thousand to one in one million increased lifetime risk. The NAS committee pointed out that the overall lifetime cancer risk in the United States is now about one in four, or 0.25. Adoption of the negligible risk standard of one in a million for pesticides would raise the risk to 0.250001.[42] That is hardly the making of an epidemic of cancer. But this is the standard that, as we discussed in the previous chapter, prompted NRDC attorney Janet Hathaway to object that carcinogens shouldn't be allowed even when the benefits outweigh the risks. The standard the NRDC desires is one that is impossible to meet and that would be economically devastating to *attempt* to meet. As Hardin explains, the law of diminishing returns comes into play. "The more contaminants you try to get out of a material—the purer you try to get it—the more it costs you." For example, "95 percent alcohol sells for a certain price. One hundred percent alcohol sells for ten times that amount. Getting that last five percent out costs like hell. The same thing is true of every one of these pollutants or contaminants."[43]

None of which factored into the decision of a U.S. federal court in San Francisco, which ruled in favor of the NRDC and against the EPA in July 1992, saying, "Congress intended to ban all carcinogenic food additives, regardless of amount or significance of risk," and, "The language is clear and mandatory." As we have seen, it was anything but, and the congressmen who passed the Delaney clause in the 1950s could no more envision the problems with MTD animal testing and increasing sensitivity of measuring devices than the founding fathers could have envisioned the need for warplanes when they allowed in the federal Constitution provisions only for an army and navy. The holding will quite possibly be struck down. The reason the NRDC brings suits in San Francisco is precisely because it knows that court will give it a more sympathetic hearing. But if the ruling stands, the language could forbid the use of over a fifth of the roughly 300 pesticides used on food crops.[44]

Further, this business about measuring increased risks in terms of one in a hundred thousand or one in a million has no meaning. Recall our discussion in the previous chapter of all the problems that arise when trying to estimate the number of deaths that UDMH would cause, and that despite this, both the EPA and the NRDC used their estimates as if they had been pulled off death certificates from the future. Those same problems apply to measuring risks. Consider that according to a 1980 report of the federal Occupational Safety and Health Administration, saccharin "shows a range of variation of more than five million-fold in estimates of human risk, although all the estimates were derived from the same set of experimental data on rats."[45] In fact, if the data had taken into account the possibility that MTD testing of rats was not able to be extrapolated to humans, the actual variance would have been *infinite*.

The most we can say about the risk of getting cancer from any animal carcinogen is that there is some *upper* limit on its effect on humans. That is, not everyone exposed to it will get cancer. Beyond that, it is all guesses. But Congress and a large segment of the public don't want to hear that. As the sour but astute H. L. Mencken pointed out: "The public . . . demands certainties; it must be told definitely and a bit raucously that this is true and that is false."[46] They are hungry for statistics and estimates and often care little about how those were generated or even who generated them. They don't want to hear someone say, "We honestly don't know." Indeed, they take that to indicate incompetence, their visceral response being, "Well, if you don't know, we'll appoint someone who does." And this is how the honest bureaucrats get squeezed out in favor of those who basically make up estimates that, if they are impossible to prove, are just as impossible to disprove. That's how the regulatory game is played.

# THE CANCER "EPIDEMIC"

But why do we have impossible standards? Why do we continue to tolerate testing that has little value? The real importance of the statement by David Rall on page 47 is that it is representative of a sector of the scientific community that came to the conclusion that using lab animals was legitimate not because of evidence that it was so, but because they wanted *something* concrete with which to begin indicting chemicals that they believed were carcinogenic. Indeed, the year Rall made that statement, 1976, was the year that the NRDC published an article in its newsletter titled "Is Cancer the Price of Technological Advancement?" In it, the NRDC dismissed nature as a significant contributor to the human cancer rate. It was "the 'chemical revolution' of the past 50 years" that was the primary cause, and "we may only be seeing the tip of the iceberg."[47]

It is a common notion, indeed the cornerstone of Efron's apoc-alyptics' thesis, that cancer rates in America are going up and that the reason is synthetic chemicals, be they poured into the air as emissions or sprayed on crops as pesticides. Barry Commoner in a 1978 article entitled "Hiroshima at Home" demanded a na-tionwide search for the victims of "environmental degradation,"[48] while Samuel Epstein, a professor of environmental science at the University of Illinois and author of *The Politics of Cancer,* charged that the price of industrial growth has been "the carnage of chemical-cancer."[49] The late Dr. Irving Selikoff, whose study of shipyard workers was crucial in establishing the risk of high-level exposures of asbestos, predicted that millions would die in the future of industrially caused cancer.[50]

For the longest time, the assertion held that the vast majority—perhaps as much as 90 percent—of cancer deaths are attributable to the synthetic products developed by the chemical industry after World War II. A *Newsweek* correspondent declared: "It's now generally accepted that about 60 to 90 percent of all human cancer is caused by manmade toxic chemicals of various sorts."[51] NCI's Umberto Saffiotti said: "Cancer in the last quarter of the 20th century can be a social disease, a disease whose causation and control are rooted in the technology and economy of our soci-ety."[52] And Dan Rather, in the 1975 CBS News special "The American Way of Death," told viewers, "It's been said that we are suffering a cancer epidemic in slow motion."[53] This extreme view, promoted by many persons and organizations including the NRDC,[54] seems to have been abandoned, quite possibly as a direct result of Edith Efron's *Apocalyptics,* but it remains "common knowledge" that much cancer is caused by industrial chemicals, including both pollutants and pesticides.

Such a view is held as a matter of faith not only by most environmentalist groups but apparently by most of the media as well. In fact, surveys of cancer incidence tend to show that when the aging of the American population is taken into account, industrial countries do not suffer higher rates of cancer. Such highly respected epidemiologists as Richard Doll and Richard Peto of Oxford University, both influential in establishing the link of cigarette smoking to disease, have stated clearly that there is no convincing evidence that there is a general increase in cancer related to the conditions of the modern industrial world.[55]

A 1990 cursory review printed in the British medical journal *Lancet,* the chief author of which was Dr. Devra Davis, purported to find an increase in cancer deaths in developed countries.[56] But the study was severely criticized by letter writers, including French researchers who stated that for their country, at least, the data presented in the original piece was simply incorrect; in France from 1950 to 1987, there was a slight increase in cancer deaths in males only, mostly attributable to increased use of cigarettes and alcohol, and a slight decrease for females.[57] A later U.S. review of childhood cancer cases found a small but statistically significant increase there as well, of about 4.1 percent from 1973 to 1988.[58]

Dr. Edward J. Sondik, deputy director of the Division of Cancer Prevention and Control at the National Cancer Institute, says the picture is not the ominous one that Davis and others have portrayed once one looks at the cancers on a case-by-case (or disease by disease) basis. "We understand the cause of certain increased problems," he says. "Asbestos exposure is responsible for the increase in mesothelioma." Likewise, he says, the increase in Kaposi's sarcoma is clearly linked to the AIDS epidemic, and the increase in melanoma is probably linked to more people spending more time in the sun with less clothing, and the increase in lung cancer to smoking. AIDS has also pushed up the childhood cancers specifically in that non-Hodgkin's lymphoma, an AIDS-associated cancer, has increased 20 percent among children.[59] Part of the increase, according to Sondik, is probably simply the result of better diagnostic techniques, which is the same point Doll and Peto had made. This may account, Sondik says, for at least a good part of the increases in prostate cancer and breast cancer. The implication of the Davis study was that the industrialized countries have rising cancer rates because they have industry. But as Sondik notes: "The industrialized countries have the best health care with the best chance for one to get a proper diagnosis." He says: "I cannot leap to the conclusion that [the Davis] article did."[60]

## THE NATURAL CARCINOGEN COVER-UP?

Enter into this controversy Dr. Bruce Ames. At one time, Ames was one of Efron's key apocalyptics and a prime exponent of the "one molecule" or no-threshold theory. He is a recipient of the most prestigious award for cancer research, the General Motors Cancer Research Foundation Prize; of the highest award in environmental achievement, the Tyler Prize; and has served on the National Cancer Institute board of directors. John Tierney, writing in *Hippocrates* magazine in 1988, stated: "It was his laboratory procedure, the Ames [Mutagenic] Test, that alerted scientists and consumers to the dangers of hundreds of synthetic chemicals. He provided the evidence—and occasionally the rhetoric—that got things banned. He was a scientific hero of the environmental movement."[61]

But then, something happened. Ames "discovered" (that is, began to think about) the existence of natural carcinogens. Efron, who herself had discovered a mass of natural carcinogen literature in 1978, wrote: "Somehow, the theoreticians, the regulators, and the apocalyptic movement itself had misplaced them. The natural carcinogens were sitting there quietly in the literature on carcinogenesis, along with the synthetics. The only difference was that they had not been publicized."[62] Ames decided to publicize those findings and the apocalyptics dropped him faster than a melon treated with DDT, although some thoughtful environmentalists do accept Ames's data on natural carcinogens.[63] Among the critics were the eighteen academics, union officials, and environmentalists who published a sharply critical letter in *Science* in 1984, the first signer of which was Samuel Epstein. The letter accused

Ames of "trivializing" cancer risks and pointedly noted that "such strategies are applauded by corporations resisting regulation of their carcinogenic products and processes."[64] (Epstein himself was blasted four years earlier in *Nature* by Richard Peto for, among other things, deliberate distortion and misrepresentation of scientific data.[65]) Ames remains one of the most respected cancer researchers in the world, he takes no industry money, and continues to publish regularly in such journals as *Science* and the *Proceedings of the National Academy of Sciences.*[66]

The Gold data base of chemicals tested in lab animals indicates that even among natural chemicals, about half are proving to cause malignant tumors in lab animals. Obviously, that puts the apocalyptics in a dilemma. The same standard that was being used to convict synthetic chemicals as potentially lethal was now proving the natural ones just as bad. This has the potential of exploding cancer policy in that it threatens the entire theoretic structure. To the rescue is the theory of evolution.

## CHARLES DARWIN, IN THE NICK OF TIME

The apocalyptics, to be fair, have acknowledged the existence of a limited number of natural carcinogens, but a highly limited number. Rachel Carson, in her landmark book *Silent Spring,* listed but a few, for example, ultraviolet rays of the sun, radioactive rocks, and arsenic. The comparative dearth of natural carcinogens she attributed to evolutionary processes whereby over time man's physiology learned to coexist with nature.[67] This theory continues to hold great sway with some. For example, in a 1989 *New Republic* article alleging a probable link between a supposed increase in cancer in the United States, NBC Science reporter Robert Bazell noted approvingly the words of the aforementioned Dr. Devra Davis, who said naturally occurring rodent carcinogens "probably don't present any threat because humans have been eating these foods for thousands of years, and if there is a danger we have evolved a way to resist it" (Bazell's words).[68] And when I talked with the senior NRDC attorney Al Meyerhoff, he gave me the same line. He qualified it, pointing out that his expertise is in law and not science, but that seems to be true of all the influential people at NRDC. They are litigators, not scientists.[69]

In fact, as Ames points out, many of our foods have been introduced into our diets only in the last few hundred years; that includes such staples as coffee, tomatoes, and potatoes.[70] More horrifying yet, the same is true of chocolate. Second, alcohol *has* been present in the human diet for thousands of years but has been proven to be carcinogenic in humans.[71] Aflatoxin, regarded even by "evolutionary theory" cancer apocalyptics as a natural carcinogen and quite possibly a human one, has undoubtedly been around as long as man. As Carson noted, nonfood substances, such as asbestos, radioactive rocks, and ultraviolet light, have proven carcinogenic in man yet they have always been here. Many of the common heavy metals, such as cadmium, lead, nickel, beryllium, chromium, selenium, and arsenic, are animal carcinogens despite having been present since the appearance of man—and since the origin of rats and mice, as well. Finally, the evolutionary theory assumes that the cancer would develop and indeed kill before the reproductive period was complete. In fact, cancer is primarily a disease of older people, those who are past normal childbearing years. Hence, it would have no effect on evolutionary development.[72]

Discussion of natural animal carcinogens terrifies the apocalyptics because it undercuts their whole approach to risk. It remains, however, that food itself is simply a complex combination of chemicals. Yes, every natural food we eat, including those purchased at the organic food store, comprise masses of *chemicals*. Further, all plants produce toxins that protect them against fungi, insects, and predators such as man. Many of these natural pesticides have been discovered, and every species of plant contains a whole set of toxins, usually a few dozen. An innocent-looking leaf of cabbage, for example, contains 49 natural pesticides and metabolites, with huge, ominous-sounding names like 4-methylthiobutyl isothiocyanate and 3-indolylmethyl glucosinolate (glucobrassicin).[73] Very few of these plant toxins have been tested in animals, but of these about half to date (27 of 52) have proven carcinogenic in MTD testing of lab animals, according to the Gold carcinogen data base. Overall, 37 of 57 of natural chemicals tested in both rats and mice have proven carcinogenic in MTD testing of lab animals. This is about the same percentage that has been found in synthetic chemicals (212 of 350).[74]

Thus, it is probable, Ames says, that because all plants contain a number of chemicals, almost every plant product in the supermarket contains natural animal carcinogens. Among those already identified as such are: apples (sans Alar), bananas, broccoli, Brussels sprouts, cabbage, carrots, celery, cocoa, grapefruit juice, honeydew melon, mushrooms, mustard, orange juice, peaches, black pepper, raspberries, and turnips. Broccoli, according to Ames, contains a compound similar to dioxin, widely claimed to be the most deadly chemical created by man and to which a chapter will be devoted later in this book.[75] Indeed, pure apple juice has been reported to contain 137 natural volatile chemicals,[76] of which only 5 have been tested for carcinogenicity,[77] and 3 of these—benzyl acetate, alcohol, and acetaldehyde—have been found to be carcinogenic in lab animals or humans.[78] Alcoholic beverage consumption, particularly by smokers, has been estimated to contribute to about 3 percent of cancer deaths in the United States,[79] although the key word is "beverage." Nobody is going around saying that the trace of alcohol in apples, many times larger though it may be than the highest amount of UDMH ever found in an apple product, is going to give you cancer. In perspective, worrying about a substance present in apple juice in such small quantities that it can only be measured with the most advanced instruments seems fatuous indeed.

In the mid-1980s, the American Cancer Society ran a series of commercials which mocked the notion that "everything causes cancer." Yet, if the results of mass-dose testing of laboratory animals are to be interpreted as applying to humans, which is to say that if the test by which Alar was tried and convicted was applied to everything else we eat, it *could* perhaps be said that everything causes cancer. In fact, the FDA was scared to death that the public would discover natural carcinogens, as evidenced by one FDA statement that Efron found buried in the middle of a long opinion on reportedly carcinogenic hair dyes. It read:

Indeed, a requirement for warnings on all foods that may contain an inherent carcinogenic ingredient or a carcinogenic contaminant (in contrast to a deliberately added carcinogenic substance) would apply to many, perhaps most, foods in a supermarket. Such warnings would be so numerous they would confuse the public, would not promote informed consumer decisionmaking, and would not advance the public health.[80]

Admitted a former FDA legal counsel later: "The number of carcinogenic substances that naturally occur in foods would ultimately require so many warnings as to be deafening."[81]

In order to establish a priority rating system for carcinogens similar to that already established for toxic substances, Ames and Gold set up what they call a HERP (human exposure dose/rodent potency dose) index, which they described in detail in the April 17, 1987, issue of *Science*. HERP rates the possibility of carcinogenicity of various chemicals by comparing the doses humans are exposed to to that which causes tumors in lab animals. Ames, Gold, and Renae Magaw said the rating system should be seen not "as providing a basis for absolute human risk assessment but as a guide to priority setting." It would be wrong to use it for direct human risk assessment, they said, because the relationship of low doses in humans and the doses fed to rodents is unknown, and because the general shape of the dose-response relationship is unknown.[82]

For example, according to the index, a liter of tap water is rated 0.001 on the scale because it contains the rodent carcinogen chloroform. A 12-ounce bottle of beer is rated at 2.8 because it contains 18 milliliters of ethyl alcohol; conventional home air, which contains the animal carcinogen formaldehyde, is rated 0.6 per 14 hours of breathing, while the same amount of breathing in a mobile home will pull in enough formaldehyde to incur a rating of 2.1. EDB, the banned grain fumigant, has a rating of .0004.[83] During the Alar scare, Ames and Gold noted in a letter to *Science* that the UDMH in a daily 6-ounce glass of apple juice has a HERP level of 0.0017 percent, less than one tenth that of either a single mushroom a day or a single peanut butter sandwich.[84] All of this, of course, assumes that there is value in MTD rodent testing, and, as noted, Ames and Gold have cast much doubt on this. Still, the HERP index constitutes an attempt to make the best of bad data.

Speaking on the *Donahue* show to promote his book *Eating Clean*, the first example activist Ralph Nader cited as indicative of the dangers in our food supply was that two years earlier imported coffee was tested by the NRDC and found to have "illegal multiple pesticide residues in it."[85] That might sound alarming, unless one realizes, as Ames and Gold have pointed out, that "in roasted coffee, among 22 [natural] chemicals tested, 16 were ro-

# Relative Risk Index

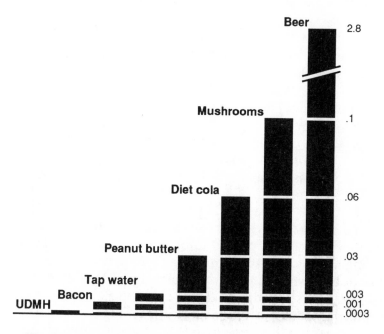

The human exposure dose/rodent potency dose (HERP) index, devised by scientists at the University of California, Berkeley, rates the degree of carcinogenesis of various chemicals based on the degree to which they have caused tumors in lab animals. According to HERP, a liter of tap water is rated 0.001 because it contains the rodent carcinogen chloroform, and a 12-ounce bottle of beer is rated at 2.8 because it contains 18 milliliters of ethyl alcohol.

Alar itself has not been found to be a rodent carcinogen but UDMH, which Alar breaks down into, has a HERP level of only 0.0017, less than one-tenth that of a single peanut butter sandwich which may contain the carcinogen aflatoxin.

dent carcinogens. Thus one cup of coffee contains 10 milligrams
of known [natural] rodent carcinogens, about equivalent in weight
to the potentially carcinogenic synthetic pesticide residues one
eats in a year." They add: "There is every reason to expect that
the thousand other chemicals in roasted coffee would produce a
plethora of rodent carcinogens if tested at the MTD."[86] Suddenly
the presence of some illegal multiple pesticide residues doesn't
seem so worrisome.

It is one of the great ironies of the synthetic chemical phobia
that some varieties of edible plants that have been bred to be
naturally pest-resistant, in order to obviate the need for pesticides,
have as a result ended up being withdrawn from the market because of acute toxicity to humans. Such was the case with one
variety of potato.[87] Similarly, a specially bred insect-resistant type
of celery proved so toxic as to cause rashes on the hands of
handlers, and upon analysis was found to have 9,000 parts per
billion (ppb) of the animal carcinogen 8-methoxypsoralen (and
related soralens), instead of the 900 ppb present in normal celery.[88]

Says Ames: "Plants couldn't survive if they weren't filled with
toxic chemicals. They don't have immune systems, teeth, claws,
and they can't run away. So throughout evolution they've been
making newer and nastier pesticides. They're better chemists than
Dow or Monsanto. They've been at it a very long time."[89]

When Ames explains it, the friendly potato doesn't seem so
friendly anymore. He notes that for all the fuss over the pesticide
DDT being stored in human body fat, humans store natural pesticides too, including the chemicals solanine and chaconine from
potatoes "because you're eating fifteen thousand micrograms a
day from a single potato." Noting that these chemicals kill insects
in the same way that the synthetic organophosphate insecticides
do, he says: "And yet you're eating only about 15 micrograms of
man-made organophosphate pesticides a day. Solanine and chaconine came into the human diet four hundred years ago. They're
teratogens, causing birth defects in animals. And nobody's worrying about them because they're natural. It's a double standard."[90]

Ames and Gold calculate that 99.99 percent of all pesticides
(by weight) are natural,[91] thus we are ingesting about ten thousand
times more natural than synthetic pesticides. It is reassuring, how-

ever, that many layers of general defenses in humans and other animals protect against toxins without distinguishing whether they are synthetic or natural. Turning around the Darwinian rationale that synthetics are bad, natural substances good, Ames and Gold write:

> In the evolutionary war between plants and animals, animals have developed layers of general defenses, almost all inducible, against toxic chemicals. This means that humans are well buffered against toxicity at low doses from both man-made and natural chemicals. Given the high proportion of carcinogens among those natural chemicals tested, human exposure to rodent carcinogens is far more common than generally thought; however, at the low doses of most human exposures . . . the hazards may be much lower than is commonly assumed and often will be zero.[92]

Much was made of EPA's John Moore having said on *60 Minutes* that if Alar were a new pesticide, he would not have allowed it to be used. That is, it was effectively grandfathered in. "Dr. Moore, I can't understand that," said reporter Ed Bradley. "I mean, you're telling me something—that if this stuff came to you today, and it was brand new, it wouldn't get on the market, but because it's already out there, we can keep using it. That doesn't make sense to me."[93] Yet that is exactly what we have done with natural pesticides and other natural chemicals that do things to rats and mice that massive levels of UDMH didn't begin to do. They were all around before the regulations were written, so they all get a free ride. Does *that* make sense to Ed Bradley? Perhaps so, as evidenced by the treatment he gave Ames on the second *60 Minutes* program about Alar.

## AMES BEFORE THE STAR CHAMBER

As a result of an apple industry backlash against CBS's first Alar show, and as the result of a campaign by the Washington, D.C.-based watchdog group Accuracy in Media,[94] CBS did another show in which they interviewed Ames. Indeed, they spent the entire Ames portion trying to discredit him. At one point, Bradley stated: "Dr. [William] Lijinsky disputes Ames's claim that 99.9 percent of all carcinogens come from natural foods," after which there was shown a clip of Lijinsky doing just that.[95] In fact, such a claim would have been bizarre. Bradley, who presumably had read Ames's articles, must have known that in several of them he states, as have many people, that about 30 percent of human cancer is attributable to smoking alone.[96] Yet when Ames confronted 60 Minutes producer David Gelber on this, Gelber responded by facsimile: "After re-reading the relevant parts of the transcript, I'm satisfied that your views were properly paraphrased."[97]

At another point Ames is quoted saying that compounds in celery and broccoli have been found to be carcinogenic. Bradley replies: "He believes further tests will show he's right. But for now, the national toxicology survey [of MTD animal carcinogens] lists just 148 substances, and the compounds in celery and broccoli aren't among them. One compound that is is the one produced by Alar."[98]

By now, it is fairly clear to the 60 Minutes viewer that Ames is not a very trustworthy witness; indeed, that he is a liar. But Bradley failed to mention that an April 1989 report by the National Toxicology Program of the Public Health Service lists both allyl isothiocyanate and 8-methoxypsoralen as carcinogens, the former as "positive" in male rats with the latter showing "clear evidence for carcinogenicity" in male rats.[99] The first of these chemicals is found in broccoli and other vegetables, while the second chemical is found in celery and other vegetables.[100] The 60 Minutes show with Ames took place in May 1989. This material also appeared in a Science article by Ames and Gold,[101] which Ames claims to have sent to producer David Gelber[102] but which, in any case, was Gelber's duty to read. Gelber later responded that it was okay for Bradley to ignore allyl isothiocylanate and 8-methoxypsoralen because they were only "suspected" carcinogens,[103] but that's exactly the category into which UDMH fell. That 60 Minutes has not done an exposé on these chemicals featuring a blowup of a stalk of celery and a piece of broccoli with a skull and crossbones on them (the way that they depicted an apple in the first Alar show) hardly changes this. Nevertheless, whatever treatment 60 Minutes or Ed Bradley may give Ames, they can't pooh-pooh away the facts, and those facts, as Cornell University nutritionist Christina Stark put it, indicate that "we've got far worse natural chemicals in the food supply than anything manmade."[104]

Indeed, it is awfully hard to readily dismiss the reality of natural chemical rodent carcinogens when more and more top scientists are saying what Ames has been saying. In a paper presented at a 1990 meeting of the American Association for the Advancement of Science, Dr. Robert J. Scheuplein, director of the Office of Toxicological Sciences at the FDA, estimated that traditional food accounts for 98.8 percent of food-related cancer risk. Of the others, spices make up about 0.98 percent, he wrote, other additives 0.2 percent, pesticides 0.01 percent, animal drugs 0.01 percent, food preparation such as broiling or pickling 0.01 percent, mushrooms and other fungi 0.0001 percent. Scheuplein didn't say human diets were without risks, merely that the public was worrying about the wrong ones.[105]

## WILL "CELL DEATH" BE THE DEATH OF MTD TESTING?

Why, then, doesn't everything give us cancer? Why doesn't everyone get cancer by age thirty? One possibility is the existence of anticarcinogens. It has been known for some time that some chemicals appear to act as neutralizers to carcinogens. Another reason for nonextinction of the human race is the balance between the activation and detoxification of both natural and industrial carcinogens. As discussed earlier, some studies have found that certain combinations of carcinogens are less carcinogenic than the same ones ingested individually.

Of course, both the effectiveness of anticarcinogens and the balance of carcinogens would be completely overridden by doses of carcinogens that are perhaps millions of times higher than an animal could expect to ingest under normal conditions. If there were something in asparagus, broccoli, and oranges that canceled out the carcinogenic effect of UDMH, it would take a lot of asparagus, broccoli, and oranges to cancel out the equivalent of twenty-eight thousand apples a day, which is the equivalent of what the rodents were dosed with in the UDMH tests.

But perhaps the most fascinating answer to the puzzle of MTD in lab animals lies in the research area that explores cell death. According to this hypothesis, toxigenicity and carcinogenicity, formerly separate and distinct, are confused in MTD testing. In MTD testing, the dose may be so high that with a given chemical administered to a given animal, some organ of the animal may become sufficiently poisoned, not to kill the animal outright, but to cause massive new cell replication to replace the cells that have been killed off. This replication then leads to mutations and cancer.

For example, massive doses of saccharin overwhelm the natural defenses of rats, causing their bladders to lose many cells, which have to be replaced. Chloroform does likewise with rat liver cells.[106] From there, come two possible effects, explains Dr. Byron Butterworth, a staffer at the Chemical Industry Institute of Toxicology, an independent research group (which receives industry funding) at Research Triangle Park, North Carolina. "First, there is a chance for errors—mutations—to show up whenever cells divide and replicate DNA. The more you necessitate this, the better the odds of a mutation are. Second, cancer is not just the presence of mutated cells but their growth and expansion. The massive killing of good cells forces the cancerous ones to rapidly reproduce to try to fill the gap."[107]

As evidence for this, Butterworth notes that the same chemicals that cause cancerous tumors at MTD levels usually cause no tumors at lower levels, even though they may still be many times higher than anyone could possibly ingest in a lifetime. That was the case with Alar and UDMH, in which neither caused tumors in lab animals below the MTD range. Indeed, overall about half of the positive sites in animal cancer tests are not statistically significant at half the MTD.[108]

"Half of [the chemicals] we call carcinogenic really aren't," says Butterworth. "They will not produce cancer at levels in which they are ingested in real life." Butterworth is not unaware of the policy implications of all this. "Our public cancer policy is dramatically off target and we're scaring people to death," he says.[109]

Indeed, epidemiologist Richard Peto, who is also the statistical theoretician for the IARC for interpretation of mouse tests, stated a similar thesis a decade earlier. He wrote:

> Any chemical which causes proliferation or necrosis in any organ that is subject to spontaneous cancers is likely to modify the onset rate of tumors in that organ, and since the aim of most animal experiments is to study a dose which is nearly, but not quite, sufficient to cause significant weight loss or mortality within three

months, it is not surprising that so many chemicals at such doses can cause cancers in animals.[110]

Thus, comments Ames, "it seems likely, therefore, that a high percentage of all chemicals, both man-made and natural, will increase cell division at the [MTD] and be classified as carcinogens, but most of these may increase cell division only at high doses and therefore may not be of interest at doses much below the toxic dose."[111]

Ames says that some carcinogens may occasionally in a workplace environment be absorbed at doses similar to what rodents were fed. Such was once the case with the fumigant EBD. In that case, the only extrapolation is from rodent to man, a lesser leap than extrapolating from rodent to man *and* from massive doses to low doses. In such a case, says Ames, the appearance of cancer in the rodent may have predictive effects for humans. But that is as valuable as the rodent tests can get.[112]

## SCIENCE VERSUS SUPERSTITION

In a letter to *Science* magazine criticizing an editorial by Daniel Koshland, Jr., which in turn had criticized environmental activists over the Alar affair, Dr. Edward Groth of the Consumers Union came out boldly and declared: "The scientific facts (estimates of how big the risk is, with all their inherent uncertainties) are just *part* of what the public knows about Alar. The policy choices— both the personal and the public kind—depend on far more than facts. . . . [It] is heavily influenced by *moral* dimensions of the risk" (emphasis added).[113]

In other words, don't confuse him with the scientific arguments, his mind's made up. That is exactly how many environmentalists feel about synthetic chemicals in general. They don't oppose synthetics because synthetics have been shown to be more harmful than natural substances. They could not oppose them for that reason, because synthetics *haven't* been shown to be more harmful. They oppose them because they are synthetic. Period.

The belief that synthetics are more harmful may stem from the notion that humanity itself is harmful and so therefore must be its creations. Note the quotation used at the beginning of this chapter: "The World Has Cancer, and the Cancer Is Man." This quote dates back several decades, but the sentiment has continued to echo, notably in Bill McKibben's book *The End of Nature,* in which the author concludes that that which people touch they spoil, no matter in what other way they affect it.[114] If a beaver dams a river, that's good and natural. If people dam a river, that is unnatural and hence bad. Beetles destroying trees are good and natural; humans chopping down trees are unnatural and hence bad. That is a very peculiar point of view, but only in its extremity. The quintessence, that humans and their creations are harmful, is widely held and is strongly advanced by environmentalists.

In her usual subdued manner, Lois Gold says: "If you're looking for big causes of cancer, it's questionable why you're looking at synthetics."[115] But the NRDC has defended this lack of concern over natural carcinogens, saying that those who broach the subject, as Hathaway put it, "want to deflect attention away from their products or other synthetic chemicals to something we can't do much about. There is no one making natural carcinogens and no one to ask to stop."[116] This sounds an awful lot like the joke about the drunk who lost his keys at the curb but insisted upon looking for them under the streetlamp, explaining, "The light is better there." It also reflects to some extent what has been called the "outrage factor." Alar gives you somebody to get outraged at; natural chemicals in vegetables and fruits don't. It's not rational, but that's the way people are. At any rate, Hathaway is completely wrong, because it happens that the carcinogens implicated in the great majority of cancers that can be attributed to a specific outside cause are by and large the same ones we have the most control over—tobacco, alcohol, and probably not eating enough fruits and vegetables.

According to Scheuplein's analysis, the risk of dying of cancer from dietary exposure to both natural and synthetic carcinogens or cancer promoters is 7.7 percent. Of this, the risk from the natural ones alone is 7.6 percent. This leaves only 0.1 percent of cancer deaths, or about 500 a year, from synthetic chemicals. Scheuplein singled out fat consumption as a special target for cancer-reduction strategies.[117] More and more researchers, in fact, are pointing the finger at both fat consumption[118] and excessive caloric intake regardless of type of nutrient consumed[119] as factors in the development of cancer.

Similarly, Doll and Peto stated that their "best estimate" is that 2 percent of cancers (about 2,000) can be attributed to pollution, with food additives and industrial products accounting for less than 1 percent (about 1,000) each. In contrast, they attributed 30 percent of cancers to tobacco, 3 percent to alcohol, and a full 35 percent (about 350,000) to diet apart from additives.[120]

Writing in *Risk Analysis,* Michael Gough, program manager of Biological Applications at the Office of Technology Assessment of the U.S. Congress, has calculated that, using Food and Drug Administration figures, cancers from food additives add up to about 1,400 cancers or 0.25 percent of the total. That would come out to about 700 deaths from food additives. As for nonfood carcinogens, which are the domain of the EPA, Gough has calculated that if EPA risk-assessment techniques are accurate and all identified carcinogens were completely controlled, about 6,400 cancer deaths annually (about 1.3 percent of the current annual total) could be prevented.[121]

By nice coincidence, carcinogens such as tobacco, alcohol, and fats also cause a tremendous amount of other fatal and nonfatal problems. One wonders how many of those people who were terrified of Alar in their applesauce nevertheless continue to smoke, drink, or overeat. None of this matters a bit to the NRDC. Their war is against man-made chemicals. The rodent tests are a weapon in that war. That the rodent tests show that natural chemicals come up carcinogenic just as often is a tremendous inconvenience that is to be ignored or pooh-poohed away.

On a *Donahue* show concerning chemicals in food, after one of the guests pointed out all the animal carcinogens that are present in natural foods, one audience member stood up and said, "I would rather take a chance on eating natural food, even though it has cancer in it, than you putting chemicals in my food to give me cancer."[122] And there you have it. For all the talk about facts and studies and science, what it really comes down to is the moral dimension Groth mentioned, or even a quasi-religious one. If a person tells you he must eat with his right hand only or do no work on a certain day or eat no meat on a certain day, you can argue science till you're blue in the face but you can't win because you're not even on the same playing field. These are religious rules, and no scholar of these religions will claim otherwise. If an environmental activist believes that somehow it's better to be given cancer by a so-called natural carcinogen than a synthesized one, that a one-in-five-thousand real chance of dying in an auto accident is acceptable but a one-in-a-million hypothetical chance of dying from a chemical is not, the only way your books and studies are going to erase that thought from their minds is if you pile them on their heads so high that you crush their skulls.

On the other hand, it's a pretty safe bet that most of us, upon hearing that the bad news is that Uncle Jake has terminal cancer but that the "good news" is that it was apparently caused by a natural source, wouldn't understand why that was good. Most of us probably see all cancer as a bad thing and our primary concern is to reduce its incidence. If that's how we feel, then the route of the environmentalist activists is not the way to go. Says Ames, "One can either chase after parts per billion of every man-made carcinogen that turns up or have some sensible regulations about pollution."[123] Most of us, given the facts, would probably prefer the latter. And if somebody's policy is going to be the rule in the land, we should not be afraid to assert science over superstition.

## REPLACING THE OLD PARADIGM

If rats and mice predict questionably for humans, if massive doses don't predict well for low doses, and if you can't place blind trust in a natural chemical, then with what are we left? For one thing, we can end the persecution of synthetics. Write Ames and Gold: "Efforts to regulate synthetic pesticides or other synthetic chemicals at the parts per billion level because the chemicals are rodent carcinogens must include an understanding of the economic and health-related tradeoffs." Synthetic pesticides have markedly lowered the cost of food from plant sources, thus encouraging increased consumption. "This increased consumption of fruits and vegetables," say Ames and Gold, "along with decreased consumption of fat, may be the best way to lower risks of cancer and heart disease, other than giving up smoking. Also, some of the vitamins, antioxidants, and fiber found in many plant foods are anticarcinogenic."[124] In short, the war on synthetic chemicals may prove to be a war on human health. A cease-fire should be declared and in its wake a new policy should be established that eliminates the natural/synthetic double standard. A chemical doesn't care if it was synthesized in a lab or on a tree, and neither should we.

As to coming up with tests that actually determine human carcinogenicity, the dropping of MTD animal models would be a major step in the right direction. Until the emperor is forced to admit he is wearing no clothes, he will never have the incentive to get dressed. Until the David Ralls of the world are forced to admit that "the only thing we have" is practically worthless, we will continue to use that which is worthless. What is needed, say Ames and many other scientists, is a lot more research into the mechanism of carcinogenesis. Once that is accomplished, it can be used to develop new tests. Until then, except for those few cases where a group of humans have been exposed to high doses of a chemical to make an epidemiological study, whether we dose animals with near-toxic amounts or read the entrails of a chicken, all we are doing is guessing.

Former IARC director John Higginson, now with the Institute for Health Policy Analysis at the Georgetown Medical Center, published an article in *Cancer Research* in 1988 calling for a reevaluation of the current general attitude toward cancer prevention. He noted that researcher Isaac Berenblum in 1980 had concluded that the most effective approach in the future would be interference in the carcinogenic process [the mechanism by which healthy cells become malignant and then spread] rather than the elimination of "incriminating" factors within the environment.[125] Higginson wrote: "Although a longtime advocate of the traditional eliminators approach to prevention, I am now convinced that recent progress in biology and carcinogenesis research confirms the essential validity of Berenblum's views, although they are largely ignored in regulatory policy and public debate." Further, he said, it appears that increasing efforts to reduce cancer based on current methods "may have relatively little impact in reducing the present burden of cancer."[126]

In fact, Higginson has also said that the efforts may be harmful because the ambiguity of the tests allows arbitrary decisions to be made, so that safe chemicals may be crucified and unsafe ones ignored. Stated Higginson in 1979:

[Some people] have found it hard to accept that general air pollution, smoking chimneys, and the like are not major causes of cancer. I mean people would love to be able to prove that cancer is due to pollution or the general environment. It would be so easy to say, "Let us regulate everything to zero exposure and we have no more cancer." The concept is so beautiful that it will overwhelm a mass of facts to the contrary.[127]

Whether intended as a prophecy or not, Higginson's statement has proven so. The goal of zero exposure to alleged carcinogenic pesticides has become the name of the game with the most powerful environmentalists, and it has overwhelmed a mass of facts to the contrary.

What many of those who promote "erring on the side of caution" when it comes to such things as pesticides don't seem to realize is that fear, like money, is a scarce resource that must be allocated. Unconsciously, people have priorities for things they fear. To push something higher up the list than it should be is to often to push other things lower than they should be, like a teeter-totter. A poll taken the year *before* the Alar scare showed that already 75 percent of Americans asked were concerned that pesticide and herbicide residues were a "serious health hazard," with another 20 percent considering them "somewhat of a health hazard." By comparison, fats, which have been linked to heart disease, diabetes, cancer, and other ills, were listed as a serious health hazard by only 61 percent of those polled. None of the other nine categories, which included cholesterol, salt, nitrites, sugar, artificial coloring, and additives and preservatives, aroused the fear that pesticides and herbicides did.[128] So, chomp another double cheeseburger, wash it down with a beer, and follow it up with a cigarette, all in the blissful knowledge that you do not run the risk of ingesting a part per trillion of a pesticide sprayed on vegetables or fruits.

Instead of this intense concentration on what may or may not cause cancer, Higginson says, interference techniques—"a wrench in the works," possibly consisting of oral doses of drugs or vaccines—is the most logical scientific method to pursue.[129] He notes that some drugs, such as oral contraceptives, have already shown efficacy in staving off some forms of cancer,[130] and indeed one such drug, tamoxifen, has recently been approved for clinical trials as a breast cancer preventer.[131]

In sum, says Higginson:

The danger of emphasis on the benefits of certain control measures [such as are presently employed] lies not in their intent and irrelevance but in their false accuracy. This may maximize trivial risks, cause unnecessary public concern, and thus divert limited resources away from more effective cancer control strategies and other more important national social and health goals.[132]

Ames has put it more succinctly: "We're spending eighty billion dollars a year trying to control pollution. [The figure has since gone up to $115 billion.[133]] Although much of this is useful, I think it will have little influence on public health. And we're spending only eight billion dollars a year on all the science in the United States."[134]

The day will come, not too long from now, when dosing animals with massive amounts of chemicals and then declaring that this predicts cancer in humans at low doses will be literally laughed at, in the same way we now laugh at witch doctoring and entrail reading. Our current cancer prevention scheme will be classified alongside leeching with the great medical follies of history. The only question is, how many hundreds of billions of dollars will be spent before then and how many lives will be needlessly cut short by policies focused on the trivial and unlikely, rather than the real dangers and truly preventable risks?

# CHAPTER 3

# A Fairly Brief, Nonboring Lesson in the Pitfalls of Amateur Epidemiology

The diagnosis of disease is often easy, often difficult, and often impossible.[1]

—Peter Mere Latham, *Collected Works*

Peter Latham, a nineteenth-century physician and philosopher, wrote: "People in general have no notion of the sort and amount of evidence often needed to prove the simplest matter of fact."[2] The focus of this chapter, epidemiology, is not concerned with the simplest matter of fact, but it comprises a lot of basic—indeed simple—concepts. It is concerned with what causes a specific disease in a specific individual.

Epidemiology is a science of association, relying on statistics plus knowledge of how illness or accidents come about (which is known as etiology). The purpose is to detect what is causing the problem and how great the problem is, in order to ultimately reduce or eliminate its incidence. Epidemiology is based on observation in populations, and is thus in contrast with laboratory studies, which develop hard cause-and-effect relationships from experimental evidence.

Certain criteria make the results of some epidemiological studies more convincing and meaningful than others. For example, a strong association specific to a single disease, such as leukemia,

78

is more compelling than slight increases in a broad spectrum of health effects, such as a potpourri of cancers and birth defects in offspring. The association also should be biologically plausible, that is, there should be a sound theoretical basis for how such and such an agent could cause such and such problem. Thus, a connection between ingesting alcohol and esophagal cancer is much more likely than one between ingesting alcohol and developing bunions, because the alcohol makes direct contact with the esophagus but not the feet. Other potential causes of disease, called confounding factors (as in "Confound it!"), must be looked at and accounted for. Often, people with one thing in common have another thing in common; for example, professional truck drivers by definition tend to sit a lot and to eat in "greasy spoons." If discovered they have a high rate of heart disease, it would not be immediately apparent which of those factors—or any number of other ones—would be responsible. Prize fighters, who throw a lot of punches, have higher rates of brain damage than most of us. Is it because they throw so many punches? Or could it be that they take their share as well?

Another basic principle is that findings are strengthened if they appear consistently in diverse populations and circumstances, particularly if it appears that more of the suspected agent causes more of the illness. If several cases of food poisoning are reported among patrons of Joe's Bar and Grill but it turns out all the victims are employees of Fred's Bar and Grill across the street, some of whom only drank from Joe's water fountain, this is not a strong indicator that there is something wrong with Joe's food. On the other hand, if a number of patrons eating Joe's "specially aged" blue cheese sauce fall ill with food poisoning symptoms and one is Joe's wife, this could be of importance.

An epidemiological exposure study usually has three parts. First, it isolates a group that has been exposed to a particular substance or other possible cause of illness. Then, it determines if the group has been more prone to particular illnesses or perhaps injury than the rest of the population. Finally, if there is an excess incidence of illness or injury, it tries to decide, by excluding all other possible factors, whether the excess is a result of exposure to the substance in question.

Most such studies are inconclusive and it may take many years to find a cause-and-effect relationship even when it turns out there was a particularly strong one, such as that linking lung cancer and cigarette smoking. Thus, epidemiology can be a crude tool, although when it does work its results are far more reliable than those of studies in test tubes and lab animals, because those factors that cause certain effects in the laboratory or in a rodent or dog will not necessarily produce the same effects in a human.

As with any profession, epidemiologists have developed their own lingo, some of which is good for lay persons to know, some of which is better ignored, being essentially the equivalent of "legalese." Epidemiologists express the mathematical possibility of increased risk by using risk ratios, which are sometimes also called "odds ratios," when epidemiologists tire of writing "risk ratio" over and over (or vice versa). A risk ratio or odds ratio of 3.0 for lung cancer means that three times as many people showed up in that category with lung cancer as in the control group. A risk ratio of 4.2 for leukemia means that 4.2 times more cases appeared than in the control group. A control group is a set of persons carefully matched to the set of persons who are being observed for the problem. Thus, an epidemiological study of women using video display terminals should have as its control women who didn't use VDTs but who did as much sitting and as much smoking as women who did use VDTs.

Nevertheless, it is not cut-and-dried that risk ratios above 1.0 mean that something special is causing the cancer or other ailment being looked at. That is because of the laws of chance and probability. Thus, if you flipped a coin four times, you might expect two heads and two tails. In fact, it often doesn't work out that way. Often you'll get three of one and one of the other. That would give you a "risk ratio" of 1.5, because you are getting 1.5 times the number of heads or tails that you expected. It doesn't mean anything is affecting the coin; it's just chance. Diseases often cluster just by chance. Just because cancer hits every fourth American doesn't mean that if you line up one hundred Americans you can walk along the line and say, "One, two, three, sorry buddy. One, two, three, I'm very sorry." (Wouldn't insurance companies love that? They could simply refuse policies to every fourth person who applies to them.) You might walk past ten consecutive people who will not get cancer, then come across two next to each other who will, just as you might flip three heads or three tails in a row.

John Allen Paulos's *Innumeracy: Mathematical Illiteracy and Its Consequences* explains this very nicely. "Most people don't realize that random events generally can seem quite ordered," he says. He then provides the following computer printout of a random sequence of Xs and Os, each with a one-half probability. Note that these could just as easily be heads or tails on a coin.

```
O X X X O O O X X X O X X X O X X X X O O X X O X X
O X O O X O X O O O O X O X X O O O X X X O X O X X
X X X X X X X O X X X O X O X X X X O X O O X X X O
O O X X X X X O O X X O O O X X O O O O O X X O O X
X X X X X O X X X X O O X X X X O O X X O X X O O X
```

Paulos discusses "the number of runs and the way there seem to be clumps and patterns. If we felt compelled to account for these, we would have to invent explanations that would of necessity be false. Studies have been done, in fact, in which experts in a given field have analyzed such random phenomena and come up with cogent 'explanations' for the patterns."[3] Indeed, we shall encounter such explanations at various points in this book. Another word for these "runs," as Paulos calls them, is "clusters." Clusters, their uses and misuses, will be discussed shortly.

To augment their risk ratios, epidemiologists use "confidence intervals." Thus, you might see a risk ratio expressed as "2.9 (0.9–3.5)." This means that, expressed in strictest terms, the risk ratio is 2.9 but anything between 0.9 and 3.5 is within the range of the results of the study. In fact, even this parameter is not that solid. Confidence intervals themselves may be off. Thus, epidemiologists will say, "This is a 95 percent confidence interval," meaning that there is a 5 percent chance that even this broad range is inaccurate. A 90 percent confidence interval means that there is a 10 percent chance it is wrong, and so on. Even then, the interval assumes the study was conducted correctly. If it were conducted incorrectly, it would have the effect of using weighted dice or an incomplete deck of cards. In that case, the results are completely thrown off and the concepts of chance and probability don't even apply.

At any rate, when not only the relative risk number is above 1.0 (the term "elevated" will often be used to describe this) but so is the bottom of the confidence interval range, then epidemiologists say that number is "statistically significant." It is very important to grasp this simple concept. A risk level elevated at 4.0 may look very serious. It says that four times as many cases of such-and-such are showing up as in the group that wasn't exposed to the suspect agent. But if few enough people are involved in the study, the confidence interval may be something like 0.8– 9.0, indicating that the elevated risk level of 4.0 may mean nothing other than that's how the coin landed. The more people that are involved in a study, the closer the confidence interval and the better the chance that an elevated risk level actually means something. This is just how the law of probability works with coins or rolling dice. If you roll two sixes in a row with your dice, it doesn't mean anything. But if you roll the dice hundreds of times and six keeps coming up far more often than it should, that could indicate there is something wrong with the dice. If you go out on two dates and both end up disappointingly, you might not have much to worry about. If you go out on ten dates and all end up disappointingly, you might want to switch to a new mouthwash. Confidence intervals and statistical significance are just concepts that describe the effort to weed out conclusions that should not be based on numbers because the numbers aren't certain enough.

## BASIC TENETS OF EPIDEMIOLOGY

Now it is time to look at the basic rules of epidemiology. Some of those rules look *really* basic, even simple, but you'd be surprised at the trouble some people have with them.

*Tenet 1: Everyone dies.* Death takes a holiday only in the movies. That seems simple enough, but many people will, in the heat of the moment, forget it. The chances are that if your local newspaper ran a story saying, "Since the hazardous waste incinerator began operating last May, 186 people have died," there would be panic—if not in the streets then somewhere. A lot of people wouldn't stop to think about how many people would have died in that same period anyway, regardless of the operations of the incinerator.

A point related to this is that while we average a little over 70 years of life apiece, that is indeed simply an average. Some of us survive to 105; others die in infancy. Cancer and heart disease tend to be diseases of the elderly but often enough a young person will die of cancer and occasionally a youth will die of heart disease as well. That is not fair, but then neither is life fair. So not only do we have to keep in mind that everyone dies, we must also remember that a lot of us die prematurely.

*Tenet 2: One fourth of us will contract cancer and one fifth of us will die of it.* Indeed, as the population ages and fewer and fewer people die of other causes, more and more will die of cancer. Why? Because you have to die of *something*. See Tenet 1. Cancer, for the most part, is a disease of old age, and the nation that has reduced its incidence of diseases killing younger people will find its cancer rates increasing. This is true of the United States.

*Tenet 3: The mechanics of how cancer develops are not well understood.* Damage to the DNA of cells and improper cell division are thought to be at the root of the formation of cancer, but beyond that, our understanding of the disease begins to get quite foggy. DNA damage to cells and improper cell division don't always lead to cancer and, further, we often don't know what causes such damage or improper division.[4]

*Tenet 4: Most cancers are unexplained.* That follows from Tenet 3. Since we don't know exactly how cancer comes about in general, it is obviously difficult to say how it came about specifically. Again, this is a concept with which many people have a great deal of difficulty.

Most lay people probably don't understand that in *all* cases it is impossible to say for sure how someone got cancer. If a person who contracts lung cancer smoked three packs of cigarettes a day for sixty years, it's a good bet that the cancer resulted from cigarette smoking, but that is by no means certain. Consider the number of heavy smokers who die in old age of diseases having nothing to do with smoking; and consider that about 15 percent of lung cancer victims have never smoked.[5]

Tumors do not come stamped with an indentification of their cause. A lump in a breast caused by consumption of excess fat looks exactly like a lump caused by excess exposure to radiation. A brain tumor caused by exposure to plutonium would look exactly like a brain tumor that occurs for no reason that can be identified. One exception to this is mesothelioma, a lung disease which appears to be almost exclusively associated with asbestos exposure, but even here there appear to be some cases where asbestos is not the cause.[6] If you read that a doctor proclaimed that X cancer was caused by Y, you may assume that either the doctor is wrongly treating his opinion as a fact, or that the media has wrongly interpreted what the doctor said. Thus, when a person says, "I got cancer from working at such and such plant, or because I lived too close to such and such factory or because I ate such and such," they cannot possibly know, nor can their doctor, nor can the wisest diagnostic physician on the face of the earth. Which leads to Tenet 5.

*Tenet 5: Being a victim of a disease does not make one an expert in how that disease is contracted.* It is a curious phenomenon that one afflicted with a disease is often treated as an expert solely because of that affliction. A man who claims he got cancer from working at a certain job is automatically given great credence. In 1991, the late football great Lyle Alzado made the news by declaring that his inoperable and ultimately fatal brain cancer was caused by anabolic steroids that he took while trying to make a comeback at the age of forty-two. "I used a certain steroid that caused me to ruin my immune system," he said. He added, "I just hope that this interview . . . will convince the other people— junior high school, high school and college students—that they can do without this stuff."[7] In fact, it is documented that taking steroids can do all sorts of nasty things to the body, though brain cancer is not among them. Further, people had been dying from brain cancer long before anyone ever had access to steroids that could be ingested or injected. Thus, neither Alzado nor anyone else could possibly say with authority that his cancer was linked to steroid use. But the Associated Press, *Sports Illustrated,*[8] Cable News Network,[9] and at least one nationally syndicated columnist[10] carried this story without any suggestion of this discrepancy. Alzado said he got his cancer from steroid use, so who are we to argue with him? Besides, his story could scare kids out of using steroids. True, but it is still bad science. In fact, a brain cancer is a brain cancer, whether it was caused by cigarette smoking, air pollution, or by some sort of spontaneous cell mutation of which we understand nothing. The sufferer of that cancer has expertise in what it's like to suffer from that type of cancer, but nothing more.

The victim's assertions may be valid in that they give insight into his feelings. That may be of interest to the average reporter and to the average reader, but not to the epidemiologist. Yet time and again we read stories in the press or see news shows on television in which a cancer victim is stating that he or she *knows* that the cancer came from exposure to a nuclear power plant.

Likewise, we will occasionally read the story about the woman who "knows" that her child got cancer from exposure to a toxic waste dump or a pesticide. In the next chapter, we will read of one such case that made national news. This is not science, it is superstition.

*Tenet 6: The physician treating the victim does not necessarily have any expertise in the cause of the problem when that problem is cancer.* If it makes no sense to treat a victim of a disease as an expert in epidemiology of that disease, it also does not make much sense to automatically attribute such expertise to the treating physician. The media seem generally to assume that anyone with an "M.D." after his or her name who is willing to speak on a given medical subject is an expert in that subject. In fact, most doctors who work outside of epidemiologically related areas (which includes the physicians you see when you are ill or hurt) took a couple of epidemiology courses way back when and now know about as much about epidemiology as you know about chemistry because you were required to take it in high school back in 1969. Further, the practice of a treating physician would not put him or her in a position to study epidemiological patterns. That is, looking at individual cases is of little use in getting the big picture.

Thus, a treating physician may make a statement like "I've never seen another case of this disease in a man of this age." The doctor may think this has great epidemiological importance, as will a reporter, as will then the reader. In fact, it probably has none. If he suddenly sees five such cases, that might mean something. But that he has practiced for many years and this is his first case means nothing. At any rate, a practicing physician who attempts to extrapolate from what he has seen to the nation as a whole is in the position of the proverbial blind men who each feel a different part of the elephant and judge therefrom what the rest of the beast looks like.

*Tenet 7: Miscarriages are common.* Studies have shown that rates for miscarriages after a recognized pregnancy vary from about 12.5 to 33.9 percent. Some of the earlier studies showing the higher end probably suffered from various errors, so a risk of about 12 to 15 percent seems most likely.[11] As for the total rate of pregnancy lost after fertilization, including those that a woman couldn't ordinarily have recognized as even having been a pregnancy, one recent study put this figure at 31 percent.[12] These are higher rates than some of us probably would have thought, the point being that when you look at a number of miscarriages in an office or a neighborhood and the figure seems high to you, it doesn't mean that it really is high relative to the expected number. Obviously these are generalized numbers. Some categories of women have a much higher risk (those over thirty-five for example, or those with untreated severe diabetes), while others have a lower one. A good epidemiological study doesn't compare miscarriages in a given group with the national rate of miscarriages; rather it tries to match up similar women (a control group) who do not have the risk factor being investigated but have much in common with those who do.

*Tenet 8: Birth defects are common.* Probably about 2 to 3 percent of all babies born in this country exited the womb with at least one major malformation.[13] Since about four million babies are born annually, that is between 80,000 and 120,000 babies born annually with birth defects.

*Tenet 9: Most miscarriages and most birth defects are unexplained.* One recent study found that 43 percent of 1,549 miscarriages studied had a completely unknown cause.[14] Of the other 57 percent, most of those were also to some extent of unknown origin. For example, it could be said that many of them were related to chromosomal abnormalities in miscarried children, but it is often difficult to tell what the origin of those chromosomal abnormalities is.[15]

According to Dorothy Warburton, Ph.D., of the Genetics Diagnostic Laboratory, Babies Hospital, in New York City, when you again consider that we usually don't know what causes chromosomal defects, we again have to assign most miscarriages to the "unknown cause" category, more so among later ones than those that occur early during pregnancy. The presence of chromosome damage can, however, be used to rule out certain causes. For example, it would rule out anything that might have happened to the other parent. One thing, according to Warburton, who is considered one of the top experts in her field, is fairly certain. "I don't think that most of the obstetrical causes that most people dream up have any support," she says.[16]

The reason for these unknowns parallels the explanation of why we don't know the origin of most cancers. There just isn't enough knowledge about what causes birth defects in the first place.

Dr. Lewis Holmes, author of the aforementioned birth defect study, says, "This bedevils us as much as it does the victims. Most people have blamed themselves, neighbors have given them ideas. They don't understand that even genetic disorders often come as a total surprise."[17]

Further, Holmes notes, even the technology that has been around for thirty years that sometimes can determine causes of defects and miscarriages is not utilized. So when a woman's family physician or gynecologist tells her, "I just don't know why you had this problem," it may simply mean that *he* doesn't know.

The importance of these "unexplained" diseases, regarding either cancer or birth defects, cannot be overstated. Miscarriage, birth defects, and cancer are always a tragedy. And people always want an explanation for that tragedy. Elizabeth D. Stierman, writing in the journal *Clinical Obstetrics and Gynecology,* notes that "anger is a common symptom of this [second] phase. [Shock is the first phase.] Parents feel cheated and may protest the unfairness of the death. In an attempt to understand what has happened, they search for the cause and meaning of the death." Stierman adds: "Blame may be directed inward, resulting in guilt or self-reproach, or it may be expressed as anger and hostility, either generally or at someone or something."[18]

Many of these people are ripe to be handed an explanation: Your cancer is a result of exposure to herbicides; your miscarriage occurred because you took a certain prescribed drug; your child's birth defect is the result of a toxic waste site a few miles away.

Now suddenly everything falls into place. The cancer/miscarriage/ birth defect suddenly has meaning. A wrong has been done and must be righted. That is how many a crusade is born, as will be seen in subsequent chapters. But part of this process is that the victim or the victim's survivors see the smoking gun of some wrongdoing in the fact that the family physician could not tell them precisely what was the cause of the malady.

Let's now consider a scenario that involves many of the afore- mentioned tenets. Mary, who has had two healthy children, now miscarries. She is angry; she is confused. How could one have two healthy children and then a miscarriage? Actually, it happens all the time, but she does not know that and, indeed, her obste- trician may not know it, since he sees only a tiny portion of all the miscarriages that take place in the country. It turns out that the woman had taken a prescribed medicine, let's call it "No- retch," for morning sickness. She's heard about thalidomide, a prescription drug that caused horrible birth defects and miscar- riages in the early 1960s, and concludes that the only likely suspect for her tragedy was Noretch. She asks her doctor, "What caused my miscarriage?" He says, "I just don't know." She thinks, "Aha! It's none of the usual causes." She doesn't know there are no *usual* causes. Now she calls a reporter, who discovers that many women using Noretch have miscarried. Or maybe Mary asks around among her friends and finds one or two who took Noretch and miscarried, and then she goes to the reporter. Or maybe the Noretch suspicion arose with another woman, and the reporter, who has gotten access to the miscarriage files at the hospital, ends up calling Mary. The reporter thinks this Noretch could be the new thalidomide. If it is, the reporter could be saving countless women the agony of birth defects and miscarriages—and, not incidentally, win the Pulitzer Prize.

The reporter interviews Mary and four other women who have miscarried or have had defective babies, and several are absolutely convinced that Noretch must have been responsible. There's just no other explanation, they say. The reporter gets ahold of a list of women to whom Noretch has been prescribed in the area and makes a shocking discovery—15 percent of all births to these women have ended in miscarriage. The reporter talks to a few doctors who have prescribed Noretch, and one of them, Dr. Casey, an obstetrician, goes through his files and discovers that no fewer than half of the six women to whom he prescribed it have miscarried. That convinces him that Noretch must be involved, and he tells the reporter as much (forgetting, for the moment, that he could be sued for malpractice for having written the prescription). He doesn't know that some other doctors in town have had several more patients on Noretch than he has and that none of them have had natal problems. He only sees his little part of the picture. Armed with these numbers, armed with the personal testimonials of the women, armed with statements by most of the doctors that in the cases of most of these women they just don't know what caused the miscarriages, armed with the statement of Dr. Casey, and given only blanket denials of culpability by the manufacturer of Noretch (what do you expect them to say?), the reporter has her story. It goes on page one.

Now every woman in town who has used Noretch and has miscarried or had defective children grabs the phone and calls the newspaper. A follow-up article appears listing half a dozen women who have taken Noretch and miscarried, and a couple who took the drug and had birth defects, most of whom are convinced it must have been the drug that was responsible. Now the story is picked up on the national wire with the title: "Noretch: The New Thalidomide?" The weekly scandal sheets and the networks pick it up from there. Suddenly, reports linking Noretch and miscarriages are popping up all over the country. The manufacturer of Noretch takes out full-page ads saying that the drug was tested for ten years before it was approved and is perfectly safe. But whom do you believe, the independent journalist, Dr. Casey, and the poor mothers, or the big faceless corporation with an obvious vested interest? And now it's time for the vultures with briefcases to get in on the act, filing $100 million lawsuits on behalf of any woman they can find who took Noretch and miscarried or had a birth defect.

If you think this scenario is fanciful, you won't after you have read a few more chapters. But note the different epidemiological principles and tenets that were ignored. The victims were treated as experts. No mention was made that both miscarriages and birth defects are common, nor that these are usually unexplainable. The situation with Dr. Casey ignored the law of probability. Further, the reporter treated Dr. Casey as though he were an epidemiologist, not an obstetrician. A physician was treated as an expert in epidemiology. Nobody ever bothered to consult with a specialist whose job it is to study such things, an epidemiologist. Why do you need an epidemiologist? This leads to the next tenet.

*Tenet 10: Epidemiology is a complex science.* Setting up a proper epidemiological study is extremely difficult even when done by top professionals. Compare epidemiological studies to quizzes given in school. In any class, there will be some students who will do well on all quizzes and some who will do poorly on all quizzes, but most will have a range that, taken as a whole, will probably give a professor a good idea of the student's ability in that class. Even this assumes that the professor's quizzes are fair evaluations. In any case, any given quiz or epidemiological study does not have much weight without the support of others.

That's why it's not unusual to hear on Monday that coffee has been linked to cancer and on Thursday that there is no link, to hear on Tuesday that birth control pills cause heart disease and to hear on Friday that they do not. There is not necessarily dishonesty or a cover-up involved; there are just so many problems that must be factored out. It can take years, even decades, to do so. That is why it is simply wrong for a scientist or, as is far more often the case, a journalist or other public crusader to build a whole case around a single study, or even around two or three.

What a good journalist *can* do is to poke holes in a bad epidemiological study. That is the essential equivalent of a nonarchitect walking into a house and seeing that it was very poorly designed, or a landlubber noting that the ship she's on is listing badly. But the building and piloting of these houses and ships is a job best left to the professionals.

*Tenet 11: Epidemiology is an inexact science.* Epidemiology cannot detect all causes of illness. If an illness is fairly common, a slight increase as caused by a specific agent may be impossible to detect. Thus, for example, Frederick J. Stare, Robert E. Olson, and Elizabeth M. Whelan, all of the American Council on Science and Health, write in their book, *Balanced Nutrition:* "Alar has been used since 1967 without a single case of cancer or any other disease attributed to its consumption at approved trace levels in apples."[19] But of course not. Almost all of us have at one time or another consumed apples and one fourth of us will get cancer. Searching among those tens of millions of cancers for those caused by Alar is like trying to determine if someone threw a brick into the backyard swimming pool by measuring the water line. Alar could cause five thousand cancers a year, but against the backdrop of a million cancer diagnoses a year among apple eaters, you would never know it. On the other hand, a brick thrown into a kitchen sink would cause a perceptible increase in the water line. The equivalent to this would be to measure those with *extraordinary* exposures, for example, workers who were exposed to high levels of Alar. Unfortunately no such study has ever been made.

*Tenet 12: Epidemiologists are only human.* They can make mistakes that overstate or understate a problem. They may, very rarely to be sure, intentionally skew their data to meet predetermined conclusions. On the whole, however, epidemiologists are more trustworthy by a factor of at least ten than the journalists who will relay their work to the public or than the regulators or politicians who will pass regulations on the basis of their studies. Epidemiologists on the whole are also quite careful and conservative in their language. If they observe, for example, twice as many influenza cases one week than the one before, they might say that this development was "significant." And if half the town got wiped out by bubonic plague, that too would be deemed "significant." Not "very significant," or "extremely significant" or "utterly horrifying," just "significant."

*Tenet 13: Associations do not equal cause and effect.* Just because people with some ailment in common have another thing in common doesn't mean that the other thing caused the ailment. When I was very small, I observed that most folks drinking diet sodas were overweight. I therefore hypothesized that gulping Tab, which was just about the only diet soda there was then, made one fat. Likewise, to sit in the sauna of any American health club is to come to the conclusion that there are a disproportionate number of heavy people in these rooms. It is probably not wise to conclude from this that saunas make you fat, any more than does Tab.

*Tenet 14: Rare diseases still have to happen to somebody.* If you read that "John, who worked for twenty years at a radioactive widget factory, was suddenly stricken with an extremely rare form of cancer, that of the little toe," your first thought is probably that the cancer has something to do with the radioactive widgets. But assuming that 100 men and women each year get this very distressing form of cancer of "this little piggie," it must be asked what of the exposures of the other 99? In one highly publicized incident, a couple's twelve-year-old was diagnosed with osteosarcoma (bone cancer) and since they lived near a plutonium-processing plant and osteosarcomas strike only about 520 American children a year, the parents assumed the plant caused the cancer. The local media seemed to share that assumption.[20] What they didn't take into account was that 519 other Americans got that cancer in that year alone, none of whom lived anywhere near the plant.

*Tenet 15: "Clusters" almost always mean absolutely nothing.* Strictly speaking, a cluster is simply an elevated incidence of disease or other problem in a given population. Cancer, birth defects, and miscarriages are the three subjects that most often come up in media accounts of clusters.

One immediately apparent problem in reading conclusions into clusters is that whether you get one or not often depends entirely on how you divide up a group. Consider a group of sixty celebrities of whom we would expect 20 percent, or 12 in number, to have cataracts. By great coincidence, they turn out to have exactly the correct percentage. We line them up in three rows in alphabetical order. Former tennis pro Arthur Ashe is first, at top left, and singer of sorts Frank Zappa is at the end, bottom right. They are represented below, with Ns being normal and Cs representing cataracts.

```
C N N N N N N C N N N C N N N N N C
N C N N N N N N N N N N N N N N N N
C N C C N N N C N C N N N C N C N N N
```

Since they have exactly the percentage of cataracts we would expect in this group, when we look at all three rows together, we find nothing unusual. No clusters. But if we look at them row by row, suddenly we find that cataracts are heavily overrepresented in the third row. Cluster! Of course, we know this means nothing, since the place one's name occupies in the alphabet is not considered a risk factor for developing cataracts.

Now let's arrange them on the basis of the length of their hair. Telly Savalas is first, edging out Mr. Clean by just a—well, you know. Savalas is top left. Country singer Crystal Gayle is pulling up the rear, because that's just about how far down her hair goes. Miss Gayle is bottom right. Our arrangement looks like this:

```
N N C C N N N N C N N N N C N N N N N N
C N N C C N N N C N N N N N C N N N N C
N C N C N N N N N N N N N N N N N N N N
```

We already know that in the overall group the number of cataracts is just right, twelve where we expect twelve. And in fact the first row has four where we'd expect four. The last row has two where we'd expect four, yet this is no cause for alarm certainly. But the middle row has six where we'd expect four. Cluster!

Now, let's rearrange our celebrities just slightly like so:

```
N N C C N N N N C N    N N N C N N N N N N
C N N C C N N N C N    N N N N C N N N N C
N C N C N N N N N N    N N N N N N N N N N
```

We've kept the same order, but now we've divided the group in half, left and right. Each half will have, on average, six persons with cataracts. On the right side there are only three. "No problemo!" as Bart Simpson would say, but he's excluded from the cohort since it's impossible to tell where his head leaves off and his hair begins. On the left side, however, there are nine where we'd expect six. Cluster!

I hope you are not enjoying this too much, because we're only going to do it one more time. Now we're arranging the celebrities by age. Bart Simpson's little sister Maggie is now first, top left, and who else but George Burns is last, bottom right.

```
N N N N N N N N N N N N N N N N N N N N
N N N N N N N C N N N N N N N N N N N C
N C C C N N C N C N C N C N C N N C C N
```

The very first thing you'll note is that I have now named seven of our celebrities and in no case did any of them ever turn out to have cataracts. That's because I don't want any angry letters from people (or cartoon characters) saying I'm telling the world they have health problems that they really don't have. The second thing you'll notice, however, is that there is a very clear pattern indicating that as the group ages, it has more cataracts. This is our only legitimate cluster.

There are virtually an infinite number of ways of breaking down groups—sex, race, address, occupation, age categories and so on, plus combinations of these categories (for example, black females living on the north end of town working as clerk typists who are between the ages of fifteen and thirty-one). If you are looking for a cluster, you will always find one, simply by arranging arbitrary categories such as the one just presented. You may find that black females living on the north end of town working as clerk typists who are between the ages of fifteen and thirty have no elevation of cancers. But if your sample group of women with cancer has two such women who happen to be 31, by tossing them in suddenly you may have doubled the expected rate of cancer. Call in the news crew! Obviously a good epidemiologist tries to avoid such arbitrary breakdowns of groups, but most reporters and citizens in general don't know the first thing about such methodology.

So what good, then, are clusters? In the hands of amateur sleuths and crusaders such as those whose reports fill our magazines, newspapers, and airwaves, they are no good at all in epidemiological terms, and very harmful in sociological terms—in other words, they serve no purpose other than scaring the hell out of people. If someone says he or someone else has identified a dozen clusters regarding VDTs and miscarriages or birth defects, the reader should say to himself, "So what? If I were given the data I could probably find a hundred."

What good are clusters in the hands of trained professionals, then? Not much there either, actually. An article in the *Journal of the American Medical Association* described how the investigations of clusters have almost always proven fruitless. "Health departments have invested large sums of time and energy investigating these so-called clusters," it said, "epidemiologists spend countless hours calculating risk ratios, attorneys endless weeks litigating civil suits. Now, say investigators in Atlanta, Georgia, at the Centers for Disease Control, it's time the public health community calls a halt to many of those investigations."[21]

At the National Conference on Clustering of Health Events, sponsored by the CDC in Atlanta in 1989, keynote speaker Kenneth J. Rothman, editor of the journal *Epidemiology,* argued that "with few exceptions, there is little scientific or public health reason to investigate individual clusters at all." Such efforts, he said, are increasingly becoming "exercises in public relations," fueled by health-conscious consumers and public misperceptions that research is the answer to every problem. Rothman said, "If the epidemic of cluster research continues, it will eventually intrude on more productive epidemiological investigation of environmental exposures."[22]

Alan Bender, chief of the Minnesota Department of Health's Chronic Disease and Environmental Epidemiology section, said at the conference that of 500 reports of suspected clusters in Minnesota, only 5 prompted enough concern for formal studies. Other states reported similar rates. For example, from 1961 to 1983 the CDC investigated 108 cancer clusters from twenty-nine states and five foreign countries. It found no clear cause for any of the clusters.[23]

There *have been* cases where cancer cluster studies have proven fruitful. In one, the investigation of a handful of cases of vaginal cancer in young women identified diethylstilbestrol as the cause, and in another the study of lung cancers among workers in the packaging industry found that polyvinyl chlorides were the cause. But in both cases, the prevalence of the disease was rare and suddenly increased in frequency. The investigations uncovered new mechanisms of disease. Yet the typical clusters trumpeted by the media involve common diseases such as cancers in general, leukemia specifically, miscarriages, and birth defects.[24]

Epidemiologist Dr. Raymond Neutra notes that in an environmentally caused cluster, as are all the types discussed in this book, "the relative risk in the [city or town] neighborhood [because there just won't be that many cases or people to measure], to achieve statistical significance, would often need to be above eight."[25] That is, you would need to find eight times what you would expect. That's something to think about the next time you see a headline that reads STUDY SHOWS THAT PERSONS LIVING NEAR

X PLANT HAVE TWICE USUAL RATE OF KIDNEY CANCER or SURVEY INDICATES WOMEN WORKING WITH Y DEVICE HAVE THREE TIMES USUAL MISCARRIAGE RATE. Indeed, Neutra goes even further, saying that when looking at a specific cluster of cases, before going off in "hot pursuit" of the cause of those cases, to use a term employed by former CDC chief epidemiologist Alexander Langmuir,[26] there should be at least five cases and the relative risk should be very high, for example twenty or more.[27]

While clusters are of little use to epidemiologists, they are a wonderful tool for crusaders seeking to indict something as a cause of disease. Tell a layman that a given office building or a given city block has had twice the cancer victims or heart attack victims as the expected rate, and he instantly assumes that something is wrong in that building or on that block.

The concept of epidemiology should be clearer to the reader now, and yet it is to be hoped that something else is clear to the reader as well. While the concepts of epidemiology are basic, the application is fraught with pitfalls. The journalist or other layperson who fancies that he can just look at a cluster of cancers or other disease and say, "Aha! There's clearly a problem there!" or who goes even further to say, "And I know what's causing the problem!" is guilty of taking the surgeon's tool unto himself and cutting away. The journalist who, upon finding that the epidemiologists disagree with him, insists that they must be engaging in a cover-up, is not only grossly ignorant, but arrogant as well. We will meet our fair share of these.

# CHAPTER 4

# Dioxin: "The Most Deadly Chemical Created by Man"

It is a shameful thing that you should mind these folks that are out of their wits.[1]

> —Martha Carrier, addressing an accusing magistrate, before being hanged as a witch in Salem, Massachusetts, in 1692

"The Politics of Poison," aired by television station KRON in San Francisco in 1979, told its viewers that dioxin is a "fetus-deforming agent one hundred thousand times more powerful than thalidomide . . . a synthetic chemical so powerful that an ounce could wipe out a million people." In this same film, which focused heavily on the alleged link of the herbicide, 2,4,5-T with birth defects and miscarriages, an Oregon woman told of developing boils on her face after a spraying and proceeded to describe in detail her miscarriage: "When I miscarried . . . the fetus wasn't even recognizable as a baby or anything. It was just a mess. . . . It looked like hamburger, like chopped meat."[2]

An op-ed piece in *The New York Times* four years later declared:

Dioxin can cause severe adverse health effects, and death, at the lowest doses imaginable. . . . millions of pounds of the two ingredients of Agent Orange are still being sprayed, despite the enormous harm they are known to have caused to human health, wildlife and the environment. . . . [It] may play a significant role in the current cancer epidemic.[3]

On the other side of the continent, a straight news story in the *Los Angeles Times* titled, "Lethal Dioxin Monster Guest in Chemical Lab," stated: "Modern wizards of science with ultra-sophisticated research tools have invented headache remedies, dandelion killers, and assorted bug poisons. They have also created a chemical monster."[4]

So far the victims of the dioxin terror have included Italians living in the town of Seveso, residents of Love Canal, residents of Times Beach, Missouri, and millions of Vietnam veterans, among others. But since dioxin is everywhere now, we are all, depending on whom you listen to, either potential victims of poisoning or potential victims of gross disinformation.

The substance in question is the compound tetrachlorodibenzodioxin, which is generally abbreviated (thankfully) to TCDD. There are in fact seventy-five dioxins, of which TCDD is only one, but it is considered by far the most toxic.[5] It is the one you have read about in newspapers and magazines and seen on gripping television shows and the one that will be addressed in this book simply as "dioxin," or "TCDD." TCDD is frequently accompanied by a compound in the furan family, TCDF, short for 2,3,7,8-tetrachlorodibenzofuran, generally considered to be significantly less toxic than TCDD.[6]

Dioxin is never intentionally manufactured. Not only is it not, as Christopher Hitchens claimed in *The Nation,* "the key ingredient in Agent Orange,"[7] in fact it serves no purpose whatsoever. Instead, it is merely an unavoidable by-product in the manufacture of certain herbicides and other chemicals,[8] just as carbon monoxide is a by-product of burning gasoline.

Dioxin is not only a by-product of herbicide production, but also of insecticides, paper milling, wood preservatives used to protect telephone poles and railroad cross-ties, and coolants for electric transformers. Incineration of plastics and such ordinary products as copy paper also releases a less toxic form of dioxin into the environment.

The question whether dioxin occurs naturally is considered by some to be of tremendous importance considering the natural/synthetic double standard applied to all potentially hazardous chemicals. While incineration at extreme temperatures is a method of eliminating dioxin, scientists from the Dow Chemical Company, which manufactured dioxin-contaminating herbicides, reported in 1978 that burning virtually anything at low temperatures produces dioxins. They found dioxins in municipal incinerators, powerhouses, and even fireplaces. "I'm convinced that dioxin has been around since the advent of fire," Dow's Ronald Kagel has said.[9] But other scientists are less convinced than Kagel. Since dioxins can now be found practically everywhere, it stands to reason that their presence in fireplace ash doesn't necessarily mean that they were created by combustion. To check that hypothesis, General Electric scientists conducted tests on twenty-eight-hundred-year-old mummies from Chile, the wrappings of which they hypothesized would contain dioxin from ancient wood fires. In fact, as they reported in *Environmental Science and Technology,* they found no presence of dioxin.[10]

Ralph Nader has told readers that "three ounces of dioxin can kill more than a million people,"[11] and *The Washington Post* reported: "The evidence is overwhelming that dioxin is carcinogenic in humans."[12] Indeed, one of the most ubiquitous expressions about dioxin is that it is "the most toxic chemical created by man." Obviously, "most toxic" has a very startling tone. There is no qualifying its severity with "one of the" or "perhaps the." No, dioxin is flat-out the worst thing that could possibly come into contact with your little body. Both the assertions that dioxin is deadly to humans and that it is indeed the most deadly chemical to come from a laboratory have been intrinsic assumptions of the American media.

And they are assumptions that are simply not borne out by facts.

Probably no scientist is more identified with the viewpoint that technology is a cause of cancer than Dr. Samuel Epstein, professor of occupational health at the University of Illinois College of Medicine in Chicago. He has already been heard from in this book and will be heard from again. Yet the single area in which Epstein has probably had the most influence has been that of dioxins. He has lent scientific credence to the proposition of deadly dioxin. Whatever other scientists were saying, a reporter could always rely on Epstein for the proper response.

The late Dr. Irving Selikoff, a principal proponent of the asbestos scare in the 1980s, has also weighed in, applying the natural evolution theory to dioxin, telling *Time* magazine in 1983: "No doubt about it, dioxin is harmful to humans. It is man-made. As a result, the human body doesn't know how to break it down. We store it in our bodies and accumulate it."[13] That is a funny remark, though, because aspartame (Nutrasweet) is man-made and it isn't stored in the body, and asbestos *isn't* man-made, yet Selikoff made much of the fact that it likes to stick around in the lungs. In fact, whether something is stored in the body has absolutely nothing to do with its being man-made or not, but only with its being water-soluble or fat-soluble. Vitamins B and C are water-soluble; they are flushed out of the body daily. Vitamins A, D, E, and K are fat-soluble; the body stores them and releases them only slowly.

## DIOXIN GOES TO THE ZOO

In an appearance on ABC's *Nightline,* Epstein averred that there is a "remarkable consistency in the chronic toxic effects of dioxin from one species to another, and also a remarkable consistency between these effects in animals and in humans."[14] That statement could not have been more false. There are few substances that are as remarkably inconsistent in the harm they cause from one species to another.

The assumption that dioxin is the most deadly chemical created by man—an assumption that is taken by most people to mean "most deadly to *me*"—would only be true if we weighed about a pound and were small stout-bodied, short-eared, nearly tailless domesticated rodents. That's right, as was pointed out in *Chemical and Engineering News* in the early 1980s: "The widely made claim that dioxin is one of the deadliest known, or that it is the deadliest man-made substance, is based on its extreme toxicity in guinea pigs." An oral dose of a mere six micrograms per kilogram of body weight killed half the guinea pigs in a laboratory experiment.[15]

But let's say that you are not a guinea pig, but rather are considerably smaller and have a little stub of a tail. That is, you are a hamster. Well, in that case you could practically season your porridge with dioxin, because tested hamsters required a dose about 1,900 times as high as the guinea pigs' to kill half the test group. Injected directly into the abdomen, the amount required to kill half the hamsters was 5,000 times as high as the oral dose that killed half the guinea pigs.[16] Rabbits, mice, and monkeys cluster somewhere in the middle—roughly 200 times less sensitive than guinea pigs and 50 times more sensitive than hamsters.[17] Once again, we find that not only can't we simply extrapolate from rodents to humans, we can't even extrapolate from one rodent to another.

In Chapter 2, the reader learned that some alleged carcinogens cause cancer only in mice and others only in rats, and may have wondered which of the two rodents he was more like. Now the question is, does the reader feel more like a guinea pig, a hamster, a monkey, or a bullfrog? Or is he prepared to accept what Dr. Epstein and many others who have been blowing the whistle about dioxin for years haven't been telling you, that if you are capable of reading this—as opposed to say, having it line the bottom of your cage—then you are none of the above; you are a member of a species that will react differently to dioxin than to any of the above.

When the statement, "Dioxin is the most deadly chemical ever manufactured by man" is amended to read, "Dioxin is the most deadly chemical *to guinea pigs* ever manufactured by man," it loses a bit of its impact.

## A DIFFERENT SORT OF CAGED TEST ANIMAL

What is the data on dioxin and humans? There exists more information than one might think. The Environmental Defense Fund (EDF) fact sheet on dioxins states that human exposure to tiny doses is dangerous and that, for ethical reasons, "scientists cannot intentionally expose humans to dioxins under controlled conditions in order to carefully measure dioxins' potency."[18] Ethical or not, one such experiment did take place in the United States. The subjects were prisoners, who in past times have often been used as guinea pigs. In the mid-1960s, a dermatologist working under contract to Dow obtained volunteers from a prison, men who had been offered small cash rewards and special privileges. Initially, he applied between 0.2 and 8.0 micrograms onto the men's skin, an amount that when applied to rabbit ears gave the animals chloracne, a skin ailment that resembles a severe form of common acne that sometimes leaves permanent scars. (To visualize a microgram, a nickel weighs about 5 grams and a microgram is 1 one-millionth of a gram.) Nevertheless, it produced no symptoms in the men. Two weeks later, a second dose of dioxin was applied to the same area of skin on the men. Still, no chloracne appeared. Thus, 16 micrograms were not enough to induce chloracne in humans. These results were consistent with those of another study done in Hamburg, Germany, which found that a minimum dose of between 50 and 100 micrograms was necessary.[19]

But here is where the subject gets interesting. The original contract with Dow ended at the 16-microgram level, but it seems curiosity got the better of the dermatologist, and without Dow's permission, he went ahead and applied all his remaining dioxin to the backs of ten of his prison volunteers. The dose used was 7,500 micrograms—almost five hundred times the amount used in the first series of tests. From this dose chloracne did develop in eight of the ten prisoners, clearing up within six months in all of them. This does not tell us much about at what level dioxin causes human chloracne, only that it is somewhere between 16 and 7,500 micrograms. What is most interesting, though, is that if this same high dose amount (relative to the animals' body weight) had been ingested by some lab animals, they would have died (see table). Indeed, an amount proportional to that placed on each man's back would have killed at least fifty guinea pigs.

As to long-term effects, the EPA did attempt to locate some of the prisoners in the early 1980s, but the effort fell apart when it was found that many of the prisoners had had many types of chemical tests applied to them and that no distinction could be made between the results of the dioxin and the other tests.[20]

## FARMERS AND FORESTERS

A rather more ethical way of testing humans for the effects of dioxin is to look at epidemiological data from people who have been exposed to the substance day after day, year after year, in considerably higher levels than that with which most of us would ever come into contact. The most important early evidence for a

**Lethal Doses of Dioxin in Various Animals and the Dose
Administered to Prisoners***

| Test animal | Dose (in micrograms/kilogram body weight) necessary to kill 50 percent of animals |
| --- | --- |
| Guinea pig | 1 |
| Male rat | 22 |
| Female rat | 45 |
| Monkey | <70 |
| Dose administered to prisoners' skin that caused no effect other than chloracne | about 100 |
| Mouse | 114 |
| Rabbit | 115 |
| Dog | <300 |
| Bullfrog | <1000 |
| Hamster | 5000 |

*Reprinted from Michael Gough, *Dioxin, Agent Orange,* p. 187; adapted in turn from *Chemical and Engineering News,* June 6, 1983.[21]

dioxin connection to soft-tissue sarcoma (cancer of the body's connective tissue) came from studies of Swedish forestry workers. Between 1979 and 1981, Swedish investigators published three papers reporting that exposure to 2,4,5-T during herbicide spraying caused a fivefold to sevenfold increased risk of soft-tissue sarcoma and a fivefold increase in malignant lymphoma (a tumor of lymph nodes and white blood cells).[22] But other early 1980s studies of herbicide applicators in Sweden,[23] and Finland,[24] failed to confirm the finding. Indeed, members of the dioxin scientific community were extremely critical of the Swedish studies, pointing out that there had been ample newspaper and TV publicity concerning the possible link between dioxin and soft-tissue sarcomas during the time these studies were conducted, and that this may have unconsciously implanted a reason for people with soft-tissue sarcoma to think that they might have been exposed in some way.[25] Such are the pitfalls of many an epidemiological study.

Since then, studies have continued to produce mixed results, with some showing an association between phenoxy-herbicide exposure and the occurrence of soft-tissue sarcomas, Hodgkin's disease, and non-Hodgkin's lymphoma (NHL),[26] and others indicating no such association.[27] Further, just because a study was negative for one or more types of cancer does not mean it wasn't positive for others. Thus, for any given cancer, most of the studies are negative while at the same time most of them are positive for *some* type of cancer. A further complicating factor is that many of these herbicides apparently contained no TCDD dioxin. Even if we were to assume that *something* in the herbicides was giving these farmers cancer, it would be wrong to attempt to implicate any given component in that herbicide.

Whatever consensus finally comes out of these farmer and forester studies, it would seem that the best method for determining the effects of high levels of dioxin is to look at those known for sure to have been contaminated with high levels. One such group, the Air Force personnel who participated in Operation Ranch Hand, dumping the dioxin-containing defoliant Agent Orange from planes during the Vietnam War, have been reevaluated every few years and so far have shown no exceptional number of soft-tissue sarcomas or Hodgkin's disease or NHL.[28] This will be discussed in more detail in the next chapter.

## OCCUPATIONAL DATA

Another group of heavily exposed persons are those who handled TCDD-containing materials where they were manufactured. There have not been many studies of these workers. One, released in 1989, surveyed forty workers who were occupationally exposed to TCDD; they had blood levels ranging from less than 20 parts per trillion (ppt)—slightly above the average American's level of about 5 ppt to as much as 750 ppt. The study looked at a wide variety of indicators of potential trouble ranging from immunological abnormalities to liver enzymes to neurological problems and found no adverse health effects in any of the workers[29] although two had suffered chloracne.[30]

Nevertheless, a much larger, more recent study has raised a warning flag. February 1991 saw the release of the long-awaited results of the National Institute for Occupational Safety and

Health (NIOSH) study of workers in plants that produced dioxin-contaminated herbicide. The study, headed up by epidemiologist Marilyn Fingerhut, looked at 1,037 death certificates available from 1,052 deaths among a total cohort of 5,172 male workers from twelve plants.[31] Using a procedure that the federal Centers for Disease Control had already employed to measure dioxin levels in soldiers who might have been exposed to Agent Orange, the NIOSH researchers measured the blood dioxin levels of 253 workers and used a formula based on the rate at which the body is known to excrete dioxin to determine what that level would have been at the time of exposure. They found that the mean (average) level of dioxin in the workers at the time of exposure was 2,000 ppt, four hundred times the average level in Americans of about 5 ppt. Among the workers in the sample who had been exposed over twenty years earlier, the mean of the estimated exposure at the time of exposure for the subgroup exposed less than one year was 640 ppt. For those who had been exposed more than one year, the mean was 3,600 ppt.[32] They found a small but significant increase in all cancers combined in the entire cohort, with a higher rate of cancer in those with the most dioxin exposure. Dividing the cohort into categories of latency (more or less than twenty or more years since exposure) and dividing the twenty-plus-year category down further into those exposed for more or less than one year, they found additional correlations to specific cancers. For example, those exposed to the most dioxin had a significant increase in deaths from cancers of the respiratory system. What the researchers *didn't* find, on the other hand, was any relationship between dioxin exposure and NHL,[33] although some have long alleged a connection, especially in regard to veterans exposed to Agent Orange.

At the very most, the NIOSH study found an elevated risk only for those exposed to tremendously high levels of dioxin. There were no excess cancers in the cohort of workers with less than a year of exposure but more than twenty years since that exposure,[34] even though the group's average concentration of 640 ppt was hundreds of times higher than the average American's exposure and higher, indeed, than that of practically any American airman who sprayed Agent Orange during Operation Ranch Hand.

Since—aside from the residents of Seveso, Italy, and other

victims of dioxin explosions—the only people exposed to such levels were the chemical plant employees being studied by NIOSH, whatever warning signals arose from the study would appear to apply only to those persons being studied.

Yet, it may be jumping to a conclusion even to assume that the workers were in danger, says Michael Gough of the Office of Technology Assessment. Gough is author of the book *Dioxin, Agent Orange,* a former member of the Agent Orange Working Group, the intergovernmental task force with responsibility for reviewing all studies related to Agent Orange (1980–85), and is a former chairman of the Veterans Administration advisory group on the health effects of herbicides. He is currently the chairman of the Ranch Hand Advisory Group in the Department of Health and Human Services. He notes that the "small excesses [from the Fingerhut study] come about from dividing workers into different categories, but when you do this you increase the possibility of creating artifactual groups,"[35] that is, groups that give false clusters, as described in Chapter 3, based simply on how someone divided them up. In other words, you can take a single large group with an average number of cancers but if you divide that group by, say, color of eyes, you may now find the blue-eyed group has an excess or if you divide by color of hair you may now find the blonds have a greater than average level of cancer.

As to the two specifically elevated cancers, that of the respiratory system may be suspect, says Gough, because of what he calls a "bizarre" method for eliminating the most important confounding factor in lung cancer, cigarette smoking. The method the NIOSH study used was to extrapolate from interviews at just two plants to the other ten.[36]

With soft-tissue sarcoma, the second cancer associated in the study with dioxin exposure, Fingerhut and the other researchers themselves pointed out that "the interpretation of the increased mortality from soft-tissue sarcoma in our study is limited by the small number of cases and the fact that the cause of death was sometimes misclassified on the death certificates of the workers *and* in the U.S. comparison population" (emphasis added).[37] Specifically, the researchers found that two of the four men who had cancer of the soft tissue listed as the cause of death did not, based on an analysis of tissue specimens, actually have that disease. Conversely, they were able to find three additional workers who did die *with* soft-tissue sarcoma (though not necessarily *of* the disease) based on hospital records.[38] The National Cancer Institute's Dr. Edward J. Sondik notes that recent autopsies of elderly men have shown that about one fourth of them proved to have cancer of the prostate, even when the apparent cause of death was something else.[39] It is not unusual for a person to have some form of cancer in his or her body for years before eventually dying of something else. To substitute *having* a given type of cancer for *dying* of it is to turn accurate statistics-keeping on its head. It is that same sort of confusion that the study talks about when it refers to misclassification in the United States comparison population. In other words, when the authors say that there were 3.0 deaths in the group of workers exposed for over one year to dioxin who died after at least twenty years later, and that this compares to an expected 0.3 deaths, they really aren't sure what the expected rate of death is.[40] It is possible to make guesses about an equation in which either the numerator or the denominator is solid. But where neither is solid, your guesses aren't much better than mush.

This point, unfortunately, went unmentioned in the accompanying *New England Journal of Medicine* editorial by a writer not affiliated with the NIOSH research group.[41] Yet, even if the denominator was correct, the tiny number of cases involved lead to a tremendously wide confidence interval range for risk ratios of from 1.9 all the way to 26.95.[42] A later study of German industrial workers exposed to massive amounts of dioxin, while the author claimed that it showed evidence of dioxin carcinogenicity, in fact found *no* soft-tissue sarcomas.[43] That study, itself, has been criticized for relying on workers' memories instead of company records and for not factoring out cigarette smoking.[44]

Notwithstanding all this, the Fingerhut study is considered to be perhaps the best conducted in the area, as the accompanying editorial put it, "a model of its kind."[45] Which shows how very difficult conducting such studies is.

In short, observes Gough, there are three possible interpretations of the NIOSH study. One is that dioxin did cause the elevated cancers, although only at extremely high levels of exposure which would not apply to anyone who didn't work in a dioxin-producing factory. A second is that there may be some other factor at the plants that is acting to increase cancer rates, a possibility left open by the NIOSH researchers, who pointed out that the workers "may have been exposed to numerous other chemicals while employed at the plants." The third possibility is that the elevated cancers occurred simply out of chance. He notes that deaths from circulatory and digestive diseases were statistically significantly lower for the workers than for the general population.[46] No one would claim that this resulted from a *protective* effect of dioxin. Likewise, a statistically significant elevated cancer risk doesn't necessarily mean it resulted from the deleterious effect of dioxin.

Looking at such data as already presented in this chapter, at least that which came in before 1984, the American Medical Association's (AMA) Council on Scientific Affairs concluded in that year:

> Adverse reactions [from dioxin] in animals include . . . [degeneration of the thymus, induction of liver enzymes, birth defects in mice, and spontaneous abortions in rodents and monkeys]. Except for chloracne, however, TCDD has not demonstrated comparable levels of biologic activity in man; that is to say, no long-term effects on the cardiovascular and central nervous systems, the liver, the kidney, the thymus and immunologic defenses, and the reproductive function—in the male, female or offspring—has been demonstrated.[47]

The AMA could make that statement today. Yet the reader with a good memory for dates will recall that the explosion of a herbicide-manufacturing plant in Seveso, Italy; the Love Canal incident; the Times Beach, Missouri incident; the horror stories about pregnant women exposed in the United States to dioxin-containing herbicide; and finally the horror stories about Vietnam veterans and their offspring, all came to light before 1984. Didn't each of those incidents prove beyond doubt that Epstein and the media were right about the effects of dioxin on humans? The Agent Orange story is so detailed that it will comprise a chapter in itself. But we will proceed to examine these other incidents. What we have to learn from them tells us a lot more about the media, about bureaucrats, and about ourselves than it does about dioxin.

## SEVESO AND "THE POISON THAT FELL FROM THE SKY"

The alleged dioxin-related illnesses at Love Canal would be used to justify the panic at Times Beach and the nation's Superfund program. But at the same time, the Love Canal panic itself was, according to some, justified on the basis of an incident that took place in the northern Italian town of Seveso in 1976 and the alleged devastation to their health that local residents suffered as a result.

On a Saturday afternoon on July 10, 1976, an explosion rocked an unattended chemical reactor at the plant of an Italian company in the town of Meda, which lies directly north of Seveso. The reactor was producing a chemical intended for use in the manufacture of the antibacterial compound hexachlorophene. A by-product of this process was TCDD dioxin. The explosion ruptured a safety valve at the top of the reactor and released into the air a vaporous cloud that slowly drifted southward onto the people of Seveso. A number of small children were playing outdoors and some of them ran around in the billowing cloud, laughing and waving their arms. But soon they began to cough and before long most of the children and many of the adults became nauseated. Later they developed headaches, diarrhea, and irritation of the skin. Some developed the sores that mark the disease chloracne. Birds began dropping from the skies and some animals on the ground sickened and died as well. The average concentration of dioxin in Seveso zone A, the most heavily exposed area, soon after the accident was measured at 230 parts per billion,[48] or 230 times higher than the level the U.S. Centers for Disease Control (CDC) would later set as a "level of concern" for lifetime exposure at Times Beach, Missouri.[49]

American newsmagazines had a field day with the Seveso incident. *Time* dutifully reported that a farmer watched his cat keel over and when he picked up the body, the tail fell off. "When authorities dug the cat up for examination two days later, said the farmer, all that was left was its skull." The magazine went on to report that "one scientist" said that "a single gram is capable of killing thousands of people" and it proceeded to list a litany of disorders that "one scientist" or another said dioxin caused in humans: damage to the liver, spleen, kidneys, respiratory tract, and nervous system, along with the possibility of birth defects.[50] (*Time* did admit two years later that there had yet to be a single human death from the effects of the explosion, but prefaced the comment with the word "miraculously."[51])

*Newsweek* entitled its first story on the Seveso accident, " 'Our Own Hiroshima,' "[52] and in its follow-up wrote of a woman who lived near Seveso who "recently delivered a child with an under-developed stomach—the eighth birth defect linked directly to the poison."[53] What the "direct" link was, other than that the woman lived near Seveso, *Newsweek* did not explain.

Perhaps the most influential in shaping Americans' view of Seveso was John G. Fuller's best-selling 1977 book, *The Poison That Fell from the Sky.* On the jacket cover we hear of the residents of the town whose

> children have sickened with disfiguring and life-threatening dis-ease; old people have died and autopsies have revealed that the chemical fatally attacked them; pregnant women have borne birth-defective babies. . . . At first these symptoms were limited to "Zone A," the area closest to the contamination. Soon there were signs that the residents of "Zone B" were affected; the contami-nation is apparently still spreading.[54]

This makes it sound like the residents of Bhopal, India, where in 1984 the accidental release of a pesticide from a Union Carbide plant quickly killed more than two thousand persons, got off easy. Fortunately, the good people of Seveso would never have recog-nized what Fuller's jacket copy was talking about. The account was essentially fiction.

Certainly it would be fair to say that if anybody were going to suffer from dioxin exposure, it would be the poor folks at Seveso. After the development of a new test to detect dioxin in blood, CDC researchers went to Seveso to measure the amount in blood samples that had been taken from exposed residents in 1976 and preserved. The levels they found were "the highest ever reported in humans." Three children who had lived in zone A and had suffered chloracne had levels of 27,821; 27,032; and 17,274 parts per trillion (ppt), which is to say they were measurable in parts per million. Recall that by contrast, studies have found that the average American has about 15 ppt TCDD in his blood. Inter-estingly, however, four people from zone A who had not suffered from chloracne also had amazingly high levels of TCDD in their blood, ranging from 1,772 to 10,439 ppt.[55]

But aside from accounts in best-selling books and newsmagazine reports, what really happened to those people? What, for example, of those women bearing babies with defects? Fuller wasn't the only one claiming birth defects resulting from exposure to the toxic cloud. *Newsweek* also reported that "the number of babies in the Seveso area that were born with deformities jumped from three in 1975 to 53 in 1978," an almost twentyfold increase. It then quoted an epidemiologist, Dr. Franco Merlo, saying, "It is not possible to say nothing is wrong."[56]

To test this conclusion, Italian researchers first looked at birth defects among children aborted by their mothers who feared the effects of dioxin contamination, and among children spontaneously aborted during the period immediately following the accident. (About ninety women were thought to have aborted their children for fear of delivering birth-defective ones.[57]) This study "failed to disclose any gross developmental abnormalities."[58] A second study looked at twenty-five induced abortions by women contaminated with the dioxin and found "no evidence of chromosomal aberrations."[59]

A third study published in the 1988 *Journal of the American Medical Association* (*JAMA*), and which remains the definitive report on the subject, looked at live births and stillbirths between the years 1977 and 1982 from women in contaminated areas and matched them with those from women in uncontaminated areas. The study concluded: "Good correlations were found between TCDD soil concentrations and both prevalence of chloracne in the resident population and domestic animal mortality." But "no correlation or association between contaminated areas and [fetal] malformations was found." Continued the report:

> Even in those infants born during the first three months of 1977 (most probably exposed to the TCDD during their first quarter of gestation), the frequency of malformations was not significantly higher than that found in the control population. Still more important is the fact that *no infant with a major malformation was identified in the most highly contaminated zone* (zone A). [Emphasis added.][60]

Noted the authors: "The most important conclusion to be drawn from this study is that the data collected contain no evidence to support the position that in the population of the Seveso area exposed to TCDD, there was a greater risk of producing congenitally malformed offspring."[61]

But what of adults? *Newsweek* also reported: "The percentage of evacuated women [from Seveso] who died of breast cancer in 1979 was double the national average."[62]

In February 1984, the International Steering Committee, which included medical experts from the United States and many other countries, reviewed all of the study reports. In summary, the committee said: "Nearly eight years after the accident in Seveso it has become obvious that besides chloracne in a very small group of cases, no adverse health effects related to the chemical produced by the accident has been observed." The committee decided its work was complete except for continued monitoring of the tumor registry through 1995.[63]

A 1986 study published in *JAMA* reported the results of more than forty-five hundred laboratory tests on about fifteen hundred Seveso-area children aged six to ten years. It found differences in only two test categories (neither representing disease manifestations), and concluded that these "observed abnormalities were slight and disappeared with time."[64]

The only study to come out of Seveso that could possibly be viewed as alarming was performed by Italian doctors and reported in the June 1989 issue of the *American Journal of Epidemiology*. The authors found that "overall, the relative risks for malignancies as a whole tended to be *below* 1.0," meaning less than average (emphasis added).[65] Among the men, however, it found increased risks for some specific types of cancers. Because there were so few men in those categories, even though the results did qualify as being statistically significant, they probably didn't mean much. The authors stated as much, though only very briefly.[66] In fact, some of the categories comprised only one case, and for the full ten-year follow-up period the statistical significance of cancer associations in the higher exposure zones of Seveso was always based on one case.[67]

Yet the legend of the Seveso catastrophe lives on to this day, passed along by those who either don't know or simply don't care that bona fide scientific studies have been done. Thus, Will Steger and Jon Bowermaster's 1990 book *Saving the Earth: A Citizen's Guide to Environmental Action* declares: "In the years following

[Seveso's contamination, dioxin] was blamed for crop failures, birth defects, and an increased cancer rate."[68] And Michael Brown, whose reporting on Love Canal would make him famous, wrote of Seveso in his 1987 book *The Toxic Cloud:* "Reports persist that the exposure caused not only chloracne but also spontaneous abortions and certain birth defects, among them spina bifida, neural tube defects, and polydactyly, the scientific term for a person born with too many fingers or toes."[69]

## THE STORY OF BONNIE HILL

KRON-TV of San Francisco, in "The Politics of Poison," asked its viewers:

> What if you and your children were receiving tiny doses of a terrible poison—a synthetic chemical so powerful that an ounce could wipe out a million people? Is that too incredible, too bizarre to believe? And if that were happening, wouldn't the government do something about it? These unbelievable questions face millions of Americans who are exposed to phenoxy herbicides every day. . . . This film is their story.[70]

It was the same story, essentially, run by *McCall's,* in its January 1980 edition, with the pathetic title of "What Happened to My Baby?"—a surefire attention-grabber in a women's magazine. It related the tale of Bonnie Hill, a woman who miscarried after having earlier had two children and who blamed it on spraying by dioxin-containing herbicides. "The doctor was as puzzled and dismayed as she was," the reader was told; "there seemed no medical reason for what had happened."[71] What the reader was not told is that, as noted in Chapter 3, miscarriages are common (about 12–15 percent of recognized pregnancies do not come to term for reasons other than elective abortion), that it is not uncommon for a woman to give birth to one or more live children before miscarrying one,[72] and that while most identified miscarriages can be attributed to smoking, alcohol, and drug abuse on the part of the mother, other causes of miscarriage cannot usually be identified.[73] These are probably facts that would be of great interest to the reader of a women's magazine. All combined, these readers will probably have hundreds of thousands of miscarriages whose causes are unidentifiable. Instead they got the story of Bonnie Hill.

Bonnie Hill's crusade began when she took a course at the University of Oregon in 1977 in which she learned that dioxin caused spontaneous abortions (meaning not intentionally induced, and often used interchangeably with "miscarriages") in monkeys. She knew that dioxin was present in 2,4,5-T, manufactured by Dow, sprayed in the forests near her home in Alsea, Oregon. She had a miscarriage in the spring of 1975 and, as women who have miscarried often do, she informally collected information on other young women who also miscarried. She talked to those whom, as a high school instructor, she had taught. She concluded on her own that there was an extraordinary rate of miscarriages around where she lived and that the best explanation was exposure to a herbicide. She then contacted the EPA, which had already announced its intentions to end the use of the herbicide but in the meantime was eager to verify its belief about the dangers of dioxin.[74]

In a study dubbed "Alsea I," the EPA sent two researchers from the University of Colorado to Oregon to collect information from Hill and the other women she had identified who had miscarried. Ten experts then evaluated this information, but were able to conclude only that it was impossible to make a judgment based on evidence obtained from nine women.

By this time it was December 1978 and spring spraying was fast approaching. Hoping to beat the clock, the Colorado researchers designed, carried out, and analyzed data from a more ambitious study, Alsea II, in what may have been a speed record in epidemiology. And the results they got reflected their haste.[75]

The problem with Alsea II was twofold. First was the choice of control areas, that is, areas where women presumably unexposed to dioxin could be compared with the women of Alsea. One such control area was urban and in no way resembled the population of Alsea or its access to medical facilities. The second problem lay in detecting spontaneous abortions and in determining what a normal number is.[76]

Despite these defects in the study, the Colorado researchers worded their conclusion in clear and stark terms: There was a dramatic increase in the spontaneous abortion index for the Alsea area relative to the two control areas, they said, and there was a significant correlation between the amounts of 2,4,5-T used in the study area during the spraying season and the subsequent increase in the spontaneous abortion index in the study area.[77] The EPA reacted immediately by banning virtually all uses of the herbicide in Oregon.[78]

Here, then, was the smoking gun connecting dioxin to human babies, not just animal ones. But a group of six scientists associated with Oregon State University (which Bonnie Hill characterized as proherbicide), including professors of epidemiology, statistics, forestry, agriculture, and environmental health and an employee of the U.S. Department of Agriculture Forest Service, tore apart the EPA's conclusions in Alsea II. They cited incomplete data collection, failure to account for patterns of and differences in medical practice among areas, and seriously incomplete data on 2,4,5-T spraying, among other things. They concluded that there was no correlation between herbicide spraying and spontaneous abortions in the Alsea area.[79]

Then it was time to critique the critics. Bonnie Hill presented, at the hearing to consider cancellation of the license to use 2,4,5-T in 1980, evidence that the Oregon State University researchers had erred and misclassified some rural areas as urban, partially undermining their own conclusions.[80]

"Who is right?" asks dioxin expert Michael Gough. Looking at all the evidence, he concludes:

Neither the [Alsea II] study nor the critique has been published in the open scientific literature, so they have not been scrutinized by the scientific community at large. No one has tried to replicate the study or design a better one. On balance, the critics are probably more right than are the original [University of Colorado] investigators. The study does not prove anything about the connection between 2,4,5-T or dioxin and spontaneous abortions, except that such a study may be impossible to do, given small populations and uncertain information about exposures and outcomes.

That, said Gough, "is not a surprise. The surprise is that Alsea II, right or wrong, is largely responsible for the cancellation of all uses of 2,4,5-T."[81]

The EPA hearings went on year after year, amassing a transcript of more than twenty-three thousand pages, before Dow finally threw in the towel in October 1983. Dow has continued to assert that dioxin has not harmed humans, but made the decision to discontinue production based on widespread adverse publicity, the resultant decreasing sales, and the costs of carrying the legal and scientific fight against the EPA.[82] Other companies gradually gave up as well with the last, Union Carbide, withdrawing from the proceedings in late 1984. Shortly after that, the EPA effectively banned the use and production of 2,4,5-T in the United States, without ever formally evaluating the evidence at the hearings.[83]

In 1979, when the Bonnie Hill story was at its peak, WGBH in Boston aired "A Plague on Our Children," a documentary about the "victims" of 2,4,5-T spraying in Oregon. It included such assertions as "About one hundred miles south of Debby Marano's house is Eve DeRock's valley and farm. . . . She is still sick two years after 2,4,5-T was sprayed there." And: "While the animal studies continue, the spraying continues. And Oregon residents are convinced that their health problems are linked to it."[84] The first assertion is but an example of reasoning that says that since something happened after something else, it must have been caused by that something else. One could just as easily have said of Debby Marano, "She is still sick two years after Jimmy Carter became President." As to the second assertion, it was merely an example of epidemiology-by-victim. But the story of the herbicide that killed babies, like that of the bogeyman who does likewise, lives on.

## NOT A LOVE STORY

UPSTATE WASTE SITE MAY ENDANGER LIVES. So ran the front-page headline on *The New York Times* of August 3, 1978.[85] The next day the headline ran, HEALTH CHIEF CALLS WASTE SITE A "PERIL"; ASKS PREGNANT WOMEN AND INFANTS TO LEAVE NIAGARA FALLS SECTOR.[86] What would follow would cause untold anguish on the part of Love Canal residents, change completely the way Americans look at toxic wastes, give United States chemical industries a black eye for perhaps decades to come, and would launch a government program costing perhaps more than half a trillion dollars.

Samuel Epstein, in his coauthored book *Hazardous Wastes in America,* wrote : "The story of Love Canal has been etched into modern history as few other events have. It has set the pace. It is the centerpiece of the hazardous waste debate."[87] What Epstein wrote in 1981 remains true today.

The story of Love Canal, as most Americans know it, is anything but a romantic tale. In 1892, entrepreneur William T. Love began building a "model city" near Niagara Falls, and commenced excavation for a canal in 1894 to service the city. The project fell upon hard times, however, and all that was left was a partially dug section of canal in the southeast corner of the city of Niagara Falls. In 1942, the Hooker Electrochemical Company completed legal transactions to begin dumping into the canal what ultimately amounted to some 21,800 tons of waste, which the company believed would be contained by the canal's clay bed. This continued until 1953, when Hooker was joined in the dumping by federal government agencies, especially the Army, again with the belief that the clay would hold the toxic chemical wastes.[88] Hooker sold the land in 1953 to the city's Board of Education.

From there, the story skips to 1976, when residents adjacent to the canal began to complain of chemical odors from the landfill. Two years later, a reporter for the *Niagara Falls Gazette,* Michael Brown, began a series of articles with such titles as "Vapors from Love Canal Pose Serious Threat," "Toxic Exposure at Love Canal Called Chronic," and "Wider Range of Illnesses Suspected." In the last, he wrote that a "random survey" conducted by the *Niagara Gazette* stated that "through the years, residents have also suffered high rates of hearing disorders, rectal bleeding, skin problems, sinus and respiratory ills, and headaches."[89] In all, Brown published more than one hundred articles in the *Gazette* on the troubles at Love Canal.[90]

Analysis revealed that the dump contained more than eighty different chemicals, including polychlorinated biphenyls (PCBs), hexachlorocyclopentadiene, benzene, toluene, tetrachloroethylene and dioxin.[91] The highest level of dioxin quantified at Love Canal, found in a storm sewer adjoining the canal, was approximately 300 parts per billion. Lesser concentrations were also found in leached material collected from remedial holding tanks, soil samples from the canal and backyards of nearby homes, and sediment and marine life of two creeks bordering the Love Canal neighborhood.[92] It was the presence of dioxin, more than that of any other chemical, that terrified the residents of Love Canal.

The townspeople were shown in photographs marching down the street carrying signs reading, WE WANT *OUT*, DIOXIN IS *HERE*, DIOXIN KILLS, and DIOXIN IS HERE. HOW LONG WILL WE BE?[93]

That same year the Love Canal story went public when, as a result of the reports, New York State Commissioner of Health Robert Whalen, in a document entitled "Love Canal: Public Health Timebomb," declared a health emergency on the second of August, citing "growing evidence . . . of subacute and chronic health hazards, as well as spontaneous abortions and congenital malformations" at the site.[94] "There is a great and imminent peril to the health of the general public at or near the said site," he stated.[95] Whalen called for limited relocations, but Governor Hugh Carey did him one up when he announced that 236 families living closest to the canal would be permanently relocated at taxpayer expense.[96] That, however, was all the more upsetting to the families who remained, since the bottom fell out of their property values. Further, they were concerned that despite their distance from the canal, they might still be at risk. Local residents, headed by housewife Lois Gibbs, organized themselves into the Love Canal Homeowners Association, which would soon grab national attention.

In February 1979, Dr. Beverly Paigen, a biologist from Buffalo, urged the evacuation of even more families based on her studies. As summarized by Lewis Regenstein in his 1982 book *America the Poisoned:* "She found . . . a much higher incidence of health disorders among those living in homes above moist ground or wet areas."[97] Before the House Subcommittee on Oversight and Investigations on March 21, 1979, she recounted the history of several families:

> [I]n family number one, the wife had a nervous breakdown and a hysterectomy due to uterine bleeding. In family number two, the husband had a breakdown. The wife had a hysterectomy due to uterine cancer. In family number three, the wife had a nervous breakdown. Both children suffered from bronchitis. In family number four, who lived there less than two years, the wife developed severe headaches after moving in. She also had a hysterectomy, uterine bleeding, and a pre-malignant growth.[98]

The EPA entered the controversy, filing suit against Hooker and commissioning a study of possible chromosome damage among Love Canal residents. Dr. Dante Picciano conducted the study, which was designed in part by Paigen. He concluded that there was evidence of an elevated level of chromosome damage, that "chemical exposures at Love Canal may be responsible for much of the apparent increase in the observed [chromosome abnormalities] and that the residents are at an increased risk of neoplastic disease [including cancer], of having spontaneous abortions and of having children with birth defects."[99] Based on this finding, Ralph Nader and coauthors would later write in *Who's Poisoning America?:* "Love Canal doesn't end with this generation's cancer or even with the next generation's birth defects. For many residents, the damage is permanent in their genes and their children's. The mutated genes will affect all of their descendants, one generation after another."[100]

High levels of chromosome damage in a given population have been associated with higher rates of cancer, although not a higher rate of birth defects, among the survivors of the atomic bombings of Hiroshima and Nagasaki. Whether the damage itself is harmful, meaning that a person with such damage is at higher risk, or whether the damage is simply a marker for a population at higher risk (say, residents living near the Love Canal) is not well understood, although an authority in the area, Dorothy Warburton, Ph.D., of the Genetics Diagnostic Laboratory, Babies Hospital, in New York City, says she would tend to favor the second theory. As to whether that damage would either contribute to or even mark someone who has developed a genetic defect that will be passed on from generation to generation, this completely depends on what sort of mutation is induced.[101] For Nader and company to simply assume that this was the case here was simply wrong, especially when to date *no agent,* including exposure to radiation following the atomic bomb blasts at Hiroshima and Nagasaki, has been shown to cause heritable human mutations in human genes.[102]

But quicker than you could say "mutation," the story was leaked to the press and appeared on the front page of the May 17, 1980, issue of *The New York Times.*[103] The media descended on the city to record the hysteria. The EPA report "was one more frightening, scary thing and we couldn't take in any more," said Lois Gibbs.[104] Coincidentally, the reporters swooped in just in time to cover the reaction of residents to the results of another EPA study, this one, to be discussed presently, on nerve damage.

The EPA reacted swiftly, advising President Carter, who on May 21 declared a state of emergency, triggering the temporary relocation of twenty-five hundred residents at a cost of $3 million to $5 million.[105] Later the relocation became permanent and the cost ballooned to more than $35 million in state expenditures for relocation and cleanup and another $20 million commitment of state and federal money in loans and grants.[106]

That's the story to the extent that most of us have heard it. It is a story that was to conclude with President Carter declaring, "There must never be in our country another Love Canal," and urging Congress to establish what became known as "Superfund," a terrifically expensive national toxic waste site cleanup program.[107]

## THE TALE RETOLD

Lewis Regenstein warned: "The residents of Love Canal may be serving as an 'early warning system' for our society."[108] Indeed, the Love Canal incident was a precursor of the Alar affair, establishing a pattern in which the media splashed the alarming preliminary news across the front pages, but by the time the carefully collected data and full reports came in, the incident had long since died down and the media had gone on to other issues. The result was not only that the situation was handled incorrectly at the time but that the impression that was left on Americans was the first impression, not the later, corrected, one.

For one thing, while the "sale" of the land to the city was seen as proof of corporate greed and indifference, Hooker actually transferred the land only after the city applied massive pressure. The transfer was for the minimum legally binding consideration, one dollar. Further, Hooker repeatedly insisted that the land was to be used for a school or parking lot or playground but that the land under no circumstances was to be excavated. In fact, November 1957 school board minutes and news accounts revealed that a lawyer for Hooker repeatedly issued strong public warnings about potential health hazards at the Canal.[109] The deed itself attempted to absolve Hooker of any liability for injury or death caused by the waste.[110] Finally, as New York consumer advocate Eric Zuesse revealed in a lengthy investigative piece for *Reason* magazine, Hooker had been so concerned that the school board would ignore its admonitions that it had board members escorted to the canal site and in their presence made eight test borings into the protective clay cover that the company had laid over the canal to make sure they saw the chemicals that lay buried.[111]

Despite all this, the Board of Education took no action to prevent digging into the canal, and the city of Niagara Falls began to construct sanitary and storm sewers at the site. The city also ignored warnings of the chemicals and the possibility of disrupting them that Hooker published in local newspapers in 1957, including the *Niagara Gazette*.[112] Later Michael Brown would write a book on the subject, *Laying Waste: The Poisoning of America by Toxic Chemicals*,[113] which simply ignored the role of the city of Niagara Falls, instead laying all the blame on Hooker. Indeed, says Zuesse, who had himself earlier referred to Hooker's actions at Love Canal as "criminal" before digging into the facts, "*Laying Waste*'s tale of Love Canal is unrecognizable to anyone who has examined the actual documents." It received three Pulitzer nominations.[114]

The EPA, too, was quick to blame Hooker. Hugh Kaufman, head of hazardous waste assessment for the EPA, described the situation thus: "What Hooker did at Love Canal, putting these wastes there, knowing about the potential for poisoning people, and then finding people were being poisoned and not doing anything about it, was just like taking a gun and pointing it at the heads of those people."[115]

And what of the alleged health effects of the Love Canal chemicals? Governor Carey, despite having ordered the first removal of families, was one of the earliest to catch on that something was amiss after the EPA recommended the removal of another 710 families. Carey told the Long Island newspaper *Newsday* that "the costly relocations of more than 700 Love Canal homeowners is medically unnecessary but has to be carried out to assuage the panic caused by the [EPA] report."[116]

## PAIGEN RITUALS

But wasn't the EPA declaration justified by the studies of Paigen and Picciano and by the nerve study? The first thing that is important to remember about Paigen is that she was neither a medical doctor nor an epidemiologist, yet she put herself in a position where she was acting as both. Further, she was never a disinterested party. She worked on behalf of the Love Canal Homeowners Association, the members of which had a great affinity for her, a fact that Lois Gibbs states in the very first page of her 1982 book, *Love Canal: My Story.*[117] Paigen's methodology should be familiar to the reader by now as the self-serving selection method. Her listing of households with a variety of illnesses means nothing, because they were not randomly selected. Any family will, over a period of years, have health problems, physical or emotional. It hardly follows that they were all, or indeed that any were, caused by some specific agent. In *any* community you can pick four or more families with serious health problems. If you can't find four with worse problems than those described by Paigen in her congressional testimony, you haven't looked very hard.

This was essentially the conclusion of a governor's panel convened by Hugh Carey and chaired by Dr. Lewis Thomas, chancellor of the Memorial Sloan-Kettering Cancer Center, which stated in 1980 that Paigen's report

> falls far short of the mark as an exercise of epidemiology. . . . [and] her data cannot be taken as scientific evidence for her conclusions. The study is based on largely anecdotal information provided by questionnaires submitted to a narrowly selected group of residents. There are no adequate control groups, the illnesses cited as caused by chemical pollution were not medically validated . . .
>
> The panel finds the Paigen report literally impossible to interpret. It cannot be taken seriously as a piece of sound epidemiological research, but it does have the impact of polemic.[118]

In fact, Paigen herself admitted that, to quote *The New York Times,* "her work was not an epidemiological study but a report of some unusual findings she came across in other research." Alas, she made this clarification a year and a half too late.[119] Another clarification that the media seemed *never* to have made (at least, not in any news story that I ever came across) was that, as Gibbs relates in her book, Paigen didn't even conduct her study—the Love Canal Homeowners Association did. What the media and other crusaders presented as a scientific epidemiological study was in fact nothing other than a number of self-diagnoses on the part of some very scared people. Paigen's role was merely that of the interpreter of the data the Love Canal residents gave her, after which she became a crusader for them.[120]

But debunking Paigen's data is one thing and establishing that there were indeed no increased health problems is another. Nevertheless, that is indeed what the New York State Department of Health found. Or, to be more specific, it is what the department has found to date since it continues to conduct tests and keep track of former Love Canal residents. Related State Commissioner of Health David Axelrod:

> Blood testing, which was designed to screen for liver and kidney abnormalities, leukemia, and other blood diseases, showed no patterns of excess abnormality. . . . None had clinical evidence of liver disease. . . .
>
> Computer analysis of the twenty-two page health questionnaire, which elicited information on some 150 different diseases or symptoms, produced no evidence of unusual patterns of illness or other disorders. Cancer incidence was within normal limits.

As to birth defects, the study found: "Efforts to establish a correlation between adverse pregnancy outcomes and evidence of chemical exposure have proven negative. Comprehensive studies of three households with unusually adverse reproductive histories did not produce evidence of unusual risk of chemical exposure."[121]

Contrast this with Michael Brown's assertion in *The New York Times Magazine* in 1979 that "the New York State Health Department investigated and discovered startling health problems: birth defects, miscarriages, epilepsy, liver abnormalities, sores, rectal bleeding, headaches—not to mention undiscovered but possible latent illnesses."[122]

Verification of the Department of Health findings regarding cancer came in a study by the New York Cancer Registry, released in *Science* in 1981, showing "no evidence for higher cancer rates associated with residence near the Love Canal toxic waste burial site." The study noted a higher rate for only one type of cancer, that of the lung, "but it was not consistent across age groups and appeared to be related to a high rate for the entire city of Niagara Falls. There was no evidence that the lung cancer rate was associated with the toxic waste sites buried at the dump site."[123]

## THE RED-FACED BARRON

As for the nerve studies, this appears to be the case of an honest researcher dragged along by the current of events. It was undertaken expressly as a pilot study, and ordinarily the head of the study, Steven Barron, would not have released it. But according to his testimony before a congressional subcommittee, the EPA requested access to his study and he consented, on the grounds that he would share with the agency only the setup of the test and not the actual results. Now Barron was confronted with his promise to the persons on whom he had performed the tests that he would notify them of their results before they heard about them from a third party. This is confusing, because he says he wasn't going to give the actual data to the EPA. At any rate, instead of having the calculations done on his data to indicate whether it was statistically significant and then mailing out letters to each of the participants, he found himself rushed to the point where he simply held a meeting with them and told them that to the best of his knowledge, some of them did appear to have nerve damage. Since the town was already swarming with reporters, that had the effect of simply releasing his data straight to the press. The rest, as they say, is history. After the statisticians got through with his data, it became clear to Barron that there had been no significant findings in the study. But by then it was too late.[124]

## THE GREAT CHROMOSOME CAPER

As to Picciano's chromosome study, an EPA review panel tore it apart. *Science* magazine, in reporting on the panel's evaluation, pulled no punches. "The much-publicized study of chromosome damage among residents of Love Canal has been discredited," it began. It went on, and "Tragically, the EPA has ended up needlessly terrifying the Love Canal residents." *Science* noted that the report was "not even meant to be scientific." According to Steven Gage, assistant administrator for research and development at the EPA, "This was a small fishing expedition. The Justice Department asked us to undertake it in connection with our suit against Hooker," he said.[125] Gage added that "in the normal course of events, the inadequacies of the pilot (preliminary) study would have been discovered and the study would have been corrected or stopped," but that the urgency to prepare for litigation and the fact that "members of the press obtained the raw results of the study before EPA management received them" torpedoed the normal process. Further, he said, in a formal press briefing, it was explained that the Picciano study had not been scientifically reviewed but that this warning was "largely ignored by most of the press accounts."[126]

The alleged smoking gun of Picciano's study was that of the four categories of chromosomal abnormalities looked at, the frequency of one type, known as "supernumerary acentrics," appeared to be elevated, indeed highly elevated. Of thirty-six members of the sample population, eight were said to have had this kind of damage, as opposed to the expected one in a hundred.[127]

To quote *Science,* though: "The EPA panel concluded that there was no evidence that the Love Canal residents had excessive chromosome abnormalities and that supernumerary acentric chromosomes existed only in the mind of Picciano."[128]

It has also come to light that Picciano had earlier resigned from the Dow Chemical study after Dow questioned his use of historical controls as opposed to the standard practice of using simultaneous ones. In fact, the director of health and environmental sciences at Dow claimed that Picciano and Jack Killian had selectively removed from their control group cells with unusually large numbers of aberrations. According to *Science,* Picciano, told of this charge, laughed, and said, "Did I do that? I don't remember doing that!"[129]

Confronted with this evidence, Lois Gibbs of the Homeowners Association was unmoved. "It scared the hell out of the residents when the government reacted [to Picciano's report] by moving people out," she said, and she wasn't about to admit, whether to herself or to reporters, that the fear had been groundless. She said the Picciano report was "very frightening to the residents," that it indicated that the residents were at risk for cancer, birth defects, and miscarriages. A Department of Health and Human Services review of the data, she said, was seen by the residents as "almost an attempt to sabotage the report."[130]

Indeed, as is so often the case, to some the good news was

bad news. The Love Canal Homeowners Association, whose homes had been purchased by the state, blasted the new chromosome study's conclusion while apparently having nothing to say about its methodology. "We've lost all our faith in government," one representative said. "It's another big cover-up," claimed another.[131]

Dr. Warburton was part of a team that investigated the chromosomal studies at Love Canal and visited the site and talked to the residents. "We tried to reassure people but they didn't want to be reassured," she says. "They wanted to sue." Observes Warburton: "What happens [in an environmental scare] is that people build their lives around it and they want to attribute any nasty thing that happens to them to these exposures. If the kid does poorly in school or the refrigerator breaks down or the husband leaves them, they can attribute it to the chemicals."[132]

But the bad good news continued to come in. On May 27, 1983, the Centers for Disease Control's *Morbidity and Mortality Weekly Report* announced a study finding that the frequency of chromosomal aberrations did not differ significantly between residents of Love Canal and control residents, notwithstanding the assertions of the Picciano study. The allegedly high number of supernumerary acentrics that Picciano found was not found in the CDC study.[133] The next year, a study appearing in *JAMA* reported that no excess illness or chromosomal aberrations were found among persons who had lived close to Love Canal.[134]

But even before the CDC data were released, the folks at *The New York Times* were feeling quite sheepish. In June 1981, after the controversy had died down, the newspaper editorialized:

> But from what is now known, Love Canal, perhaps the nation's most prominent symbol of chemical assaults on the environment, has had no detectable effect on the incidence of cancer. When all the returns are in, years from now, it may well turn out that the public suffered less from the chemicals there than from the hysteria generated by flimsy research irresponsibly handled.[135]

At any rate, this admission came too late. Without a doubt, the residents of Love Canal suffered, and suffered terribly. They suffered not from chemicals, but from fear spread by the media, slipshod scientists, and assorted opportunists.

"People are very, very frightened," said Lois Gibbs, three days after the decision was made to move out twenty-five hundred residents. Many Love Canal residents suffered from a vague assortment of psychophysiological problems such as depression, irritability, dizziness, nausea, weakness, fatigue, insomnia, and numbness in the extremities, she said. Mental health and psychosomatic illness were not the only results of the Love Canal horror show. Gibbs also claimed that among the 237 families involved in the 1978 evacuation, 40 percent of the couples had separated or divorced as the result of the wear and tear of two years of stress and uncertainty, though we must keep in mind here her tendency to exaggerate.[136]

## THE MOUTH THAT ROARED

The supreme irony of Lois Gibbs's attestation to the terrors of the Love Canal residents was that she was so instrumental in causing it. Gibbs serves as living proof that sometimes one person *can* make a difference—and shouldn't. At the time the Love Canal controversy began, Gibbs was a young and attractive wife and a mother of two. After she decided that her son's epilepsy and some other health problems she identified were probably caused by Love Canal seepage, she demanded that local education officials close down the school built over the canal.[137] When they refused, she began a petition and education drive that snowballed into the formation of the Love Canal Homeowners Association and from there meetings with everyone from local health officials to state health officials to the governor to President Carter, and even with Jane Fonda and her husband Tom Hayden.[138] Reporters took an instant liking to her. *People* magazine in 1982 gave her the heroic crusader profile treatment that it had earlier given to asbestos crusader Paul Brodeur and would later give to Meryl Streep, calling Gibbs "the Love Canal heroine."[139] That same year, CBS presented a two-hour docudrama, "Lois Gibbs and the Love Canal," starring Marsha Mason.[140]

Gibbs's main tool, amplified a thousandfold by her media supporters, was sheer belligerence. When New York State Health Commissioner Whalen ordered a partial evacuation of the area, Gibbs screamed at him, "You're a murderer! You're killing our children by not ordering all the families out!"[141] At another point in the drama, angry residents led by Gibbs held two EPA officials hostage in the Homeowners' headquarters.[142]

The problem with Lois Gibbs wasn't that she wasn't a scientist—most of us aren't, after all. It was that she didn't seem to think much of those who were, and she had a very loud mouth. "You don't have to be a scientist," she said on a national television program. "You don't have to do a survey to find out—common sense'll tell you, there's something wrong in Love Canal."[143] And after the surveys and tests *were* done, Gibbs was still promoting that amorphous concept called "common sense" over science. Gibbs is now the founder and executive director of Citizens Clearinghouse for Hazardous Waste, where she continues to do the talk show circuit and to dispense her own very special version of scientific material[144]—and continues to be rewarded for it. In 1990 she received a $60,000 award from the Goldman Environmental Foundation of San Francisco.[145] Echoing a sentiment that describes all too many environmental crusaders, she answered *People* magazine's query about resuming a private existence, saying, "I'll never go back. My life was aimless before. Now I have a goal."[146] How unfortunate that that which finally gave her purpose in life proved to be so horribly destructive.

Yet the wider problem is that the media lionized this woman and appointed—or anointed—her an expert. In assigning blame for the Love Canal hysteria, no one put it better than Gibbs herself. "The news media has made Love Canal what it is," she said. "They have helped us force government to do what they have done thus far. . . . That's a direct result of us doing a survey, pushing it through the media, and eventually, having them confirm it. So the media has been great. It really has."[147] (Samuel Epstein, too, has been quite complimentary of media coverage of dioxin in general.[148])

Yet there's one thing for which Gibbs didn't give the media credit. The media didn't just present Gibbs to us, they helped make her what she became in the first place. The genesis of Gibbs's activism was not when she realized that something was making her children sick and asked herself why. The order was actually reversed. It was after reading Michael Brown's articles in the *Niagara Falls Gazette* that she began to tie every illness her children had ever had to the canal.[149] This pattern would continue to be repeated throughout the Love Canal crisis. On the cover of both *Laying Waste* and Brown's later alarmist book, *The Toxic Cloud*, it reads that Brown "broke the Love Canal story."[150] Wrong. Brown didn't break the story, he helped create it.

## DR. VICTIM

If one were to try to put a finger on the worst aspect of the media coverage of Love Canal, it would have to be their constant focus on the "victims" themselves. Nowhere has there been a better example of victims being presented as experts with the consequence that the real experts were portrayed as engaging in a cover-up since they disagreed with the victim-experts.

Over and over, the media shoved their cameras and notebooks into the homes of Love Canal residents and presented their self-diagnoses to the world. *U.S. News & World Report* ran an article on Love Canal packed with victim-epidemiologists, including Marge Bates, who said, "I lost a baby after carrying her for nine months. She weighed only three pounds and was stillborn. My doctor couldn't explain why, after nine months, she weighed only three pounds. It had to be the chemicals." A man told the magazine, "We couldn't figure out why my wife developed epilepsy when no one else in her family had ever had it."[151]

It is interesting how a doctor's failure to explain a miscarriage or epilepsy or cancer or whatever—things that usually have no "explanation" in the usual sense of the word—is repeatedly taken by victims, and faithfully reported by the media, to indicate *ipso facto* that it must have resulted from exposure to toxic man-made chemicals. It's a non sequitur, making as much sense as saying, "Since I don't know why my car won't start, it must be the ignition system," or "Since I don't know what color my blind date's hair is, it must be blond." But when it comes from a victim of a health malady, the media just eat up this kind of logic. It's so full of pathos, they just can't resist.

What the media quickly discovered was that some victim-experts at Love Canal were much more attractive than others. A survey of articles about Love Canal residents indicates that while 99 percent were apparently never heard from, some in that 1 percent appeared over and over. One such person was Barbara

Quimby. The media knew it had a great victim in Mrs. Quimby and the Quimby family. She popped up in *U.S. News & World Report, Time,*[152] the *Donahue* show,[153] *Maclean's,*[154] and myriad other places. *McCall's,* just six months after its profile of Bonnie Hill, ran a whole story on the Quimby family. "Our Fear Never Ends" cited a large variety of illnesses the Quimbys had suffered, along with some of their relatives who at one time or other had visited the house, dating all the way back to 1952. Even Pugsley, the dog, was said to suffer vomiting. The medical authority cited to tie all these ailments to the Love Canal leakage was Dr. Beverly Paigen.[155]

The media picked the worst-off family they could think of and broadcast their faces and their words from coast to coast. The idea was that the Quimbys were sadly all-too-representative of the horrors of the seepage from Love Canal. But the fact that the Quimbys turned up in magazine after magazine while 99 percent of all Love Canal residents were ignored indicated quite the opposite. The Quimbys got attention for the same reason anyone gets attention—because they were exceptional.

## A HYSTERICAL PROBLEM, BUT NO LAUGHING MATTER

Upon close inspection, the complaints of the Love Canal residents seem an awful lot like simple everyday problems, or, in fact, like psychosomatic illnesses. This is not to imply they were a bunch of loonies. But when you tell a group of people that something is supposed to be making them sick, as these people were told again and again, two things invariably happen. First, some people with real ills latch on to the supposed new agent as the cause of their troubles. Second, people develop psychosomatic troubles. Suddenly they are experiencing new pains and aches. Their throats are sore. They feel lethargic. They become victims of nondescript illnesses for which doctors can provide no explanation—and by now we all know what "no explanation" means.

Nowhere did it become more apparent that Love Canal was a site of mass hysteria than on a *Donahue* show that featured Lois Gibbs and Mrs. Quimby and several other residents of the Canal. Appearing on the show with white carnations to signify that they were being held hostage (a variation on yellow ribbons put out for the hostages in Iran), they then proceeded to indict the EPA, the mayor, and President Carter for covering up the dangers. Finally, they even asserted that the local doctors were covering up. "I've got urinary and bladder infections, and I went to the hospital—I was in the hospital for two weeks to find out what was causin' it, and they told me to see a psychiatrist afterwards," said one. "The pediatricians are not very sympathetic," said another. "They say, 'Your children are not any sicker than any children in the rest of the city.' "[156] (*Christian Century,* in its scare coverage of Love Canal, stated: "Doctors were reluctant to treat them,"[157] as if the doctors knew they were sick but refused to administer aid.)

At this point it became apparent to Phil Donahue that this looked like mass hysteria. "I don't want to beat you over the head with this, but . . ." he said, "you take another 50 people off the street, give them the same situation, and they see neighbors going to the doctors with ailments, they see lawyers, they see all that federal money, and they say, 'Me, too. I got a headache. I got a bad pancreas.' " To which Lois Gibbs could only answer, "Well, that's not true in the Love Canal."[158]

Such mass hysteria is far from unheard of. In March 1944, the local health office in the Newburgh-Kingston area of New York began receiving citizen complaints after it announced it would begin fluoridating the water supply. Some complaints stated that the fluoridated water was discoloring their saucepans, others that it was giving people digestive troubles. One woman complained that the "fluoride water" had caused her dentures to crack. In fact, all of the complaints were made before fluoride was added to the water supply. They stopped abruptly after a Newburgh newspaper criticized the town's imaginary ills.[159]

A much more recent case of mass hysteria occurred in 1988 in a town fifty miles outside of Atlanta, Georgia. It involved parents who believed that, as the result of small natural gas leaks in their children's school building, their children got gradually sicker during the day until they requested to be excused, and that when they got home they showed such symptoms as pallor, dark circles under the eyes, headaches, nausea, and vomiting.[160] After being told that their children couldn't be getting sick from the small amounts of released gas, parents picketed the school and uttered such comments as "I don't know what their reason is for keeping quiet" and "I don't trust them, and I feel like they have been dishonest with me."[161]

The health authorities investigated the leak and the complaints and agreed there was no reason for the reported illnesses. But what made this sociogenic illness cluster especially interesting was that it *wasn't* one. That is, it appears the illnesses were simply in the minds of the parents. Children weren't even going home any more often than they had been, except when their parents pulled them out of school for several days because of their worries. The authorities, in their write-up in the British medical journal *Lancet,* called this "mass sociogenic illness by proxy."[162]

Of course, it is always sad to see people scared for no good reason. Fear in and of itself greatly lowers the quality of life. When it leads to collateral consequences such as the breakups Lois Gibbs cited at Love Canal, it does that much more to lower the quality of life. Indeed, it ruins lives.

But one of the saddest possible outcomes of such unnecessary fear is that while the mechanisms of cancer development and fetal development problems are still little understood, stress has long been thought to have the capacity to cause either and there is increasing medical evidence to substantiate this.[163] One has to wonder, how many people put under great stress by fear of developing cancer or fetal problems from nonexistent environmental dangers end up really getting cancer or having miscarriages because of their fear? More readily identified are those women whose children have been potentially exposed to alleged teratogens who have undergone voluntary abortions. For example, as noted, at Seveso about ninety women aborted their children out of fear of dioxin contamination having affected them, yet no baby upon autopsy proved defective. Those were ninety babies who had otherwise been wanted but who died directly because of false fears. Babies were born dead, certainly, but it wasn't from the dioxin.

A related tragedy is that, as Samuel Epstein noted, Love Canal would become the center of the debate on hazardous waste. As real a problem as hazardous waste is, like all problems it deserves no more attention than reality dictates. A recent poll presented in *Science* magazine of the public's top environmental concerns places active hazardous waste sites and abandoned hazardous waste sites at the very top of the heap. By contrast, neither of these even made the list of the EPA's twelve top concerns.[164] It is the public's perception of this risk, and not the EPA's, that has influenced Congress's spending on Superfund. Reauthorization of Superfund legislation quietly passed Congress in the fall of 1990, providing an additional $1.5 billion through September of 1994 for cleaning up abandoned waste sites. Yet, as *Environment* magazine has noted, "recent estimates of the cost of hazardous waste cleanup suggest that a rethinking of current strategy is in order."[165] The EPA has estimated that the cleanup costs for the 1,175 sites on the National Priority List may reach $30 billion, an average cost of more than $25 million per site.[166] According to a 1989 Office of Technology Assessment report, national cleanup costs over the next several decades may total more than $500 billion unless major technological innovations bring them down.[167] But other analysts have put the figure at $1 *trillion*. Of this, $200 billion could be spent on "transaction costs" alone. This is spending that has nothing to do with the actual cleanup, most of it being spent for corporate attorneys' fees in thousands of lawsuits that companies file against the government because they don't want to be held liable.[168] The final cost of Superfund could dwarf that of the savings and loan bailout.

Now whip out a pocket calculator and do a bit of figuring. There are about 125 million taxpayers in this country. At $30 billion, that comes out to $240 for each of us, which is not particularly cheap, considering we still have to pay for national defense, entitlement programs, roads, interest on the national debt, and free mailing privileges for members of Congress. But the $500 billion price tag comes out to $4,000 for each taxpayer. Now we're talking real dough.

Now consider that diagnostic mammograms are the best defense against breast cancer, that each costs $100, and that many women cannot afford them. That $30 billion could provide 300 million free mammograms to such women, saving perhaps millions of lives. Those are real lives saved, not the potential ones in some mathematician's model that assumes X number of deaths per toxic waste site. Again to quote *Environment:* "The benefits of the [Superfund] clean-up are highly questionable. An investigation of risk levels at unremediated hazardous waste sites that are slated to be cleaned up . . . found that 70 percent of the sites currently

present risks at a level that EPA considers acceptable *after* re-
mediation efforts have been made" (emphasis added).[169] This,
then, is the legacy of the hype over dioxin and incidents such as
that of Love Canal: massive expenditures, massive trauma, and
a massive shift of funds away from any number of areas where
they could do more good.

But then, let's not forget that formula that says ignore expenses
and ignore the data, just assume the worst-case scenario and
spend, spend, spend. Yes, it's the old nonargument, this time
presented by *Newsweek,* which stated: "Without definitive answers to what dioxin does to human health, many scientists believe
the EPA should err on the side of caution."[170] Unfortunately, as
always, this recommendation does not apply to caution in draining
the taxpayers dry or needlessly scaring the hell out of people.

## PURSUING THE LAST MOLECULE (AGAIN)

With dioxin, as with all carcinogens and suspected carcinogens,
the EPA has used the worst-case, linear-dose-response model;
that is, it has said there is no safe level of dioxin. In so doing,
the EPA has set its intake level at 0.006 picograms per kilogram
of body weight per day. That is a total amount for ingestion from
food, water, and breathing. By contrast, Canada and some European countries have dismissed the linear model as unrealistic,
and have set their limits about 170 to 1,700 times higher than the
EPA's at 1.0 to 10.0 picograms per day. But, as toxicologist Michael Gallo of the Robert Wood Johnson Medical School in New
Jersey, observes: "It's the same chemical on both sides of the
Atlantic."[171]

Nevertheless, the conclusions of a disparate group of thirty-
eight researchers and regulators meeting at the Banbury Center
at Cold Spring Harbor Laboratory on Long Island, New York,
in 1990 may eventually change this peculiarly American view of
dioxin—and other suspected carcinogens. The meeting, which
was sponsored by the Chlorine Institute (dioxin is a by-product
of chlorine bleaching), but was organized by Gallo and representatives of the FDA and the National Institute for Public Health of
the Netherlands, offered a way to clear up the mess. Most at-
tending scientists agreed that before dioxin can cause any of its

many toxic effects, birth defects and cancer included, it must first bind to and activate a receptor. Following that rationale, it could then be said that there is a "safe" dose or "threshold" below which no harm is done. The concession of such a threshold would overturn the EPA's long-standing model. But, as Gallo says, "this is bigger than dioxin."[172] If the EPA concedes there is a threshold for dioxins, it is essentially doing likewise for other carcinogens that work through receptors—such as the much feared PCBs. Which doesn't mean the EPA will change the model. As the *Science* reporter who wrote up the conference put it, not for "a molecule as politically charged as dioxin." Gallo called dioxin a powerful "litigen," making reference to the numerous suits alleging dioxin spills and contamination; and Michael Gough predicted "a tremendous uproar from environmental groups and Congress."[173] Considering the uproar they've continually made over studies showing no ill effects from dioxin, such a prediction was a safe one indeed. In fact, John Moore, when he was assistant administrator at EPA, twice unsuccessfully tried to revise both the dioxin risk number and the model.[174]

Curiously, Ellen Silbergeld, a toxicologist formerly with the EDF and now at the University of Maryland, reacted to the conclusions of many of the Cold Spring Harbor scientists by cautioning against "replacing one stupid model with another."[175] While she was at EDF, no one was a bigger promoter of the old "stupid model" of no threshold than was Ellen Silbergeld. On the subject of birth defects in children of Vietnam veterans exposed to Agent Orange, Silbergeld was there promoting the theory that dioxin is dangerous at extremely low levels,[176] and she told *Ms.* magazine that women may be particularly sensitive.[177] She promoted the no-threshold theory concerning Love Canal[178] and Times Beach, as well.[179] Likewise, on the subject of the minute amounts of dioxin sometimes found in bleached paper, she was quoted saying: "The levels of dioxin in paper products seem to be very low, but these are products that we use intensively, and they should have a very high standard of purity."[180] Whenever the media was looking for a toxicologist willing to say alarming things about minute amounts of dioxin, Silbergeld was there for them with her handy no-threshold theory of toxicity. Acting on Silbergeld's advice, the EDF has become to dioxin what the Natural Resources Defense Council was to Alar and remains to other pesticides. Now suddenly Silbergeld was attacking her old standby as stupid in order to discredit the new consensus theory. What a difference a day makes!

Six months after the Banbury meeting, Vernon N. Houk, assistant surgeon general of the United States and the director of the Center for Environmental Health and Injury Control at the CDC, told the *St. Louis Post-Dispatch* that he regretted having urged the evacuation of Times Beach in 1982. The EPA had bought out Times Beach and relocated all of its occupants after dioxin was discovered in relatively high concentrations in its soil.[181] Had he known then what he knows now about dioxin, he said, "I would not be concerned about the levels of dioxin at Times Beach." His statement, made at an international environmental health conference, came just weeks after a cleanup of the town's contaminated soil began, with an estimated price tag of $200 million. Said Houk, if dioxin is a human carcinogen, "it is, in my view, a weak one that is associated only with high-dioxin exposures."[182]

Karen Webb, director of the division of environmental and occupational health at the St. Louis University School of Medicine, noting that studies of Times Beach residents found "no significant chronic illness," added her opinion that "the data seem to point out that if TCDD is a carcinogen at all, it is not a very potent one."[183]

"We should have been more upfront with Times Beach people and told them: 'We're doing our best with the estimates of the risk, but we may be wrong,' " Houk said. "I think we never added, 'But we may be wrong.' "[184] Houk said that his belief that the dangers of low doses of dioxin had been overrated, "is becoming more and more accepted around the world," though not yet by the EPA. "I don't know why," he told the *Dispatch,* "maybe they're afraid to back off." Donald G. Barnes, director of the EPA's Science Advisory Board, was quoted as saying the agency "is going in the same direction" as Houk in rethinking dioxin toxicity. "I, personally, have felt for some time that the agency has been over-estimating the risks," he said. "Their method is designed to give an upper bound on what the risk is."[185]

## QUELLING THE COUNTERREVOLUTION

But, as it turns out, neither the EPA nor the other political interests involved in the dioxin debate were going to give up that readily. In June 1992, the House of Representatives Human Resources and Intergovernmental Relations Subcommittee of Government Operations held its own hearing on the potential dangers of dioxin. The one nongovernment scientist testifying who caught the media's attention was Ellen Silbergeld, who stated flatly that "we know that dioxin is a human carcinogen" and that "our toxicological studies suggest that we have not yet found the no-effect level."[186] Likewise, the EPA's Linda Birnbaum, director of the Environmental Toxicology Division at the Health Effects Research Laboratory, said of the assertion that dioxin does not pose a cancer risk to humans at low doses, "This hypothesis is not true."[187] Finally, the late Congressman Ted Weiss (D-N.Y.), who, as will be seen in the next chapter, led a rather unseemly campaign against the federal Centers for Disease Control's finding that dioxin-containing Agent Orange is not a carcinogen, stated that dioxin "is unsafe at any dose."[188] Yet, the studies on which all three of these people based their conclusions are no more than the ones discussed in this book.

At any rate, some dioxin alarmists are already prepared with a counterproposal in case the evidence against dioxin as a low-dose human carcinogen becomes too overwhelming to contest. Here is the new tack they have taken: Whatever the final verdict is on dioxin as a carcinogen, its negative effects in that arena may be dwarfed by the harm it can do as a hormone. Karen Schmidt, writing in *Science News* in early 1992, stated that while "most dioxin researchers now suspect that only very high doses of TCDD—as occur accidentally or in certain occupational settings—may increase the risk of cancer in humans," this "redefinition does not necessarily imply that the chemical is harmless at lower doses." She goes on to say that "TCDD's ability [as an environmental hormone] to mess with the immune system—not its carcinogenicity—may represent its greatest threat to public health."[189]

But then, less than three months later, in a story for *U.S. News & World Report,* Schmidt stated that dioxin is "not only a potent carcinogen" but the chemical "looks more dangerous to human health now than ever," again citing its alleged effect on the immune system as a sort of hormone.[190] The frightening article devoted but one sentence to human epidemiological studies such as Seveso that showed no such effects from massive exposure to dioxin, instead relying almost exclusively on animal data and quotes from such authorities as, yes, Ellen Silbergeld and Linda Birnbaum. But who wants to hear about what dioxin didn't do to humans at Seveso when we can hear what it *did* do to female rats at the University of Wisconsin? James P. Whitlock, of the Department of Pharmacology at Stanford University School of Medicine, says that the debate over what effect dioxin has as an environmental hormone and whether as such it can prove harmful in humans is "pretty general, because none of [the charges of harmfulness] is proven," and says also that if other chemicals—including natural ones—had been studied as intensively as dioxin, similar findings might result, à la the Bruce Ames argument made concerning carcinogenic chemicals.[191] (See in Chapter 2, "The Natural Carcinogen Cover-up," page 60.)

Says an exasperated Michael Gough, "We've always known it has had hormone-like activity—but so do hormones! I've been pointing this out for years. Now they're trying to turn it into something evil." In a statement made before the House Human Resources and Intergovernmental Relations Subcommittee, which "reinstated" dioxin as a cancer-causer, Gough said, "They're just redrawing the boundaries. . . ."[192]

But this is how witch-hunts are conducted. The guilt and the punishment are foregone conclusions, and all that is left is the hearing of evidence. In the comedy movie *Monty Python and the Holy Grail,* a villager declares loudly that the woman on trial as a witch "turned me into a newt!" When another villager observes that he certainly does not appear to be a newt, he sniffs, "Well, it got better." More compelling evidence is found (the accused is found to weigh the same as a duck), and the hapless woman is summarily disposed of.[193] Likewise, dioxin has been declared a witch, and the environmental groups, the EPA, and much of the media seem determined to see it burned at the stake, whatever the evidence.

# THE CORPORATION IS ALWAYS WRONG

Had it been left to Samuel Epstein, that Cold Spring Harbor meeting would never have taken place, nor would any of the studies since 1983 and Houk would never have had the data to make his confession of sorts. For 1983 was the year Epstein told *Nightline*'s Ted Koppel, "We have more than enough evidence to take the position that dioxin represents a major potential human hazard. . . . How much more information do we need? The time for debate is over: The independent scientific community accepts the data. It's industry and industry consultants that are still fighting a rearguard action."[194]

The Veterans Administration consultant who also appeared on the show completely disagreed, but Koppel buttressed Epstein's position by saying, "It would seem logical, would it not, that industry, which seems to have been responsible for a great deal of dioxin getting into the atmosphere and into our total environment, that they would have a vested interest in suggesting to the public at large that it ain't all bad?"[195] Six years later, hosting a show on a different issue—electromagnetic fields—Koppel presented essentially the same argument, saying, "Let me put the question to you from the vantage point of the consumer, who's going to look at the [power] industry and say, 'Those folks have got so many billions of dollars at stake here, and so much money to use, that the evidence would have to be absolutely overwhelming before you guys would do anything.' "[196]

The short answer to the first Koppel assertion is yes, of course industry is going to downplay risk from its products. But the long answer is that this is simply something to be taken into account. This book takes it into account. Monsanto scientists have collected a wealth of data on employees exposed to fairly heavy doses of dioxin from plant explosions in the 1960s. They claim no long-term health effects from such exposure. That material has all been excluded from this book. There is plenty of other material, however, from independent scientists that happens to indicate the same things that Monsanto says its data shows. The important point is that whether it's Uniroyal and Alar or herbicide companies and dioxin, you can't convict industry of wrongdoing on the basis of its profit margin. Until you have established that an evil act has been committed, it is utterly worthless to proceed on the basis of motive. Simply invoking corporate motives also completely ignores the motives on the other side. Samuel Epstein, for example, has staked his entire career on the thesis that industry is pumping out carcinogens that are killing us left and right. Thus, when a new alleged industry carcinogen comes along, he is among the first to jump on the bandwagon because it seems to confirm his life's thesis. Still, that doesn't necessarily mean that every time he impugns an industry chemical, he is wrong. Once having established that he is wrong, however, *then* one can point to his consistent antichemical record to help establish why he took that position.

## THE PAPER CHASE

But while the EPA reevaluates dioxin, yet another drama related to the chemical is unfolding in American river communities. The issue involves the creation of dioxin during the process of bleaching paper; dioxin may show up in that paper and in wastewater downstream from the mill.

Improvements in detection processes have had a major impact on the dioxin controversy. Michael Brown, in his book *The Toxic Cloud,* related that a recent breakthrough allowed dioxin to be detected in the air. He wrote of one such test:

> Then, in a jolting set of peaks on the graph . . . scientists unmistakably identified 2,3,7,8-tetra dioxin in the ambient, free-flowing air in the most polluted part of Niagara Falls.
> Dioxin of the worst isomer was in the air, captured in cartridges containing an absorbent gel.
> It was above the detection limit of a part per quadrillion.[197]

Then, after leaving a break of four lines, he moves onto the next subject. Such a break we can call, for lack of a better term, a "gasp space." That is, what comes before it is supposed to be so shocking that the writer leaves a space after it so that the reader can mentally gasp or say "Omigod" or whatever the reader is wont to do when shocked by a writer's brilliant insight or revelation. But perhaps the reader wouldn't be so quick to gasp if she knew, first of all, that there is no evidence of lasting human harm from dioxin even in levels in parts per million, which is a billion times more than parts per quadrillion. And the reader might not be so shocked if she discovered that until a few years ago, nobody worried about parts per quadrillion of dioxin, simply because it couldn't be measured at that low a level.[198] Thus, dioxin can be found now in places where previously there was no evidence it existed, paper mill products and wastes being among them. When the Food and Drug Administration (FDA) and the American Paper Institute, a trade association representing the pulp and paper industry, conducted a study of wastewater from paper mills, the study found dioxin at a level that simply wouldn't have been detected a few years earlier. That level was a median of 24 parts per *quadrillion*.[199]

Comments Marshall Hann, a graduate in physics and CEO of the Georgia-Pacific Corporation:

> Dioxin is produced in pulp and paper in quantities so extremely minute that we have only recently been able to detect them. One part per quadrillion—the quantities that we are talking of—is like one second in 32 million years. We are committed to reducing dioxin levels to nondetectable levels. But what is nondetectable? It just means that we can't detect it today. Tomorrow, as we advance our technology, we may be able to measure it again.[200]

At some point, perhaps ten years from now or if not then fifteen or twenty years, scientists may be able to detect dioxin in virtually everything we eat and drink. Perhaps at parts per sextillion, perhaps not until parts per septillion, or not until parts per octillion. But eventually that day will come. What will we do then? Will all Americans begin blaming their cancers and vomiting dogs on these parts per sextillion of dioxin? Or for that matter, at parts per sextillion of benzene or formaldehyde or anything else you want to name because at some parts per something, eventually we will find molecules of everything in everything.

## A FISH STORY

In late 1990, a jury awarded Wesley Simmons, a retired Gulf Coast fisherman living in southeast Mississippi, $1.04 million of the Georgia-Pacific Corporation's money because he was exposed to dioxin from eating fish that swam in the water downriver from the company's mill. Simmons never alleged to be in anything other than good health. But he said he noticed that the river was getting "blacker and blacker" and, "then I started seeing catfish with big heads and bodies that were dried up to nothing."[201] It probably goes without saying that at present there are a dearth of scientific studies establishing that dioxin causes catfish heads to swell up and catfish bodies to shrink. But such testimony, in combination with the undeniable fact that Georgia-Pacific was indeed putting dioxin into the river water and discoloring it, was enough for the jury. Perhaps it is more accurate to say that it was enough for a truly new type of fish in the area—sharks. For Simmons's attorneys netted *one half* of his award, plus court costs and expenses.[202] Earn half a million and save the world from tiny amounts of a chemical of dubious human toxicity at the same time—not a bad way to earn a living. As one would guess, many other attorneys have decided they want to save the environment, too. Approximately twenty-seven cases similar to Simmons's are, as of this writing, on the dockets.[203] Those attorneys, represented by such groups as Trial Lawyers for Public Justice, have learned that serving "public justice" can be quite profitable. As of April 1991, lawyers had brought over $5 billion in suits in the state of Tennessee against two paper companies, the Georgia-Pacific Corporation and the International Paper Company, alleging that they had threatened the health of those coming into contact with downstream water and fish that had been in that water.[204] Another in North Carolina sought $5 billion from the Champion Paper Company alone.[205]

Yet not everybody is cashing in, even aside from all American consumers who find themselves paying more for their paper products to line the pockets of attorneys. Some people downriver of paper plants have become absolutely terrified of getting cancer. An article in the *Knoxville* (Tenn.) *News-Sentinel* in 1990 told of the fears of the residents of Hartford, Tennessee who, two years earlier, had dubbed their town Widowville and became an overnight sensation, a mini-Love Canal when, as the *News-Sentinel* put it, "doctors, researchers, regulators and reporters from around the world descended on the small town, eager to prove or disprove the residents' contention that the polluted river running through their midst was killing them." The scientific conclusion was that the river was not polluted, although Greenpeace placed signs along the river warning people against eating the fish.[206] But like the residents of Love Canal, those of Hartford, who have not been relocated, do not feel satisfied. One complained that "cancer and heart disease are still the thing in Hartford," apparently unaware that as the leading causes of death they are "the thing" throughout America, although not in less fortunate parts of the world where "the thing" is often malaria, tuberculosis, and diarrhea.[207]

America's war on dioxin has resulted in very little but the expenditures of great amounts of fear and great amounts of money. Already, says American Paper Institute spokesman Tom Kraner, paper mills have spent "many hundreds of millions of dollars" to reduce tiny levels of dioxin to even tinier levels.[208] Considering that those expenditures will probably result in saving zero lives and preventing zero illnesses, it doesn't take much imagination to come up with alternative ways of spending this indirect tax that regulators have placed on paper mills (and which not incidentally they are passing on to consumers, as they must); they could save hundreds or thousands more American lives or, if spent in third world countries, could save many more than that. And while the expenditure of these tremendous sums of money is still in its early stages, the fear is not about to go away either. In fact, there may be over a million Americans living in daily fear of dioxin poisoning. They are our Vietnam veterans, those known to be exposed to or who were potentially exposed to the dioxin-containing compound Agent Orange. It is to their plight that we now turn.

# CHAPTER 5

# The [Agent] Orange and the Green

An ultratoxic herbicide was rained down leaving an endless harvest of genetic defects and cancer.

—*The Poison Conspiracy*[1]

"Only you can prevent forests." That was the unofficial motto of participants in Operation Ranch Hand. And that was what they did. From 1962 to 1971, the Air Force Ranch Handers dumped an estimated 19 million gallons of herbicides for defoliant purposes over between 10 and 20 percent of the South Vietnamese landscape. While several herbicides were employed, Agent Orange proved the favorite. Eleven million gallons of it were dumped.[2]

In the mind of most of the public and the general media, Agent Orange is guilty of all charges of toxicity, and those who ordered its spraying are guilty of wanton disregard for human safety, indeed, of genocide. In criticizing the United States war effort against Iraq, one newspaper columnist declared: "It becomes quite clear that whatever atrocities are attributed to [Iraqi dictator] Saddam Hussein, they pale in comparison to the Trail of Tears, Wounded Knee, the Sand Creek [Colorado] Massacre, slavery, lynching, Agent Orange and countless other inhumane acts European-Americans committed in the cause of progress and

144

victory."[3] And shortly after the war, *USA Today* ran a cover story that inside the paper was headlined KUWAIT BLAZES COMPARED TO AGENT ORANGE.[4] The reference was to the myriad oil refineries set on fire by Iraqi soldiers, which made parts of the country dark even at midday, the airborne pollutants of which were clearly posing a threat to the health of Kuwaitis and allied soldiers. The newspaper did say that "others warn against comparing the oilfield fires of this war to soldiers' exposure to Agent Orange in Vietnam," thereupon paraphrasing an obscure chemistry professor who said Agent Orange shouldn't be compared because it is far *more* dangerous.[5]

Hollywood also weighed in against the defoliant with, among other movies, a made-for-TV one called *Unnatural Causes,* starring John Ritter, whose character *USA Today*'s reviewer called "a hero in the war against Agent Orange." Said the reviewer: "Unabashedly crusading, the film, written by the immensely talented John Sayles, details yet another Vietnam nightmare—the cruel effects of Agent Orange, the deadly defoliant. . . . Agent Orange rained death not only on vegetation but on unsuspecting soldiers." The reviewer concluded that *Unnatural Causes* "is one of the simplest, most eloquent television movies in an age [*sic*]."[6]

America's use of herbicides in Vietnam began in 1962, increasing slightly until 1965 when Agent Orange was introduced; it reached a peak in the years 1967 through 1969. The herbicides were stored in color-coded drums, from which their names were derived; those names included Agents Orange, Orange II, Green, Purple, and Pink. Agent Orange comprised a fifty-fifty mixture of the herbicides 2,4,5-T, and 2,4,D.[7] Operation Ranch Hand spraying of Agent Orange ended in 1970, although there is a general belief that Agent Orange continued to be used in small quantities around base perimeters for another year.[8] The main use of the defoliant was to deny cover to Communist Vietcong guerrillas so that they could be spotted and engaged by American aircraft and so that their movements could be tracked. About 8 percent of Agent Orange was used against enemy food crops such as beans, peanuts, potatoes, and mangos.[9] Finally, about 2 percent of Agent Orange was used by other branches of the military for special purposes such as maintaining clear fields of fire around military bases or denying cover to enemy troops along riverbanks. This minor spraying was done with truck-mounted sprayers, backpack sprayers or from helicopters, while most of the defoliant was dumped from the backs of cargo planes.[10]

The most important factor causing the end of Agent Orange spraying in 1970 was the release a year earlier of a report linking 2,4,5-T to birth defects in mice. Agent Orange was already being phased out in 1970 when the American Association for the Advancement of Science (AAAS) sent a team of scientists to Vietnam, led by Harvard biologist Matthew Meselson. This was despite his having gone on record as one of the organizers of a 1966 petition opposing the use of herbicides in Vietnam. In addition to reporting the considerable damage to Vietnamese fauna, the AAAS committee reported that it had gotten unconfirmed stories of health effects on Vietnamese civilians, as well. Next a team from the National Academy of Sciences went over and inspected. It, too, could find no records to support claims of health problems but nonetheless attached great significance to the statements of Vietnamese who lived in the highlands that animals and children had been killed by the sprays.[11] In a war where psychology and image counted more than battlefield victories, the United States could not tolerate being accused of engaging in chemical warfare against civilians. The spraying stopped.

Since 1979, more than two hundred thousand Vietnam veterans, concerned about exposure to the defoliant, have come to Department of Veterans Affairs (VA) hospitals for an Agent Orange Registry medical examination.[12] The vets go because it has become "common knowledge" that Agent Orange had a harmful effect on both veterans and their offspring. After all, Agent Orange manufacturers agreed to a huge out-of-court settlement; the federal government agreed to pay compensation to veterans; and, most important, the media has made it clear that Agent Orange is guilty of everything with which it has been charged.

Typical was a pathetically titled article in *Woman's Day*, "Did Agent Orange Kill My Babies?" which quoted Lily Adams, a woman who had served in Vietnam and began reading early, alarming reports about Agent Orange. "I was like a crazy woman," she told the magazine. "Was that why my son was going through all that pain? Was that why my other babies died? Just because I went to Vietnam?"[13] *Woman's Day* also set up the classic victim-as-epidemiologist scenario. First, it quoted the chairman of the White House Agent Orange Working Group (AOWG), a panel of thirty-four federal scientists and health officials established in the Carter administration who review studies of Vietnam-era defoliants, saying there was no evidence of harm; then it gave the rebuttal to Adams. "Lily disagrees. Ever since Vietnam, she has been plagued by illnesses that doctors found hard to diagnose and even harder to treat."[14] The first person was probably a doctor with years of training who studied every Agent Orange report, while the second person's relation to Agent Orange was exposure to it. Whom do you think most *Woman's Day* readers believed?

But probably far more important in influencing public opinion are articles like the one in *USA Today* mentioned above that don't bother to *argue* that Agent Orange poisoned United States veterans; they just *assume* it. To argue is to allow at the very least that there is something to argue against. Merely assuming something, however, eliminates that element of dissent.

The original impetus for the suspicion that Agent Orange has poisoned our veterans is that it contains dioxin. Dioxin is that substance that allegedly caused the Oregon miscarriages, the disintegrating cats of Seveso, and some of the myriad health problems at Love Canal. It is ironic, then, that the very lack of extraordinary health problems in those places constitutes some of the best evidence that there should be none such among veterans exposed to Agent Orange. Yet there is much additional evidence, compiled specifically from veterans, that indicates that neither the dioxin in Agent Orange nor anything else is causing health problems to either veterans or their offspring.

## CANCER AND OTHER DISEASES IN VETERANS

It is common to hear Vietnam veterans claim they were exposed to massive amounts of Agent Orange and hence appreciable amounts of dioxin. But against the many stories of ground troops being drenched with Agent Orange or other herbicides is the fact that the spray rate from the planes was only three gallons per acre. Further, the majority of Ranch Hand missions were flown over jungles, where about 94 percent of the spray would be caught on tree leaves.[15] Subtract further from that remaining 6 percent of three gallons per acre the amount of the spray that would land on hats, fatigues, ponchos, and other protective items and that didn't soak through to the skin.[16] Although there are some recorded instances of an entire one-thousand-gallon load being dumped in an emergency, such "aborts" accounted for less than 1 percent of all Ranch Hand missions.[17]

But how about dioxin in soil, where infantrymen slept and dug in and lay in ambush? Dioxin degrades rapidly in sunlight, half of it disappearing in two hours. That doesn't leave much after two or more days. Dioxin that reached the ground before it degraded would bind to the soil, becoming resistant to degradation but also to absorption by anyone who wasn't actually rolling in or otherwise exposing himself to dirt. Even this would be a tiny amount of that which he might have received from direct spray.[18]

Dioxin can also drain into water, where it may be absorbed by drinking or perhaps bathing in it, but dioxin is insoluble in water, tends to bind to soil particles, and sinks to the bottom of any water supply.[19]

## EVALUATING THE RANCH HANDERS

But isn't there any group of veterans whom we can say definitely received relatively high exposure to Agent Orange and thus high doses of dioxin? Yes: the members of Operation Ranch Hand, the ones who did 90 percent of the spraying. Indeed, blood testing of those sprayers and handlers has indicated that they have many times the level of dioxin in their systems found in veterans who fought on the ground. The concentration of dioxin in their blood at the last sampling, 1987, ranged from 0.0 to 617.7 with a median of 12.4 parts per trillion (ppt). The Air Force comparisons (controls) who had no Agent Orange exposure had a range of 0.0 to 54.8 ppt with a median of 4.2 ppt.[20] The average level in the comparisons is the same as the average concentrations (less than 5.0 ppt) found in the fat of veterans of ground warfare in Vietnam, as well as in that of veterans who did not serve in Vietnam. The health of the Ranch Handers is evaluated every few years. The latest evaluation showed that skin cancers on some parts of the body were higher in the Ranch Hand enlisted flyers than in a nonexposed control population, although the report said this may be a statistical anomaly since such problems were not noted in the enlisted ground crew, which, as a group, had higher levels of blood dioxin than the enlisted flyers.[21] There was no elevation of other types of cancer, including non-Hodgkin's lymphoma (NHL) and soft-tissue sarcoma.[22] The report found a correlation between dioxin and decreased testicular size, but it could make no comments on how that might affect fertility.[23] Further, measuring testicles is, as one might imagine, a ticklish procedure and the possibility of error must be assumed.

Interestingly, there was also an elevation of diabetes in the latest evaluation. That is one of the few diseases that no one has ever blamed on Agent Orange or dioxin. But the same men with diabetes also tended to be fatter than the control subjects. Thus, there are several possibilities. Perhaps dioxin or something else in the Agent Orange caused both the diabetes and the obesity. Or something in the Agent Orange caused overall ill health, which led to obesity and the obesity led to diabetes. Or the Agent Orange-exposed men coincidentally became fatter independently of the Agent Orange and that led to the diabetes. Or both the increase in fat and the increase in the level of diabetes were coincidental.[24] It will be several years before we get the answers; it should again be emphasized that these men were exposed to tremendously high levels of Agent Orange compared with the average American soldier, a subject that will be discussed shortly.

One of the cancers most commonly attributed to Agent Orange is soft-tissue sarcoma, probably because of the Swedish studies mentioned in the previous chapter that indicated a connection between use of phenoxy herbicides and this type of cancer. To test the soft-tissue sarcoma hypothesis, the Veterans Administration launched a study of 13,469 Vietnam-era patients who had sought treatment from Veterans Administration medical centers, that concentrated on soft-tissue sarcomas. It found no difference in prevalence between veterans who had served in Vietnam and those who did not.[25]

These studies are a strong indicator of a lack of extraordinary cancer among servicemen exposed to Agent Orange, but they must also be looked at in conjunction with all the other dioxin studies discussed earlier in this book. Even the Ranch Hand personnel had levels of exposure generally far below that of Seveso residents and those of the trichlorophenol workers evaluated in the National Institute of Occupational Safety and Health (NIOSH) study.[26] Jeanne Stellman, a Columbia University professor of public health and perhaps the one scientist most identified with the proposition that dioxin-containing Agent Orange has had adverse health effects on Vietnam veterans, said of the NIOSH study: "There is much more we need to know before we can extrapolate these results back to veterans." She added, however: "But there is enough here, from a policy point of view, to give veterans the benefit of the doubt and attribute some of these cancers to dioxin exposure."[27]

This is a non sequitur. As noted in the previous chapter, the NIOSH study measured the blood levels of 253 workers for dioxin and found that the mean level of exposure, using the half-life extrapolation, was 2,000 parts per trillion (ppt). Among the workers in the sample for whom exposure had ended more than twenty years ago, the mean of the half-life extrapolated levels (meaning the average level they had back when they were carrying the most dioxin in their bodies) for the subgroup with less than one year of exposure was 640 ppt, while for those with more than one year of exposure the mean was 3,600 ppt.[28] Thus, the group that clearly showed no cancer effects nonetheless had 50 times the exposure of Vietnam veterans, while the group that may have shown some cancer effects had *250* times the exposure.[29] How this provides "enough . . . from a policy point of view, to give veterans the benefit of the doubt and attribute some of these cancers to dioxin exposure" simply cannot be explained in scientific terms.

Another reason that Stellman shouldn't have been too happy about the NIOSH study is that it explicitly stated that there was no elevation of NHL among even the most highly exposed workers.[30] Along with soft-tissue sarcoma, this is one of two types of cancer that the United States government has allowed Vietnam veterans to receive compensation for, regardless of the failure to prove that Agent Orange was the cause.

## THE STELLMAN STUDIES

In the mid-1980s, Stellman and her husband Steven Stellman, who is assistant health commissioner for biostatistics and epidemiological research for the city of New York, were retained by the American Legion to investigate the possibility of veterans' ills being linked to Agent Orange exposure. The Legion is an advocacy group and there is no doubt what outcome they desired, although this by no means proves that this influenced the Stellmans' conclusions. A better hypothesis is that the reason the Legion picked the Stellmans is that they thought they would reach the "proper" conclusion, but even that is certainly not a matter of public record. What is a matter of public record is that the Stellmans did reach the "proper" conclusions where others did not, and to this day the American Legion and others who maintain that Agent Orange caused sickness among American vets have relied on those studies.

The Stellmans sent questionnaires to 6,810 Vietnam and Vietnam-era veterans, asking about their current health, as well as where they served in Vietnam and the dates they were at each location.[31] According to the Stellmans, their data show that veterans exposed to Agent Orange face an increased risk of elevated blood pressure, benign fatty tumors, a wife's miscarriage, visual and skin sensitivity to light, and symptoms of depression. The researchers say they adjusted for combat stress in their analysis. They did caution against putting too much weight on the exact magnitude of the risk increases. They also said that study design didn't allow them to look for a connection between Agent Orange and cancer or birth defects.[32]

Those who had been looking for such results were highly impressed with the Stellman studies. "What the American Legion study does is confirm everything we've been saying for the last 10 years," said James Sparrow of Vietnam Veterans Agent Orange Victims.[33] Others, however, were less impressed. The federal Centers for Disease Control (CDC) claim they contacted the American Legion and the Stellmans concerning the study in order to conduct a scientific review, but that advance copies of the publication, the original study protocol, and the study questionnaire were all denied to them. Thus, the CDC did no review of the study.[34] The Agent Orange Working Group, however, did. It found that the data in the report "did not support the conclusions drawn by the authors." It also said that the sampling for the subjects was nonrandom, that there was a low response rate (which detracts from a study's validity even if the original selections were random), and that self-reported combat exposure was not compared with military records. "Because of these problems," the AOWG said, "the results of the American Legion report are of little or no value in further understanding the Agent Orange issue."[35]

Similarly, the team of Air Force researchers studying the Ranch

Hand cohort stated of the Stellmans' study in its March 1991 report:

> Design limitations in this study are such that few conclusions can be drawn beyond that, in self-reported questionnaires, Vietnam veterans perceive themselves to be in worse health than non-Vietnam veterans. Furthermore, given the evidence cited above [which will be discussed later in this chapter] that most Vietnam and non-Vietnam veterans do not differ in the current body burden of dioxin, the exposure indices employed in this study must now be considered invalid.[36]

Finally, Hellen Gelband of the Office of Technology Assessment Health Program, an agency of Congress, prepared a full report evaluating the American Legion-Stellman study. The Gelband evaluation was negative virtually throughout, and found that "this study has major flaws that call into question the validity of virtually all the findings reported" and that "the American Legion study has such serious problems that, even though some of its conclusions might be correct, the evidence produced by the study cannot be relied upon for an understanding of the consequences of having served in Southeast Asia during the Vietnam era."[37]

## BIRTH DEFECTS AND MISCARRIAGES

While stories of men who have served their country and are now suffering from terrible diseases are heartrending enough, nothing is more pathetic than tales of women who lost their babies or whose babies were born with awful defects. And in the latter category, pictures prove much more valuable than the proverbial thousand words—a picture such as the one in a *Newsweek* article about the Agent Orange trial, showed a pretty little girl in a wheelchair with a deformed right arm, whom it identified as a daughter of a Vietnam vet.[38]

Yet the scientific rationale that dioxin may cause birth defects and miscarriages in humans is shaky indeed. The basis is that in some of the animal studies, dioxin exposure did appear to cause such defects.[39] Having noted previously, in Chapter 2, the problems with using animals to test for human health risks, there are further reasons for questioning the results of animal studies concerning dioxin and birth problems. First, exposure in the tests was quite high, often so extreme as to cause overt health effects in the exposed female animals as well.[40] Second, although in some cases smaller amounts that did not affect the mother animals have caused defects—cleft palates in mice offspring, for example—it is still almost impossible for humans to consume proportionately large doses. Some Australian scientists have calculated the proportional dose for a 110-pound woman to match that which, when given to the mice, produced those cleft palates. The woman would have to ingest a half ounce or more of dioxin-containing 2,4,5-T per day, an amount that Dr. Meselson has said would be enough to kill five hundred thousand people.[41] If the source of the herbicide was meat from animals that had grazed on sprayed vegetation, the woman would have to consume between 13,200 and 198,000 pounds of that meat daily or drink 3,975 to 238,000 gallons of sprayed water daily to take in an amount of dioxin equivalent to that which caused birth defects in mice.[42]

If we used monkeys as our model instead of mice, we'd have to note that monkeys do not react to dioxin with birth defects; rather, they miscarry. Applying the equivalent amount that caused those monkey miscarriages to a pregnant woman would require her to consume about 30,000 pounds of meat containing the highest reported levels of dioxin daily for a week.[43]

The third caveat in extrapolating from the animal studies to humans is that in those studies, the miscarriages and defect effects occurred when a pregnant animal was exposed to dioxin, not an animal that later became pregnant as was the case with women who were exposed to Agent Orange in Vietnam.[44]

This brings up what may be the most important difference between the animal studies and the human circumstances. Usually when we speak of health problems in veterans' offspring, we are not talking about women who served in Vietnam, but about women whose *husbands* were exposed. That is an entirely different situation. Nevertheless, responding to the anecdotal information of Vietnam veterans, amply magnified and relayed by the media, that they were suffering vastly disproportionate numbers of birth defects, the CDC undertook a study of the matter that it presented in the *Journal of the American Medical Association* in 1984. Among 13,000 babies born with birth defects in the years 1968 through 1980 in the Atlanta area, it looked at the 7,529 that according to an international classification system were regarded as having serious defects. It then broke these down into ninety-six separate categories of defects, conducted an investigation to find out which of those were fathered by veterans, and broke those veterans down into categories of non-Vietnam veterans and Vietnam veterans, and then further broke down the last groups into those classified as exposed to Agent Orange based on the veterans' own recollections and to those classified as exposed based on military records.[45]

"The most important conclusion to be drawn from this study," wrote the authors, "is that the data collected contain no evidence to support the position that Vietnam veterans have had a greater risk than other men for fathering babies with all types of serious structural birth defects combined." Among the vast numbers of specific defects that the researchers looked for, it did find a handful that indicated slightly higher risk ratios among Vietnam veterans who probably had higher Agent Orange exposures than other veterans or that showed slightly higher ratios among Vietnam veterans as compared to other veterans. But these were more than balanced out by areas in which Vietnam veterans had lower risk ratios. In fact, the most significant deviation from the expected number of birth defects was that Vietnam veterans had only about half as many babies with defects classed in the group "complex cardiovascular defects."[46]

The authors noted that their study jibed well with previous ones, including one of Australian Vietnam vets[47] and one of Vietnamese children born between 1962 to 1973 to mothers possibly exposed to herbicides.[48] Neither showed any increase in birth defect frequency. One much-touted study the CDC researchers also mentioned was that of families of North Vietnamese veterans, conducted by the North Vietnamese government and headed up by Ton That Tung, who had served in sprayed areas in the south. The study presented case histories of birth defects but it failed to provide adequate controls.[49] Indeed, both the World Health Organization and the Cancer Assessment Group of the EPA concluded that Tung's data was not conclusive and was inadequate to link Agent Orange or its constituents to the effects it alleged it caused.[50]

This assumes the Tung study was even an honest one. It bears noting that this study was published not only while the war was still going on but while American troops were actively involved in combat in 1971. It seems to have occurred to none of the journalists citing this work that it might have been designed for propaganda purposes. Certainly it was used that way. Reported *Rolling Stone* magazine in a highly sympathetic article: "The North Vietnamese sent antiwar groups photographic evidence— one baby had three legs, no neck and a bulbous sack for a jaw, another had a mouth beveled like a duck's—and as public outrage grew and even government reports confirmed the dangers of Agent Orange, the Pentagon elected to abandon Ranchhand [*sic*]."[51] Such publicity is an awfully good reason for a doctor working for the North Vietnamese government to fudge data, one would think. Yet, along with *Rolling Stone, Newsweek,*[52] the *Bulletin of the Atomic Scientists,*[53] and *The Nation*[54] all took Dr. Tung and his work quite seriously, without suggesting a possible conflict of interest. Tung's studies were also crucial to Fred Wilcox's influential book, *Waiting for an Army to Die.*[55] Interestingly, Wilcox noted that Bonnie Hill, whose role in getting dioxin-containing herbicides outlawed in this country was discussed in the previous chapter, went to hear Tung speak and was greatly influenced.[56]

In their conclusion, the CDC researchers observed that:

> Many fathers, whether Vietnam veterans or not, have had the misfortune of having babies with birth defects. Although specific types of structural birth defects are rare, when all types are combined they usually affect roughly two percent to three percent of stillborn and live-born babies. If by 1984, each of these men have had an average of one baby since the time of their service, they will have had 52,000 to 78,000 babies born with serious defects if they have had the usual risk of two percent to three percent. If these men have had an average of two babies each, then these figures would be doubled. Although these numbers may seem alarming, they are based on nothing more than assumptions about the fertility of Vietnam veterans and the usual rate at which birth defects occur.[57]

The wider meaning of this statement is something to ponder. It means that *People* magazine or *American Legion* or *Newsweek* or anyone else can present an article featuring not just three or four or five Vietnam veterans whose children have birth defects, as is usually the case, but any number of such case histories, limited only by the length of the article and the writer's ability to track these veterans down. They could present the case histories of dozens of such veterans, of *hundreds* of such veterans, of *thousands* of such veterans—*and it wouldn't mean a thing*. The reader will almost certainly be convinced of the Agent Orange-birth defect connection after just a few such case histories, as indeed will have been the writer of the article himself, who will have listened to sad tale after sad tale and perhaps will have seen the children firsthand. But no such connection exists.

Some health problems are the result of modern man-made chemicals. But these, like polyvinyl chlorides and diethylstilbestrol and thalidomide are discovered through careful scientific investigation. You're not going to learn anything useful from personal testimonials of hysterical parents on *Donahue* or personal testimonials in *Newsweek* or *U.S. News & World Report* or from family physicians or from environmental activists or from crusading reporters. You will discover such health problems in the findings of epidemiologists, cancer researchers, toxicologists, and others who specialize in those areas. They are people who generally do not call press conferences, do not publish books with major companies, do not appear at citizens rallies, and do not write op-ed pieces for *USA Today*. They just quietly go about their business year after year, occasionally publishing in medical or scientific journals, and hoping that somewhere out there is a journalist who will interpret those studies and correctly relay them to the masses.

## GUILTY BY ANECDOTE

To most Americans, the "proof" of the harm caused by Agent Orange isn't in the Stellman studies or anybody's studies, especially since most of them show no harm. Rather, the proof is in the testimony of the alleged victims themselves, as relayed by the media.

The fallacy that says that something that happened after something else must have happened *because of* that something else, formally known as *post hoc ergo propter hoc* ("after this, therefore because of this"), pops up regularly in the dioxin debate. Lewis Regenstein, author of *America the Poisoned*, notes that among the cases collected by the environmentalist group Friends of the

Earth of unborn children allegedly affected by their mother's exposure to 2,4,5-T was the following: "In a small settlement in northern Wisconsin of less than 40 families, all five pregnant women lost their babies after spray drifted over their homes."[58] If a town meeting were held on that same day as the spraying it could just as easily be argued that the town meeting caused the miscarriages. After all, they all took place after the event in question.

This fallacy is regularly observed in the case of Vietnam veterans who have developed medical problems since their tour. They were in Vietnam, and now they have cancer, or now they have digestive problems, or now they have children with defects. That's all these intrepid investigative reporters need.

While it's common for the media to grant victims of a given disease the status of an epidemiologist, with Agent Orange, sometimes that expertise was attributed to all Vietnam veterans. *Health* magazine printed an "as told to" article in 1987 by alleged Agent Orange victim Elmo Zumwalt III, who had been a river-boat commander in Vietnam. Zumwalt's case was remarkable in that his father, Elmo Zumwalt, Jr., was commander of the U.S. Navy in Vietnam from 1968 to 1970, and in that role he had ordered the spraying of Agent Orange along the riverbanks to destroy the foliage from which enemy soldiers could hide as they shot and killed river-boat sailors. For the media, the irony was too tempting; they played up the story for all it was worth.

In one 1987 article, the younger Zumwalt was said to have asked, concerning lymphoma, "Why . . . have physicians at the National Cancer Institute and at other major medical centers suddenly been seeing so many 20-and 30-year-old Vietnam veterans afflicted with the cancer?"[59] Actually, they hadn't. Considering that the youngest legal age for an American soldier in Vietnam was seventeen and that the spraying of Agent Orange had ceased by 1971, those exposed to the substance would have been at least thirty-three years old in 1987. Zumwalt's twenty-year-olds with lymphoma hadn't yet made it into kindergarten when the spraying of Agent Orange had ceased. Didn't this simple calculation occur to the actual writer of the article, *Health* editor John Grossman, or to anyone else?

Another Vietnam vet, Alan Belcher, who was involved in screening veterans for Agent Orange exposure in the Chicago suburbs, told a local newspaper that "About six men have died in [McHenry County] of cancer that could be related to Agent Orange exposure." The front-page story continues: "The death toll began with a McHenry man named Joe Thome." The reporter then quoted Belcher, who averred that Thome's death "really brought the whole issue to a head for us. If Joe can die, anyone can die."[60] Think about *that* for a moment. Consider, too, that this was the full epidemiological information supplied by the newspaper. A veteran who didn't even pretend to have any medical expertise—who indeed seemed incognizant that all humans eventually die—says six men have died whose deaths "could be related" to Agent Orange. What did they die of specifically? What was their exposure level to Agent Orange? Did they even serve in areas where it was sprayed? The reader has no idea. Yet this sort of amateur epidemiology can have a real impact on the thinking of many readers who may assume poor Mr. Belcher had some idea of what he was talking about.

Besides the *post hoc ergo propter hoc* fallacy, another one that regularly comes into play with Agent Orange is that of *appeal to emotion*. With this fallacy, you ignore the real issues in favor of pulling heartstrings through a display of pathos. Thus, Lewis Regenstein quoted from a *Washington Post* article about a Vietnam veteran who brought his severely deformed daughter to a congressional hearing on Agent Orange. "During the emotion-laden hearing," wrote the *Post* reporter, "Kerrie [actually, Kerry], a frail child with short brown hair, sat in her wheelchair gazing wide-eyed at the television cameras. . . . Kerrie was born eight years ago with 18 birth defects: missing bones, twisted limbs, a hole in her heart, deformed intestines, a partial spine, shrunken fingers, no rectum."[61] To this Regenstein in his book added: "Unfortunately, the U.S. government has no help it can give to Kerrie because of the damage Agent Orange may have done to her. She should try to understand that the dangers of the chemical remain officially unproven."[62]

In fact, what she, Regenstein, the *Washington Post, People* magazine (which ran a short profile of Kerry for the same reason Regenstein did),[63] and Clifford Linedecker, the author of a 1982 book about Kerry and Agent Orange,[64] all should try to understand is that the horribleness of a set of birth defects has no intrinsic bearing on whether the defects were caused by whatever is being accused. If poor Kerry had "only" nine birth defects, the case against Agent Orange would be no weaker; if she had thirty-six, it would be no stronger. The amount of damage is relevant only *after* causation has been demonstrated, when addressing the issue of compensation for injury already established as caused by the one from whom compensation is sought. It does not serve as proof of causation.

## THE CASE OF PAUL REUTERSHAN

In 1983, Fred Wilcox published what would become one of the more influential Agent Orange books, *Waiting for an Army to Die.* The *San Francisco Chronicle* compared it to Rachel Carson's *Silent Spring,* while California assemblyman and former Jane Fonda mate Tom Hayden called it "my bible on the issue of Agent Orange."[65] Among the ten books listed in the bibliography were Michael H. Brown's *Laying Waste,* John G. Fuller's *The Poison That Fell from the Sky,* and Clifford Linedecker's *Kerry: Agent Orange and an American Family,* all mentioned in this or the previous chapter. In an extremely lengthy and highly sympathetic review in the *New Republic,* C.D.B. Bryan, author of *Friendly Fire,* noted Wilcox's claims of having interviewed practically everyone under the sun but felt obligated to point out that "nowhere in the book do I find evidence that he interviewed any representative from the chemical companies; nor for that matter, from the V.A."[66]

True to the pattern of these and virtually all the books in his bibliography, Wilcox is long on anecdotes and emotion and short on data. *Waiting* reads merely like one of myriad popular magazine articles about Agent Orange giving veterans cancer, except that it provides greater detail and more horror stories. Indeed, the horror story—more specifically, the testimonials of dying veterans who apparently believe that Agent Orange brought on their demise—is the cornerstone of the book. First and foremost was that of Paul Reutershan, who was to become the most famous alleged victim of Agent Orange other than Elmo Zumwalt III. Wrote Wilcox on page one of his introduction:

> In the spring of 1978, a twenty-eight-year-old Vietnam veteran who appeared on the *Today* show shocked many of the program's

viewers by announcing: "I died in Vietnam, but I didn't even know it." As a helicopter crew chief responsible for transporting supplies to the 20th Engineer Brigade, Paul Reutershan flew almost daily through clouds of herbicide being discharged from C-123 cargo planes. He observed the dark swaths cut into the jungle by the spraying, watched the mangrove forests turn brown, sicken and die, but didn't really worry about his own health. Agent Orange, according to the Army, was "relatively nontoxic to humans and animals." On December 14, 1978, Reutershan succumbed to the cancer that had destroyed much of his colon, liver, and abdomen.

In the months before he died, Reutershan founded Agent Orange Victims International, and spent all of his waning energies trying to inform the American people about his belief that his cancer was the result of his exposure to an herbicide called Agent Orange.[67]

Through Wilcox's book, that *Today* show appearance, and the fact that he began the Agent Orange lawsuit against the chemical companies, Reutershan became symbolic of Agent Orange victims everywhere. But what evidence is there that this caused his disease? Surely not that he got cancer. One million of us get cancer each year and half die of it. Over 1 percent of Americans now living have served in Vietnam (2.8 million) and 1 percent of one million is ten thousand. So why, with over 700,000 expected cancers in a given population, is there any reason to assume that Reutershan's—or the cancer of any given veteran—is related to Agent Orange?

The best possible reason is that those one million cancers are not spread evenly over the population. Cancer is far more often a disease of the aged; deaths from cancer are ten times more frequent in those aged sixty-five and older than in younger age groups.[68] But, because so much progress has been made in reducing premature deaths from infectious disease, heart disease, accidents, and other causes, cancer is still the number one killer of adults aged twenty-five to forty-five. Reutershan died of a cancer in his pelvis that grew out of control so quickly that pathologists couldn't tell in what organ or tissue it had begun. About 980 white men and about 790 white women between the ages of twenty-five and twenty-nine died from cancer the same year.[69] Thus, death from cancer at age twenty-eight is uncommon, but hardly unknown. In 1988, 1,835 persons died of cancer between the ages of twenty-five and twenty-nine,[70] all of whom were too young to possibly have been exposed to Agent Orange.

Likewise, Wilcox makes the point that "hundreds" of men with testicular cancer had joined the class action suit against the makers of Agent Orange. Always ready with an anecdote, he relates the story of veteran Ron DeBoer. "And even when he first began feeling ill," writes Wilcox, "when the lump in his groin began to swell and he suspected it wouldn't go away, he [DeBoer] dismissed the articles his wife was clipping from the paper about a herbicide that had been sprayed, quite possibly, upon the area of Vietnam where he had served."[71] To read that, one might think the only way to get testicular cancer is through exposure to Agent Orange. It looks like the fellow said to himself, "Look, this Agent Orange business is phony, therefore I don't have testicular cancer." In fact, testicular cancer strikes most often at the age at which these veterans were during the suit and an estimated twenty-three hundred testicular cancers will occur among those veterans.[72] Testicular cancer is the most common cancer in males between the ages of twenty and thirty-four.[73] That "hundreds" would join a suit and that Wilcox would relate the story of one—or ten or twenty or thirty—does nothing to prove an elevated incidence of the disease among veterans.

In fact, the "evidence" for the Agent Orange connection to Reutershan's cancer is nothing more than that he claims his cancer was related to the herbicide and that he served in Vietnam. Even the business about flying "almost daily" through Agent Orange clouds is certainly wrong. The normal procedure for spraying was three times at two-week intervals. That took care of the area for a year.[74] Assuming Reutershan's timing was perfect and that each time he flew to the 20th Brigade base it was at the exact time the spraying was going on, he flew through Agent Orange clouds on three days. One could ask further how much Agent Orange would end up on Reutershan when he was in the cockpit of a helicopter, but the point is made.

This is not to call Reutershan a liar. But once he had decided that Agent Orange must have been the cause of his problem, the more he believed himself to be exposed. This is a common phenomenon among both those who are victims of a disease and those who are afraid they may become so. Reutershan was a man who, probably like most men in their twenties who are told they will not make it to anywhere near their allotted three score and ten, that they will not have children and grandchildren and grow old gracefully, reacted bitterly and demanded to know "why me?"

The mathematician might have told him "odds—somebody's got to die young," and a clergyman might have told him it was part of God's plan. But Reutershan felt more comfortable with his own theory.

Yet there is more to the psychological aspect of Agent Orange than the mere searching for meaning and purpose that often accompanies diagnoses of cancer as well as miscarriages. As one ill veteran put it: "I'm very bitter. We were used as young kids are used in every war. But what makes it especially terrible is that we were wasted for no good reason."[75] Agent Orange is the angry veteran's way of striking back. They got no parades, no brass bands, no bragging rights. What they got was spat upon and labeled "baby killers." Yet they simply did their job just as every American soldier has done his job since the French and Indian War. Vietnam veterans fought hard, fought bravely, and never lost a single major military battle, even though far more often than not they were heavily outnumbered by the enemy. But regardless, the war was lost and that has made all the difference. That makes their efforts, in the eyes of some, "wasted" and, as the one veteran put it, makes them very bitter. The vast majority have accepted this emotion, walled it off, put it behind them, and gone on with their lives. A small but vocal number, however, have vented their anger and frustration by lashing out at the military. Some have joined veterans organizations that fought against United States military action in the Persian Gulf, and others have crusaded against Agent Orange. This is a psychological condition for which we must have understanding and compassion, but it must not take us down the path of giving in to unreasonable demands by acquiescing to untruths. A few veterans groups and thousands of angry veterans do not a scientific case against Agent Orange make. Further, it must be asked, how compassionate is it to let perhaps millions of Vietnam veterans consider themselves ticking time bombs when in fact they are not, and to let them think they are more prone to sire defective children when they are not?

## "ORANGEMAIL": AGENT ORANGE ON TRIAL

Prevented by law from suing the government and frustrated by the refusal of the VA to pay their claims without proof of causation, veterans and their families instead brought suit against the seven chemical firms that manufactured under military contract Agent Orange and its dioxin-tainted relatives with their various color names.[76] The suit ended in 1984 in a settlement for $180 million and was the biggest mass damage award ever negotiated. Yet, if the purpose of the suit was to obtain both compensation and vindication, the settlement achieved neither. For compensation purposes, attorneys for the plaintiffs estimated the $180 million would average out to only $850 per plaintiff, although that would ultimately depend on how many veterans made claims.[77] Some pointed out that the $180 million was interest-bearing, and thus the plaintiffs would get more, but by the time this increase was discounted for inflation, the bottom line wouldn't change that much. Thus, looked at in this way, the sum was peanuts, but it appears the trial judge made it clear that it was all the plaintiffs could hope to get.

In fact, while one of the veterans' attorneys crowed, "Today the chemical companies surrendered . . . a quarter of a billion dollars is a hell of an admission" (he arbitrarily tossed in six years' of interest),[78] it appears the chemical companies were prepared at one point to increase their offer—indeed, even to double it— but Judge Jack Weinstein stopped them, believing the existing offer of $180 million was sufficient in light of the weakness of the case. The plaintiffs' attorneys introduced very little evidence showing a statistical correlation between exposure and injury, and there was no evidence proving that any individual's injury was the result of exposure to Agent Orange. The chemical companies settled because they faced the prospect that if the judge submitted the case to the jury, the jury would sympathize with the veterans' plight and return a staggering verdict.[79]

This plight of the chemical companies prompted *The New York Times* to coin the term "orangemail." This colorful description, according to the *Times,* consists of

> hordes of personal-injury lawyers [who] sign up alleged victims of a toxic chemical, creating the prospect of such costly litigation that the manufacturers are driven to settle, even if no connection between injury and chemical can be proved. . . . Agent Orange is orangemail in its purest form. A thousand tort lawyers jumped on the settlement bandwagon even though the court found their case to be substantially without merit. . . . Yet the makers of Agent

Orange faced the prospect of endless litigation, and the risk of losing many cases before juries apt to put compassion ahead of dispassion.[80]

But before allowing oneself to have too much sympathy for the chemical companies, observe that, as with Uniroyal and Alar, these companies had a chance to stand up for what they had been saying all along, that there was no scientific evidence that their product had caused any harm. They thus allowed some people, like the widow of a veteran who died of leukemia, to think and assert that even though the evidence she put together didn't show that her husband died of Agent Orange exposure, "they [the chemical companies] are guilty, or I wouldn't have gotten a check."[81] When the going got tough, the tough went shopping for an easy way out. Two companies then proceeded to pursue claims against the U.S. government for allegedly misusing their product.[82]

## THE CDC CLIMBS ONTO THE CROSS

The CDC in Atlanta is one of the most respected federal agencies in the country. Under the tutelage of Dr. Alexander Langmuir, it instituted a brand of "gumshoe" epidemiology that has been imitated throughout the world yet never excelled. Like any section of the bureaucracy, it may sometimes have a tendency to overstate problems and thus overemphasize its own importance, but it remains the world's epidemiological leader. Indeed, when other countries have a perplexing epidemiological problem, they often attempt to bring the CDC onto the case. Likewise, when it became apparent that the Veterans Administration could not handle the job Congress gave it in 1979 of ascertaining the effects of Agent Orange on veterans, the agency turned that task over to the CDC. What it should have given the agency as well, however, was a cross and nails.

The CDC began its attempt in 1983 with what it called a "validation study," in which it attempted to identify veterans who had been exposed to Agent Orange, using military records of troop movements and herbicide spray missions. After four years of wading through records of troop movements and attempting to correlate them with records of Agent Orange spraying, they found that accurate correlations could not be made, for a variety of reasons that will be discussed presently. Nevertheless, a new development would prove far more valuable. In 1986, researchers reported a new test that involved analysis of a small amount of fat in less than a pint of blood that made it possible to determine levels of exposure to dioxins in Agent Orange even fifteen to twenty years after exposure; and later studies backed up the method's effectiveness.[83] Previously, it had been necessary to withdraw ten grams of fat from either the subject's buttocks or abdomen, a painful procedure which some men were reluctant to undergo. Either system of analysis, of blood or fat, incorporates the principle that the half-life of dioxin in the body is about seven years. Thus, it is possible to look at levels of dioxin in the body today and calculate back to what it was at given points in the past.[84]

Blood or fat testing for dioxin is far more valuable than finding out who was where on what day and comparing that with the time and place that Agent Orange was sprayed, because no matter how accurate one's data on troop movements, it still cannot tell you how much exposure each man received. A direct test is always more accurate than a surrogate.

The results of the Agent Orange validation study, released in July 1987, showed no association of blood levels of dioxin and several different military-records-based estimates of the likelihood of Agent Orange exposure. There was also no meaningful correlation between dioxin levels and veterans' self-reported exposure estimates. Among the 646 Vietnam veterans for whom dioxin levels were obtained, the median amount of 3.8 ppt, consisting of men with less than 1.0 ppt up to one man with 45.0 ppt. The median dioxin level for the ninety-seven non-Vietnam veterans was also 3.8 ppt. The two veterans with the highest levels had 25.0 and 45.0 ppt. The 45.0 ppt soldier reported no exposure, military or civilian, to herbicides, while the 25 ppt one reported 180 days of indirect military exposure, defined as walking through, or clearing vegetation in, a previously sprayed area, along with one day of home use of dioxin-containing herbicide. Both of those men reported their health to be "excellent." As a result of these findings, the CDC concluded that it could not conduct a scientifically valid study of Agent Orange exposure based on military records; nor was it possible to divide veterans into statistically significant groups based on their dioxin blood levels. There simply was not any apparent connection between where soldiers served in the country and their harboring of dioxin.[85] In endorsing the CDC report, the OTA stated flatly: "There cannot be a general study of Agent Orange on ground troops."[86]

But instead of writing off the whole project, the CDC worked with the material it had available. It did know who had been stationed where and it had good records indicating how those people had been diagnosed. The CDC published its report, called the Selected Cancers Study, in May 1988 in the *Journal of the American Medical Association*,[87] although the final version was not released until February 1991.[88] The study had essentially four conclusions. First, Vietnam veterans have roughly a 50 percent increased risk of developing non-Hodgkin's lymphoma (NHL) fifteen to twenty-five years after military service in Vietnam. Second, veterans who served in locations other than Vietnam do not have a similar increased risk of NHL. Third, the increased risk of NHL among Vietnam veterans cannot be explained by Agent Orange exposure because the veterans who showed the highest risk for NHL were those least exposed to Agent Orange or with virtually no possibility for exposure, such as those who served on board ship the whole time. For example, of thirty-two Navy veterans the study found with NHL, twenty-eight had served on oceangoing vessels in so-called "blue water" while none had served on boats in so-called "brown water," which would have allowed them to come into contact with Agent Orange sprayed along the riverbank.[89] NHL has been much on the rise in recent years; this increase is connected not with dioxin or Agent Orange exposure, however, but with AIDS.[90] (One researcher suggested to me that the Navy veterans may have a higher percentage of those who engage in high-risk activity for AIDS than do the Army or the Marines, although there is no data on this.) Finally, Vietnam veterans are not at increased risk for any other type of cancer, including soft-tissue sarcoma.[91] The CDC did find total deaths to be 17 percent higher among veterans than among nonveterans, but most of this was from external causes, such as motor vehicle injuries, suicide, and homicide. Further, this overall rise was similar to that found among men returning from combat areas after World War II and the Korean War.[92]

These obviously were not the results that Agent Orange critics wanted to hear. The study even found that there was no correlation between NHL and veteran self-reports of suspected contact with Agent Orange. As to why nonexposed veterans had that higher level of NHL, the researchers could only speculate, saying it might have had something to do with some unexamined characteristic of men who went to Vietnam, it might have resulted from something specific to Vietnam service such as a viral or other type of infection, or it might have been caused by some characteristic of the men who served in Vietnam but developed later, such as stress or behavioral change.[93]

Perhaps most disappointing to those looking to indict Agent Orange was the lack of association between Agent Orange and soft-tissue sarcoma. The study found that the risk of acquiring that type of cancer among Vietnam veterans was 88 percent of that of men who served in the military during the Vietnam war but never served in Vietnam. Even looking at specific types of sarcomas, it found no increased risks in any category.[94]

The popular science magazine *Discover* said of the CDC findings: "They contradicted a prevailing myth: that most of the more than 2.5 million men who served in Vietnam, on top of having to fight an ill-conceived and unpopular war, on top of coming home to indifference and even scorn, had actually been poisoned by their own government and careless and greedy chemical manufacturers."[95]

Obviously, for those with an interest in keeping the myth alive, the results were devastating. They called upon their allies in Congress, who in several hearings bullied the CDC researchers over the study.

Most galling to the congressmen and the various veteran advocacy groups was the CDC conclusion that not only were dioxin levels in servicemen too uniform to compare one with another group, they were uniformly low. As the director of the CDC study Robert Worth said: "We have evidence for the first time that only a very small proportion of ground troops show significant exposure to Agent Orange. In essence, you can walk through an area or be around where they're spraying, and it doesn't necessarily mean that you'll get a significant dose."[96] Indeed, the very highest level found in any of the veterans tested, 45 ppt, was less than one tenth of that which would later, in the Fingerhut-NIOSH study, prove to be the average level for civilian employees working with dioxin who had less than a year's exposure to dioxin—640 ppt—a group that showed no excessive rate of cancer.

But for all the stream of rhetoric that poured forth from angry congressmen and others alleging harm from Agent Orange, this aspect of the CDC study was virtually ignored. One New Jersey study has been repeatedly proffered to show that in fact United States ground troops were exposed to high levels of Agent Orange. As *The Nation* put it: "New Jersey's commission made the news last fall, when it announced that the levels of dioxin in the blood and fat of exposed veterans it studied were ten times higher than those of two control groups."[97] In fact, the study comprised a grand total of ten contaminated men, which by definition disqualified it as possibly being representative of the exposure of servicemen as a whole. Yet that was never the purpose of the study. The researchers intentionally sought out the most contaminated men they could find, and all but one of them had worked directly with the dispersal of Agent Orange. The main purpose of the study was to determine to what extent dioxin remained in the body and how it could be measured.[98] It was not made so that people like *The Nation*'s reporter could crow about how much dioxin veterans absorbed.

Most opponents of the CDC study, however, simply concentrated on the fact that the CDC said the original intent of the study, to compare troop movements to where Agent Orange was sprayed, had not been carried out. Indeed, in August 1990, both the American Legion and the Vietnam Veterans of America filed suit to force the CDC to resume the Agent Orange study.[99] It didn't matter that what the CDC had done was incomparably superior to what it originally intended. The idea was that if the CDC had only done the study the other way it would have found the desired results. It was rather like boasting that one could beat up that snarling tiger in the cage if the bars suddenly vanished, knowing full well that the bars were not about to disappear. Thus Senator Tom Daschle (D-S.D.) denounced the CDC report on the Senate floor as "nothing short of incredible. It confirms what I have suspected all along: The CDC does not want to do the study."[100]

To counter the CDC assertion that it was not possible to determine exposure to Agent Orange from troop movement records, angry congressmen waved about the study conducted by the American Legion's hired hands, Jeanne and Steven Stellman.

Indeed, it was the same study that the Ranch Hand study researchers, the Agent Orange Working Group, and Hellen Gelband of the OTA had vigorously ripped apart. The Stellmans made no claims of being able to estimate doses received by individual soldiers, but they said that wasn't necessary, since the likelihood of being exposed was good enough to draw conclusions about later health effects. Said Jeanne Stellman: "We *can* evaluate exposure. There are troops [for comparison] who were in areas that were never exposed" (emphasis in original).[101]

In a July 1989 hearing before the House Government Operations Subcommittee on Human Resources and Intergovernmental Relations, chairman Ted Weiss (D-N.Y.), since deceased, held up the Stellmans' study as an indictment of the CDC's efforts and proof that such an analysis could be done. Accusing the CDC of not using detailed troop location information, as the Stellmans said they had done, Weiss declared the CDC study "either politically rigged or monumentally bungled."[102] But the director of the CDC study, Vernon Houk, replied it was neither. Rather, he said, the records of company movements were just not detailed enough to determine whether individual men were exposed. "Even at the company level, the men would be dispersed over 20 kilometers. And the spray did not disperse [drift] more than two kilometers." As evidence of this lack of correlation, Houk cited the results of the aforementioned lab testing, which had only become available in 1986 and which could detect dioxin in the blood even twenty years after exposure. Using this, the CDC tested the blood of 646 veterans whose records indicated they had been fighting in areas that were sprayed and found that only one had a dioxin level above that considered to be above what one would expect in the system of a person who hadn't served in a sprayed area. Houk said that this forced the CDC to conclude that "very few ground troops were exposed to Agent Orange."[103]

Jeanne Stellman didn't think much of this explanation. She said: "We dumped 12 million gallons on Vietnam; someone had to be exposed."[104] But OTA's Gelband pointed out that even though troops were located in the general area, they were not sent into sprayed locations until defoliation had occurred, often several weeks later, and that this was long enough for most of the dioxin to have been degraded by sunlight.[105]

As *Science* magazine reported, while the Stellmans were the heroes of the Weiss hearing, they had been on the defensive the day before at a hearing held by the House Veterans Affairs Committee, in which a series of witnesses cast doubt on their methods. Houk testified that their questionnaire-based health reporting was essentially useless. "People who think they were exposed always report more adverse health effects," he said, noting that this was shown by the CDC studies. "Self-reports need to be validated." Other witnesses and some committee members also challenged the likelihood that veterans could remember with accuracy where they were fighting in Vietnam and when they were doing that fighting some twenty years later.[106] Moreover, recall that the AOWG specifically noted that self-reported combat exposure in the Stellman study was not compared with military records.[107]

Congress's own OTA stamped its imprimatur on the CDC report. Hellen Gelband testified before the Committee on Veterans' Affairs:

> OTA finds the Selected Cancers Study to be well designed, conducted, and analyzed. The case-control design is the only practical approach to studying relatively rare diseases in a large population, but it has some inherent difficulties that must be recognized and addressed, to the extent possible. CDC did this admirably with thorough and complete analysis.[108]

If anything, said Gelband, CDC might have *overstated* the significance of the finding of a higher level of NHL in veterans, a matter of some significance since it was on the basis of the CDC's findings that VA Secretary Edwin Derwinski made the decision to compensate Vietnam veterans suffering from NHL.[109] Said Gelband:

> In our view, CDC has, in its interpretation, perhaps minimized the possibility that the elevated risk seen in the study is due to chance, bias, or confounding [variables not accounted for], which are common problems with case-control studies. CDC is more convinced than is OTA that the result represents a real excess risk, but no one can say for sure, and the range of possible explanations should be given due consideration.

At any rate, she said, "the Selected Cancers Study provides strong evidence that Agent Orange is not an important cause of the cancers included in the study."[110]

Seeing that help was unavailable from *that* source, Weiss ordered another agency of Congress, the U.S. General Accounting Office (GAO), to conduct an investigation of how the CDC used the $70.4 million it received from the VA to conduct the aborted Agent Orange study and completed the Selected Cancers Study. Of the four agencies with investigative powers that serve Congress, GAO has received the reputation of being not so much the watchdog it is supposed to be, but more of a lapdog. Essentially, when someone from the House or Senate majority asks the GAO to find out "Isn't it true that . . . ?" the GAO has a strong tendency to reply, "Yes it's true that . . ."[111] Thus, it wasn't surprising that the GAO had negative findings on the CDC's action. What may be surprising, however, is how those findings were used. The Associated Press story carried August 21, 1990 and tagged "GAO Says $6.6 Million Misspent," stated: "Rep. Ted Weiss (D-N.Y.), chairman of the House human resources and intergovernmental relations subcommittee, called the report 'direct evidence that the political manipulation of the Agent Orange study resulted in the waste of millions of taxpayer dollars.' " It went on to state that "Rep. John Conyers, D-Mich., chairman of the House Government Operations Committee, said, 'The suppression of this information, combined with the millions of taxpayers' dollars wasted in the process, makes this cover-up by the White House and CDC a disgrace.' "[112]

Demagoguery from a congressman is not surprising. What is—or should be—surprising is that the White House was nowhere mentioned in the GAO report. Nor was political manipulation nor was suppression of information. All the GAO report said was that $6.6 million had been needlessly spent.[113] Much of this was lost when the CDC prematurely paid for work on the Agent Orange study that never came about because the study was canceled and the CDC failed to get the money back. The study also pointed out that about $20 million of the allocated money was never spent, thus saving the taxpayers that much.[114] A federal government agency with poor spending practices is about as unusual as fleas in a dog kennel, yet that is all the GAO found. In its thin (thirty-page) report it made no mention of lawbreaking, manipulation, cover-ups, or anything of the sort. The summary Weiss and Conyers gave was utter fiction, nothing less—fiction legitimized by the AP's story, which gave no description of what was actually in the report.

There was, to be sure, *a* government body that did find that the CDC engaged in political manipulation, collusion with the White House, and a general cover-up. But that government body was the House Committee on Government Operations, chaired by none other than John Conyers, and the specific subcommittee was Human Resources and Intergovernmental Relations, headed by none other than Ted Weiss. Most of the charges they made have already been discussed. The White House-connection charge relies essentially on motives. Allegedly the White House feared tremendous costs from acknowledging an adverse health effect of dioxin, in compensation not only to veterans but to persons living near toxic waste dumps and the like; *therefore* the White House did what it could to derail the Agent Orange study.[115] But as the dissent from the committee's report noted:

> After subpoenaing virtually every imaginable document prepared, reviewed or witnessed by the White House regarding Agent Orange, the most the Committee Report can tell us is that the White House opposed legislation which presumed that simple exposure alone to Agent Orange constituted a service-connected disability meriting compensation. We are then asked to conclude that this opposition provided the impetus for its plot to cover up the truth about Agent Orange. This conclusion is simply not supported by the facts.[116]

In addition, it pointed out the implausibility of blaming the White House for a cover-up "when Congress was intimately involved in the Agent Orange proceedings since their inception," pointing out the involvement of the OTA and the House Veterans Affairs Committee, both of which supported both the CDC's activities and its conclusions. Thus, the dissent noted, "the Committee Report cannot accuse the White House of engineering a coverup without also implicating Congress."[117] In fact, of all the federal agencies or bodies that had anything to do with the study— OTA, GAO, AOWG, Office of Management and Budget, the House Veterans Affairs Committee, the CDC, and Conyers's Committee on Government Operations—the *only* one to so much as hint at intentional wrongdoing on the CDC's part was the Conyers committee. Hence, no doubt, there was a desire to suggest that *some* other body, such as the GAO, had backed the committee's decision, even though the GAO did not.

## *TIME* TAKES UP THE BANNER

But if Conyers and Weiss and the Agent Orange conspiracy theorists found a dearth of ears among the scientific community, the case was quite the opposite among the fourth estate. Most prominent was *Time* magazine's article of July 23, 1990, "A Cover-Up on Agent Orange?" which could leave no doubt in the average reader's mind that the title, sans question mark, was an accurate statement of the facts. *Time*'s article by Ed Magnuson reported: "Critics charge that the [CDC] and one of its senior officials, Dr. Vernon Houk, helped scuttle [the CDC Agent Orange study]. Houk maintains he recommended that the study be canceled on strictly scientific grounds. Yet there is evidence that the CDC suppressed reports from the National Academy of Sciences (NAS) that directly challenged its position and spurned extensive help from the Pentagon, leading the White House to kill the study." *Time* went on and on about the cover-up of the report, which had been conducted by the NAS's Institute of Medicine, and how the CDC kept it from the White House's attention. It related that retired Army Major General John Murray was hired by Defense Secretary Caspar Weinberger to review the Pentagon records, but that as a nonscientist Murray did not feel competent to challenge Houk and White House scientists. "Unknown to Murray and the White House, the Institute of Medicine, an arm of the National Academy of Sciences, then turned in a contracted consultant's report to the CDC on the Agent Orange study," wrote *Time*'s Magnuson. "It concluded that the Pentagon was fully capable of 'determining locations and filling gaps' in the troop movements and criticized the CDC's study for excluding many of the veterans most likely to have been exposed. The CDC never turned the Institute's report over to the White House." Said Magnuson: "Murray presented his conclusion at a White House meeting on May 27, 1986. The White House moved to kill the study unless other ways could be found to identify exposed soldiers." *Time* related this story to Murray who replied, "I may have been a babe in the woods."[118]

The problem with all this intrigue rooted up by Magnuson and his reporter, Jay Peterzell, was that it never happened. Samuel O. Thier, president of the Institute of Medicine and Paul D. Stolley, chairman of the Advisory Committee on the CDC Study of the Health of Vietnam Veterans, in a letter to *Time,* noted: "The 1986 report was intended for internal use by the Institute and was not transmitted until this July [1990], when the agency requested it, following *Time*'s inquiries. Thus the CDC could not have suppressed it."[119] It would have been very interesting to hear *Time* relate why its staffers concocted this story and what actions it takes against writers who weave yarns in what is supposed to be a newsmagazine. (Not coincidentally, perhaps, it was Magnuson who falsely informed *Time*'s readers a decade earlier, in an article with the alarming title "The Poisoning of America," that Love Canal residents had "high incidence of cancer, birth defects and respiratory and neurological problems."[120]) All the magazine said in the reply, was *"Time* regrets the error concerning the 1986 report. The story should have said only that a 1987 report was suppressed." Considering that the 14-paragraph article devoted only four sentences to the 1987 report, this was a bit like saying, "Okay, so he didn't kill his wife and chop her into pieces, but he did slap her once."

But what of the one kernel of truth in what *Time* told its readers, that the Institute of Medicine had been highly critical of the CDC report? *Time* said of the 1987 Institute of Medicine report: "It urged that each of the agency's major conclusions be deleted because the evidence presented by the CDC did not support them." It called the report "devastating."[121] Well, apparently even that tiny little kernel of would-be truth is also false. In April 1990, a representative of the Institute of Medicine, Dr. M. Donald Whorton, reported that the institute felt "the data collected in the Selected Cancers Study are a valuable resource" and "that the CDC staff has carried out the best possible study under the circumstances. In the committee's judgment, their work meets the highest professional standards."[122] There was not a single uncomplimentary word in his entire testimony.

This testimony came three months *before Time*'s damning article appeared. Of course, it was not mentioned in the *Time* piece. *Time* relied on the fact that few of its readers keep track of congressional hearings.

Earlier in this book, *Time* science editor Charles Alexander was quoted declaring, on the subject of environmental issues: "As the science editor of *Time* I would freely admit that on this issue we have crossed the boundary from news reporting to advocacy."[123] The fabricated Agent Orange story has made it all too clear just what that means.

## THE ADMIRAL FIRES A BROADSIDE AT THE CDC

The *Time* Agent Orange article also hammered the CDC study by bringing in the opinion of Admiral Zumwalt. Noted *Time:* "The most forceful complaints about the CDC have been leveled by former Chief of Naval Operations Elmo R. Zumwalt, Jr. . . . Last month Zumwalt told a House subcommittee that the CDC's work on Agent Orange had been 'a fraud.' He singled out Houk for having 'made it his mission to manipulate and prevent the true facts from being determined.' " *Time* then immediately quoted Weiss as saying the CDC report was "rigged."[124]

But what made Zumwalt an authority on White House cover-ups? VA Secretary Edwin Derwinski had put Zumwalt in charge of a review (meaning no new data, just a look at previously done work) of studies possibly relating to Agent Orange toxicity. Zumwalt's remarks about Houk and the CDC, as well as disparaging assertions about dioxin and Agent Orange authority Michael Gough,[125] were made to Weiss's subcommittee in the third (and presumably final) hearing on Agent Orange. It is unfortunate that *Time* did not go into that report further, as it and its circumstances are so telling of the entire Agent Orange debate.

Two of the principal authors, according to Zumwalt, were Jeanne Stellman and the Environmental Defense Fund's Ellen Silbergeld,[126] so it was clear the way the report was going to go. Indeed, Zumwalt began by saying:

> There is an overwhelming body of credited scientific research supporting the conclusion that certain cancers and other illnesses are associated with exposure to Agent Orange. Tragically, there is also credible evidence strongly suggesting that the probable cause of birth defects among children of Vietnam veterans can be traced to their parent's exposure to Agent Orange.[127]

Nonetheless, some very interesting observations are to be made about it. The first was that Zumwalt was put in charge. Having had a son who died, allegedly from Agent Orange exposure, he was hardly a disinterested party. He explained to the subcommittee that he had "suspected" prior to being put in charge of the review that Elmo III might have died from Agent Orange but believed "that there was insufficient scientific evidence to support a linkage between his illnesses and Agent Orange exposure."[128] But note that in a 1986 book cowritten by the Zumwalts and told to John Pekkanen, Zumwalt stated:

> I too am convinced, based on what I have read, and conversations with people, that Agent Orange can cause cancer and birth defects, and in the case of many Vietnam veterans, has done precisely that. I realize the final scientific word is not in yet, but I think that because of all the veterans Elmo and I contacted, and all the illness and medical problems they told us about, we are ahead of the scientific evidence.[129]

Moreover, while he indicated that he had begun his literature review a matter of "several months" before his June 26, 1990 testimony, the March 10, 1989 *USA Today* quoted him saying that the settlement between the herbicide companies and the veterans "represents a mere pittance. . . . It is by no means an acceptable solution for them."[130] In no uncertain terms, Zumwalt had made his mind up on Agent Orange long before he was put in charge of the review study. He had also decided that his and his son's personal interviews were valid epidemiological studies.

Another strange observation is the laundry list of ailments the report tied to Agent Orange, allowing Zumwalt to conclude that "it is at least as likely as not that there is a relationship between exposure to Agent Orange and the following health problems" which included NHL, soft-tissue sarcoma, and chloracne but also lip cancer, skin cancer, bone cancer, Hodgkin's disease, leukemia, lung cancer, kidney cancer, nasal/pharyngeal/esophageal cancers, prostate cancer, testicular cancer, liver cancer, brain cancer, and a host of noncancer-related diseases.[131] Many of these had *never* been connected to Agent Orange in any published report.

Here is how the Zumwalt report tried to make the link. It went into the NHL connection at great length, citing studies previously discussed in this book. But for its connection of Agent Orange to cancers of the respiratory organs and the digestive tract, it cited all of one study on which it conceded it was taking a position different from that of the author, the Monsanto Company, a manufacturer of Agent Orange.[132] For lip and bone cancer, as well as cancer of the nasal cavity and sinuses, it cited a single study among Missouri farmers using herbicides. Likewise for the cancers of the rectum, liver, and kidney, and for leukemia.[133]

It is bad enough to build one's whole case on the basis of a single study. In fact, it's just plain bad science. But it gets worse. For the second group of cancers just listed—rectum, liver, skin, kidney—and for leukemia there was in fact no statistically significant increase in incidence.[134] Zumwalt's report tied these diseases to Agent Orange on the basis of a single study that didn't even show a statistically significant correlation. Worse yet, dioxin was never mentioned in the study, nor were either of the herbicide components of Agent Orange, 2,4-D or 2,4,5-T. Indeed, the parameters of the study were incapable of evaluating specific causes of increases in varieties of cancer. The closest the authors got to the subject was their statement that

> the evidence may be strongest for a role of agricultural chemicals including herbicides, insecticides, and fertilizers. The use of agricultural chemicals has increased dramatically over the past several decades. In general, ecological studies that have attempted to correlate county-specific risk estimates with pesticide use or type of crop production have yielded no clear pattern of exposure and cancer risk.[135]

From there it went on to review some of those studies.[136]

Finally, for some of the alleged Agent Orange-connected cancers, such as that of the testicles, the report cited *no* evidence at all, not so much as a single nonstatistically significant elevation in a single report that didn't happen to concern dioxin. *Nothing*.

What did the witnesses on the other side of the issue have to say to the subcommittee? Sorry, there weren't any. Silbergeld testified, as did other contributors to the report. But no one was invited from the CDC or elsewhere to dispute their testimony. While it is hardly uncommon for a congressional subcommittee to stack the witnesses in one particular direction, it is most unusual for witnesses on one side to be completely excluded. In fact, Weiss did say that officials from the Veterans Administration had been asked to attend but could not,[137] yet there was no mention of any scientific personnel from the CDC or elsewhere having been invited.

In sum, the Zumwalt report was overseen by a man whose position had been decided years earlier; it made incredible assertions that had no basis in the scientific literature; and worst of all it cited specific scientific literature that it claimed backed up those assertions when in fact the literature said no such thing. VA chief Derwinski had no business appointing Zumwalt, Zumwalt had no business taking the position, and Weiss had no business publicizing it and using it to bash the CDC. Finally, if Stellman and Silbergeld did put their imprimatur on the report, they and the other authors have compromised their respective scientific fields.

But they did more than that. As Zumwalt himself put it so eloquently, all over this country:

> When you sit down with Vietnam era veterans, they believe in their hearts, and many of them have the anecdotes, but they are not scientists, to really prove, if you will, in nonscientific ways that something terribly wrong has happened.
>
> That then spreads out across the population, and some in barroom conversations, in living room conversations, in conversations among friends all over this country, you have speculation about what may or may not have happened, what the consequences may or may not be.
>
> And I would submit to this committee that that is a form of nightmare. . . . We owe them a full report, and we owe them the truth, however painful or difficult that truth is, for anybody to accept.[138]

It is sad that such a highly respected, highly ranked naval officer as Zumwalt would have allowed himself to become part of that perpetuated nightmare.

After Zumwalt spoke, guests invited by the Weiss committee also took turns hurling insults at the CDC. Silbergeld of the Environmental Defense Fund said of the unit that worked on the Selected Cancers Study: "I think that this unit has been identified as malfunctioning; if I were a surgeon, I'd say, let's either lance it and drain it, or excise it, but let's not just let it sit there and fester."[139]

But it was the guest who testified immediately after Silbergeld spoke who finally truly explained the issue. Declared Mary R. Stout, national president of the Vietnam Veterans of America:

> I guess, to sum up all of what this means to us and what it means to Vietnam veterans, is that if we must now presume that the

scientific community cannot be trusted—and in some cases obviously we are assuming that—then a political decision must be made on this issue to provide compensation to veterans.[140]

And there you have it. The scientific community refused to come up with the "correct" conclusions. It has therefore betrayed its trust and must be ignored—and vilified to boot. Stout's dictate, of course, goes far beyond Agent Orange or even dioxin in general. In every major topic discussed in this book—and many not extensively addressed here—somebody with power has decided that the scientific community cannot be trusted. It must therefore, when the need arises, be bullied into adopting the correct line and, failing this, it must be ignored.

Certainly Stout had Congress's ear. In January 1991, Congress voted to provide permanent disability benefits to veterans suffering from non-Hodgkin's lymphoma and soft-tissue sarcoma. The bill clearly fell into the if-you-don't-vote-for-this-you're-a-bad-person category, as evidenced by the unanimous vote in both the House and Senate. However, it did not reflect the opinion of all the members, whatever that opinion might be worth; many still believed that Agent Orange did not cause cancers in Vietnam veterans. One of those who voted for the bill was Congressman Sonny Montgomery (D-Miss.), who continued to insist that studies showed no such connection but that debate over the bill was getting in the way of other important veterans issues. Senator Alan K. Simpson (R-Wyo.) said that while he was satisfied with the bill as a compromise, he still felt that "we should not pass bills based on frustration and pressure from veterans groups."[141]

Despite Congress's action, the Agent Orange issue has not been put to rest. New data continues to come in, with the marked characteristic that it looks quite similar to the old data. But what should be the final word on the CDC study came out in the March 1991 *American Journal of Public Health,* published by the American Public Health Association. Unlike the CDC study, this one, conducted by Han K. Kang and others, measured dioxin levels in adipose tissue (fat) in Vietnam veterans, non-Vietnam veterans, and civilians. It found that:

In this study, military service in Vietnam was not associated with elevated dioxin levels in adipose tissue with or without adjustment for demographic variables. In addition, no Vietnam service char-

acteristics measured singularly or in combination were good pre-
dictors of dioxin levels in adipose tissue.[142]

In fact, while it found that the mean level of Vietnam veterans
was slightly higher than that for non-Vietnam veterans (13.4 parts
per trillion as against 12.5 ppt), civilians had the highest levels at
15.8.[143] The researchers found that the mean levels of dioxin did
rise slightly with those who had combat military occupational
specialties (that is, were combat soldiers) and with those who had
been within two kilometers of sprayed areas within three days of
spraying. But no matter how they broke down the categories, they
couldn't come up with one that was as high as the mean civilian
exposure.[144]

The researchers did find that the levels of dioxin they had
measured in both civilians and military were considerably higher
than the amounts reported by others, but said that that was probably explained by the blood for their cohorts having been collected
several years earlier than the blood collected for other studies.[145]
Michael Gough explains that atmospheric levels of dioxin are
considerably lower now than they were in the 1970s and continue
to drop. Therefore, up to a point, the earlier a person's blood
was removed the more dioxin would be in it. This has nothing to
do with Agent Orange.[146]

In conclusion, said the researchers: "The results of our study
did not support the hypothesis that most U.S. troops were heavily
exposed to dioxin in Vietnam. . . . These results are consistent
with those of CDC."[147]

In an editorial accompanying the Kang study, Gough fired a
broadside at the Weiss House subcommittee. "Convinced by
whatever reason that veterans were exposed," he wrote:

It not only dismissed but belittled and denigrated the CDC study
and, to be consistent, it may do the same to the Kang *et al.* study.
Its dismissal of the CDC study was writ large, commanding newspaper space and TV time. It chucked aside the scientific process,
including publication in the peer-reviewed literature, as having
little value. It said CDC had done wrong or dishonest science. No
convincing evidence was offered to support either charge; the
charges were simply repeated over and over. Science—buffeted on
all sides as too definite or too wishy-washy, as too slow or too quick
to produce results, as overblowing risks or hiding them—can only

suffer further when politicians damn it because the results are not what they want.[148]

## CRUSADERS WITHOUT A CAUSE

*Washington Post* ombudsman Richard Harwood, in a 1990 column, told the story of *Baltimore Evening Sun* science writer Jon Franklin, a two-time Pulitzer Prize winner who was assigned an investigative report on Agent Orange. As a college student, Franklin had taken part in protests against Dow Chemical, a producer of both napalm and Agent Orange. "It would be, I thought, *the* story of my science-writing career," Franklin said. "I gathered about me the righteous fervor that is the armor of the crusading reporter, and I went to work."[149]

But a funny thing happened on the way to the Holy Land. After months of countless interviews and a thorough review of the scientific journals, Franklin came to a dismaying conclusion: No medical evidence supported the dioxin horror stories. He also came to another conclusion. "The Agent Orange story was a myth created by a group of Vietnam-era protesters, seized upon by the Viet vets and disseminated by the press. That discovery and the more shaking discovery that my colleagues [in the press] didn't care much about the truth of the matter and had never bothered to look into the substance very deeply changed my life," he said. He quit his job as a reporter and is now the journalism dean at Oregon State University.[150] As Hargrave concluded on the subject, "often we [in the media] are more diligent in defining the responsibilities of others than examining our own."[151]

Noting that science, especially epidemiology, is intertwined with policy, Gough says: "We fool ourselves if we think that good science, by itself, will assure that science will be treated fairly, used appropriately, and not besmirched when it does not meet some political test."[152] No one familiar with the story of the dioxin scare and the vicious disinformation campaign concerning Agent Orange could ever suffer such an illusion.

# CHAPTER 6

## Food Irradiation: Drumsticks and Double Standards

[Food irradiation is] the massacre of the American food supply.
—Dennis Mosgofian, director, National Coalition to Stop Food Irradiation[1]

Mankind's fascination with the possible effects of radiation on animal life, along with its fear and misunderstanding, was illustrated vividly in a spate of 1950s horror films like *The Beast from 20,000 Fathoms,*[2] *Godzilla,*[3] *Them!,*[4] *The Giant Behemoth,*[5] and *Attack of the Crab Monsters,*[6] in all of which exposure to man-made radiation through atomic explosions caused otherwise benign organisms to grow to tremendous proportions and begin feeding on human prey.

Ironically, at the same time, in the 1950s, shoe stores used X rays to measure customers' feet (really as a gimmick to draw customers into the store),[7] and some United States soldiers were intentionally exposed to radiation from nuclear fallout.[8] A few decades earlier, women working for watch manufacturers had used their tongues to narrow the points of the brushes they used to apply radium to watch dials, and suffered from bone cancer and various cancers of the head because of it.[9]

182

Enter now the use of ionizing radiation* on food, better known as food irradiation. General availability and public acceptance of irradiated food has always been perceived as being just around the corner. In 1957, *Science Digest* enthusiastically rhymed, "Frozen foods are antedated, ask for yours—IRRADIATED!" while a 1981 *Science 81* stated: "After more than 20 years, irradiated food may be coming out of the deep freeze."[10]

Yet, it was not until 1986 that the U.S. Food and Drug Administration (FDA) allowed the process for grains, vegetables, fruits, and spices. One state, Maine, has banned irradiated foods, while two, New York and New Jersey, have passed moratorium legislation. Even in the other states, irradiated food is rarely sold. Irradiated food has been authorized for use in thirty-eight countries as of this writing[11] and is in active use in twenty-four of those countries.[12] Japan, for example, always ready to lead the way in high tech, each year produces 15,000 to 20,000 metric tons of irradiated potatoes alone.[13] But in the United States irradiated food is clearly still in the deep freeze and, indeed, will remain there forever if some activists have their way. For, taking their cue and much of their logic from the antifluoridation movement, anti-irradiationists are waging a desperate war to keep their fellow citizens from availing themselves of the fruits of this technology, digging up conspiracy theories and bizarre alleged health effects and pitting the forces of fear and intimidation against those of science.

## KILLER IRRADIATION

Make no mistake: Food irradiation kills. That's the purpose. A person exposed to 100 kilorads of radiation (a rad is a unit used to express an amount of absorbed radiation; a kilorad is a a thousand rads) would be dead in less time than it takes to eat an apple.[14] Some anti-irradiationists make much of the high dosage

---

*"Ionizing radiation" is that which most of us think of as just "radiation"; that is, that which is emitted when nuclear weapons explode or which we receive when we are X-rayed. A discussion of the full band of radiation will be presented in the next chapter.

of radiation used, as if it were being aimed at the eater, not the food. Said Wally Burnstein, an osteopath and the head of the New York City-based anti-irradiation group, Food and Water, Inc., on a national television talk show: "One hundred thousand rads of radiation they call low level. Six hundred rads—as you know from Chernobyl—600 rads kills a person. One hundred thousand rads is going to be used in our apples."[15] But consider: Yeast bread is normally baked at temperatures in excess of 400 degrees Fahrenheit for about half an hour. No human being could possibly withstand that temperature for that duration. By Bernstein's logic, the baking of bread should be outlawed. The important distinction is that the food is irradiated (or baked), not the consumers thereof.

Irradiation is the use upon food of ionizing radiation (also called ionizing energy), either from radioactive isotopes of cobalt or cesium, or from devices that produce controlled amounts of electrons or X rays. It is a process completely different from microwaving, which is nonionizing and generates heat in most products. Irradiation is currently used to sterilize more than 50 percent of the nonheat-sterilizable medical devices used in the United States.[16] When food is irradiated, most of the radiation passes through the food without being absorbed. The small amount that is absorbed, depending on the dose of irradiation employed, kills insects, extends shelf life, or merely prevents fruits or vegetables from ripening too fast.[17]

In the irradiation treatment process, food in containers (metal boxes, sacks, cans, crates, even airtight plastic packaging) is placed on conveyor belts and guided into closed lead- or water-shielded chambers where it is exposed to radiation in specific doses. Explains John Cox, a scientist and founder of Citrex, a research and development firm in Gainesville, Florida, "Food irradiation works for the same reason radiation therapy works. Cells that are metabolizing faster are affected more, like cancer cells in humans, insects in a grapefruit, the eyes of a potato and bacteria in meat."[18]

Uses for food irradiation fall into three broad categories: high, medium, and low doses. High doses both retard spoilage and sterilize food, killing disease-causing microorganisms and insects. After this treatment, the sterilized food can be stored in sealed containers for years at room temperature without being spoiled by microorganisms. Refrigeration is no longer needed. As such, the process is somewhat analogous to canning, which uses a heat treatment to kill the microorganisms. (Canned food, however, is also cooked. Irradiation doesn't cook food.) Low doses of irradiation alter biochemical reactions, such as those involved in fruit ripening, and sprouting in tubers and bulbs. Such irradiation interferes with cell division, which is necessary for the reproduction of parasites and the sprouting of vegetables.[19] It also disinfects insects from grains and fruits and renders certain parasites harmless, such as the trichinae in pork and flukes in fish. In the medium dose range enough spoilage bacteria in food has been killed to provide an extended shelf life and kill most disease-causing organisms, including salmonellae, shigellae, campylobacteria, Yersinia, parasitic protozoa, and worms.[20] Food irradiation at substerilization doses is called radurization or radiation "pasteurization."

"We see the day when you can go into a supermarket and buy a barbecued chicken that has been cooked, vacuum-packed and irradiated. It can sit on the shelf for eight years, and all you'll have to do is heat it up," predicts physicist Martin Welt, founder of a food irradiation company, Radiation Technology.[21] As to how good that eight-year-old chicken will taste, well, that will be discussed later.

"Not only will radiation save tremendous amounts of food," said the late Dr. Eugen Wierbicki when he was chief researcher at the USDA's Eastern Regional Research Center, "it will also mean that consumers in the Midwest, for example, will be able to buy fresh fish shipped in from the East or West Coast. The season for fresh fruits and berries will be extended considerably."[22]

Moreover, scientists in India have also reported that a special treatment involving irradiation has solved one of man's oldest and most perplexing dietary problems—producing beans that don't cause flatulence.[23]

Everything sounds okay so far, but we're talking not about medical instruments but food. So how does it taste? Usually it's identical in taste to how it would have been when fresh. But irradiation isn't for all types of food. Some soft foods, particularly fruits, may be softened even further when irradiated. Further, says Marcus Karel, formerly professor of nutrition and food science at the Massachusetts Institute of Technology (MIT) and now at Rutgers, "there is no hope that milk will ever be preserved by irradiation." Exposure affects sulfur bonds and makes the milk taste bad.[24]

## WHO NEEDS IT, ANYWAY?

"The need for this particular industry remains a mystery,"[25] said then-Congressman Douglas Bosco (D-Calif.), who in 1987 introduced unsuccessful legislation into Congress to ban irradiation of pork and produce among other things.[26] "It has no up side. It doesn't really do anything," says the former editor of the San Francisco-based National Coalition to Stop Food Irradiation (NCSFI) newsletter, Irv Rothstein.[27] After all, there are numerous methods of preservation already—freezing, canning, salting, shrinkwrapping, drying—who needs another one?

Forty percent or more of chickens sold to consumers in the United States are contaminated by salmonella bacteria that cause illness, according to the U.S. Department of Agriculture.[28] The illness salmonellosis can produce fever, diarrhea, vomiting, and even death. The number of U.S. cases of salmonellosis is estimated at 2 million to 4 million annually with approximately 2,000 deaths, 9.5 percent of which are from chicken.[29] Add to this another estimated 2.1 million cases annually of campylobacter infections resulting in 2,100 deaths with about half of these from chickens.[30]

Food safety and public health experts speaking at a 1988 conference cosponsored by the American Medical Association and the Institute of Food Technologists reported that despite scientific, educational, and regulatory measures to preserve the safety of the food supply, the incidence of foodborne disease is on the rise in the U.S.[31] FDA officials estimate, for example, that at least one of every ten Americans will suffer from some form of foodborne diarrhea each year.[32] One indication of the rise came in a report that, in 1981, there were 568 foodborne disease outbreaks reported to the CDC, compared with 366 in 1970.[33] Douglas L. Archer, Ph.D., director of the Division of Microbiology at the FDA, said the problem lay not so much in the food supply per se, which remains the safest in the world, but rather in the way food is handled. "If it's instituted correctly, and if the public accepts it, food irradiation could obviously have a dramatic impact" on foodborne disease, said Archer.[34]

Trichinosis and toxoplasmosis are two diseases resulting from eating infested pork. Time lost from work by people infested with these parasites by eating pork can be reduced by between $180 and $280 million annually if the pork is irradiated, according to a 1985 Office of Technology Assessment (OTA) report. The estimated cost for the irradiation was put at $80 million, giving a net annual benefit of between $100 million and $200 million. According to the same report, if chicken were irradiated for control of salmonella and campylobacter, annual costs because of time lost from work would be reduced by $341 million to $635 million. With the cost for irradiation estimated at $155 million, control of these infectious bacteria in chicken would result in a net benefit of between $200 million and $500 million annually.[35]

Irradiation may also have a promising future as a replacement for postharvest fumigants such as ethylene dibromide (EDB), which was banned by the EPA in 1984 as a suspected human carcinogen.[36] In this role, irradiation could also facilitate interstate and international shipment of fruits and vegetables and help prevent the periodic medfly infestations in California that lead to the massive spraying of malathion. One disadvantage of irradiation for insect control, however, is that it does not leave any active agent in an unpackaged food to protect it against reinfestation. Thus, such disinfestations would have to be accompanied by protective packaging, as is canned food.[37]

Congressman Bosco displayed a disturbing ignorance in asserting that "irradiation is a post-harvest treatment and can only be used in addition to pesticides, not in place of them."[38] As noted earlier, irradiation is currently being used as a replacement for the pesticide ethylene oxide. Several other chemicals are currently used to protect crops postharvest. Irradiation can replace some of them, though not others.

But the health advantages that food irradiation would bring to the United States are small compared with the potential in Third World countries. "With the availability of readily accessible fresh meats in the United States, I doubt that sterilized meat will become a large part of the food-irradiation industry in this country," said USDA's Eugen Wierbicki. "But there is terrific potential in Third World countries where refrigeration and modern transportation systems are lacking."[39] Likewise with grains and other plant foods. In fact, according to the World Food Program of the United Nations, around one fourth to one third of all food worldwide is lost to spoilage and infestation. Estimated African losses alone could feed forty million people, and Indian losses could feed eighty million people. Said one UN official, "In Africa for 1991 there are 30 million people in dire need. If we were to reduce these food losses significantly, Africa would not have nearly as much trouble."[40] The ability of food irradiation to save lives and alleviate human suffering on a global scale is incalculable but may prove immense.

This last argument is one that irradiation opponents are very sensitive to—and eager to counter. One irradiation opponent says that the claim to help the world food shortage is a "technological fix" that should be recognized as unworkable, since hunger is "as much a political, cultural, and socioeconomic problem as it is a scientific and technological problem."[41] Gary Null, citing the case of Ethiopia where political corruption kept food from getting to starving people, says: "To claim that food irradiation is going to feed the world necessarily implies that it is capable of solving all of the political and sociological factors contributing to world hunger."[42]

But advocates of food irradiation never claimed that it was "going to feed the world" as in "every hungry person in the whole world" any more than World Health Organization (WHO) personnel providing yellow fever vaccinations have claimed their vaccinations are capable of eradicating all disease. Reasonable people don't seek out or offer panaceas. Like the WHO vaccinators, they are just trying to do their part to better the human condition.

In the February 1978 issue of the *Bulletin of the Atomic Scientists,* Willard Libby, the late Nobel laureate and member of the Atomic Energy Commission, warned: "Surely the millions who live in the shadow of starvation deserve the benefits of a more rapid introduction of irradiated foods. Wasteful as man has been in the past, he can no longer afford to waste time, technology *and* food" (emphasis in original).[43]

## WHO ARE THE ANTI-IRRADIATIONISTS?

One driving force behind opposition to irradiation that seems to have gotten very little attention is the interest in green. No, not green leaves or grass—green as in money. Just as organic growers and stores helped promote fear of pesticides, so too have they done with food irradiation. Chief among the lobbyists for the anti-irradiation bill in Maine, the first state to ban the process, was the Maine Organic Farmers and Growers Association, along with a group calling itself Citizens Against Nuclear Trash.[44] Similarly, one UK magazine has reported that "the British Frozen Foods Federation has expressed concern over monitoring and regulatory procedures" of food irradiation.[45] Jolly nice of them to be so concerned about the safety of their competition.

But most irradiation foes aren't in it for the bucks, so what does motivate them?

On the whole, it appears that the people who find food irradiation to be dangerous are the same ones who have a horror of any recent chemical or process devised by man. University of Illinois professor Samuel S. Epstein, already known to the reader for his doomsaying on pesticides and dioxin and his statement that "30 to 40 percent of cancers in the general population" may be due to pollution from the large petrochemical plants,[46] told the *Progressive*: "Food irradiation is an extraordinarily dangerous experiment in public health. I would strongly counsel any consumer under no circumstances to eat irradiated food." Eating such food, he says, "is like inviting someone to play Russian roulette and not telling him there's one bullet in the revolver."[47]

Donald Louria, chairman of the Department of Preventive Medicine and Community Health at New Jersey Medical School, one of the best-known opponents of food irradiation (although he maintains that he isn't an "intransigent" one[48]), invoked the old synergism argument discussed in Chapter 2, telling a congressional panel, it "takes us right back to Rachel Carson."

> In essence, what we're now being asked is whether we're going to add another substance that they will say, in the dosage used, is not demonstrably harmful. But [this] does not in any way take into account the odd mixture of allegedly safe substances from our highly industrialized society, pesticides, a little bit of radon, a little bit of asbestos, et cetera.[49]

It may be telling that one of the foremost irradiation opponents considers radon, a gas that has been seeping out of rocks since the beginning of the earth, a "substance from our highly industrialized society," but that he would suggest a harmful synergistic effect between food irradiation and radon, or irradiation and asbestos, is little short of bizarre. What Dr. Louria is basically doing is invoking the natural-is-good, unnatural-is-bad article of faith, assigning radon to the unnatural category for the sake of convenience.

Jacques Leslie, writing in *The Atlantic,* averred: "Of the hundreds of scientists in this country who have done extensive research on the wholesomeness of food irradiation, only few have publicly expressed opposition to it, and the several other scientists who are actively against food irradiation are not experienced in the field."[50] His remarks closely echo those of dental experts about antifluoridation fanatics in the 1950s and 1960s. For every several thousand dentists who would say that fluoridation at prescribed levels was safe, there would be an occasional doctor who would say, as one article in the *American Mercury* put it, that "repeated doses of infinitesimal amounts of fluorine will in time gradually reduce the individual's power to resist domination" by the communists.[51]

By contrast with such fringe figures as Epstein and Louria (among other things, Louria has supported a completely untenable claim that fallout from the Chernobyl nuclear plant accident caused a sudden increase in deaths not just in the area immediately surrounding the plant but in the *United States*), there are virtually nothing *but* scientists with irradiation training on the pro-irradiation side. The problem is, while they're glad to talk to reporters who bother to call them, these scientists are too busy being scientists to take to soapboxes. Industry, also, has refrained from spending much to debate the issue. Instead each company refrains from using irradiation, but remains waiting like penguins on an ice floe to see who will be the first to jump in and whether he will get eaten. The tiny industry-funded flack, the National Coalition for Food Irradiation, was allowed to go bust, leaving part-time advocacy up to such organizations as the American Council on Science and Health in New York and the Committee for a Constructive Tomorrow in Washington, D.C.

## THE FDA UNDER FIRE

Opponents of food irradiation have concentrated their fire on the FDA; indeed, when the agency announced its preliminary proposal in 1981, the agency received hundreds of letters from citizens concerned about "radioactive food."[52] The FDA is by law the primary federal regulatory body responsible for granting permission for use of irradiation on food. That has been its function since 1958, when the U.S. Congress—"apparently without really understanding what it was doing," as the *Bulletin of the Atomic Scientists* put it—amended the Food, Drug and Cosmetic Act of that year to include irradiation as a food additive.[53] Since then, the approval process has slowed to a crawl, with the FDA granting approvals for individual foods one tiny increment at a time. Based upon the scientific evidence in petitions submitted, the FDA could stop that process entirely, even reverse it. Conversely, it could speed it up.

Irradiation opponents say that the FDA has given approvals with reckless abandon. Said Louria: "The FDA has done a slipshod job here. We need a lot more study before we can accept food irradiation."[54] But by comparison with major international regulatory bodies, the FDA is downright slow. In 1977, for example, a joint committee of the World Health Organization (WHO), the International Atomic Energy Agency, and the United Nations' Food and Agricultural Organization gave irradiation their seal of approval. Four years later, the WHO committee declared that food irradiated with up to an average dose of 1,000 kilorads should be considered safe for human consumption without toxicity testing or labeling, but the FDA was more conservative and limited the maximum dose for blanket approvals to 100 kilorads for fruits and vegetables.[55]

Indeed, WHO has been unequivocal in its endorsement of food irradiation. A 1981 WHO document states:

> All the toxicological studies carried out on a large number of irradiated foods, from almost every type of food commodity, have produced no evidence of adverse effects as a result of irradiation.
>
> Radiation chemistry studies have now shown that the radiolytic products [chemicals created in the irradiation process] of major food components are identical. . . . Most of these radiolytic products have also been identified in foods subjected to other, accepted types of processing. . . . The nature and concentration of these radiolytic products indicate that there is no evidence of toxicological hazard.[56]

In the United States, there is a general consensus among scientists working in areas related to the process that food irradiation is worthwhile and safe. For example, in April 1982 more than forty scientists, engineers, and policymakers with expertise in food irradiation met in Washington, D.C., to evaluate low-dose radiation as an alternative quarantine treatment for fruits and vegetables. After three days of discussion and deliberation, participants concluded that "the use of irradiation for commodity disinfestation and quarantine treatment is feasible and that, with the exception of [certain federal regulations including those since changed by the FDA], no insurmountable research, engineering, or institutional barriers should precede the use of radiation treatment of commodities."[57]

Yet the FDA waited until 1985 to approve irradiation for use on pork,[58] for which it is a proven killer of the trichinae worm, the cause of trichinosis,[59] and in 1986, the FDA allowed the use of irradiation on fruits and vegetables and increased the level of radiation allowed for dried herbs, spices, and vegetable seasonings.[60] The regulation by no means slipped through unnoticed; indeed, in the two years before final approval it received more than five thousand public comments.[61] Finally, in 1990 the FDA allowed the irradiation of poultry.[62]

Rarely has the FDA been accused of being too quick to approve use of either a food or a drug. Indeed, during the AIDS era it finally came to widespread attention that there's one characteristic for which the FDA can be counted on, its tremendous caution, which leads to equally tremendous delays. Long before the AIDS controversy, lifesaving drugs were routinely available in Europe that were still undergoing FDA testing. Beta-blockers to reduce heart attacks were themselves blocked by the FDA for ten years, during which time an estimated ten thousand Americans a year died from ailments that the drug could have prevented.[63] The reason for this delay, according to FDA Commissioner Donald Kennedy, "was the suspicion that a number of B-blockers might be tumorigenic, and the resulting [FDA] requirement that long-term animal studies be undertaken to investigate this possibility." Similarly, in December 1988, the FDA announced its approval of misoprostal. This was the first drug to prevent the gastric ulcers that are caused by aspirin and similar anti-inflammatory drugs taken in high doses by arthritis sufferers. These drugs cause an estimated 10,000 to 20,000 deaths a year through internal bleeding and other complications. Misoprostal is reported to produce a fifteenfold reduction in these gastric ulcers. So effective and important did it appear to the FDA that the agency put the drug on its approval fast track. Yet because of the tremendous amount of time required of the applying pharmaceutical company in the preapproval process for testing and evaluation, misoprostal was available in forty-three foreign countries—in some since 1985—before it became available in the United States.[64] As with heart disease, arthritis is generally a disease of older people; hence the risk that the drug will contribute to cancer some decades down the road is diminished.

The seeming callousness of the FDA is really just a result of bureaucratic incentives. According to Sam Kazman of the Washington, D.C.-based Competitive Enterprise Institute, the FDA's tremendous caution derives from the time it delayed the approval of thalidomide, which was to result in thousands of defective births in countries where it was approved. The FDA came out of that looking like heroes. Now, says Kazman, "every new drug is potentially another thalidomide. From the FDA commissioner to the bureau heads to the individual National Drug Application reviewers, the message is clear: If you approve a drug with unanticipated side effects, both you and the agency will face the heat of newspaper headlines, television coverage, and congressional hearings."[65]

To allow an FDA official to explain it in his own way: "The FDA is a conservative organization. What we decide ultimately affects more than 250 million Americans. We can't afford to take unnecessary risks."[66] Choose whatever rationale you wish, but the FDA doesn't say something is safe that it doesn't absolutely 100 percent believe is safe. (The one exception to this is AIDS drugs, in part because AIDS is an always fatal disease and thus the worst a bad drug can do is to speed up the dying process, and in part because of intensive lobbying by AIDS groups.) If, as with beta-blockers, the FDA won't take the risk of approving drugs that are (1) potentially lifesaving and, (2) affect only a portion of the population that usually has too few years of life left to develop cancer from a newly introduced carcinogen, it certainly isn't going to hastily give its okay to something, such as irradiation, that is not designed to save lives, that may be used by the entire population, and that may be ingested by all age groups, including infants.

But if there seems to be a consensus among regulators and

scientists and even the cautious FDA that food irradiation is safe and worthwhile, various self-styled consumer or public interest groups strongly maintain otherwise. And they have caught the attention of a good part of the public. A 1987 poll of consumers by the Food Marketing Institute, a Washington-based retailers and wholesalers group, found that 43 percent of the respondents believed the use of gamma rays on foods was a serious hazard—an increase from 37 percent who answered that way just a year earlier. Twenty-nine percent considered the process somewhat dangerous, 20 percent were unsure, and a mere 8 percent believed the process was safe.[67]

But the poll that really counts is the one in the nation's food stores. Irradiated food has made a poor showing there, though there are reasons for this poor showing that have nothing intrinsically to do with unhealthiness or unpalatability of the food. Food companies claim that they are holding back on selling irradiated products not out of fear of health problems but out of fear of adverse publicity. For instance, General Foods spokesman Cliff Sessions told *Hippocrates* magazine: "Society seems to be a little nervous about accepting radiation, so we are, too." Therefore the firm uses no irradiated spices. Meanwhile, an official of the American Spice Trade Association has stated: "The major food companies recognize that irradiation is viable, but everybody's afraid to touch it." To which he adds: "Let's face it, the companies that pioneer irradiation are going to be crucified."[68]

Who are these would-be crucifiers? And what are their arguments that keep irradiated food out of the hands of the American consumer?

## A THREAT TO HEALTH?

Many Americans seem to be under the impression that irradiated food becomes radioactive. In fact, that may be one of the only arguments *not* used against irradiated food. Irradiated food is no more radioactive when it comes off the conveyor belt than when it went on, something even vociferous anti-irradiation activists such as Food and Water, Inc., the most prominent anti-irradiation organization, admit.[69]

One groundless claim came up when Walter Burnstein, the head of Food and Water, Inc., asked on national TV about the possibility of sending irradiated food to Ethiopians, said flatly: "The [irradiated] food will cause birth defects and you don't want to send starving people food that causes birth defects."[70] With perhaps the sole exception of Burnstein, irradiation foes have never claimed that the process causes birth defects, either in animals or humans.[71]

But if anti-irradiationists don't generally make claims that irradiated food is radioactive or that it causes birth defects (or miscarriages for that matter), they do have a formidable laundry list of objections—health-based and otherwise.

## RPs, URPs, AND THE FDA

When ionizing energy splits food molecules, small numbers of new ones are created. These are known as radiolytic products, or RPs. These tiny radiolytic products are the focus of the health aspect of the irradiation food fight.

In the early 1980s, an FDA committee first looked at the issue of differences between irradiated and nonirradiated food, and found RPs to be the only one of import.[72] They then asked whether those should be of concern. They cited data showing that a low radiation dose would generate no more than 30 parts of RPs in a million parts of food. Of those 30 parts, about 90 percent, or 27 parts per million, have been identified as identical to natural food components and therefore are presumably safe.[73] The remaining 10 percent, or 3 parts per million, they found to be chemically similar to natural food components. But playing it conservatively, they decided nonetheless to label them "unique radiolytic products," or URPs.[74] Assuming that more than 10 different URPs would be formed, the concentration of any one URP would thus be less than one in a million; thus the committee concluded that the chance of any single URP of unusual toxicity being formed in significant amounts would be negligible—"negligible" being a term of art meaning "less than one in a million" but also meaning negligible from a health perspective. The committee also noted that they probably overstated the total number of URPs.[75]

But now FDA researchers are saying of the URPs that they aren't unique, after all. Rather, they are probably existing chemicals that have not been detected yet in the human diet. "There's no food that is completely known," pointed out then-FDA biochemist Clyde Takeguchi. "You can't identify everything that's in an apple. The basis for establishing safety is not absolute safety. It's reasonable safety."[76] Indeed, he could have pointed out that what we do know about an apple indicates that it includes at least one known human carcinogen, alcohol.

More vociferous, perhaps, is Dr. Edward Josephson, currently professor of science and nutrition at the University of Rhode Island. A veteran of more than thirty years in irradiation research, he has also held the posts of director of the National Food Irradiation Program and senior lecturer at MIT. In testimony before a congressional subcommittee, he made the following forceful claim: "In over 30 years of research, *no* compounds that are unique to foods processed with ionizing energy have been formed. *I repeat, no URPs have ever been found.* Anyone voicing a contrary opinion should be challenged to provide the URPs' chemical formula or name, the amount formed, the food in which the URP was found, the conditions of irradiation, and the reference to the published report" (emphasis in original).[77]

Moreover, while FDA officials recognize that at least one significantly carcinogenic RP, benzene (which we breathe in significant amounts every day because it is a by-product of gasoline combustion), has been caused by irradiating meat at a high dose, that meat was irradiated at a dose more than fifteen times greater than that currently approved by the FDA.[78] George H. Pauli, an FDA consumer safety officer who has supervised the agency's food irradiation deliberations, found that this amount of the chemical was one hundredth of that reported in nonirradiated eggs.[79] While many of us avoid eggs, it's usually because of cholesterol, not benzene.

Irradiation critics like the Ralph Nader group Public Citizen Health Research Group in Washington, D.C., contend that the only way to prove that alleged URPs are safe is through traditional maximum tolerable dose testing of animals.[80] That's essentially the same thing as killing irradiation, which may well be what they have in mind. This is because a standard toxicological evaluation of a food additive involves dosing animals with levels far higher than would normally be found in any diet, in order to find the maximum quantity that produces no ill effects (called appropriately enough the "no-effect level"). This quantity is then divided by a safety factor, usually 100 (an arbitrary number that comes about because we have a base 10 system) to determine the maximum amount allowable in human diets.

With food irradiation, though, the "additive" is the food itself. A rat would pop like a balloon long before you could stuff it with enough irradiated food to find the maximum no-effect level,[81] although at least one major study has been done in which mice, rats, rabbits and beagles were given large amounts of irradiated food over a two-year period, with no ill effects.[82] Further, if the animal was fed one type of irradiated food out of proportion to its normal intake of that food, the study might produce effects caused not by irradiation but by the test diet's nutritional imbalance. Scientists have tried to circumvent these natural limitations by defining the RPs as additives, meaning that instead of giving the rat or mouse gigantic whole wheat muffins, they could just be given the RPs created in the irradiation of the muffins. But that, too, is problematic since RPs exist in such low concentrations that the needed amount cannot be supplied. Also, many RPs may not even have been identified. Thus, toxicological testing can do little more than provide rough parameters as to the safety of irradiated food. Historically, the FDA has permitted the use of chemical and nutritional data in place of animal studies.[83] Regulations allowing the use of X rays for food inspection, microwaves for heating food, and ultraviolet radiation for treating foods were all based on chemical analyses.[84]

As to that nonanimal testing, it too swirls with controversy. That's because, to listen to irradiation opponents, the FDA has based its decision that irradiation is safe on only 5 studies out of a data base of 409.[85] That does sound very suspect, especially given how often opponents repeat it. In fact, the claim simply is not correct. What the FDA actually said was that when it reviewed all those studies, it found that while each individual study looked at very specific areas, together they covered a very broad span. Some looked for the possibility of birth defects, others for specific types of toxicity to the fed animal itself. Only five "were considered by agency reviewers to be properly conducted and reported, fully adequate by 1980 toxicological standards, and able to stand alone in the support of safety."[86] It's not as if the FDA said, "Oops, all the rats had tumors in this one; it's no good." The other studies were taken into account. As FDA officials have put it:

> Although most of the study reports were inadequate by present-day standards and could not stand alone to support safety, many contained individual experimental components which, when examined either in isolation or collectively, allowed the conclusion that consumption of foods treated with low levels of irradiation did not appear to cause adverse toxicological effects.[87]

## A SMOKING GUN MADE OF POLYPLOIDY

For the most part, it appears that anti-irradiationists don't pretend to have found any pattern of adverse reactions among this vast number of studies. Instead, they seem fairly content to call the very existence of the alleged URPs essentially a threat, to point out that no MTD animal studies were used, and to hang their hats on essentially one set of studies conducted in India.

Working under the hypothesis that malnutrition can increase one's vulnerability to drugs, scientists at India's National Institute of Nutrition (NIN) in the 1970s devised a study to test the effect of irradiated food on severely underfed children. Three groups of five children, ranging from ages two to five and all suffering from a disease of malnutrition called kwashiorkor, were hospitalized so that they could recover their strength. One group was then fed freshly irradiated wheat, another irradiated wheat stored for twelve weeks, and the third nonirradiated wheat. The authors of the study stated that four of the five children in the first group developed polyploidy, a chromosomal abnormality that has been linked to cancer. Children in the second group displayed far fewer polyploid cells and children in the third group showed none whatsoever. Concluded the authors: "These observations clearly indicate that the appearance of polyploid cells is due to the feeding of irradiated wheat," and recommended storage of such wheat "for periods beyond 12 weeks, before it can be considered safe for human consumption."[88] Other NIN studies also showed polyploidy or lethal (to the chromosome) mutations in animals fed irradiated wheat.[89]

The polyploidy findings have proven very influential—the

smoking gun, as it were, of the dangers of eating irradiated food. For example, the Canadian Parliament's Standing Committee on Consumer and Corporate Affairs relied on the Indian study in recommending a ban or moratorium on irradiated food,[90] although Parliament as a whole rejected it. But the statements of the Indian polyploidy study authors have been rebutted in a report of the Council for Agricultural Science and Technology [CAST], an association of twenty-eight scientific societies and others located in Ames, Iowa, and has been refuted elsewhere on the grounds that the experiments were improperly carried out, used faulty techniques, or the data presented did not support the conclusions of the authors.[91] Further, notes the *Harvard Medical School Health Letter,* "the number of children studied was very small, and all of them were seriously malnourished to begin with. These and other flaws of this study invalidate any conclusions that might be drawn from it about irradiated food."[92]

As to the "other flaws," the studies' conclusions conflicted with those of a similar experiment on rats and mice at the Bhabha Atomic Research Center in Bombay, prompting the Indian Ministry of Health to ask two independent scientists to look into the discrepancies. These scientists harshly criticized the NIN studies, finding that the number of polyploid cells detected in the children fed freshly irradiated wheat "is well within the normal range of occurrence in healthy human beings," while the number of polyploid cells found prior to the beginning of the study—none—contradicted the conventional understanding that all human beings have some level of polyploid cells. The scientists also questioned the studies' claim that in the two children who were examined after they had stopped eating the irradiated wheat, all abnormal cells disappeared within twenty-four weeks. Those cells, according to the two scientists, should have lasted for years. These, with other problems, led the scientists to conclude that "the bulk of the NIN data are not only mutually contradictory but also at variance with the well-established facts of biology."[93]

In a 1986 letter to a member of the Atomic Industrial Forum, the Indian government expressly disavowed the reports of polyploidy, stating: "The issue of polyploidy of irradiated wheat including the studies of NIN have been very carefully evaluated and the outcome is 'unconditional acceptance of wheat and ground wheat products irradiated for the purpose of disinfestation.' "[94]

The FDA has also dismissed the NIN studies as unreliable science.[95]

Yet opponents of irradiation never fail to cite the NIN study as proof of irradiation's harm. Articles presenting the study as evidence have appeared in *Glamour*,[96] *Health*,[97] *The Progressive*,[98] and *Boston*[99] magazines. The study was also cited in Food and Water, Inc.'s official comment on a proposed FDA rule on irradiation written by Richard G. Piccioni, Ph.D.[100]

## COOKING UP CANCER?

Because he is one of the few scientific authorities to have come out against irradiation, Piccioni is often quoted as a source by those opposed to irradiation.[101] In his comments submitted to the FDA in 1990 regarding proposed regulations that would allow poultry irradiation, Piccioni, a senior staff scientist with Accord Research and Educational Associates, a public health research group in New York City, tacked on an appendix with an exhaustive listing of studies purporting to show adverse health effects at the cellular level in lab animals fed irradiated foods. Many of these are the same studies considered by the FDA and rejected as having severe problems, though Piccioni makes no distinctions. One of these is the aforementioned Indian study of malnourished children.[102] Yet even this list managed to include a mere three distinctive chemicals that it linked to carcinogenicity. One of the three, benzo(*a*)pyrene, Piccioni noted, was found when a mixture of starch, oil *and* benzo(*a*)pyrene was irradiated.[103] Now, some of us might think it unfair to demand that irradiating a carcinogen should result in the creation of a noncarcinogen, but that is only because we lack Mr. Piccioni's keen scientific eye.

While irradiation opponents spread fear over the possibility that some day in the future something produced by the irradiation process might somehow be linked to cancer, what they ignore is that *all* traditional methods of cooking food have been discovered to produce carcinogens and mutagens (again, using the maximum tolerable dose test in animals) and the same is true of *all* types of food preparation, including salting, smoking, and fermenting. The following are some examples from the exhaustive collection, taken from government studies, in Edith Efron's *The Apocalyptics*.[104]

- Polyaromatic hydrocarbons (PAH) have been identified in charcoal-broiled steaks: benzo(*a*)pyrene, benzo(*a*)anthracene, dibenz(*a,h*)anthracene, and chrysene. All are reported carcinogens, varying from weak and possibly uncertain to potent.
- Three of the above four PAH have also been reported in fish broiled over a gas flame.
- Polycyclic aromatic hydrocarbons including benzo(*a*)pyrene have been produced in roasted coffee beans and extracts of tea leaves at high temperatures.
- Benzo(*a*)pyrene has been found in the charred crusts of biscuits.
- Nineteen hydrocarbons including benzo(*a*)pyrene were isolated from carbohydrates, amino acids, and fatty acids when cooked at temperatures reached by baking bread and by cooking fats in boiling sauces.
- Smoking foods (cheeses, meats, sausages, fish, ham) over wood or charcoal produces benzo(*a*)pyrene and benz(*a*)anthracene.
- Salted fish contain a variety of nitrosamines, which give rats nasal and nasopharyngeal (nose and pharynx) cancers.

In 1991, a study of the *International Journal of Cancer* reported that boiling meat and serving it with meat gravy, in addition to frying it, can increase the risk of getting cancer from eating that food. The author of the study speculated that the problem with highly browned meats is the creation of at least ten cancer-causing chemicals that form at temperatures above 212 degrees Fahrenheit, the boiling point of water at sea level. Above 300 degrees, the formation of such chemicals increases "logarithmically," she said. Commented another doctor on the study: "We are eating small amounts of potent carcinogens."[105] (As always, the caveat here is that the chemicals cause tumors when fed to rodents in massive doses.) We're not talking here about the *possibility* of the formation of one rodent carcinogen, but the *confirmed presence* of ten or more depending on the cooking temperature. Irradiation opponents are so busy witch-hunting among irradiated foods' radiolytic products that they can't hear the sausage on the grill cackling, "I'll get you, my pretty, and your little dog, too!"

Opponents also don't like to mention that the irradiation process can be substituted for some types of food preservation that have been linked to cancer. For example, irradiating cured meats like bacon reduces the need for nitrites, which inhibit botulism but have also been shown to cause cancer in animals fed massive doses of the chemical.[106] Since those seeking to condemn food irradiation are, as a rule, the same ones who claim massive-dose testing of animals is the final word in determining whether a synthetic chemical is carcinogenic or not, this puts them in, to say the least, an awkward position.

Piccioni's approach to irradiation was made clear when, at a 1987 food irradiation debate in Washington, D.C., he explained: "Food is not a defined substance. You don't know what's in food to begin with, and when you expose food to radiation you have no idea what the changes are."[107] Now *there's* something to think about. If you don't know what's scratching at your door, be it a big friendly dog or a foaming rabid one, you say "I hope it's not exchanged for the other, whatever the other may be, because I'm not even sure which it is now." What we *do* know about food is that it's loaded with chemicals that in massive doses have been shown to cause cancer in animals. In addition, food often has chemicals such as alcohol that have been shown to cause cancer in not-so-large doses in humans. By contrast, try as they might, food-irradiation opponents have been able to identify practically nothing created by irradiation that is carcinogenic, even at massive doses given to lab animals. On what basis do we ban irradiation but not the food being irradiated, other than that carcinogenic food is an old issue and the irradiation controversy is fairly new? It's the old-carcinogen-good, new-carcinogen-bad concept tossed at Alar, with the difference that irradiation does not create carcinogens, not even under the same faulty measure applied to Alar.

## NUTRITIONAL LOSS

One charge commonly made against irradiated food is that, aside from inflicting direct harm, it allows for the possibility of malnutrition because it robs foods of nutritional value. Donald Louria has stated "about nutrient decrement": "There's study after study showing that there's damage to foods by irradiation."[108] Likewise, Ellen Hass, executive director of Public Voice for Food and Health Policy, a group strongly opposed to both pesticides and food irradiation, says: "There are nutrient losses. Look at all these good vegetables, but when you irradiate them, what happens to the nutrients? Do they stay there? Not as much. Consumers will be getting a bum deal when they have irradiated food."[109]

Edward Josephson replies to this that most of the numbers used to show nutrition depletion from irradiation come from old data on radiation-sterilized foods gathered prior to 1964.[110] But at any rate, again a little perspective is in order. The processing of food causes nutrient loss, as does the cooking. We all know that "enriched bread" is enriched because milling whole wheat bread into the white version strips out vitamins. Take a nice vitamin-packed vegetable like broccoli or spinach and boil it up on the stove and watch a good part of the vitamins go down the sink when you drain the food. The comparison to make regarding food irradiation is with other preservation processes. And irradiation compares quite favorably. Josephson says that the new technology irradiates food at lower temperatures than it did previously and "won't cause any more destruction of nutrients in food than canning or other food-processing technologies." He notes also that 90 percent of vitamin B-1 (thiamine) is preserved in irradiated sterilized food such as pork and ham as against 20 percent of it in food that has been heat-sterilized.[111] Likewise, the FDA's Sanford Miller avers: "In low-dose [exposure levels] the nutritional losses are insignificant and less than with other preservation techniques."[112] And in 1986, the Council for Agricultural Science and Technology issued a report on the use of food irradiation that stated that foods so treated are "safe to eat [and their nutritional adequacy] compares favorably with that of fresh foods or with that of foods processed by well established conventional methods."[113]

## THREE PORK CHOP ISLAND

Another seriously offered argument against consuming irradiated foods is the alleged danger to workers in irradiation plants. Congressman Douglas Bosco made this point in an article in the newspaper *USA Today* and in testimony in support of his bill before the House Subcommittee on Health and the Environment. He cited a single case from eleven years earlier (1977) in which a worker had accidentally walked into a radiation chamber "and received a near-lethal dose of radiation."[114] In 1988, according to the National Safety Council, 10,600 American workers in all occupations died from job-related accidents (6,700 non-motor-vehicle) and 1.8 million suffered disabling injuries on the job (1.6 million non-motor-vehicle). They died in car factories, paper mills, and bakeries. They died at plants that freeze food, can food, and wrap food. They died especially growing and harvesting food. Farm residents have a job-related death rate three times higher than that of other workers.[115] Applying Bosco's reasoning concerning food irradiation workers to the whole of the food industry would result in starvation for the entire populace. In fact, food irradiation plant workers are probably safer than other food disinfection and sterilization workers. An official of Mc-Cormick and Company has noted that the alternative to irradiating spices, gassing them with ethylene oxide, poses an even greater potential danger to employees because high doses have been shown to cause health problems and in that ethylene oxide is potentially explosive.[116]

Likewise anti-irradiationists cite over and over again the experiences at two irradiation plants, those of Radiation Technology, and International Nutronics, as evidence of the dangers irradiation plants pose to the public.[117] Radiation Technology had its license revoked after the Nuclear Regulatory Commission (NRC) accused it of lying to investigators about disconnecting a safety lock on a radiation room door. International Nutronics was indicted on charges of conspiring to cover up a 1982 accident in which radioactive water seeped into soil at its Dover, New Jersey, plant.[118] If irradiation plants were that dangerous, you wouldn't find critics being forced to drag out these two relatively innocuous incidents time and again. And to listen to them, one would think that no other industry in the nation, no other factory, has ever had a problem with emissions. The difference is that while it is always possible that there might be accidental emissions at an irradiation plant, emissions into the air and water at other plants can be both intentional and massive. On the basis of these two accidents and an alleged third one, which it alluded to but did not describe, the British magazine *New Statesman and Society* stated in a large breakout quote: "The U.S. irradiation industry has been plagued by a 'litany of accidents.' "[119] When only two or three minor accidents occur among the nearly forty plants that have existed for over a period of decades, with no evidence of injury, and those accidents are described as a "litany," what value does the word have?

The NCSFI, on the other hand, has claimed six accidents as evidence of the low level of safety at these plants. In fact, none of the accidents was related to food processing nor did it cause harm to anyone outside the plant. Some involved exposure of a single worker; some resulted in no such exposures.[120] Further, although four of the incidents involved leaks of isotopes into the shielding pools, in each case the leaking capsules had been constructed with a technology no longer being made, although some of the old-style capsules themselves are still used.[121] The leading current supplier of the new capsules, Nordion International, claims to have built twenty-five thousand and delivered them around the world without their suffering a single leak in transit or in use.[122]

Of course, eventually material used to irradiate the food must be disposed of, and disposal of radioactive waste is always a serious thing. According to *Health* magazine: "Perhaps the most far-reaching worry about the use of irradiation has less to do with food safety than with the storage and shipping of nuclear wastes." The article goes on to explain that cesium 137, "the substance proposed for the DOE's gamma-ray irradiators, is a water-soluble element. Therefore, an accident could contaminate underground drinking water supplies for over 100 years."[123] Groups like the Washington, D.C.–based Environmental Policy Institute and Health and Energy Institute also worry that widespread use of food irradiation would dramatically increase the amount of radioactive materials being used and transported. The amount of radiation that would go in and out of one typical food irradiation plant every five years, it is argued, would be five times the total volume of low-level nuclear wastes produced by *all* sources in 1981.[124]

Obviously, it is impossible to say that a truck or train car will never have an accident, but it is possible to protect their contents so that accidents couldn't possibly disturb them. Cobalt 60 has been transported for medical use for forty years without incident. Very little cesium 137 is even available for use and, therefore, very little would be on the road. If it were, it would be doubly encapsulated into welded stainless steel jackets and shipped in lead caskets approved by the DOE and the NRC,[125] just as cobalt 60 currently is.[126] Use of particle accelerators or X-ray machines would completely eliminate the problem of transporting radioactive material, since they stop emitting ionizing radiation as soon as they are switched off. Further, for processing thin pieces of food or food in powder or granular form, these machines are much more efficient than cobalt 60 or cesium 137, although machines could prove too expensive for use with thicker pieces of food.[127]

## FEEDING THE ARMS RACE

One sure indicator that a scientific process or a product is being politicized is when you see two disparate issues being closely tied together by opponents of that process or product. Thus, opponents of nuclear power plants tie concerns over the safety of such plants to their opposition to nuclear weapons. Likewise with those expressing concern over the safety of nuclear weapons plants. An op-ed piece in the Denver *Rocky Mountain News,* expressing opposition to the nearby Rocky Flats plant, which processed plutonium for nuclear weapons, was entitled "Rocky Flats a Cancer on Denver and the World."[128]

The anti-irradiation folks likewise have managed to hitch their wagon to nuclear weapons, which should and do cause real fear and anxiety. Dennis Mosgofian, the NCSFI's former director, has gone so far as to call food irradiation "the engine to drive a crucial component of the arms race."[129]

Irradiation opponents cite the DOE's role as administrator of a program, launched in 1985, to build six demonstration irradiation plants, at a cost of about $32 million. While most irradiation plants in the world use cobalt 60, supplied by Nordion International, as their isotope source, government planners originally hoped to use cesium 137 in the demonstration plants. Unlike cobalt 60, cesium 137 is a by-product of nuclear-weapons manufacture.[130]

One claimed reason for advocating the use of cesium is that there already exists a relatively small amount that has been kept in underwater storage tanks at Washington State's Hanford Nuclear Reservation awaiting storage in a permanent geological repository.[131] But, say irradiation opponents, there is an additional, sneakier connection to the military. If a demonstration plant showed that cesium was beneficial in food irradiation, food irradiation plant operators might then ask for access to another, much larger source of cesium, the spent fuel from commercial nuclear reactors. Since spent fuels also contain an abundant amount of plutonium, reprocessing of it, which would be necessary to extract the cesium, would be the first step toward purifying the plutonium for military use. As an NCSFI publication in the 1980s stated: "The separation processing of cesium will allow for the reprocessing of plutonium for the new generation of 17,000 warheads the Reagan Administration has requested within the next 6–7 years."[132]

In fact, a 1982 amendment to the Nuclear Regulatory Commission's budget authorizations bars using spent commercial fuel for military purposes, and the DOE has shown no interest in repealing the amendment. The needed reprocessing facilities don't even exist in this country.[133] Further, the impetus for six demonstration irradiation plants came not from the DOE but from Congress, where supporters of irradiation regularly put money for the program into administration budgets.[134] Finally, none of the planned demonstration plants specified any intention of using cesium as an energy source, and after budget cutting caused the program to be cut back, the two plants that survived chose to use electron beams, not cesium.[135] This doesn't seem to be an effective way to create a demand for cesium, but perhaps it is just a reflection of how sneaky the conspirators really are.

George Giddings, an irradiation-technology consultant who now works for the Joint Division of the International Atomic Energy Agency and the Food and Agricultural Organization of the United Nations in Vienna, Austria, calls the cesium argument "the single most inflammatory aspect of the food irradiation debate. . . . It has fueled the controversy far beyond its significance." Giddings replies to the nuclear conspiracy theory by pointing out that, among other things, "present and future U.S. weapons grade plutonium needs can likely continue to be satisfied by the easier and cheaper production directly from uranium."[136]

Giddings thinks the whole nuclear weapons theory seems rather farfetched,[137] but obviously others disagree. Author and New York talk show host Gary Null writes:

> Why should the DOE have anything to say about what America eats? What is the FDA, whose primary mandate is to ensure the safety of our food supply, thinking about when it ramrodded [*sic*] through its approval of irradiation? The Reagan administration, strong on exotic weapons programs like Star Wars, was also a supporter of food irradiation.[138]

Hmm. The same administration that supported a strategic ballistic missile defense system also supported food irradiation. Perhaps something *is* afoot here. *The Nation* magazine obviously thinks so. It devoted several pages of a 1987 issue to Ken Terry, an editor at *Variety* magazine and a nuclear weapons freeze activist whose piece was entitled "Why Is DOE for Food Irradiation?" Terry suggests the answer immediately: "to justify the extraction of plutonium from commercial nuclear wastes for use in nuclear weapons."[139] It seems not to occur to him that the DOE thinks the extraction of plutonium for nuclear weapons needs no justification. Nuclear weapons require plutonium; the nation requires nuclear weapons. The fact that Ken Terry doesn't think the United States should have a nuclear arsenal doesn't change this. Incidentally, Terry cites Richard Piccioni as a fellow conspiracy-watcher.[140]

If one wants to argue that food irradiation is bad, that is one thing. And if one wants to argue that having nuclear weapons is bad, that's another. But the two are separate issues. Beware the person who tries to tie such disparate issues together: He is probably indicating they don't have enough evidence to defeat each one separately.

## THE MICROBE THAT ATE MANHATTAN

*Consumers' Research* magazine is not to be confused with *Consumer Reports*. Indeed, it may often be seen as an alternative to the latter's perceived biases against chemicals and technology. But the *Consumers' Research* columnist who reports on food irradiation, Beatrice Trum Hunter, is no fan of the process. In one column, she states: "Although radiation kills salmonella, some bacteria might resist irradiation—bacteria that are more virulent and dangerous than salmonella [and] over time, these bacteria might be singled out and strengthened. And through mutations, irradiation might produce dangerous variations in bacteria and viruses, which would be highly resistant to destruction."[141] Notes the *Harvard Medical School Health Letter:* "This scenario is not inconceivable, but there's no historical precedent for it, and no experimental evidence suggests that this is a likely hazard in the real world" (as opposed to a laboratory dish).[142] This is but another example of the activists holding the process up to a standard by which other methods of preservation would fail. According to Mac Peat, a Chicago-area spice processor, 5 to 10 percent of bacteria typically survive gassing, while irradiation's kill rates are nearly 100 percent.[143] When other food processes are less than 100 percent efficient in killing organisms, that's okay; when it's food irradiation it's a scenario for The Bacterium That Ate Boston.

A seemingly more plausible concern, voiced by Sidney Wolfe of Public Citizen Health Research Group, a Ralph Nader organization, is that "irradiation kills bacteria and [other] microorganisms. But minutes after you zap [food items] they could become re-infested."[144] He's right. But once again, there is a double standard because that is exactly what happens to food that is heat-treated for canning but then not canned quickly and properly. It causes botulism, a sometimes fatal illness. Protecting irradiated food is no different from protecting food prepared for canning.[145] Josephson has testified before Congress that irradiation can provide "the same margin of microbiological safety as the heat sterilizing process" (canning).[146]

Similarly, Beatrice Hunter says that "irradiation also fails to control—and might actually encourage—aflatoxin, a virulent mold contaminating many foods." In studies conducted in India, she writes, "irradiated samples of wheat, corn, sorghum, pearl millet, onions and potatoes were all contaminated with higher levels of aflatoxin than nontreated samples."[147] But Josephson notes that to do this, "they had to use an unnatural system that would never be encountered in practice. First the Indian researchers heat sterilized the food [as is done in the canning process], which destroys naturally-occurring immunity of food. Then they inoculated the food with aflatoxin, then they irradiated it."[148] But there's no reason to ever heat-sterilize food before irradiating it.[149] Further, he says, making note of data published in the *Journal of Food Safety:* "Actually irradiation can destroy aflatoxin at a high enough dose, but they never tell you this."[150]

## MORE FROM THE LAUNDRY LIST

Some items on the laundry list of objections thrown at irradiation proponents are just plain silly. For example, Linda Mason Hunter, in her book *The Healthy Home,* makes four quick, unsubstantiated statements as to why "irradiated food is not safe," the first of which is that "the food cannot be eaten for 24 hours, to allow for radioactive decay."[151] First, the statement is false. According to George Giddings, who once ran an irradiation plant, irradiated food can be eaten right off the conveyor belt.[152] At no point is irradiated food dangerous or unhealthy. Second, distribution systems are such that by the time the food goes to a warehouse, is then shipped to the store, then put onto shelves, it would be impossible to consume within twenty-four hours anyway. Finally, of all the arguments one might make against a method of food *preservation,* surely the weakest is that it can't be eaten right away. If it were meant to be eaten right away, it wouldn't be preserved by any method.

Another argument used against irradiation invokes circular reasoning. Activist Ralph Nader says one of the main reasons for preventing food irradiation is that "people are rebelling against it all over the country."[153] But to the extent that consumers have "rebelled" at all against irradiated food—which is a very small extent at any rate—it is essentially because of the misleading activities of Ralph Nader and other alarmists. One who cranks up a smoke machine should not be allowed to insist that where there's smoke there must be fire.

A related anti-irradiation argument employs what may be called an "impossible threshold." It says that I'll be convinced if only X is demonstrated but then defines X as something that is essentially impossible to demonstrate. Thus, the Food Irradiation

Network (FIN), which is vociferously anti-irradiation, takes the reasonable-sounding position that it is opposed to food irradiation "unless and until all outstanding issues are fully resolved." [154] The problem is that the FIN gets to define what "fully resolved" means. As far as the FDA is concerned, for all the foods it has approved for irradiation, the issues *are* fully resolved. Congressman Henry A. Waxman (D-Calif.), perhaps cognizant that more than twenty years ago the Atomic Energy Commission was already able to announce that "food irradiation has been more thoroughly tested than any other method of food preservation," [155] pointed out during congressional hearings on food irradiation: "If we require that food irradiation be proven safe, we may be requiring something that can never be proven one way or the other, therefore we would lose the possibility of an advance in the technology." [156] But as far as FIN is concerned, that's the whole idea. On any scientific issue that can be named—from fluoridation to whether the earth is round—it is possible to find an opposition group that seeks to provoke controversy. FIN's logic is: (1) As long as there is controversy over a practice, it shouldn't be implemented; (2) we're creating controversy over it; therefore (3) it shouldn't be implemented.

## MAKING PEACE WITH SALMONELLA

In 1982, the editor of *Prevention* magazine, noting that some organisms in food can keep in check other, harmful organisms, then remarked: "We know that people and animals have lived for millions of years eating natural, nonirradiated food. And while there is plenty of evidence that sometimes that food has spoiled and caused illness or death, we should not kiss off so quickly the idea that the life in food that we can't understand totally is without long-range value." [157] Our ancestors also had no canning, no refrigeration, no salting—and short lives. But again, agrarian utopianism lifts its head. Let us live in harmony with all the beasts of the earth, including those little things wriggling around in our food. Who needs irradiation? The birds don't use it, the bees don't use it. Our ancestors swinging in the trees didn't use it. Let's not use it, let's fall in love—with nature.

And natural is *always* best. Stated a Mr. Spring Friedlander of

Oakland, California, a member of NCSFI, in a letter to the *Co-op News* of Berkeley: "When I shop, I seek mold as a confirmation that the food I am buying is not irradiated."[158]

Time and again, irradiation opponents cite arguments against the process that if applied to other food-processing procedures would look absurd. It depletes vitamins, they say. So does canning. Workers may get hurt on the job at irradiation plants, they say. Almost two million workers are already hurt or killed on the job. Irradiation creates new chemicals, they say. So does roasting, frying, broiling, and boiling. Well, we haven't been able to identify each of those new chemicals, they say. We haven't been able to identify each chemical in the food *before* it's irradiated.

A critical writer in *Boston* magazine who apparently has more knowledge about pesticides than Congressman Bosco, pointed out that irradiation would in fact cut down on pesticides and fumigants but "only on those used after the food has been grown, harvested, and stored."[159] *Only?* For health purposes, that is exactly the type of pesticide we should be looking to replace, because that is the type that would leave a residue, potentially toxic or carcinogenic. Why is irradiation being less than a miracle cause for disparagement? Do we look at all the things canned food *can't* do, frozen food *can't* do, salting *can't* do? The anti-irradiationists insist that we apply standards of both safety and usefulness that if applied to other products or systems that have been in use already for many years would possibly wipe out most of the scientific advances of the twentieth century. Josephson observes: "In the 180 years since Nicholas Appert in 1809 discovered canning by heat to preserve food, the canning process has never been subjected to a systematic study for wholesomeness."[160] In other words, canning was just grandfathered in, as have been all preserving processes prior to irradiation, just as the anti-chemical crowd has grandfathered in all natural chemicals and indeed natural carcinogens while waging war against synthetic chemicals.

What the anti-irradiation argument really comes down to is: It's new technology, therefore we don't like it.

If people want to be technophobes, that's fine. No doubt somewhere in the penumbrae of the Constitution there is granted a right to be phobic. But there is no right to force your phobia down someone else's throat.

## FREE TO CHOOSE

This brings us back to an earlier question. Why food irradiation? In light of all the palpable advantages, let's turn the question around. Why not ask: Why not food irradiation? If despite grandiose efforts, irradiation opponents have been unable to support their claim that the process is in any way dangerous, why should approval be stopped? Nobody questions Detroit when it comes out with a new automobile. Nobody says, "Look, we've already got plenty of four-door mid-priced sedans. Let's keep yours off the market." Indeed, market is the key word. If there's really no room for that new car or that new food-processing method, consumers will avoid it and it will fail. That's why it's curious that of the laundry list of objections to irradiation, one is that it is too expensive.[161] There's no reason to think that will prove true. The only commercial food irradiation being done in the United States right now is on spices, and Chicago spice processor Mac Peat says that although irradiation is a much more efficient killer of bacteria on spice than conventional methods, it is just as cheap.[162] But if it were to prove true, then irradiation would be unable to compete and that would be the end of it.

Donald R. McNeil has written: "The continuing success of [these people] raises several questions regarding this role of science, the scientists, and public health agencies in a democracy. It demonstrates the power of a small, volatile minority which directs its appeal to the emotions of a community."[163]

The subject McNeil was addressing was not food irradiation. His words appeared in a 1961 issue of *The Nation* and concerned water fluoridation. Certainly his words could be applied to the anti-irradiationists. Ironically, now *The Nation* often turns its pages over to small, vocal minorities appealing only to emotion on scientific issues, including food irradiation. But there is at least one difference between these two groups of fanatics (other than that one comprises mainly the fringe of the political right and the other that of the left). The only really good point the antifluoridationists had was that the profluoride forces were shoving their experiment literally down all people's throats. If you drank the city's water, you had no choice but to drink fluoride. The anti-irradiationists are in exactly the opposite position. They *don't* want people to be able to choose.

During food irradiation hearings of the U.S. House Subcommittee on Health and the Environment, Congressman Sid Morrison (R-Wash.) made a nice point by noting that in experiments in stores, if irradiated and nonirradiated strawberries are put side by side and so labeled, consumers will initially reject the irradiated ones. They will do this, he said, "until the ones that are not irradiated begin to look worse than the ones that are irradiated, and then they will buy the better-looking product, even with the sometimes frightening label of irradiation on it."[164] In fact, marketing surveys conducted in fourteen countries since 1984 have found that consumers not only buy irradiated foods when given the opportunity, but in many cases actually prefer the irradiated product and may pay more for it. For example, papaya purchasers in southern California, by a ratio of eleven to one, favored the irradiated fruit. A survey of purchasers of irradiated apples found that most preferred them over nonirradiated apples, despite the higher price, because of what they perceived to be superior quality.[165]

Food irradiation opponents seem to be aware that given a free flow of information and enough time, their cause will be lost, and their tactics reflect this. For example, the first irradiated fresh fruit sold in the United States, Puerto Rican mangoes, were quickly snapped up by shoppers in a North Miami Beach produce market. A large sign indicated that the fruit was the first irradiated produce item sold in the country.[166] However, two years later, when two southern California supermarkets carried irradiated Hawaiian papaya, the move was met with a parking lot demonstration by anti-irradiation forces.[167] One month later, the Southern California Grocers Association collectively decided not to sell any irradiated food for the time being, notwithstanding the grocers' eleven-to-one preference for the irradiated papaya. They represent 65 percent of the market in the region.[168] The Grocers Association has made it clear that it will not sell irradiated food as long as protests may be anticipated.[169]

Obviously, such pressure makes supermarkets nervous. One executive, who requested anonymity, said he would not want it known that his company, a major food processor, has even looked at the possibility of using irradiation "because we don't want to become a target for all those activists to picket or boycott."[170] In New York City, a spokesman for the Pathmark, Sloan's, A&P, and Food Emporium chain said the stores would probably decline to sell irradiated produce if it were offered to them because of the potential for bad consumer reaction. "I avoid those kinds of issues like the plague," said Raymond Smith, director of produce operations for Sloan's Supermarkets.[171] The anti-irradiationists know this and use it to their full advantage. They know they don't have to win the debate, but merely to keep up the pressure. For the catch-22 of food irradiation is that more companies won't use it until it is publicly accepted but that it won't become publicly accepted until more companies use it. Thus, a spokesman for the Campbell Soup Company said in 1987: "We're not going to use irradiation until we're sure the public will accept it. If it gets a clean bill of health and has widespread usage, then we might change."[172]

It's not that people wouldn't know that their food was irradiated. FDA regulations require irradiated food to carry a symbol marking it as such. In addition, there must be a label statement that the food has been "treated with radiation" or "treated by irradiation."[173] Some food processors opposed the use of "irradiation" or "radiation" because of the negative association with the words, conjuring images of radioactivity; instead, they preferred to substitute "picowave treatment" or "ionizing energy." Further, an international committee that comprised a joint committee of the WHO, International Atomic Energy Agency, and the Food and Agriculture Organization, stated: "It was . . . not thought necessary on scientific grounds to envisage special requirements for the labeling of irradiated foods."[174] But what the FDA has done is to say, regardless of the proven safety of this process, we're still going to give people the option of rejecting it on a food-by-food basis.

While it may be argued that irradiated food in poor Third World countries, labeled or no, doesn't really leave those consumers much choice, that's because their only other option is going extremely hungry or literally starving. The theoretic possibility that a food may cause cancer in a small percentage of its consumers doesn't have much relevance to those ingesting only half the calories a day that they should. Such a situation is distinctly different from one in which the Nestlé Foods Corporation was accused of sending its milk formula to poor countries and urging mothers to use it instead of their breast milk. In that case women had a real choice and had been urged to make the wrong one.

The real worry of the anti-irradiationists is that consumers might look squarely at food clearly marked with that symbol, grab the item, and drop it into the shopping cart. Giving consumers a choice is absolutely the last thing anti-irradiationists want.

## THE COERCIVE UTOPIANS

Rael Jean Isaac and Erich Isaac, in their book *The Coercive Utopians,* wrote:

> The utopians do more than reject our economic institutions: Ultimately their attack is directed against modern technology and science itself. In a very real sense, the coercive utopians are twentieth century Luddites. They do not smash machinery in the crude bashing of their forebears, but in a more sophisticated way demonstrate, lobby, propagandize and bring suit.[175]

Noted Willard Libby in the *Bulletin of the Atomic Scientists* 1978: "The success of [irradiation] processes will depend ultimately upon their costs, consumer acceptance, and labeling requirements, as well as evaluating whether the technology fulfills a perceived consumer need."[176] The irradiation foes intend to see that none of these ever come into play. As with pesticides, the agrarian utopian vision of the anti-irradiationists cannot tolerate diversity of choice or opinion. Their vision of the world as it should be cannot stand either of these. Just as those who oppose all pesticides insist that we must all eat organic food, irradiation foes insist that we must all eat nonirradiated food. They cannot tolerate man-made chemicals on or in food; they cannot tolerate man-made (or at least directed) radiation. And most of all, they cannot tolerate toleration for those with opposing views.

Americans live in a country with myriad religious and moral beliefs, which contradict those of other people; this includes beliefs involving food. We accept that it is perfectly all right for Orthodox Jews to keep kosher, for Roman Catholics not to eat meat on Fridays during Lent, for Muslims to abstain from pork, and for Hindus to abhor beef. But none of those groups are given the right to dictate what will be served to persons who do not belong to their faiths. If Orthodox Jewish parents send their child to school and don't want her to eat nonkosher food, they must provide their own alternative. They can also urge others to adopt their ways. What they cannot do, and indeed do not attempt to do, is make everyone eat kosher.

Not so the coercive utopians. They are brownshirts dressed in green. Stated one German Green party representative, "Grassroots democracy sounded wonderful before we were elected to Parliament. But now that we are in power, centralized solutions seem far more effective."[177]

Scientists are now developing genetically engineered food. Such food, both vegetable and animal, can be made more nutritious, cheaper, and more delicious. For example, the biotechnology industry is already contemplating "designing" cows and pigs with extra genes to code for hormones that produce a higher ratio of lean meat to fat, and making plants that produce useful oils. But when Great Britain became the first country in the world to approve a genetically engineered food, a yeast whose genes were modified to produce carbon dioxide more quickly and so make bread rise faster, no bakery in the country would touch the substance.[178] There may be some excellent arguments to make against specific types of genetically engineered food, just as one can argue that a specific synthetic pesticide is bad without indicting all synthetic pesticides. But in this case, it appears there was nothing more than a simple aversion to technology.

Such genetic engineering holds incredible promise for foods that do everything from helping fat people stay thin to helping thin people gain weight to providing nourishment to people who don't eat enough or just don't eat what they should. Will special interest groups keep these products forever off our store shelves because they aren't just like the foods raised on the farm back when plows were pulled by animals? Whether they succeed will depend in part on whether the products are potentially profitable enough for industry to fight for them. In part it may depend on whether legitimate scientists are willing to do more than place articles in technical health and science publications. But ultimately it may depend on whether the vast majority of American consumers, those who don't share the romantic vision of a world with nothing but "organic" waste, "organic" transportation, and "organic" food—meaning, sometimes, insects and mold—will finally throw off the yoke of the self-appointed elite and decide for themselves what is in their best interest.

# CHAPTER 7

# Currents of Misinformation: The Shocking Facts About Electrical and Magnetic Fields

[Electromagnetic fields are] the most pervasive—and covered up—public health hazard Americans face.[1]

—Paul Brodeur's *Currents of Death*

"The room is equipped with Edison Electric Light. Do not attempt to light with a match. Simply turn key on wall." So ran one of many similar notices that began to appear in hotel bedrooms during the 1880s. But along with the admonition not to try to ignite the light bulb came a further statement to allay fears. "The use of electricity for lighting is in no way harmful to health, nor does it affect the soundness of sleep."[2] The reassurances did not convince everyone, however. James Thurber wrote of his grandmother, in a 1933 essay, that she "lived the latter years of her life in the horrible suspicion that electricity was dripping invisibly all over the house." She spent her days turning off the wall switches that led to empty sockets, "happy in the satisfaction that she had stopped not only a costly but a dangerous leakage."[3]

Did Thurber's grandmother know something most of her contemporaries didn't? Were her fears, if exaggerated, nonetheless justified?

Author and journalist Paul Brodeur says so, and so do a lot of other people. From his treatments of asbestos, the ozone layer,

218

and microwaves and electricity, Brodeur has established a mighty reputation as an exposer of public health hazards that have been covered up by the authorities. Clearly there are folks out there who think very highly of Brodeur and his work. Awards for his articles include the Sidney Hillman Foundation Award, Columbia University's National Magazine Award, an American Association for the Advancement of Science/Westinghouse Science Writing Award, and an American Bar Association Award.[4]

Whatever one thinks of Brodeur or his work, he has been tremendously influential. Dr. M. Granger Morgan, physics professor with the Department of Engineering and Public Policy at Carnegie-Mellon University in Pittsburgh, wrote of *Currents:* "Brodeur's book is already shaping the way many concerned, technologically untrained citizens, including some decision makers, frame and think about these issues."[5] Brodeur's material on the dangers of extremely low-frequency electric and magnetic fields (EMF) has been serialized in *The New Yorker,* for which he has been a writer for many years. *The New Yorker* may or may not be the "best magazine in the world," as it bills itself, but it certainly is influential. Brodeur has published two articles on EMF in *Family Circle* and has been cited favorably in a variety of magazines, including *Time,*[6] *Woman's Day,*[7] *Business Week,*[8] and many others. An ABC News *Nightline* program was built around him and his thesis.[9] No environmental alarm is so identified with a single person as the alarm over EMF is identified with Paul Brodeur.

The Brodeur thesis, in a nutshell, is that extremely low-frequency electric and magnetic fields can be hazardous to human health in a variety of ways. We're not talking about the electric chair, electrified fences, or broken power lines that fall onto people and fry them instantly. We're talking about a much more insidious foe, one that causes disease to develop only after a long period of time and which not only cannot be seen or heard but can't even be felt. The instruments of death: power lines, power substations, house wiring, electric blankets, and video display terminals. Depending on whom you listen to, other electrical appliances may be a risk, too. Worries over such a health hazard have focused on cancer—especially leukemia and brain tumors—and developmental abnormalities, and to a lesser extent on endocrine and nervous system disorders, including chronic depression. It's a technophobe's worst nightmare, that the source of so many of man's recent improvements in health and comfort—from air conditioning to refrigeration to appliances to personal computers—are killing us and our unborn offspring. Or so many of us believe. Consider:

- Boulder, Colorado considered burying a single fifty-year-old power line at the cost of $5 million.[10]
- To calm public protests, a Canadian utility proposed buying all the homes along a ninety-mile power line that was under construction. But residents became so upset that the government ordered a halt to work on a segment of the line.[11] One protestor staged a "live-in" in a tent on top of an as-yet-unstrung power cable that was to go over her backyard. Utility officials pointed out that someone so concerned about safety shouldn't be sitting on a veritable lightning rod.[12]
- A judge in Palm Beach, Florida, ruled in 1989 that children could not play in schoolyards near overhead power lines because the EMF emitted by the lines may eventually be found to cause or promote cancer.[13]
- Residents of an affluent section of Denver used their clout to move a proposed underground power cable away from their neighborhood.[14]
- Elsewhere in Denver, sixteen miles of power line threatened to hold up the development of the Denver International Airport. The power line cut directly across the new airport site and some officials worried about moving it closer to residences because of, as the *Denver Post* put it, "concerns that high-voltage power lines might be carcinogenic." One idea was to bury the line—at a cost of $106 million.[15] What was most amazing in the brouhaha over the Denver airport power line proposal was that most of the thirty-four-mile route was to run through largely vacant farmland likely to remain so for the foreseeable future.[16] The tens of millions to be spent burying the line was therefore only for the protection of the corn and its attendant crows.
- The Klein Independent School District in Texas forced Houston Lighting and Power to spend $8.6 million to remove a transmission line from school property.[17]
- While electric generating capacity grew by 10 percent from

1983 to 1987, transmission and distribution capacity grew by only 4 percent, according to Sanford Cohen at the investment firm of Morgan Stanley and Company. "Transmission capacity is not going to get built because of this controversy," he says.[18]

As always, opportunistic businesses have cashed in on the health fears, and have actively promoted those fears through their advertising. One company, Walker Scientific of Worcester, Massachusetts, sells a hand-held battery-powered monitor complete with ten-segment LED display to measure emissions from TVs, computer screens, or nearby power lines.[19] One New Jersey company makes money on many of the popular scares of the day. The cover of its brochure features electric power lines strung over a house with a little stick figure at the front door with dashes coming out of its head to express alarm.[20]

What are the financial ramifications of taking action on EMF on a national scale? According to Ram Mukherji, an electromagnetism expert at Southern California Edison power company: "We are talking about rewiring America. We would have to reduce our standard of living." The potential costs of personal injury lawsuits filed by cancer patients and others against utilities and other companies "are just incredible," says San Francisco lawyer Stephen M. Snyder. "They would dwarf things we've dealt with so far like Agent Orange, the Dalkon Shield and asbestos."[21] So far, only a few such suits have been filed in connection with EMF fields, but "there are dozens of these suits in preparation," according to Louis Slesin, editor of "Microwave News," a newsletter which watches and comments on the EMF controversy.[22]

But are you really at risk? Should you run for the phone and call Healthwaves? According to a draft report prepared by the EPA and released in October 1990, EMF exposures are "a possible, but not proven, cause of cancer."[23] But Dr. Eleanor R. Adair, a fellow at the John B. Pierce Laboratory in New Haven, Connecticut, and a member of the Institute of Electrical and Electronics Engineers (IEEE) Committee on Man and Radiation, says absolutely not. Adair, who is also a senior research associate and lecturer at Yale University, and editor of the book *Microwaves and Thermoregulation,*[24] is a severe critic of what she calls "electrophobia," defined as "the irrational fear of electromagnetic fields." In a 1990 commentary in *IEEE Spectrum,* she wrote:

> Electrophobia is flourishing! If no voices are raised to challenge that buildup, the cost to the U.S. taxpayer in meaningless research, product redesign, and electric power distribution retrofit (excluding billions in litigation costs) may soar into the trillions of dollars in the next decade. Meanwhile, attention and funds will be diverted from other, proven hazards.[25]

Dr. Edwin L. Carstensen, a physics professor in the Department of Electrical Engineering at the University of Rochester and author of the book *Biological Effects of Transmission Line Fields,*[26] concurs. "If you look at the scientific basis for the whole thing," he says, "there's nothing there. A few studies seem to give a borderline indication of an effect, someone else tries it, and it disappears."[27]

Who is right? Is there any risk at all, and even if it appeared there were, would the degree of risk be enough to justify such massive expenditures?

## THE WERTHEIMER-LEEPER STUDIES

Wendy Wertheimer is a Boulder, Colorado, psychologist who acquired a special interest in childhood leukemia. In 1974, on her own time, she began investigating leukemia clusters in the nearby Denver area, working on the hypothesis that the disease might be linked to an infection. She found no such link, but she did begin to think she had found another. It seemed to her that there was a connection between addresses of victims of childhood leukemia and power line transformers. That piqued her interest and she began discussing the issue with a physicist friend, Ed Leeper, who fashioned a crude gaussmeter used to measure magnetic fields. Wertheimer used this to verify her hypothesis that EMF dropped off sharply a few houses' distance from the transformers, as indicated by her observation that this is where most of the leukemia cases were clustered. At that point, she began a methodological comparsion of all childhood cancers and compared them to a map she had made of homes that she classified into high- and low-current, depending on their exposure to EMF. This classification she referred to as "wire codes." In 1979, she and Leeper published the results of their study in the *American Journal of Epidemiology*. They reported finding "electrical wiring configurations [such as terminals and sub-stations] suggestive of high-current flow . . . near the homes of case children [those who had contracted cancer]. The finding was strongest for children who had spent their entire lives at the same address, and it appeared to be dose-related."[28] Although the paper gave no risk ratios, a later calculation showed the children had two to three times greater risk of leukemia than would otherwise be expected.[29] As a result of the Wertheimer-Leeper work, research on EMF will be conducted into the twenty-first century.

The conclusions of the first Wertheimer-Leeper study were questioned in the scientific community because of various limitations in its design and methods. Those included the experimental and thus unvalidated use of wire codes and a failure to take account of such potentially important confounding causes of disease as exposure to ionizing radiation or passive exposure to cigarette smoke. The similar results of their second study have been questioned because the study was conducted mostly with a nonblind exposure assessment. In other words, they knew ahead of time who had concern and who had been exposed to the highest amounts of EMF.[30] A Rhode Island study repeated the Wertheimer-Leeper experiments, with negative results, yet Swedish epidemiologists got results they suggested supported Wertheimer and Leeper.[31]

But to really understand the Wertheimer-Leeper study and the issue at large, a little must be known about the science of electric and magnetic fields and how they may affect the animal physiology.

## HOW ELECTRIC AND MAGNETIC FIELDS WORK

The electricity that comes out of outlets uses AC, or alternating current, as opposed to batteries that produce DC, or direct current.[32] DC flows steadily in one direction, but AC alternates back and forth. In North America this frequency is sixty times a second, which is identified as 60 hertz (Hz) power. In Europe and some other parts of the world the frequency is 50 Hz. Europe also uses

220 volts instead of America's 115, which is why you need to buy an adapter if you plan to bring your hair dryer to the Old Country. But that is a different matter, having nothing to do with frequency. both 60 and 50 Hz are at the low end of the electromagnetic spectrum, and hence are referred to as "extremely low frequency" or ELF.* When discussing potential dangers of EMF at ELF, it's simpler to just use one or the other abbreviation. This book uses EMF, except when quoting others who use the different terminology.

Transmission lines produce two kinds of fields: electric and magnetic. While they are often spoken of together, "electromagnetic," it is important to draw distinctions between the two. Electric fields are the forces that electric charges exert on other charges at a distance because they are charged. They are measured in volts per meter (V/m). When those charges move, they create additional forces on each other, which are carried through space by magnetic fields. A magnetic field is the force that a moving charge exerts on another moving charge because of that movement. Magnetic fields are often measured in Teslas, but in popular work, the most common unit of measurement is the Gauss, which equals 1 ten thousandth of a Tesla.

A group of charges all moving in roughly the same direction is called an electric current. All electric currents produce magnetic fields. Electric and magnetic fields are found throughout nature and in all living things. The magnetic field of the earth, which makes a compass needle point north, is made by flowing charges, or currents, in the earth's molten interior. The molecules in our bodies and in all other living and nonliving things are held together in part by fields. The messages in our nervous systems involve fields.

---

*The electromagnetic spectrum is divided as follows: Up to 300 hertz is extremely low frequency; 300 hertz to 10 kilohertz (a kilohertz is a thousand hertz) is very low frequency; 10 kilohertz to 1 megahertz (a megahertz is a million hertz) is low frequency; 1 megahertz to 30 megahertz is high frequency; 30 megahertz to 300 megahertz is very high frequency, which we know as VHF and which is used for television broadcasts; 300 to one gigahertz (a gigahertz is a billion hertz) is UHF, which is also used to broadcast television. One gigahertz to 3,000 gigahertz is microwave transmission, above which is infrared, then visible light, then ultraviolet light, and then ionizing radiation. The top of the ultraviolet light band falls into the ionizing radiation category.

Because 60-Hz power is so widely used in our society, there are 60-Hz electric and magnetic fields almost everywhere we go. The strengths of those fields diminish as you move away from electrical objects just as the light and heat of a fire grows dimmer as you move away from it.

Other factors will also affect field strengths, such as the voltage of the object creating it. Thus, a high-voltage power line usually produces stronger electric fields than a low-voltage power line. Current does not have to be flowing in the object for an electric field to exist; it need merely be plugged in.

Magnetic fields pass through most common objects without being significantly affected, a point that becomes extremely important when one considers burying power lines to reduce potential adverse health effects. Soil does not stop magnetic fields. Electric fields, conversely, are affected by objects, especially those that can conduct electricity. Trees, yard walls, and normal houses can also partially shield electric fields. How much they do so depends on the construction material. A typical house shields about 90 percent of the electric field from outside.

Sixty-Hz fields are often confused with X-ray or microwave radiation, but there are several important differences. X rays (and other forms of ionizing radiation such as gamma rays) produce effects in living systems because the energy carried by the X rays is so large that it can directly break apart molecular bonds, including DNA. Scientists think that is why X ray exposure can lead to cancer. Microwave radiation also cannot break those bonds, but it is absorbed by the water in tissue, causing heating. That's how microwave ovens work. Your kitchen microwave will cause you no harm, but maintenance workers or other persons who may be directly exposed to a powerful microwave antenna, such as is used for radar or communication, can be harmed from the overheating of their body tissue. The energy carried in 60-Hz electric and magnetic fields is much too small to directly break either molecular or chemical bonds or to heat tissue.

The fear of EMF combines two of man's gut-level emotions: the fear of the invisible and the distrust of new technology. The word "radiation" also sends some of us into fits, in great part because it is invisible and associated with new (and sometimes terribly destructive) technology. Brodeur likes to tag his EMF articles with the word "radiation" in the title. Thus, a Brodeur piece in *Family Circle* was entitled "Radiation Alert,"[33] while his series of articles in *The New Yorker* was entitled "Annals of Radiation."[34] Perhaps Brodeur's purpose in this is to conjure up visions of Hiroshima, Nagasaki, and Chernobyl. In fact, not only are there various types of radiation that are utterly harmless to us, such as TV signals, or even good for us in the proper dose, such as sunlight, the EMF about which he writes is not radiation of any type.*[35]

Now, what does all this have to do with cancer?

## CELLULAR-LEVEL EFFECTS OF EMF

Carnegie-Mellon researchers Morgan and Nair cite several reasons for the failure of scientists until recent years to even consider the possibility of adverse health effects from EMF:

- The heat produced in body tissue from currents induced in the body by power-frequency fields is less than 1/10,000 of the body's own background rate of heat production.
- (As noted) power-frequency fields carry too little energy to break chemical and molecular bonds and so do not do the sort of biological damage which ionizing radiation produces.
- Electric fields induced in the body by external sources are typically far weaker than the fields that occur naturally inside the body, especially those due to the potential differences set up by "ion pumps" that move ions into and out of cells.
- The currents established in the body by power-frequency fields are often no larger than the currents induced in it by movement through the earth's magnetic fields.[36]

---

*There are two types of electric and magnetic fields, those that travel or propagate long distances from their source (also called electromagnetic waves) and those that are confined to the immediate vicinity of their source. The power-frequency fields that people encounter are of the nonpropagating types because power lines (and appliances) are much closer to people than one 60-Hz wavelength, which is several thousand kilometers. Only a tiny portion of the energy in power lines goes into propagating fields. Because the power-frequency fields of public health concern are not of the propagating type, it is inappropriate to refer to them as "radiation."

On the other hand, Morgan and Nair say, cellular-level experiments point to the cell membrane (outer surface) as at least one site of EMF interaction. The cell membrane is known to be affected by chemicals that cause cancer. In one laboratory, EMF has been shown to increase production of a cell enzyme that is essential for normal growth (ornithine decarboxylase, or ODC). Nevertheless, EMF does not cause the very high ODC levels that are associated with cancer promotion, according to Charles Rafferty, a biophysicist who manages most EMF laboratory studies for the Electric Power Research Institute (EPRI), an organization funded by utilities.[37]

Likewise, it is possible that EMF is not in and of itself a cause of cancer, but rather that it may make it easier for an actual carcinogen to cause cancer. The best-documented physiological effect of EMF in animals, according to Rafferty, is the suppression of nighttime synthesis of melatonin, a hormone secreted by the pineal gland of the brain, under exposure to electric fields. "If this observation is accurate—and we are now examining this—the possibility that EMF could affect human health through the alteration of pineal gland function must be taken seriously," he says. Suppressed melatonin levels have been associated with the growth of cancer, while administration of melatonin, under certain laboratory conditions, can slow cancer growth.[38]

On the basis of his knowledge of the laboratory studies, Rafferty does not see the evidence of biological effects from exposure to magnetic fields as clear and unequivocal. "I think that overstates what we know, as well as the strength of the experiments," he says. The problem is that although some good laboratories have done some well-designed experiments, there has still not been good replication among laboratories. "All the positive results from all studies everywhere get thrown into the same bag, but in general, they have not been replicated or explored thoroughly," he says.[39] Likewise, Morgan and Nair point out that while the observations "are consistent with the hypothesis that [EMF] may play a role in cancer or tumor development, none of this constitutes proof or even necessarily a strong indicator that it does."[40]

Nevertheless, in *Currents,* Brodeur constantly refers to "32 published studies demonstrating ELF effects."[41] He doesn't point out that these thirty-two studies are in contrast to hundreds of animal and cellular studies showing no effects.[42] More important, the strong implication is that these are *harmful* effects. But that assumption is simply false.

Just what do we mean when we say "biological effects"? Not a whole lot, really. Says William Feero, who is chairman of the IEEE Power Engineering Society's Working Group on Biological Effects of Power Frequency Electric and Magnetic Fields: "There is a scientific principle that says no matter what you do, there is a discernible effect somewhere else."[43] As the Carnegie-Mellon researchers have pointed out:

> A biological effect is not necessarily a significant health consequence. In jogging half a mile, a variety of changes occur in the human body; pulse and respiration rates change, as do various hormone levels. These changes are biological effects. Such an effect may be of no consequence to overall health, or it may lead in some way to either beneficial or detrimental changes in health.

They also note:

> The human body is made up of highly adaptive systems that involve multiple processes of control. For this reason, an observable biological effect from exposure to a particular condition does not necessarily imply any health consequence; the body may simply adjust to the new condition.[44]

In other words, even if it were clear that something had a terribly adverse effect on cells in a petri dish, it may have no effect in a human body that has all sorts of interactive defenses. (Likewise, a drug that is extremely effective on the cell level might be useless in the body. Many drugs have been found that have proven highly effective against the AIDS virus (HIV) in test tubes but have proven useless when given to patients with the disease.)

A study showing biological change has no intrinsic connection to cancer or any other health problem. Indeed, we now know that frequent introduction of an electrical current into a broken human leg bone has a distinct biological effect on that bone. It is used to help bones heal faster.[45]

## EPIDEMIOLOGICAL STUDIES

What, now, do the human studies tell us? At this writing, twelve United States studies have examined occupational EMF exposure

and leukemia. All these show an increased risk of leukemia ranging from 1.4 (40 percent higher than expected) to 3.2 (220 percent
higher) when all leukemias are considered together. The most
extensive to date is an ongoing study of New York City telephone
workers being conducted at Johns Hopkins University in Baltimore. Involving 50,582 present and past male employees, it shows
a higher risk of leukemia for young workers who continue to be
employed by the telephone company. In particular, cable splicers—the group with the highest exposure—showed a high cancer
incidence not only for leukemia (seven times that of nonline workers) but for all cancers, including those of the gastrointestinal
system, prostate, and brain. While the actual numbers of cancer
cases found among New York workers in the Johns Hopkins study
were small, the incidence rate for subjects with line-related jobs
was higher than that for other telephone company employees.
The cable splicers showed a statistically significant 1.8-times-
higher overall incidence of cancer when compared with other
telephone workers. On the other hand, compared with New York
males as a whole, the cable splitters actually had a *lower* rate of
cancer.[46] Not too many people are going to argue that merely
being employed by a phone company reduces one's risk of cancer.
All it shows is that when you're working with small enough numbers, all sorts of things may show up in your data.

Of several other occupational studies made elsewhere—five in
Sweden, two in the UK, and one in New Zealand—two of the
Swedish studies show no significant association between leukemia
and field exposure, while the rest show a correlation, with risk
ratios of between 1.3 and 3.8.[47]

Eleven studies have linked brain tumors to occupational EMF
exposures. Five were part of research already described, while
the rest focused on brain cancer and occupational exposure in the
United States. All showed relative risks between 1.5 and 8.0. That
figure of 8.0 from one study sounds pretty scary, but if the link
between disease and exposure were so strong, why have five other
occupational studies done in Sweden—four of them looking for
cancer incidence in electrical workers, and one examining the
occupational distribution of over four thousand brain tumors—
found no excess risk for central nervous system tumors or brain
cancer in electrical occupations? On the other hand, several studies also appear to link occupational EMF exposure with breast
cancer in male workers.[48]

## WHAT DO THE STUDIES MEAN?

In May 1989, the Office of Technology Assessment (OTA) released a report by three researchers from the Department of Engineering and Public Policy at Carnegie-Mellon University in Pittsburgh; the report's authors were the aforementioned M. Granger Morgan and Indira Nair, and H. Keith Florig. The one passage from that report that has appeared in practically every news story on EMF since then is "As recently as a few years ago, scientists were making categorical statements that on the basis of all available evidence there are no health risks from human exposure to power-frequency fields. In our view, the emerging evidence no longer allows one to categorically assert that there are no risks."[49] Unfortunately, many of these stories omit the next sentence: "But it does not provide a basis for asserting that there is a significant risk." For example, concerning the occupational studies just discussed in this book, the OTA report stated: "The results of all studies taken together indicated a small positive association or no association." It did find that, "although ELF field exposure cannot be definitely or uniquely identified as a causative agent, some aspect of [certain] manufacturing and repair jobs . . . does place the workers at increased risk of brain tumors," and that, "based on the set of studies discussed above, it is fair to say that there is an indication that occupational exposure in 'electrical occupations' is associated with enhanced leukemia risk." But it immediately added: "Remember that 'associated' means 'occurs together with'; it does not imply a causative link. . . . No confounding variables and household and other exposures have been taken into consideration in these studies."[50] In other words, it is highly possible that whatever gave the electrical workers higher rates of cancer than nonelectrical workers bore no relation, per se, to their electrical work but may instead have borne a relation to things that electrical workers do or don't do in everyday life compared with nonelectrical workers. Says Savitz: "There may be some sort of sociologic process by which certain types of people with different baseline cancer risks select certain kinds of careers."[51] If we found, for example, that assembly line workers at a Ford factory had higher rates of cancer than Ford executives, it would clearly be jumping the gun to say that assembling cars is necessarily a risk factor. Ford executives earn much more than do their workers, they have different diets, they are of different racial and ethnic backgrounds, they have different rates of smoking and drinking, get different amounts of exercise, live in different communities, and have access to different health care. So, too, will electrical workers have non-work-related differences with nonelectrical workers. If there were a really massive difference between electrical workers' rates of cancer and those of nonelectrical workers, that would be some evidence that there might be more at play than simply these background variables. But when half the studies show no elevated risks of cancer, you do not have that massive difference.

Another important phrase in the OTA report (it occurred where the ellipses appear in the above quote) reads: "The job classifications do not clearly indicate the actual occupational exposure to fields."[52] Likewise, says Savitz, "because these studies are based on job titles rather than on exposure data, we really don't know if the individuals with cancer have been exposed to elevated field levels."[53] If it turned out that some of the recorded cancers were occurring in these people, it could destroy any meaning in the test results.

On the issue of adult cancers caused by residential exposure, there was "not enough evidence to judge the possibility of an association." With childhood leukemia, the aspect of EMF upon which Brodeur focuses the most and which has gotten the most attention in general, the report found that: "Collectively the studies do not provide good evidence that ELF exposure increases the risk of leukemia." But, they added, carefully hedging their conclusion, "At the same time the evidence precludes categorical statements that no such risk exists."[54]

Eleanor Adair, on the other hand, thinks that categorical statements as to EMF's harmlessness are entirely in order. "In truth," she says, "no study, whether laboratory research or epidemiological survey, has demonstrated a causal link between low-level ELF fields and human cancer, the major theme echoed and reechoed in the media. None!" Adair adds: "Nearly all epidemiological research published to date—whether relating VDTs to birth defects or power lines to cancer—suffers from recall bias [that is, people trying to remember information that is important to assess their exposure], lack of appropriate case controls, inadequate or no measurement of ELF fields, and a myriad of uncontrolled and unevaluated confounding variables."[55]

One problem with imputing harmful effects to EMF from the

studies is that the increased level of cancer isn't very high even when there is an increase.

"We're not talking about strong associations like those found with smoking and lung cancer," explains Leonard Sagan, EPRI's field effects researcher. "It's widely acknowledged that smoking increases the risk of lung cancer about 10-fold. With the field effects of epidemiology on the other hand, we're seeing incomplete evidence for weak association," he says. "Savitz's numbers, for instance, suggest that there might be a little less than a doubling in the cancer incidence (from about one to about two in 10,000 per year) for children living near high-current-configuration lines. But the range of experimental error for these results extends down to where there may be no increase in risk to this population."[56] Sagan isn't saying, So what if EMF merely doubles a child's chance of getting cancer? He's saying that a mere doubling in light of all the difficulties in researching the phenomenon indicates that there's a good chance that EMF is causing no extra cancers at all.

Similarly, Morgan says that "in evaluating results from experiments on the possible biological effects of weak low-frequency electric and magnetic fields, investigators looked for similar patterns. Often they did not find them. Instead effects appeared and disappeared as what appeared to be very small—many said irrelevant—changes were made in experimental conditions." Long experience, he says, "has led scientists to think experimental results that are marginally significant and that come and go in apparently random ways are usually not real."[57]

The now-you-see-it-now-you-don't phenomenon has been common in research on exposure to EMF. H. B. Graves, a biology professor at Pennsylvania State University, has labeled it the Cheshire Cat phenomenon, after the cat which periodically appeared and disappeared during Alice's visit to Wonderland.[58]

On the whole, the medical community does not seem particularly impressed with the possibility of danger from EMF. An editorial in the *Journal of the Royal Society of Medicine* stated: "An objective assessment of the epidemiological evidence must, I think, lead one to the conclusion that it is weak and unconvincing";[59] while another in the *British Medical Journal* concluded: "At most the carcinogen potential of extremely low frequency electromagnetic fields must be weak."[60]

But all this is very general. Much can be learned about the

EMF phenomenon and even more about the Brodeur phenomenon by looking carefully at the work done by Savitz and his
fellow researchers.

## THE SAVITZ STUDIES

As noted, the Wertheimer-Leeper studies are controversial and
flawed in that they used a system for measuring exposure to fields
that may, in fact, not be an actual measure; they also failed to
account for a wide variety of confounding variables. Far less suspect are the studies of David Savitz, formerly of the University
of Colorado at Boulder, now at the University of North Carolina
at Chapel Hill. Those studies are very important to Brodeur in
shoring up the weaknesses of the Wertheimer-Leeper ones. Wrote
Brodeur in *Currents:*

> Far and away the greatest blow to the effort of the utility industry
> to deny that 60-hertz electric and magnetic fields could pose a
> health hazard came on November 20, 1986, when Savitz and his
> colleagues announced the results of their long-awaited replication
> of Wertheimer and Leeper's childhood cancer study: Their findings
> showed that "prolonged exposure to low-level magnetic fields may
> increase the risk of developing cancer in children." Indeed, Savitz
> not only found a statistically significant association between all
> types of childhood cancer and external magnetic fields but also
> determined that for children in certain high exposure groups—for
> example, children who lived in homes very close to high-current
> wires—the risk was more than five times that of the control pop-
> ulation.[61]

Yet, Brodeur's version of Savitz's work and Savitz's version—
along with that of his fellow researchers—are so different as to
make it difficult to comprehend how they could have come from
the same body of work.

The Savitz study, which like Wertheimer-Leeper's was conducted in Denver (Savitz then lived in Colorado), was sponsored
by the New York State Power Lines Project (NYSPLP), a research
program controlled by an independent scientific advisory panel
set up by the state to evaluate possible health effects of EMF.

Savitz's team attempted to eliminate as many problems as possible from the methodology employed by Wertheimer and Leeper
and others. Many of the earlier confounders were eliminated and

wire coding was blinded, meaning that the researchers would not be familiar with the location of ELF sources and hence exhibit a bias. But in addition to using the Wertheimer-Leeper wire codes, the Savitz group used a second system that they thought might be a more accurate indicator of actual exposure to EMF. They took actual measurements of electric and magnetic field strengths in various places in the houses of the cancer victims and the controls.[62]

In terms of exposure to electric fields, no correlation with cancer was found. With magnetic fields, a slight correlation between *low-power* exposure levels and cancer was indicated, according to Savitz, but interestingly none at higher power levels.[63] None of the power level correlations were statistically significant, though.[64] It was only when using the Wertheimer-Leeper coding system that a few statistically significant correlations appeared. Even there, however, they were not strong. Brain cancer showed a slight correlation when persons exposed to low-strung wires were compared to those exposed only to higher ones, with about twice as many cancers as would be expected. Total cancers also were slightly significant under that same index, with about 50 percent more cancers than would be expected. But when persons exposed to very high wires were compared to those exposed only to buried ones, neither total cancers nor brain cancer nor any other cancer showed a significant correlation.[65] The category that Brodeur says was "more than five times that of the control population" was, in fact, barely statistically significant, consisting of a mere eight cancer cases with which there were only two control people to compare them.[66]

The Savitz study attempted to control for several major potential confounders, but despite all this care, as Savitz makes clear, if every time the fields were high, another agent was also present, the positive association observed between the field exposure and cancer might actually be one between the exposure to this other agent and cancer. One such confounder Savitz specifically mentions is the traffic density near the homes. Indeed, two years later Savitz was the primary author of an article appearing in the *Scandinavian Journal of Work, Environment, and Health,* in which he found indications of "an association between traffic density near the home occupied at the time of diagnosis and childhood cancer," which was [not explained by other potential causes]. The odds ratios were 1.6 to 2.0 for all cancers except lymphomas and soft-tissue sarcomas, very close to what Savitz found for childhood leukemias in the New York Power Lines Project.[67] The presumed mechanism for carcinogenesis would be benzene in the vehicle exhaust, benzene being strongly suspected as a cause of adult leukemia,[68] plus other particles in the vehicle emissions.[69] Frank Barnes, electrical engineering department chairman at the University of Colorado in Boulder, and coauthor of the NYSPLP study, noted that the EMF correlation found was barely statistically significant—not enough so to justify vast expenditures on rerouting transmission lines. "It is very noisy data," he says, "noisy" being an epidemiologist's term for something that may be statistically significant yet still remains within the range of chance. "It's noisier than anything I've ever had a part in publishing, and it's quoted more than anything I've ever published."[70]

## DESPERATELY SEEKING (TO CONFIRM) SAVITZ

Just as Savitz evaluated the Wertheimer-Leeper conclusions, so are other studies now seeking to evaluate his. The most prominent as of this writing was an EPRI-funded one made public in February 1991. Just as Savitz had added a second method of determining exposure, measuring power line strengths, to the Wertheimer-Leeper method of simply measuring the distance to those power lines, this new study, conducted in Los Angeles County, added a third. A recording device was placed in each child's bedroom to measure such fields every minute for twenty-four hours. Instant spot measurements were made around the home. Using telephone questionnaires, the study also attempted to assess patterns of EMF exposure to electrical appliances. The questionnaire additionally contained questions to evaluate exposure to agents other than EMF, such as household chemicals and cigarette smoke.[71]

No association was found between childhood leukemia and measures of exposure to electric fields. This correlates with Savitz's results. As to *magnetic* fields, the study found that using the Wertheimer-Leeper wiring code, there was a statistically significant increased risk. Using the Savitz spot measurement system, there were elevated risk levels but none that were statistically significant. Using the new twenty-four-hour measurement system, the Los Angeles group again found no statistically significant elevations in the odds ratios; indeed, there was no correlation between measured magnetic and electric fields and disease.[72]

In sum, the California study found essentially what Wertheimer and Leeper had using the Wertheimer-Leeper method and it found what Savitz had using the Savitz method. Using yet a third method, it got yet a third set of results that would, if verified in further studies, indicate that power lines have no connection to leukemia. The big question is which measurement system is best. One's first temptation is to go with the Los Angeles method since it seems to be the most exact. But since the actual exposure that resulted in the leukemias occurred years earlier (since that is the incubation time for a leukemia case), it may be that the exposures recorded in the twenty-four-hour measurements, while more exact indicators of what the children are being exposed to *now,* don't have any more bearing on what they were exposed to *then* than do the other testing methods.

If this sounds rather confusing, that's because it is—even to the top experts in the field. It is going to take many more studies, perhaps using new methods of measuring exposure, before things are sorted out. The one thing that appears clear is that nothing is clear—in stark contrast with the assertions of Brodeur.

The California study came out after Brodeur's book and related *New Yorker* articles, so Brodeur can't be blamed for not having considered it. But the bottom line on the New York State Power Lines Project is that no one involved with it gave it either the interpretation or the importance that Brodeur assigned to it. Indeed, Brodeur's book is built around these shadowy data. Over and over again, Brodeur cites the Savitz study as confirming the Wertheimer-Leeper data and the Wertheimer-Leeper data is his proof that power lines cause cancer. But not only does Savitz disagree with Brodeur as to the meaning of his data—that is, whether any cancers are being caused by EMF—he also disagrees with the policy implications. Brodeur calls for drastic measures such as avoiding the use of electricity or shielding power lines,[73] but when asked if he believes these steps should be taken, Savitz replies: "Probably not. There is so much uncertainty that it doesn't seem wise for individuals or society at large to expend a lot of resources to avoid a danger that may not exist. If there was a little 59-cent device that would eliminate exposure it would be worth it, but in reality there is so much uncertainty and the costs of reducing exposure are so high that it is difficult to justify such expenditures."[74]

Indeed, knowing that his studies would be used to promote fear, Savitz published an open letter to "Persons Concerned About Reports of Electromagnetic Fields and Childhood Cancer." In it he stated, "there is a suggestion of a possible hazard which has yet to be resolved. Given these circumstances, it seems that interest or concern may be justified, but our study is not sufficiently convincing to warrant drastic action by homeowners."[75]

Dr. Samuel Milham, Jr., of the Washington State Department of Heath and Social Services plays a role similar to Savitz's in *Currents*. His studies on extreme worker exposure to EMF and a possible relationship to cancer are key to the Brodeur thesis and occupy fourteen pages of *Currents*.[76] Yet, like Savitz, when quoted Milham doesn't back up the Brodeur thesis at all. "My mind is still open on whether the general public has a significant risk," Milham told one newspaper in late 1989. "But to put things in perspective, I don't think the risk is an inordinate one. In other words, a whole lot of cancer can't be related to electric fields and power lines."[77]

Whether intentional or not, misrepresenting a researcher's work is very serious business. Since there are no notes in *Currents*, only with difficulty can one check Brodeur's assertions against the actual data. It is a fair guess that over 90 percent of those reading Brodeur's books or articles don't even know where the closest medical library is, that even fewer have the ability to search the library for the appropriate data, and fewer still have the inclination to do so. The people who shell out their money to buy a book trust that the author, whatever his biases, has relayed accurately the information gathered by others.

## WHERE ARE ALL THE CANCERS?

How can one tell if epidemiological studies are correct? One possible way is to see how their results would play out in the real world. One of the best indicators that those epidemiological studies claiming a correlation between cancer and EMF are incorrect is the way their results apply to the population at large. *Science* reporter Robert Pool has calculated: "If the implications of the Savitz study are true, then roughly 15 percent of childhood cancers are due to power line exposure." He notes further that the dean of the School of Public Health at the State University of New York in Albany, David Carpenter, thinks it is reasonable to guess that another 15 to 25 percent could be caused by appliances. "But if 30 to 40 percent of childhood cancers are caused by EMFs, there should have been a big jump in these cancers over the last 40 years." Concludes Pool: "Epidemiologists don't agree on exactly how much cancer rates have changed over time, but it would be hard for them to miss something this large."[78]

Indeed, epidemiologists and other scientists agree. "There's been an enormous increase in our consumption of electrical power over the last 30 years, so we're all constantly pervaded by EMFs," says John Boice, Jr., chief of the National Cancer Institute's Radiation Epidemiology Branch. "During the same period, the incidence rates for childhood leukemias have been relatively stable, not what one would expect to see if increasing EMF exposure were having a major effect."[79]

A related assertion is Milham's. If EMF does cause cancer, it certainly can't be causing it very often. Or to put it another way, if you do a lot of driving and never see a pink car, it doesn't necessarily prove there are no pink cars on the road but it is a pretty good indicator that if there are some, there aren't a lot.[80]

## BLANKETS, HAIRDRYERS, AND POWER COMPANIES

Ultimately the "they" in Brodeur's story of cover-up of EMF dangers is the power companies. Brodeur concludes his second *Family Circle* article with a quotation by the mother of a ten-year-old boy with cancer of the thymus, a founder of Residents Against Giant Electric (RAGE), declaring, "Believe me, it's far better to spare a child from cancer than to continue to protect the economic interests of the electric utility industry."[81] In a previous *Family Circle* article, Brodeur stated that the answer to industry's refusal to act to alleviate EMF dangers "lies, as it did in the recent case of the cancer-producing chemical Alar . . . with public awareness and insistence that preventive measures be enacted."[82]

It is true that most utilities have not acted to reduce fields on their own, contending that the regulatory agencies should direct them to do it if necessary. "We're in the business of providing power," said Robert Bell, vice president of Consolidated Edison Company of New York in New York City. "We'll do it however the public tells us to."[83] That brings up a vital point that Brodeur fails to recognize in his conspiracy theory. Power companies always have regulatory agencies and always do what those agencies tell them to. The way such utilities function is that they are granted a monopoly to serve a given area. The quid pro quo for receiving the privilege of not having to compete is that the utilities' practices and prices are subject to control by a regulatory body. The regulatory body is supposed to allow the utility to make a fair profit and nothing more. Some utilities have managed to cajole the regulators into allowing them to make far more than a fair profit, but never does a utility work for less than a profit. Otherwise it would shut down. Brodeur claims the utilities are covering up hazards because they don't want to pay to alleviate them, but while such an accusation may sound reasonable with asbestos manufacturers or the maker of a chemical like Alar, it hardly applies to a company with a predetermined profit margin. If Con Edison or another utility is forced to pay to bury or move power lines, it will simply get its regulator to pass the price along to the customers. That's what makes it so easy for Con Edison to "do it however the public tells us to," because whatever the public says to do is that for which the public will end up paying.

It is quite possibly because of this need for a centralized bad guy that Brodeur concentrates on EMF emissions from power lines and virtually ignores those from appliances, his two exceptions being computer terminals and electric blankets. Yet the level of EMF emissions from appliances can be many times that which one could possibly receive from power lines. For example, if you are near a garbage disposal while it's operating, you may be exposed to 1 to 5 milligauss normally, with a maximum magnetic field of as many as 33 milligauss. An electric kitchen range will expose you to from 1 to 80 milligauss with a maximum of 625. An electric can opener has a typical range of 30 to 225 milligauss with a maximum of 2,750 and an electric razor normally puts out fields of 50 to 300 with as many as 6,875 milligauss.[84] (The maximum exposures comprise direct contact with the object.) Obviously, exposure levels vary according to how close one is to the appliance, since magnetic fields drop off rapidly. You may always be so far away from your stereo except while turning it on or off that you receive virtually no exposure from its fields. Conversely, electric razors and blow dryers are always used within the range of the fields. An electric alarm clock puts out 1 to 12 milligauss normally with a maximum of 450, but that clock may be inches from your head when you sleep or it may be six feet away. Nevertheless, compare these exposure levels with those at which Wertheimer-Leeper and Savitz were getting their significant results, a range of 2 to 3 milligauss.[85] Says University of Washington bioengineering professor and vice chairman of the IEEE's Standards Coordinating Committee on nonionizing radiation, Arthur W. Guy: "The magnetic field exposure from power lines is just a drop in the bucket" compared to that from appliances.[86]

Indeed, among the studies of the effects of EMF lines can be found those indicting appliances. The aforementioned California study found that children who used electric hair dryers or sat in front of black-and-white televisions had a significantly higher risk of cancer.[87] None of which is to say that appliances are necessarily dangerous, but merely to point out the inconsistency in portraying power companies—huge and impersonal though they be—as the devil while ignoring what may be a greater area of concern. Yet Brodeur has even gone so far as to suggest that those who note that the EMF emissions from appliances are much higher than those from power lines are doing so to cover up the power line problem,[88] which is similar to Janet Hathaway of the Natural Resources Defense Council saying, in Chapter 2, that those who dare to point out that natural chemicals fed to rodents in massive doses cause cancer as often as synthetic ones are simply trying to cover up for the synthetics.

As noted, however, Brodeur does make an exception for VDTs and for electric blankets, both of which do result in lengthy exposure to the user. VDTs will be discussed in Chapter 10. As to electric blankets, the evidence is as sketchy as for power lines, hardly warranting the title *USA Today* put on its review of Brodeur's book, "Beware Your Electric Blanket." Again, the main protagonists in the scientific world are Wertheimer and Leeper. The authors reported a seasonal pattern, indicating a higher rate of spontaneous abortion, longer gestation periods, and lower birthweights in babies born to users of heated waterbeds and electric blankets. But the study was fairly small and involved uncontrolled variables such as the possibility that the heat was damaging fetuses.[89]

In 1990, Savitz and two other researchers looked at the possibility of cancer resulting from the exposure of children, both within and without the womb, to electric blankets. Savitz's team interviewed Colorado residents to assess their exposure to a wide variety of household appliances but only attempted to look at the risk imposed by those concerning beds: bedside electric clocks, heated water beds, heating pads, and especially electric blankets. When they looked at prenatal and postnatal exposure together, there were no statistically significant elevations from any of the appliances, including electric blankets, for any type of cancer. When just prenatal exposure was looked at, there were no statistically significant elevations of cancer involved with the use of any but electric blankets.[90]

As to prenatal exposure to electric blankets, the Savitz researchers also found in general no statistically significant elevations. But when they broke this category down even further, they did find that a few of these did have significantly elevated odds of getting cancer. For example, brain cancer had an odds ratio of 2.5 but the bottom range of the confidence interval was 1.1, meaning it was barely within the range of significance. They also found a significant increase for brain cancers for children exposed in the first trimester. The researchers found no statistical associations for children exposed after birth to electric blankets. The bottom line, according to Savitz? "Results are limited. . . . Nonetheless, electric blankets, one of the principal sources of prolonged magnetic field exposure, were weakly associated with childhood cancer and warrant a more thorough evaluation."[91]

As to adults, while Brodeur has Wertheimer hinting at the possibility of a connection between adult leukemia and electric blankets and mattress pads,[92] as of this writing, a few studies have shown no increased risk of adult cancer from electric blanket use, while none have shown an increased risk.[93] Still, it is a relatively new area and not much work has been done. Nevertheless, some people are not waiting around for results. Northern Electric Company of Chicago has already introduced a Sunbeam electric blanket with magnetic fields one thirtieth that of earlier models.[94]

## ATTACK OF THE EPIDEMIOLOGIST MOTHERS

Epidemiology-by-victim, as is so often the case with other health scares, plays an important part in the EMF scare. Here though, it may be more apt to describe it as epidemiology-by-victim's-mother. *Business Week* reported on an anti-power-lines activist named Sharon Rausch, who "had a young son who died in 1978 from a brain tumor, and she suspects power lines near her son's school may have contributed to his cancer." No reason is given for her suspicion.[95]

The *Worcester Sunday Telegram* reported on the Taylor family, whose infant son died of a brain tumor and who lost several dogs to cancer, as well. Stated the article: "Mrs. Taylor said the couple had suspicions about the power lines from the start, because they feared that defoliant sprayed under the lines to kill vegetation might be leaking into the groundwater. Later, their suspicions turned to the power lines themselves, and the electromagnetic fields (EMF) they produce."[96] Considering that over one million human cancers develop each year and goodness knows how many in dogs, one might consider the possibility that something completely unconnected to the power lines prompted the formation of the cancerous growths. But as is so often the case with miscarriages and birth defects, there is a psychological need for explanations and recriminations. "It was God's will" or "It was sheer chance" isn't enough for these people.

To quote Francine Kritchek, cochair of "1 in 9," an organization for breast cancer patients, researchers should turn their attention to the environment—be it power lines, herbicides, or anything else man-made—because "women are tired of being told it is because of their educational background, their high socio-economic status, their ethnic background and their age that they are prone to this illness."[97] That years of epidemiological study may confirm this seems a rather unimportant point to her and to some victims. What is inexcusable is reporters and other crusaders who use these sad stories in lieu of scientific evidence.

Certainly, in one way at least, EMF have had an impact on health—mental health. An official with Northern Virginia Electric Cooperative reported that at a meeting to discuss a plan to run a 115-volt distribution line to a new electricity substation outside a residential subdivision, "I had to deal with a lady breaking down and crying at the back of the room because she was convinced it would cause irreparable harm to her two children."[98] Morgan and Nair report that the Department of Engineering and Public Policy at Carnegie-Mellon University in Pittsburgh "receives a constant stream of telephone calls and letters" from terrified people. "One pregnant woman," he says, "asked whether she should get an abortion because she had slept under an electric blanket early in her pregnancy."[99]

It is time now to take a closer view of the one man who made this terror possible.

## THE CULT OF BRODEUR

It is important to look carefully at Paul Brodeur's work in part because he has been so very influential in the EMF and VDT debates, but also because his techniques are the purest techniques of the journalist-alarmist. Nobody, not even Michael Brown of the Love Canal controversy, has shown the ability of Brodeur to pull fear out of thin air. As one EMF alarmist put it in a letter to the editor of the *Albuquerque Tribune:* "To get the whole story, get *The New Yorker* magazine . . . it will scare the very devil out of you!"[100] A study of Brodeur is a case study in how the crusading journalist operates and how he is rewarded.

The Brodeur methodology appears to comprise first the identification of a potential problem, usually a cluster of cancer cases. It appears that he then goes to epidemiologists and other authorities who have expertise that Brodeur doesn't have, and who have a dispassionate attitude that he lacks as well. Those experts say there is no evidence of a problem. Then Brodeur claims that there is not only a problem, but a massive cover-up as well. To disagree with Brodeur is then to be involved in the cover-up. The word "cover-up" appears on the covers of both *Currents of Death* and his 1977 book, *The Zapping of America,* subtitled *Microwaves, Their Deadly Risk, and the Cover-Up.*[101]

Brodeur's *The Zapping of America* detailed the health horrors of microwaves emitted from radar, microwave ovens, and other devices. The book, much of which appeared first in *The New Yorker,* gave many a suspicious mother "facts" to explain her refusal to purchase a microwave oven. If you are old enough to remember when Radar Range was used generically to describe microwave ovens, you are old enough to recall the fear of microwave ovens that early on prevented many Americans from buying these tremendously useful devices. But gradually the fears of the new wonder device gave way to science. In 1980, only 15 percent of all American households had microwave ovens; by 1989 that figure had risen to between 75 and 80 percent, as reported in a *Wall Street Journal* article with the apt title, "The Microwave Cooks Up a New Way of Life."[102]

Much of *Currents of Death* is repetitious of *Zapping*. The diseases are the same: cancer, miscarriages, birth defects, and cataracts. Many of the sources of these problems claimed by Brodeur are the same. In both books Brodeur dwells to a great extent on radar stations in general and a military radar in Masschusetts in particular.[103] But the most important similarity in the books is his apparent disdain for epidemiology. As will be seen, Brodeur is a master in at least two different areas: The first is locating cancer and birth defect clusters and making them appear clearly tied to whatever he's seeking to indict. The second is characterized by "never apologize, never explain." Both come together nicely in his story of the effects of the microwave bombardment of the United States embassy in Moscow.

Around 1973, it became known that the American embassy in Moscow had been continuously irradiated by the Soviets with microwave rays from as far back as 1953 up to the present. Despite a United States investigation into the phenomenon, called Project Pandora, there was much speculation but little actual knowledge of why they might have been doing this. The prime support for Brodeur's thesis in *Zapping* that microwaves cause cancer comes from his assertion that persons living in the embassy suffered serious health effects from this bombardment. The embassy and the alleged health woes of its occupants pop up throughout the book.[104] Noted the journal *Science*:

> The atmosphere was ripe for a conspiracy theory, and one duly emerged in 1977 in a widely noticed book, *The Zapping of America*, by Paul Brodeur. The federal government, the military, the electronics industry, not to say "all of the academic and research institutions financed by the military-electronics industry complex," have been colluding to avoid bringing to light the malign health effects of microwaves, Brodeur reported.

He had, said *Science* sardonically, "laid bare what must have been one of the largest and most successful conspiracies known to history."[105] After *Zapping* appeared, a study commissioned by Congress concluded that the embassy employees actually had *better-than-average* health.[106] In *Currents,* Brodeur criticized the government study, declaring that it

> had underestimated the health hazard of microwave radiation at the embassy by failing to point out that the death rate—particularly from breast cancer—was extraordinarily high [he doesn't say how high] among women living in apartments on the third through seventh floors of the embassy during the late 1960s and 1970s, when the irradiation of the embassy had become a source of major concern to the State Department and the CIA.[107]

But look closely at Brodeur's wording and see what he says by what he's leaving out. He mentions only breast cancer, so he's first ignoring the appearance or nonappearance of every cause of death or illness that is not cancer. He is also ignoring all types of cancer that are not of the breast. That automatically excludes all cancers in children, since children virtually never get breast cancer. Men rarely get breast cancer, so he is ignoring all male cancers as well. He is also ignoring all the workers save those on floors three through seven. We don't know how tall the building was, but at the very least he is ignoring the first two floors. Finally, he is ignoring the years prior to the late 1960s, even though the study covers years dating back to 1953. Now, he says, take just this tiny group of people who satisfy all his requirements—and voilà!—a cluster. Microwave irradiation is guilty!

One might suspect that those persons Brodeur wants you to ignore don't do much for his argument. And one would be correct. First, looking at causes of death of both embassy males and females as separate groups and even breaking these down further into six different cohorts—including all cases, cancers only, and heart disease only—the government study found fewer of all these than one would expect in a similar demographic group and fewer than in comparison embassies.[108] It looked at other groups, at adult dependents, and dependent children, and found lower death rates than would be expected. The only problem definitely present to a greater degree among children in the Moscow embassy was mumps—microwave mumps, perhaps?[109]

All Brodeur has proven is that if you take *any* group and break it down just right, to exclude people who don't help you make your case, you can always, always, find a cluster of *something*. His work is a showcase for all the pitfalls of bad epidemiology, for why epidemiologists say that clusters almost never mean anything. But it does seem to win him lots of awards.

## BRODEUR IS IN THE EYE OF THE BEHOLDER

People and journals without expertise in science areas, such as *Publishers Weekly,*[110] *Library Journal,*[111] and *USA Today,*[112] tended to be highly impressed with *Currents*. The scientists, however, were not so complimentary. M. Granger Morgan, who along with David Savitz is probably the researcher identified most with this area of science, wrote in *Scientific American* that Brodeur has authored "a dramatic and riveting story, one that should sell lots of books." But, he said, "there are outstanding studies done with great care by very careful investigators. There are also poorly conceived or poorly executed studies done by people who do not exercise appropriate care." Brodeur's book, Morgan continued, "treats them all alike. If they found a positive effect, they must be right. If they did not find a positive effect, usually they go unmentioned." He did this, said Morgan, "presumably in the interest of sustaining his cover-up theory."[113]

Brodeur informs his readers that all of the scientists who do not state flatly that electromagnetic fields are dangerous are either engaged in a cover-up or are incompetent. Thus, Brodeur informs us that Edwin Carstensen, who believes there is no danger from EMF, is not a medical doctor. Indeed, he is not an oncologist (cancer doctor), not a cell biologist, not an epidemiologist, not a statistician. His degree is in physics. Carstensen may have studied cell biology for ten years, Brodeur tells us, but he has no formal degree. Brodeur also informs us that "none of the 116 publications listed in his resume [as of the date of the 1985 testimony] dealt with the health effects of magnetic fields emitted by transmission lines."[114] He sees no purpose in mentioning that some of the top EMF experts, such as Morgan and Nair, are physicists, or that two years later Carstensen published an entire book on the subject, the aforementioned *Biological Effects of Transmission Line*

*Fields*. For that matter, all the things that Carstensen is not also apply to Brodeur.

Savitz associate Howard Wachtel says the Savitz study doesn't lead to the conclusion Brodeur would have it lead to, so Brodeur dismisses him as just an electrical engineer.[115] Yet, Brodeur repeatedly cites the authority of Robert O. Becker, discussing him and his theories in 18 pages of the 314-page *Currents of Death*.[116] Becker is an orthopedic surgeon.[117] And what of Wendy Wertheimer, who is basically to Brodeur's book what Christ is to the New Testament, appearing, according to Brodeur's index, on 155 of Brodeur's pages?[118] She, he is quick to note on page one, is an epidemiologist. In fact, she is no medical doctor and did not get her degree in epidemiology; instead her doctorate was in psychology, as he subsequently admits.[119] There is no evidence in *Currents* of her having any formal epidemiological training. This certainly doesn't mean her work can be dismissed out of hand; it can't. But it would have to be if we applied to her Brodeur's rules for the opposition.

Another smeared scientist is Dr. Philip Cole, who takes the same position on EMF as does Carstensen. Cole is a medical doctor and not just any epidemiologist but the head of an epidemiology department, so Brodeur can't go after his credentials. Instead, he identifies Cole as having "appeared at a 1987 congressional hearing to support the position of EPRI. . . ."[120] Mind you, Brodeur didn't say he just happened to support the position of EPRI; he said Cole appeared at the hearing *to support* it. There you have it. To say that there remains doubt about the carcinogenicity of EMF is "to support the position of EPRI."

If Wertheimer is the Christ figure in Brodeur's book, David Savitz is Saint Paul, appearing on thirty-two pages and repeatedly cited as backing up Wertheimer's work. But Savitz doesn't seem to think much of the man who glorified him as one of the few heroes in a sea of conspiring villains. In his review of *Currents* in the *Journal of the American Medical Association*, Savitz wrote:

> If held to the standard of a balanced, scientific review of the evidence, *Currents of Death* simply fails. There is little evident attempt to separate legitimate criticism of the scientific evidence suggesting health harm from irrational resistance based on the implication of that evidence. Personal or institutional bias is invoked as the only possible reason for failure to accept what the author (but few

others) considers irrefutable evidence. Deficiencies in some studies are not mentioned, while contradictory evidence receives strong criticism.[121]

None of this negative criticism by the scientific experts seems to have hurt Brodeur's credibility with the media, however. If anything, perhaps it has enhanced it by showing him to be the threat to the mass conspiracy that he says he is, a true Cassandra. That one of his erstwhile allies, Savitz, has abandoned him just shows how powerful "they" are.

Thus Brodeur continues to retain the faith of *The New Yorker*. In July 1990, he pumped out his most terrifying article yet, another "Annals of Radiation," with the subtitle "Calamity on Meadow Street." "Calamity on Meadow Street" makes *A Nightmare on Elm Street* look more like *Miracle on Thirty-fourth Street*. In it, Brodeur detailed the vast number of illnesses that have befallen a tiny community situated around an electrical power line substation. Ailments ranged from brain cancer to kidney ailments to miscarriages to a wide variety of birth defects to epilepsy to suicide. It's a huge article, so he could retell the story of the cluster of child-cancer deaths in Fountain Valley, California, and he even allowed himself a Hitchcocklike walk-on with one of the local physicians saying he'd read "an article in a women's magazine about a study showing cancer in children who lived near high-current power lines."[122]

Brodeur also told of Montecito Union School in Montecito, California, where the cancer rate was "at least a hundred times what might have been expected."[123] In fact, he was later forced to admit that he had wrongly calculated and that the odds ratio was more like fifteen times.[124] He insisted that this was still tellingly high, but recall from Chapter 3 California Department of Health Services epidemiologist Dr. Raymond Neutra who advised that before someone goes off in "hot pursuit" of a cancer cluster in a neighborhood, the relative risk should be very high, for example twenty or more. This time around, Brodeur decided he needed to get really graphic to scare his readers. So he treated them to the niceties of brain cancer surgery. One victim he quoted as saying, "He removed my forehead bone in two pieces and took out a meningioma—a generally nonmalignant but often fatal tumor—which was the size of a small grapefruit and had got entangled in my optic nerves and stretched them out as fine as ribbon. In order to take out the tumor, he had to sculpt out a small piece of my brain." Brodeur's relaying of the details goes on and on, literally *ad nauseam.*[125]

In early 1992, Trial Lawyers for Public Justice, a group which has also sought to cash in on dioxin fears, filed suit against two Connecticut utility companies on behalf of one of the women whose cancer was chronicled in Brodeur's article.[126] The article also prompted another accolade for Brodeur, a National Magazine Award nomination, which the journal *Mediaweek* describes as the "Oscars of magazines," with which "the industry demonstrates why we should read magazines and how good they can be."[127]

Yet as Brodeur admits, the epidemiologists who studied the exact data he looked at found no more cancers than could be accounted for by probability, indeed nothing exceptional at all— save perhaps for a populace scared out of its wits by Brodeur. Brodeur seemed rather puzzled, or more probably, miffed, in this article at Savitz's downplaying of Brodeur's alleged calamity to a local newspaper. Savitz also declined an invitation from the local newspaper to advise people to reduce their exposure to EMF.[128] Brodeur isn't bothered by being on the opposite side from the experts; as always, it just shows how wide the conspiracy really is.

In June of 1992, the Connecticut Academy of Science and Engineering released a report that the state general assembly commissioned in light of the publicity over "Calamity on Meadow Street." The conclusion: "There is no evidence that there are any health effects" from the Guilford power station. While the academy said there was no way to completely rule out the possibility that the magnetic waves might cause illness, the epidemiologist who headed the study said, "I can't prove that a meteorite won't fall on New Haven tomorrow, but I'm reasonably sure it won't." The *New York Times* report on the article then quoted Michael B. Bracken, professor and vice chairman of epidemiology and public health at the Yale School of Medicine, saying, "Diseases don't fall evenly on every town like snow." He added, "There are clusters of any kind of cancer," but "in Guilford, it's not even a cluster because the cancers aren't related. These are individual tragedies."[129]

Nonetheless, major magazines like *U.S. News & World Report* have bought completely into the Brodeur thesis. *U.S. News*'s 1987 article was entitled "An Electrifying New Hazard," expressing apparent ignorance on the part of whoever came up with the title that power transmission lines have been around since just after the turn of the century. The article managed also to cite numerous studies on adverse health hazards of EMF without so much as hinting that there was a single study indicating no ill effects.[130] Specialty magazines have also found a way to capitalize on Brodeuresque fears. The April 1991 cover of *Radio Electronics* featured a magnetic field meter on its cover to illustrate its enclosed article on how to build the devices. Concerning the dangers of magnetic fields, it recommended Brodeur's articles in *The New Yorker*.[131]

## WHAT TO DO IN THE MEANTIME?

Ironically, the two solutions that occur to most people to protect against EMF exposure may not only be worthless but actually harmful. One is to increase the height of power lines. The problem with this is the studies, including the NYSPLP study of Savitz and the Los Angeles one, that indicate that low levels of exposure could be more harmful than higher ones. That applies also to the advice that some have given on placing appliances farther away from one's body (the electric clock next to the bed, for example). Notes Raymond Neutra: "There's a possibility that by moving away from something you make it worse."[132] That seems a very strange concept, because the standard rule for things that harm the body is more is worse. If a little arsenic makes you sick, more will kill you. If a little of some chemical may give you cancer, a lot of that chemical has a much higher chance of giving you cancer. But, explains Nair, our conception of what causes cancer is based on our observation of chemical and radiation inducers. Assuming EMF are harmful, they would be inducing harm in a completely different way, by interfering with the timing of certain cell operations rather than by tearing apart molecules as carcinogenic chemicals and ionizing radiation do. "Therefore," says Nair, "it's perfectly understandable that [harm to the body caused by EMF] won't be linked to intensity of the field."[133]

The other "solution," which has already been implemented in a few areas, is the frightfully expensive one of burying cables.

George Koodray, spokesman for Jersey Central Power and Light, says it has been calculated that burying all of that utilities' above-ground power lines would cost about $100 billion. The extra costs, he explains, result from a need for extra wire, oil pumps to dissipate heat, removal of vegetation, higher labor costs, more costly splicing, soil erosion control, and a considerably more onerous application procedure due to environmental concerns. The $100 billion is a worst-case figure, since it includes lines that are out in the middle of nowhere and that perhaps nobody would insist be buried. But consider that the company's total assets, according to Koodray, are less than $2 billion.[134] This is a company that serves one part of one state in the country. It is easy to see why Eleanor Adair speaks in terms of trillions of dollars of expenditures for a national program.

But costs aside, burying cable for health reasons is sheer folly. The growing consensus among scientists is that electric fields are pretty much off the hook, although the studies continue. Neither the NYSPLP study nor the Los Angeles study found increased risk for exposure to electric fields. It is magnetic fields that are suspect. But while soil will block electric fields, it does not stop magnetic ones. Burying cable to protect from magnetic fields is like wearing a vest made out of paper to protect against bullets. (Some have suggested that encasing the underground wires in a pipe containing petroleum can effectively block the magnetic fields. But such piping would be terrifically expensive and would allow petroleum to escape into aquifers each time someone accidentally broke into the line.) Indeed, burying cables may be worse than nothing, because if a cable is strung overhead, it is at least twenty-two feet off the ground and that's the closest you can get to it. If it's buried, it may be as little as two feet under the surface of the soil, and that's how close you will get to it.[135] Thus people outside of and inside of houses will find themselves exposed to higher levels of magnetic fields—though again it must be emphasized that we don't know if higher levels are necessarily better or worse. Something that we do know, however, is that buried power lines are much more likely to be disrupted than overhead ones and are more difficult to repair when they are. "We all take electric power so much for granted," one power company spokesman told me, "that we don't realize that people die because of power outages." Nair says sardonically that the only "advantage" to burying cables is "out of sight, out of mind."[136]

Indeed, some utilities officials and others seem to suspect that much of the clamor to have utilities bury or move their lines is simply a matter of aesthetics. Said Hamilton S. Oven of the Florida Department of Environmental Regulation: "The people who don't want it in their backyard will latch onto anything to get it removed." At the time he said that, a campaign was being waged against a power line running through pristine wilderness in New Mexico and the opponents said they were prepared to use the health argument.[137] Did they fear squirrel leukemia, perhaps?

## ONCE MORE, "ERRING ON THE SIDE OF CAUTION"

Brodeur concludes *Currents,* saying: "The *de facto* policy that power lines, electric blankets and video display terminals should be considered innocent until proven guilty should be rejected out of hand by sensible people everywhere. To do otherwise is to accept a situation in which millions of human beings continue to be test animals in a long-term biological experiment whose consequences remain unknown."[138] He is joined by David Carpenter, an official with the New York State Department of Health, whom author Gary Null quotes as saying the studies on EMF "are sufficiently worrisome that we should begin to change the way we wire our homes and not delay for another five to ten years for additional epidemiological studies."[139] Note once again the old cry of "No time for studies, let's act!" And note once again the ubiquitous "E" phrase, with Brodeur writing, "A far wiser policy with regards to the potential hazards of electromagnetic fields would be to let the existing data speak for themselves—indeed, to err on the side of caution by assuming that they are valid."[140]

The problem is, industry will *never* be able to prove EMF safety beyond Brodeur's reasonable doubt. He's using the same "impossible threshold" tactic that food irradiation opponents use when they call for a ban on the process "until all outstanding doubts are fully resolved," with "fully resolved" being defined not by scientists but by irradiation opponents. Dr. William Clark, in his classic 1981 essay "Witches, Floods, and Wonder Drugs:

Historical Perspective on Risk Management," wrote: "The Inquisition asked, 'Are you a witch?' and proceeded to examine the evidence to see if you were. Today . . . we ask 'Is this a risk?' and proceed accordingly. In neither case is there any conceivable empirical observation which could logically force an answer 'No!' "[141] There cannot be, because those who are prosecutors, and then set themselves up as judge and jury over what is "beyond a reasonable doubt," will never be satisfied. They demand the logical impossibility of proving a negative. If a hundred tests come back negative, they can always insist on test 101 because, theoretically, that one might be positive.

But, writes Null, "science, and much of society for that matter, is all too ready to ignore things that it fails to understand."[142] Most of "society" wouldn't call spending $15 million a year on studies "ignoring," it is simply a matter of refraining from spending perhaps hundreds of billions or trillions on something *simply* because we don't understand it. To be fair to Null, he doesn't call for spending the money; in fact he doesn't call for spending anything at all. But as is so often the case with environmentalists, he doesn't like to talk money. Instead, he offers some simple hints for self-protection, which include wearing "a Teslar watch, which collects destructive waves of extremely low frequencies, converts them to an eight Hz field (the pulse of the Earth's natural field), and surrounds you with the eight-Hz cocoon to protect you from other electromagnetic fields."[143] Yes, and the watch will be delivered to your door by a little green man in a shiny suit.

On the other hand, M. Granger Morgan and Indira Nair do deserve to be taken seriously. The data, they say, just don't justify drastic action. Instead, they suggest we employ what they call "prudent avoidance." Morgan and Nair note that "many citizens, regulators, and public health officials—and even some utility officials—have become unwilling to settle for public education programs. They urge that steps be taken to modify exposures." But, they counter, "since we do not know if fields pose a risk, the prudent action is to keep people out of fields when that can be done at modest cost. But expensive controls should be avoided since we do not know if they would be beneficial." They go on to chide the legal and regulatory system, which they say "tends to force everything into one of two categories: safe or hazardous."[144]

Carstensen, for his part, thinks that even "prudent avoidance" is going too far; that based on the evidence it makes no more sense to take slight or cheap steps to avoid EMF exposure than it does to avoid black cats crossing one's path.

If it isn't exactly clear what strategy we should take regarding possible risks of EMF exposure, what is clear is that it would be easy to overreact and that this potential threat must be looked at in the same way we look at all real and potential threats—in perspective. Write Morgan and Nair: "Many forget that all of us face thousands of risks every day and that life is inherently a process of balancing and trading off those risks." They add:

> Even if fields are involved in 10–30 percent of childhood cancers in the United States—as David Carpenter of the School of Public Health of the State University of New York in Albany has publicly speculated they might be—the risk faced by most children would be small. The average child has about a one in 10,000 chance per year of developing leukemia. Even if 30 percent of this figure came from field exposures, that would be an average individual risk of only about one in 33,333 per year—far smaller than the other hazards children face.

"Without minimizing the importance of every life," they conclude, "it is important to keep a sense of perspective."[145]

David Savitz in his previously discussed open letter went on to say: "If the risk really were 1.5 to two-fold greater among persons with elevated magnetic field levels, the risk would be 1.5 to two cancers in 10,000 children per year. . . . this would be very important, but minor relative to childhood injuries or risks from known cancer hazards to adults such as cigarette smoking or asbestos exposure."[146]

The bottom line, then, is that by the time one ends up multiplying the *possibility* of EMF causing cancer in children by the *probability* that it would if indeed this turned out to be the case, we must live in a very safe country indeed to be very worried about such risks and a very rich one to want to spend vast amounts of money to reduce that risk. The bottom line, too, is that persons who refuse to buy houses near power lines or transformers, or cities that spend millions of dollars to bury electric lines, have been reading too many *New Yorker* articles and been engaging in too little risk assessment. Yet, it does appear that when people realize that they themselves will have to pay those costs, whether through taxes or increased power bills, a bit of sanity returns. The Boulder power line mentioned at the beginning of this chapter will remain unburied. The city told the residents that if they were so worried they could form a special district and pay the cost themselves. "No way!" said the residents. And the mayor said the same. "Spending millions of dollars on undergrounding the line, when there are some real ambiguities about the research in terms of documented health risks, was not something I could do," he said.[147]

Just so, if each time we considered X billions or trillions of dollars to alleviate any perceived problem, be it with dioxins, types of air or water pollution, or EMF sources, we instead considered the good that this same amount of money would do elsewhere, it is quite possible that the environmentalists might realize it isn't worth all that to eliminate the last quadrillionth of this or the theoretical one cancer in a million caused by that. It is a sobering thought that per capita medical spending in Africa is about $2 a year and that as a result millions of Africans die yearly from such ridiculously curable diseases as diarrhea. It's also sobering to know that our own nation may soon face new epidemics of childhood diseases because the cost of vaccinations have skyrocketed in recent years and parents and communities can't afford them. The $5 million it could cost to bury a small stretch of power line that will quite possibly save zero lives could be spent to vaccinate every child in the area around that stretch of power line with every vaccination he or she could possibly need, which in turn would protect unvaccinated children from infection.

In any case, what actions should be taken to reduce mortality and sickness from EMF will have to be determined on the basis of the studies done and those yet to be done, and on good science and good policy, which in turn is based on cost-benefit schemes. Terrifying the hell out of readers or viewers with talk of children with "unexplained" brain cancer when in fact *all* brain cancer is unexplained, painting utilities as devils, accusing the scientific community and utility companies of engaging in a massive cover-up—none of these leads to intelligent policy. They are good for putting money into one's pockets, they are good for TV ratings and magazine sales, they are good for building a reputation as a crusader who happens to lack a cape—but they are very bad for people.

# CHAPTER 8

# A Fairly Brief, Nonboring Lesson in Risk Taking

Of what are Americans fearful? Nothing much, really, except the food they eat, the water they drink, the air they breathe, the land they live on, and the energy they use.[1]

—Mary Douglas and Aaron Wildavsky, in *Risk and Culture*

It could be a scene from a modern horror movie. It's 1989. A man is lying out on the beach, using only a factor-two sunscreen. He's drinking Perrier mixed with apple juice, eating Chilean grapes, and flirting with a beautiful woman with whom he will later have sex. Can you hear the ominous background music? Death looms in every corner—skin cancer from tanning, other cancers from the benzene in the Perrier and the Alar in the apple juice, AIDS from the tryst with the woman.

Or so it would seem if you are not familiar with the concepts of odds and of relative risks. In fact, there are a lot of folks out there who are trying to tell you how to run your life who do not understand these concepts themselves. Others do understand them but hope that you do not.

I do not propose an objective standard to rate risk, as some have. There are too many subjective considerations in any risk-rating scheme for that to be possible. Nevertheless, as Mary Douglas and Aaron Wildavsky note: "Since an individual cannot look in all directions at once, social life demands organization of bias.

People order their universe through social bias. By bringing these biases out into the open, we will understand better which policy differences can be reconciled and which cannot."[2]

Following are some of the specific tenets of odds and risk taking that can help us to organize our biases. They will be followed by fallacies that confuse the process. Finally will come some general rules that help us pull everything together.

*Tenet 1: Everything is a gamble, and everyone is a gambler.* You may never have stepped inside a casino or played the lottery, but you are a wagerer nonetheless. In fact, you spend much of your day gambling; you just don't think of it that way. Most people, for example, don't think they have enough time in the day and consider their time a scarce and precious resource. Therefore, anything they do in that time is a gamble that there isn't something they would rather be doing. Your reading this book is the result of a gamble that this would be a more productive use of your time than the other things you could be doing—mow the lawn, call your mother-in-law to wish her a happy birthday, clean out the attic.

Some gambles, obviously, are much more important. Yet even these we engage in constantly. To cross the road is to gamble that a crazed driver who has just watched the 1970s cult film *Death Race 2000* is not prowling the streets of your town looking for that big score. Every year thousands of pedestrians are mowed down, and most of them never considered crossing the street to be a gamble, never thought the words "road kill" would appear on their death certificate.

Marriage is one of the most important gambles you will ever make. When you propose or accept a proposal you have gambled that this is the best you can do, that no one else will come along who will have that same combination of nice things and tolerable not-so-nice things that you seek in a mate. Sometimes you win but sometimes you end up singing to a third party, "Where were you when I was falling in love?"

A classic gamble in which most of us engage is called insurance. With life insurance, for example, you gamble that you'll die during the course of a policy or early enough in a policy for your premium to pay off. The insurance company gambles that by the time you grow angel wings, what you will have paid in premiums, together with the interest on those premiums, will amount to more than they will have to pay out. Incidentally, you usually lose on insurance gambles because if you didn't, insurance companies couldn't stay in business. That's why it doesn't pay to buy insurance unless you really need it and why you should always get the highest deductibles you can afford.

*Tenet 2: Many gambles involve the possibility of death.* It is part of the risk-free society's value system (more on this peculiar institution later) that nothing is worth the risk of death. Often this is expressed in dramatic either/or terms as in the formulation "Is getting a tan worth dying of cancer?" or "Is a few moments of pleasure from sex worth losing your life?" or "Are pesticides worth getting cancer?" The answer may well be yes, if the odds are good enough. Every time we hop in the car, take a walk, or eat salmon pâté, we are assuming a real, if small, risk of death.

Consider the following two scenarios: (1) You park your car across the street from the hardware store, where you plan to purchase a smoke detector for your house, when a huge semitruck carrying smoke detectors runs you down. (2) You are at the all-night convenience store, the kind that is robbed three times a week and four times during the holidays, attempting to buy condoms to practice "safe sex." Unbeknownst to you, it is in the process of being robbed when you vociferously complain that the store has run out of the brand of prophylactics that have a stick of bubble gum in each pack. (Hardly worthy of a complaint, since it's the same nasty gum that is in trading cards packages.) The robber, a veritable bundle of nerves who probably also doesn't appreciate the need for bubble gum sticks in condom packages, promptly brings your problem to an end forever.

It is this "nothing is worth even the possibility of death" fallacy that fuels so many of the false environmental debates. Whether it is pursuing the last molecule of dioxin or the last fiber of asbestos, it simply ignores the reality that we encounter each day more objects capable of causing death than you'll find in all the Agatha Christie novels combined.

*Tenet 3:* Something *is going to kill you.* The chance of dying is close to one hundred percent. Granted, Catholics believe the Virgin Mary ascended directly to heaven, and the Old Testament of the Bible says Elijah did as well, but that's pretty heady company to aspire to. And remember, too, poor Lazarus had to die twice.

So far, there is no cure for death. Some day the President may declare a "war on death" and create a Cabinet-level position to oversee it. We could then get Jerry Lewis to host a yearly telethon admonishing us that "death can be cured in your lifetime." Until then, however, we'll just have to accept it.

But wait, it gets even worse.

*Tenet 4: Anything can kill you.* No, not *practically* anything, but *anything*. Witness the following death circumstances as collected by the authors of *The Book of Lists* and *The People's Almanac,* Irving Wallace, David Wallechinsky and Amy Wallace. Zeuxis, a fifth-century Greek painter, laughed so hard at his own painting of an old hag that he broke a blood vessel and died. Claudius I of Rome choked to death on a feather which his physician shoved down his throat to induce vomiting after Claudius's wife served the emperor poisoned mushrooms. Detective Allan Pinkerton accidentally bit his tongue and died of gangrene. Jerome Napoleon Bonaparte, the last American Bonaparte, died of injuries sustained when he tripped over the leash of his wife's dog in New York's Central Park.[3]

Nothing is so irrelevant or innocuous that it cannot kill you. Pick anything. Pick your teeth. The *New England Journal of Medicine* reported on a case a few years back in which a man accidentally swallowed a toothpick and suddenly died as a result of it six months later when it perforated his intestine.[4] A quicker death was suffered by Agathocles, Tyrant of Syracuse, who choked to death on a toothpick in 289 B.C.[5] In Tampa, Florida, a dairy delivery man received his just deserts when he was crushed to death under a rack of Nutty Buddies.[6]

And just as nothing is completely safe, no *place* is either. How about the bathroom? People slip and fall in tubs and break their heads and necks. They dry their hair with a blow dryer while sitting in the bathtub, drop the device, and deep-fry themselves. Toilets are notorious as instruments of death. Many heart attacks occur on "the throne." The King himself, Elvis, met his maker in the bathroom, albeit not on the toilet.

It's enough to make you never want to get out of bed—but

you're by no means safe there, either. If the toilet is one favorite place for heart attacks, the predominant site for coital activity looms as another one. Coitus itself, we are often reminded, can prove fatal. A few years ago, an obese man was having sex with a woman on a piano with a hydraulic lift. By accident the piano began to rise and while the woman was able to scramble off in time, the man was crushed. And he probably thought the worst that could happen was herpes. Yet, one can die suddenly alone in bed as well. One Thornton, Colorado, man was sleeping in the basement of a house when an occupant of the floor above him dropped a revolver, which discharged sending a bullet into the sleeping man's head. He survived, but talk about rude awakenings!

*Tenet 5: Practically nothing is guaranteed to kill you.* But now the news starts to get better. If it's true that anything can kill you, virtually anything is survivable as well. People have been shot full of more holes than swiss cheese and stabbed more times than a pin cushion and have lived to tell of it. There are cases on record of persons falling thousands, even tens of thousands of feet, and surviving without the use of a parachute. Cancer patients given but weeks to live have gone into remission and lived full lives. Rasputin consumed poisoned tea cakes and wine, and was shot twice, but only died after being bound and thrown into the Neva River where he drowned.

*Tenet 6: The chance of injury is high but dropping. The chance of illness is dropping.* According to the National Safety Council's booklet *Accident Facts:* "While you make a 10-minute safety speech, two persons will be killed and about 170 will suffer a disabling injury. Costs will amount to $2,700,000."[7] This ought to discourage anyone contemplating making such a speech!

Still, in terms of accidents, America has definitely become a safer place in which to live. Between 1912 and 1988, accidental deaths per 100,000 people were reduced 52 percent, from 82 to 39. It would have been a much greater reduction, but automobiles have helped take up the slack. The reduction in the overall rate has resulted in 3 million fewer people being killed accidentally.[8]

Likewise, the incidence of life-threatening disease has dropped dramatically. A revealing statistic is that if the mortality rates from 1940 applied to 1988, 4 million Americans would have died in 1988. Instead, 2.2 million died.[9] This is something to think about when you hear that the use and manufacture of toxic chemicals, dangerous machines, and nuclear materials in the postwar period has turned life into a veritable minefield.

*Tenet 7: People affect their own odds.* Death on a two-lane highway is as close as giving the steering wheel a sharp tug to the left in the presence of an oncoming car. But how do we deal with that? We don't give the wheel that tug. This introduces the concept of creating one's own odds.

Sometimes there is little you can do about your odds one way or another. If cancer runs in your family, you have a higher chance of contracting cancer than the national average. If it doesn't, your odds are lower. But if you smoke, drink, and overeat, you considerably increase your chance of cashing in your chips before your game of life was biologically determined to end.

## RISK EVALUATION FALLACIES

*Fallacy 1: People feel more comfortable when they are in control of a situation and their perception of that control tends to be exaggerated.* This is probably one reason why so many of us dislike flying, including those of us who do it frequently. But one common misperception people have is an exaggerated idea of the degree to which they are in control of situations. First, we all make mistakes. Most of the time, depending on the activity, the mistake is not harmful. Lose control of your car because you spilled hot 7-Eleven coffee on your lap and chances are you will still regain control before hitting anyone or getting hit. But eventually these things catch up to you and you lose control and an accident does occur. Second, even if you're in perfect control, something may happen to you that is unavoidable. You can be a stunt driver for the latest installment of *Smokey and the Bandit,* but if that drunk driver jumps the meridian and smashes sideways into your car, your sheet metal will crumple just like anyone else's. Finally, you just may not be as competent as you think. Lousy drivers all have one thing in common besides being lousy drivers—they all think they're good drivers. And who among us has not heard the drunk person say he drives better with a little alcohol in his blood?

Perversely, we often prefer a risk we control that threatens our lives far more than factors beyond our control. Thus, many of the same people who are terrified of pesticides, power lines, and video display terminals that might have anywhere from a chance in a million to zero chances of causing cancer will not take a second to buckle their seat belts, even though this can halve their one in five thousand chance of dying horribly in a car accident.[10]

*Fallacy 2: People tend to apply a grandfather clause to risks. Old risks are considered much better than new risks, even if the old risks are much greater.* Alcohol is a proven human carcinogen, while benzene is strongly suspected of being one. In 1990, a North Carolina laboratory found that bottles of Perrier contained about 14 to 20 parts per billion of benzene.[11] So Perrier went back to the store. The company recalled 72 million bottles and shut down its business while it cleared up the contamination problem.[12] Instead, fizzy water connoisseurs settled for Canada Dry for a while, took that home, and mixed it with their gin. Gin, at 80 to 94 proof, is at least 40 percent alcohol. In other words, gin contains 400 million parts per billion of a known carcinogen, alcohol. Not to mention the nasty things alcohol does to brain cells, livers, and little children who end up under the tires of cars driven by drunken drivers.

Consider another example, the woman who only buys expensive pesticide-free vegetables, refuses to go within five feet of a video display terminal, and has thrown out all the electric blankets in the house but continues to drink or smoke. We all know the type. People make peace with old hazards. We have made peace with automobiles. We think little of their toll of more than forty-five thousand dead per year. We make peace with cigarettes, which take hundreds of thousands of lives per year. Radiation from nuclear power plants is relatively new, however, even compared with the automobile. For this and other reasons, the mere possibility of any loss of life owing to nuclear plants is considered an utter horror.

We spend much of our time pursuing trace amounts of modern chemicals like dioxin that, so far as we know, have killed no one, even while we continue to gulp down alcohol, puff away at cigarettes, and clog our arteries with fat. Those are enemies, but they are old ones. We became used to them all long ago. But the presence of pesticides on vegetables in parts per quadrillion or dioxin in water at parts per quintillion—now *that's* considered terrifying.

*Fallacy 3: Outrage may be a factor in assessing risk.* As shown repeatedly in this book, there appears in many humans an ever-ready willingness to blame all mysterious health problems on industry and government. One audience member on *Donahue* typified the attitude. "I live near Starrett City," he said, "and I never had sinus [*sic*], and now since I moved there, because they got the dump, I got sinus."[13] We may not know what "sinus" is, but the point is made. Recall, also, the family in Chapter 7 who originally thought that herbicides must be responsible for their child's cancer but then settled on electric and magnetic fields from a nearby power line. The idea that anything other than industry could have caused the cancer didn't even occur to them.

*Fallacy 4: There seems to be a human need for fear. No matter how safe we may be as a society, we will always find new things of which to be afraid.* Comments Nicholas S. Martin, executive director of the Consumer Health Education Council: "Paradoxically, the healthiest people in history live in constant fear of death."[14] Fear seems to fill a certain psychological need in many of us. Take away major fears and we will replace them with minor ones and elevate them to a major level. Columnist George Will has stated: "Only man is perverse enough to feel most alive when the news is most lurid."[15] Likewise, fear seems to make some of us feel more "alive," just as soldiers report that they feel most alive when they are under such heavy fire that they feel like "goners." Fear can also be a pleasant alternative to boredom.

Whatever the psychological underpinnings, as science continues to eliminate more and more visible threats, society feels a need to exaggerate those threats that remain. This helps explain why a Lou Harris poll taken in 1980 indicated that twice as many people in the general public thought there was more risk in society than twenty years earlier,[16] even though the opposite was true. As the visible threats recede, we always manage to find "hidden" ones—hidden both in the sense that they may have been there for some time but only just now have been discovered, and in the sense that they may damage us unawares. Thus, while our ancestors sat around the cave fire boasting of how they protected their household from a saber-toothed tiger, and our more recent ones might have done similarly with a tale of a marauding bear, an article in *Good Housekeeping* was entitled "How I Saved My Family from Asbestos Contamination." Man against microscopic fiber: the ultimate battle.

People in poor countries do not share our worries about parts per quadrillion of pesticides; they worry about starving to death for lack of pesticides. You wouldn't find mothers in Ethiopia or Bangladesh dumping applesauce down the drain because it contained Alar. Indeed, they would be aghast at Americans doing such a thing. Cancer is almost certainly not a big worry in those countries. Cancer there essentially means you survived enough bouts of famine and contagious diseases to make it into old age. Cancer is another way of saying you were lucky. What has been dubbed the "risk-free society," that is, a society engaged in an endless effort to reduce all levels of risk to zero no matter what the trade-offs, is an outgrowth, albeit not a necessary one, of affluence.

Many of the health hysterias in recent years have had their roots in the risk-free society. This obsession is only of very recent vintage and seems to be stronger in the United States than in other developed countries. The late Henry Fairlie, writing in the *New Republic,* contrasted the nation's reaction to the deaths of three astronauts in the first *Apollo* spacecraft with the deaths of seven astronauts in the *Challenger* space shuttle nineteen years later. In the first instance there was a congressional hearing and some delay, but "the Apollo program went smartly ahead, with the full understanding and support of the nation, and within eighteen months Apollo 11 landed on the moon, ahead of the deadline set by John Kennedy." After *Challenger,* "the prevailing mood in America so panicked NASA that it took almost three years to send up another shuttle." Commented Fairlie: "In the 19 years between those tragedies, the idea that our individual lives and the nation's life can and should be risk-free has grown to be an obsession, driven far and deep into American attitudes."[17]

One example of such obsession was the Great Suntan Scare of '88. It began with popular news commentator Ted Koppel checking into a hospital for treatment of a cancerous condition that he said had probably resulted from a very severe burn two decades prior. Suddenly the papers were filled with stories on the evils of the sun *tan*. Doctors were quoted asking how having darker skin could possibly be worth the chance of death. Fashion designers were quoted as saying the tan was "out" and pale, white skin was "in." One would never have guessed from all this that people have been getting tans since the beginning of time, that sunscreens are better than ever, that the rate of surviving skin cancer is better than ever (Ted Koppel is alive and well), and that in the very year of the Great Suntan Scare, there was made widely available a new ointment, Retin-A, that was shown not only to reduce the possibility of developing skin cancer but to cosmetically improve overexposed skin as well.

Ultimately, the problem with the risk-free society is that in exchange for those hypothetical days we may be adding to our lives by giving up things we would otherwise be doing, we are giving up things we *want* to do. How many of us would extend our present life span by one or two years if the quid pro quo were that we would have to spend the rest of our lives in prison? What "risk-free" living means is that we are trading off quality of life for length of life.

This is not a difficult concept, yet it is one that seems to be lost on those shouting the latest alarm. If sporting a tan means a lot to you, then by all means get a tan. Just know, too, that you risk a chance of getting skin cancer from it or eventually ending up looking like an old saddle, depending on how much time you spend under the sun or in a tanning booth, on your ethnic background, and on other factors.

Just as we trade off quality of life to lengthen life, so too by spending money on eliminating environmental problems do we trade off that money for other purposes. If you spend 5 percent extra each time you buy a paper product because the paper companies have been forced to squeeze the last part per quintillion of dioxin out of their waste, that's money that you would have spent for something else. Likewise, if your power bill goes up 10 percent because the utility was forced to expand the right-of-way near its power lines and to buy up houses to do it as a result of fears of electric and magnetic fields. In extreme cases, workers lose their jobs because of environmental regulations. Ask the poor coal miners of West Virginia who were driven out of their jobs by the acid rain provisions of the Clean Air Act of 1990. This in a state that already was one of the poorest in the nation.

None of this is intended to disparage environmental regulations in general; it is merely to point out that they carry a price in terms of the quality of life and that that price must be weighed against the benefit in a rational, nonhysterical manner.

*Fallacy 5: People fear that odds accumulate, but usually they do not.* One reason a lot of us have trouble with odds is probably because of baseball. Not baseball per se, but rather baseball sportscasters. Why? Because you always hear about batters who are "due" for a hit. For example: "Rostenkowski hasn't had a hit in five games, so he's really due." It seems to make sense at first. But try it with coins. If you flip a coin for an hour or so and keep track of the results, you will make at least two observations. One, you will find that you have developed a nasty blister on the tip of your index finger. Two, you will note that the pattern of flips before an individual flip will have no effect on that last flip. In other words, you can flip five heads in a row and still the chance of getting tails on that sixth flip is only one in two. It is true that over the long run you can eventually expect to get about half heads and half tails, but that doesn't mean that a string of heads must therefore be followed by a tail on any given flip. The situation is somewhat similar with the baseball batter, except that his odds of breaking his string are even worse. For one thing, he has less than a fifty-fifty chance on average simply because no one has a .500 batting average in the big leagues. Second, the very fact that he has been hitting poorly indicates that probably he will hit poorly this time, too. Eventually he will probably break out of his streak, but probably not on *this* specific at-bat. In other words, when you hear those magic words, "He's due," it's a darn good indicator that the batter will not get a hit.

Does this reasoning apply outside of the ballpark? Sure. A driver who has gone without an accident for fifteen years, far from being "due" for an accident, is far more likely to go another fifteen years without an accident than one who had an accident just last year and is therefore not "due" to have one for some time to come. No doubt, however, when baseball sportscasters get on a bus they make sure they get a driver who has just had an accident, knowing that he is not "due" to have another for years to come.

Some odds, of course, do accumulate. Strictly speaking, the best way to increase your chance of dying of cancer is to grow old. The vast majority of cancers are in older people. Likewise with heart disease. The best way to avoid cancer is to die in the age range of fifteen to forty. That way you've skipped the childhood cancers and haven't really had a chance to move into the elderly cancers. This is just a general recommendation, of course.

*Fallacy 6: People tend to fear most that which happens least.* It is a paradox, but often those activities that carry the least risk nevertheless inspire much fear merely because they are so rare that when they occur they gather tremendous attention. You read and hear about every plane that crashes or even has a major malfunction but virtually the only automobile crashes you'll ever read or hear about are those that are local. Read the paper each day and you will hear about each and every fatal shark attack in the country and many of the nonfatal ones. Recall the Quimbys from Chapter 4. They were chosen to represent a more or less typical victimized family from the Love Canal, but if they were so typical why were they the one family getting all the press attention?

This is simply the way the media works. Dog-bites-man doesn't sell; man-bites-dog does. One would get the idea from the papers that dogs never bite men, that only the opposite is ever the case.

The most risky thing you can do in ordinary life is to drive an automobile. On an average trip, you have about a 1 in 4 million or 5 million chance of being in a fatal accident. That seems awfully tiny, until you consider the number of trips you take in the course of a lifetime. The risk of ultimately being in a fatal accident is somewhere between 1 in 100 to 1 in 2,000.[18] And we aren't just talking death here, folks. Death is inevitable, but mutilation and paralysis are not. Yet, virtually nobody ever claims to be afraid of dying in a car crash. People will refuse to fly because there are 300 or so American airline fatalities a year. They will refuse to swim in the ocean because perhaps 3 or so Americans each year end up as Chicken of the Sea for sharks. They will refuse to have a nuclear power plant near their home even though such plants in Western countries have never caused a single fatality. But almost 50,000 automobile deaths a year fazes most folks very little, certainly not so much that they refuse to get in cars.

Again, this irrationality can play out in the environmental arena. A woman who doesn't put her child in a car seat for short trips will nonetheless show up at a town meeting, tears streaming down her face, as she demands that the local utility move the power line away from her house so that the child won't get leukemia. A custodian who smokes heavily will nonetheless demand that the building he tends have its asbestos removed, even though by giving up smoking he could not only dramatically reduce his chance of contracting lung cancer, emphysema, or numerous other diseases but probably eliminate even the tiny chance of getting asbestos-related disease.

*Fallacy 7: You can't personalize risk.* Actually, strictly speaking, you *can* personalize risk. But you shouldn't. It is a worthless endeavor.

Some years ago, *Saturday Night Live* did a skit in which it was first announced that "every fourteen seconds a person in New York City is assaulted." (I forget the exact number of seconds, actually, but fourteen will do for our purposes.) Thereupon we were introduced to the hapless man who, even as we looked on, was indeed assaulted every fourteen seconds.

To use a real-life example of personalizing risk, one female doctor who studies HIV-infected prostitutes has said: "It's true that in the dating situations I find myself in, the chance [of HIV infection] is slim. But it's 100 percent if you're the one who gets it."[19] Likewise, one could say, "It's true that the government says use of this chemical will cause at most one cancer per one million users, but if you're that user it's one hundred percent." John Allen Paulos cites a virtually identical statement in his book *Innumeracy: Mathematical Illiteracy and Its Consequences.* The speaker, writes Paulos, will "then nod knowingly, as if they've demolished your argument with their penetrating insight."[20] Indeed, the statement sounds profound, until one realizes that this is true of any risk-taking. How about: "It's true that the chance of being mauled by a tiger in Manhattan is slim. But it's one hundred percent if you're the one mauled."

*Fallacy 8: Odds cannot be generalized.* Probabilities often vary not just from situation to situation but from person to person. Most people appreciate this at some level. Most women don't spend much time worrying about prostate cancer; most men don't sweat out the results of their ovarian cancer tests.

But consider this. "It's hard to believe that women are safer on an empty street at night than they are in their own homes," says the host of CNN's *Sonya Live*. It should be hard to believe, because it's untrue. What Sonya has done is to extrapolate the risks of some—women who live with battering husbands or boyfriends—to the whole, women in general. No one would ever think of extrapolating a woman's chance of breast cancer to cover all people, male and female. No one would think of extrapolating the odds of a black person suffering from sickle-cell anemia to all people, including whites and Asians. Usually when the media engages in such a faulty procedure, it's trying to make a point which doesn't happen to be warranted. Men are not a bunch of women-beating thugs, whatever Sonya might think. Similarly, most of us live far away from toxic waste sites, but have been convinced nonetheless (as discussed in Chapter 4) that toxic waste sites are our number one environmental risk. In fact, of the top five risks listed by the public, all are localized: hazardous waste sites, exposure to work-site chemicals, industrial pollution of waterways, nuclear accident radiation, and radioactive waste. Broader possible threats such as vehicle exhaust, indoor air pollution, and X-ray radiation are rated far behind.[21]

## GENERAL TENETS OF RISK EVALUATION

*General Tenet 1: Risk itself is absolute but the value of all risk is relative.* Some have suggested that risk, like beauty, is in the eye of the beholder. Wrong. Beauty is truly subjective, as anyone who has ever watched a beauty pageant can attest. The judges *never* pick the prettiest woman. With risk, however, your chance of being killed or injured or rewarded by a certain activity does not change with the way you look at it. Your probability is as solid as your probability of flipping "tails" with a coin. What *is* subjective is your evaluation of that risk, *plus* what that risk may mean to you. You may think you can drive better while you are drunk, but you cannot. (Or if you can, you shouldn't be allowed on the road, *period.*) Your risk hasn't changed because of your belief, only your perception or evaluation of that risk.

Here is a scenario that tries to clarify this fallacy. There used to be an extremely popular game show called *Let's Make a Deal,* hosted by Monty Hall, in which would-be contestants dressed up like rutabagas, cabbages, guinea pigs, houseboats, and in general like idiots in order to catch Hall's attention and become players on the show. In a typical case, Hall would offer a contestant— dressed, let's say, as an artichoke—money. Let's say he offers $2,000. The artichoke could take the money or could take a choice of what was behind curtain number one, number two, or number three. Invariably, behind one curtain would be a dud—a can of Alpo or something. Behind the other two would be very nice prizes (one probably a car) worth considerably more than $2,000, which would be given to the show in exchange for a fifteen-second hyped-up description by some guy with a booming voice whom you never saw.

Now, here we go. Assuming that the show's producers didn't pull a fast one and put Alpo behind *two* curtains, the artichoke's actual odds of getting something worth more than $2,000 from choosing a curtain is two in three. This is *not a relative* thing. The guy may be as much an idiot as his costume indicates and may think that his chances are, say, five out of six of getting a good prize. Or maybe he never watched the show before and figures that there is something nice behind all the curtains. But that being the case he is simply, objectively, wrong. What is relative is his perception of those odds. If he thinks his chances are five out of six, then that is what he thinks. His *perception* is *relative.*

Now, let's say that right before he got on the show he was paid a visit by Mac the Knife, and Mac told our artichoke that if he didn't hand over $2,000 that he owed Mac in the next ten hours, Mac would take him apart leaf by leaf. By taking the money from Monty Hall, the artichoke has just guaranteed that he will live to play another day. Taking a curtain gives him one chance in two of ending up in a salad.

Now change the scenario just slightly. Mr. Knife decided to tack on an extra $500 in interest to that $2,000 debt (which was mostly interest anyway, of course). Now the $2,000 is worthless to the artichoke, who had already tried in vain to borrow money. (Would you lend money to a man who dressed up like an arti-choke?) Taking the $2,000 guarantees a painful death for our green friend. Going for what is behind the curtain gives him one chance out of two of living. Thus, depending on what Mac demanded, we have two situations in which the value of taking a risk has completely changed. This scenario shows that the value is *relative,* even though the risk itself remains identical. Unfortunately, I can't tell you what the artichoke chose. The suspense was killing me, so I switched to *The Price Is Right.*

This concept of one risk being good for one person and poor for another is called "relative risk." It has nothing to do with the possibility that your fiancée's mother could turn out to be the Wicked Witch of the West. The concept of relative risk is grounded in a very basic and obvious point, which doomsayers on a given issue fail to grasp but which by now has been drilled into the reader's head: that *everything* in life carries a risk.

Driving to the drugstore to buy a six-pack of beer entails a risk. We all have known people who have died in car accidents and at some level we appreciate that there is some danger in being in an automobile. Yet we take that risk daily because we consider it small enough to be justified by the likelihood of even such trivial gains as being able to enjoy a beer.

Basically, consciously or otherwise, we divide risks into three categories: risks that are so high that we avoid them altogether, risks that are so low that we don't even consider them risks (even though a few people may actually die from them each year), and in-between risks that we'll take only while exercising what we consider due caution. For the average person, a too-high-risk activity would be jumping from an airplane and waiting until seven hundred feet above the ground to pull the ripcord; a low-risk activity would be taking a bath (although a few hundred Americans each year drown in bathtubs); and an in-between risk would be taking a drive on the freeway—unless you're in Los Angeles and driving without a bulletproof vest, which would be high-risk. Thus, the average person would simply not sky-dive in the above manner, would take a bath without considering special precautions, and would drive on the freeway but do so cautiously.

Inherent in our everyday judgments about risk taking is the concept that the risk is not considered alone; rather it is weighed against the potential reward. Consider how many risks you would refuse to take if someone offered you a dollar to do so, but would readily accept if someone offered you a million dollars? Note that when a state's lottery jackpot increases dramatically, the number of people buying lottery tickets also shoots up, even though their risk of losing goes up accordingly. Similarly, a low risk can make a low reward tolerable. Driving to the store to pick up a six-pack doesn't sound like much of a reward considering that there is a risk of death by automobile accident, but the probability of that happening is so low that it's tolerable.

The willingness to take a risk varies not only with the size of the reward, but also with the values and temperament of the person contemplating it. What is too high a risk for some people to even consider taking is low enough for others to take. A rich man would probably never consider playing a round of Russian roulette for $10,000, but a poor man whose wife will die without a $10,000 operation might consider the opportunity a gift from heaven.

Alarmists and people subjugating science to political ends don't want you to consider relative risk in this way. Indeed, many of them haven't the slightest idea of what relative risk is. They will tell you that there is a chance that X pesticide or Y food process or Z manufactured product will give you cancer and that therefore it must be banned. That the chance may be smaller than your chance of having an airplane fall on you is utterly inconsequential to them. They want it to be inconsequential to you. That anything may end up killing you is also something they don't want you to consider. And understanding of how odds work is the last thing they want you to have. They want to be able to present you with a simple model that says that since this or that has been alleged to be harmful, it must be banned or at least heavily regulated.

Note the similarity between this fallacious thinking and the assertions by some environmentalists that synthetic chemicals shown to cause cancer in rodents should be banned while natural ones with the same properties should not. When someone says we are outraged that the government allows Alar on the market when a certain dose of Alar's breakdown product in one study on one type of animal showed that it might be carcinogenic, but they couldn't care less that our food is crawling with natural chemicals that have caused cancer in several species of animals at much lower doses in many tests, what they are saying is that they simply don't like Alar. When they demand that food irradiation be banned because it might someday be proved to cause cancer even though we know that animal testing has linked numerous other types of food preparation to cancer, they're saying that they simply don't like food irradiation. And likewise when they tell you that the negligible risk standard of as much as one cancer caused per million people using a synthetic pesticide is one cancer too many but that it's okay that one in five thousand of us die each year in automobile accidents, they're saying that to them automobiles are okay and synthetic pesticides are not. That reflects *their* values and/or *their* vested interests, those which we explored in the previous chapter and elsewhere in the book. But they may not be *your* values. In order to apply *your* values, you need to know how risk-taking works.

*General Tenet 2: In order to make proper risk evaluations, people must have accurate information.* Mind one, having proper information doesn't necessitate proper risk evaluations. We've just finished going through a laundry list of fallacies in the risk evaluation process. Still, it's amazing how, as a result of the media's love of man-bites-dog stories and as a result of politics, a lot of people have very little idea of what is risky and what is not.

Much of the problem is that other people have set before you their values and presented them as objective. If you heard someone say, "The maximum potential for harm from this pesticide has been estimated at one death per million users and this is something we should all be terrified of," you might not be so willing to jump on the bandwagon as when you hear simply, "We should all be terrified of this pesticide." But what can you do when people don't give you the whole story or when they put their own spin on the news? Sometimes, there's little you can do. But often you can read between the lines, figuring out the problems with what they're saying by what they say and what they don't say and by who's saying it. This will be the focus of the next chapter.

# CHAPTER 9

# Prejudice and Logic: How to Spot a Smelly Argument

He flattered himself on being a man without prejudices; and this
pretension itself is a very great prejudice.[1]

—Anatole France

No one can know everything about everything, though some of
us pretend that we do. Even a so-called Renaissance man will find
there are areas of knowledge about which he knows nothing. Yet
we are constantly bombarded with information and put in situations where we need to apply that information. How do we cope?

We get by through the use of prejudice. Most of us seem to
consider prejudice to be a bad thing, especially because in recent
years it has become equated especially with "racial prejudice."
But a prejudice is really just an inclination to think and act in a
certain way without having all the facts in.

The key to effective utilization of prejudice is to distinguish
between that which is valid and that which is not. At one time a
foreign product meant shoddy quality, and thus for a long time
after foreign cars had begun to surpass American cars in quality,
a lot of Americans still refused to buy them, citing a lack of quality
as their reason. That was a bad prejudice. We have already discussed in these pages many of the bad prejudices of environmentalists, such as assuming that natural chemicals are better for you

than synthetic ones, or assuming that if a business is at odds with a crusader that the business must be lying and the crusader telling the truth. Those are prejudices that have not been borne out historically or scientifically. They serve no useful function, save as a sort of propaganda tool to be used by those who want you to buy into them. On the other hand, it is a good bet that a business will fudge somewhat when discussing the safety of a given product. That happens so often that to recognize it is a valid prejudice. The problem is in not recognizing that crusaders fudge too, in the belief that their holy cause justifies the means.

Provided below are some rules governing good prejudices, followed by rules of logic. Between them, they can help you figure out situations even where you may not be an expert.

## THE RULES OF PREJUDICE

*1. Has the source been reliable in the past?*

*Example:* As discussed in Chapter 7 (EMF fields), the thesis of Paul Brodeur's book *The Zapping of America,* that microwave transmissions are harmful to people and that the threat was being covered up, proved fallacious. Over a decade later he wrote *Currents of Death,* in which he alleged that electric and magnetic fields were harmful to people and that the threat was being covered up. Brodeur, in the evaluation of his second book, deserves to be judged by his failure with the first book, especially because the topics are closely related.

*2. Regard with great skepticism any article on public health issues in* USA Today, People, *or the women's magazines.* At some point, a media organ must decide whether it wishes to provide primarily information or primarily entertainment. *USA Today* and *People* magazine, as this book demonstrates, have thrown in their lot with the latter while pretending to have the credibility of the former. As for the women's magazines, of which *People* is essentially one, one of their problems is that their writers and editors are trying to switch from the "Fifty Simple Ways to Slim Down That Figure" image to one including complicated issues like toxic wastes and cancer epidemiology. They all fall under the definition of health issues but have little else in common.

Further, as anybody who has ever waited in a supermarket checkout line knows, no line appears on a women's magazine cover more often than "What Every Woman Must Know About . . ."

The idea is that early death or heartbreak is the inevitable fate of any woman who dares to pass up that issue of the magazine. Thus, these magazines are alarmist by their very nature. This week it's what every woman must know about husbands who cheat; next week, about power lines or video display terminals.

*3. Consider what they're not saying by what they're saying. Assume they're making the strongest case they could and ask yourself: If this is their best shot, what* aren't *they saying?*

*Example:* Again, we will go to Brodeur. Recall from Chapter 7 his criticism of the government study finding no health problems at the United States embassy in Moscow; Brodeur declared that the study had underestimated the health hazard of microwave radiation at the embassy by failing to point out that the death rate—particularly from breast cancer—was extraordinarily high among women living in apartments on the third through seventh floors of the embassy during the late 1960s and 1970s, when the irradiation of the embassy had become a source of major concern to the State Department and the CIA.

He is in so many words admitting that the government study was correct, since only by drawing from a very narrow proportion of embassy staffers—those of one sex suffering from one specific type of cancer on a few specific floors during some specific years— could he demonstrate so much as the possibility of a problem.

*4. Remember that the people who are being quoted in a story were specially selected by the writer and may be completely unrepresentative.*

*Example:* During the media-generated Love Canal panic discussed in Chapter 4 (dioxin), the media presented the same few persons and families over and over, all of whom were depicted as being terrified. Those residents who thought the fuss was much ado about very little were simply not presented to the reader or viewer, or at least not until years later.

*5. Always look for context.* If someone tells you that a certain population has suffered X amount of cancers or Y amount of birth defects, remember that any population has a normal number of those diseases. If the source of your information doesn't tell you the size of the population or how much of this disease is to be expected in that population, the figures are meaningless.

*Example:* In his book on Agent Orange, *Waiting for an Army to Die,* discussed in Chapter 5, Fred Wilcox tries to make the reader think it is of great importance that "hundreds" of men with testicular cancer had joined the class action suit against the makers of Agent Orange. In fact, testicular cancer strikes most often at the age at which these veterans were during the suit (testicular cancer is the most common cancer in males between the ages of twenty and thirty-four) and an estimated twenty-three hundred testicular cancers will occur among all Vietnam veterans. That "hundreds" would join a suit and that Wilcox would relate the story of one—or ten or twenty or thirty—does nothing to prove an elevated incidence of the disease among veterans.

*6. Beware guilt established by anecdote.* Alarmist writers who lack hard data will often substitute with anecdotes. Instead of giving data to establish that Agent Orange causes cancer, you just quote four veterans who are willing to say that they believe they got cancer from Agent Orange. If you want to indict VDTs as a cause of birth defects, you simply quote a woman who had a defective child that she claims is related to VDT usage. Then throw in lots of gory details.

*Example:* Fred Wilcox, in Chapter 5 (Agent Orange) relates the story of veteran Ron DeBoer. "And even when he first began feeling ill," wrote Wilcox, "when the lump in his groin began to swell and he suspected it wouldn't go away, he [DeBoer] dismissed the articles his wife was clipping from the paper about a herbicide that had been sprayed, quite possibly, upon the area of Vietnam where he had served."

*Example:* Paul Brodeur's work in general consists heavily of anecdotes. Thus, as discussed in Chapter 7 (about EMF fields) in a *New Yorker* article titled "Annals of Radiation: Calamity on Meadow Street," he relates, in horrifying detail, the stories of two residents of Meadow Street who underwent brain cancer surgery. Brodeur has by no means established that their cancers were related to a power substation, as he would have us think; instead the horrifying stories tend to pull us away from this central issue.

*7. Do they cite sources?* Beware the disembodied source, such as "experts say." The passive voice is often used to present a disembodied source.

*Example:* A press release of the Environmental Defense Fund (EDF), stated in the passive voice: "Dioxin is the toxic chemical held responsible for the cancers related to Agent Orange in Vietnam and was found in the communities of Love Canal and Times Beach."[2] Held by whom? By the EDF, of course! To put the sentence in the active voice is to require saying *who* is holding dioxin responsible.

*8. If someone does cite sources, look at what those sources are.* Material that relies heavily on op-eds, editorials, and letters to the editor for the basis of their positive evidence (unless it's using these sources simply to dispute them) is highly suspect. Also, if they do cite sources, look to see where they *aren't* using a citation but certainly should. This is a variation of the theme discussed above at number 3.

*Example:* In his book *Design for a Livable Planet,* Jon Naar makes the terrifying statement: "At this rate, the world's tropical forests will be effectively eliminated by the end of this century."[3] There is no note at all, nor is the font of Naar's information present in the text itself. Why, in a chapter having twenty-eight notes, does Naar feel this assertion doesn't need one?[4]

*9. What are an "expert's" credentials?* "Credentials" here don't necessarily mean having a certain academic degree. The most important credentials a person can have is a good track record. Who would you rather have working on your car, a person with a degree in automotive engineering who misdiagnoses your car's problems almost half the time, or one who has never had an hour of formal training but always fixes your car right the first time? Obviously, a degree or title can be important, but also see if it's one that matches the area in which the person claims expertise. The main reason this problem arises with scientific issues is the willingness of the media to treat anyone with an M.D. after his or her name as an epidemiologist. An epidemiologist is someone who studies disease or accident patterns. He or she has had special training in both etiology (disease transmission) and statistics. The average M.D. knows practically nothing about epidemiology, having taken but a course or two on the subject way back in medical school. But often reporters, unable to get an epidemiologist to back up a dire claim, will run to another type of doctor—*any* type of medical doctor—to get an alarming statement. This is like finding that no baseball manager will predict that the Cleveland Indians will win the pennant, so instead you go to a football coach. Yet the media does this all the time.

*Example:* As noted in Chapter 4 (dioxin), Dr. Beverly Paigen, whose studies provided the only "epidemiological" evidence of harm to Love Canal residents induced by toxic waste, was not an epidemiologist at all, with the result that her findings were haphazard and worthless. But because no epidemiologist had found such apparently exciting data, the media elevated Paigen to the status of an expert.

*10. When an authority admits "I don't know," he's more likely to be an authority.* He's showing humility, which is the first step in gaining knowledge, and he's showing honesty.

*11. Newspapers and newsmagazines tend to be more trustworthy than television news.* As noted, *USA Today* is an exception, but then it is really the exception that proves the rule since it is basically television in typeset. On the other hand, don't think that the only reason television news and *USA Today* are less trustworthy is that they run shorter pieces. Articles in *The Washington Post* are often encyclopedic, but that doesn't necessarily make them accurate.

*12. Has the exponent set up an impossible threshold?* That is, has he or she required the opposition to present proof that simply cannot be presented but in fact need not be presented to establish the opponent's case?

*Example:* FIN, the Food Irradiation Network, discussed in Chapter 6 (on food irradiation), describes itself as "an informal worldwide coalition of like-minded groups and individuals opposed to food irradiation *unless and until all outstanding issues are fully resolved*" (emphasis added). In how many scientific areas are all outstanding issues fully resolved? As Mays Swicord, chief of the radiation biology branch of the Food and Drug Administration's Center for Devices and Radiological Health, put it: "I don't know of any area of public health where the evidence is completely in."[5]

*13. Are they trying to build a case for fear by simply repeating statements of fearful people?* Frequently, an article will begin with the fearful statements of several persons, then go from there without making a real effort to establish that there is anything to be afraid of.

*Example:* The Love Canal story, described in Chapter 4, consisted to a great extent of terrified people running around terrifying other people. The press set events in motion by indicating there were severe health effects from the buried waste and then kept things going by reporting on the people it had terrified.

*14. Are nonauthorities diagnosing themselves or their neighbors?*

*Example:* As noted in Chapter 4 (dioxin), *U.S. News and World Report* ran an article on Love Canal packed with victim-epidemiologists, including Marge Bates, who said: "I lost a baby after carrying her for nine months. She weighed only three pounds and was stillborn. My doctor couldn't explain why, after nine months, she weighed only three pounds. It had to be the chemicals."

*Example:* In Chapter 5 (Agent Orange) *Woman's Day* first quoted the chairman of the White House Agent Orange Working Group (AOWG), a panel of thirty-four federal scientists and health officials established in the Carter administration who review studies of Vietnam-era defoliants, saying there was no evidence of harm; then it gave the rebuttal to Lily Adams. "Lily disagrees. Ever since Vietnam, she has been plagued by illnesses that doctors found hard to diagnose and even harder to treat." The reader is left believing that surely Lily knows best.

*15. Movie and television stars should be regarded as experts only in being movie or TV stars.* In recent years, Congress, the media, and many environmentalists have decided that movie stars are authorities on all issues. It's one thing to have Ed Mc Mahon endorse Alpo, or to have Robert Urich endorse a Denver radio station, but another thing to present a star as an authority. Yet the press release for Paul and Anne Ehrlich's *The Population Bomb* touts the endorsement of Robert Redford;[6] Meryl Streep is presented as an authority on pesticides (Chapter 1); various actresses who have played farmers' wives in movies are treated as experts on farm problems (Chapter 10); and Elizabeth Taylor and Madonna are considered authorities on transmission of the AIDS virus.[7]

## LOGICAL FALLACIES

Some years ago, the Coca-Cola Company ran a very successful commercial in which singers on a hillside (aptly called the Hillside Singers) crooned about their wish to, among other things, "buy the world a Coke and keep it company." Myself, I'd like to throw the world into a formal logic class. In lieu of that rather costly scheme, I offer the following short lesson in formal logical fallacies as they apply in the context of this book.

*1. Post hoc ergo propter hoc (After this, therefore because of it).* This is one of the most common logical fallacies one sees in the pseudoscientific arena; it is a subset of a larger set of fallacies called "false cause," in which something is associated with something else because of mere proximity in time. One often encounters—in news stories or documentaries—people assuming that because one thing happened after another, the first thing caused it, as with "I was exposed to dioxin, and now I have cancer, therefore the exposure caused my cancer." Simply because something happened after something else doesn't mean that it resulted *from* it. One might as well say, "President Kennedy was shot shortly after Joe was born; therefore Joe's birth caused the death of the President." This is probably the origin of many of our older superstitions. Someone had a black cat cross his path and at some later point ill befell her. Someone else walked under a ladder and again at some point in the near future he had an accident. It's a sad reflection on society that the source of these foolish old superstitions is the source of our foolish modern superstitions.

*Example:* From Chapter 4 (dioxin): "About one hundred miles south of Debby Marano's house is Eve DeRock's valley and farm. . . . She is still sick two years after 2,4,5-T was sprayed there."

*2. Circular reasoning.* Here, an unsubstantiated assertion is used to justify another unsubstantiated assertion, which is, or at least could be, used to justify the first statement. For instance, Joe and Fred show up at an exclusive club. When asked if they are members, Joe says, "I'll vouch for Fred." When Joe is asked for evidence that he's a member, Fred says, "I'll vouch for him."

*Example:* One reason for opposing food irradiation given by Ralph Nader is that "people are rebelling against it all over the country."[8] The reason they're "rebelling" is because Nader and others like him have told them to. He's saying the food preservation process should be opposed because it is being opposed.

3. *Straw man.* Here the speaker attributes an argument to an opponent that does not represent the opponent's true position. For instance, a political candidate might charge that his opponent "wants to let all prisoners go free," when in fact his opponent simply favors a highly limited furlough system.

*Example:* In Chapter 6 (food irradiation), author and radio show talk host Gary Null cites the case of Ethiopia, in which political corruption kept food from getting to starving people. Null said: "To claim that food irradiation is going to feed the world necessarily implies that it is capable of solving all of the political and sociological factors contributing to world hunger." In fact, irradiation proponents never claimed the process could feed the world, simply that it could make a significant dent.

4. *Ad hominem.* One of the most often-employed fallacies, *ad hominem* means "to the man" and indicates an attack that is made upon a person rather than upon the statements that person has made. The classic example is: "Don't listen to my opponent, he's a communist" or "Don't listen to my opponent, he's a homosexual."

*Example:* As discussed in Chapter 2 (cancer testing on animals), opponents of the American Council on Science and Health (ACSH) will often try to discredit the organization just because it receives funds from industry. The arguments and proofs proffered by the ACSH are not even dealt with by these people.

5. *Non sequitur.* This means "does not follow," which is short for: The conclusion does not follow from the premise. To say, "The house is white; therefore it must be big" is an example. It may be a big house but there is no intrinsic connection with its

being white. On the other hand, "He's the pope; therefore he's Catholic" does follow logically. You simply cannot be elected pope unless you're a Catholic. A sequitur can either be established by common knowledge, as in the case of the pope being Catholic, or through an argument that has just been presented. "Joe has a Corvette convertible and is therefore popular with women" isn't necessarily a logical deduction; in fact it may not even be true, but it is acceptable as a sequitur. "Joe has a Corvette convertible and is therefore unpopular with women" is not acceptable, that is, it is a non sequitur, because there is no intrinsic reason why this should be the case.

*Example:* Recall the above quote from Marge Bates who said that since the doctor couldn't explain why she had miscarried, "it had to be the chemicals." Since most miscarriages can't be explained, *why* did it have to be chemicals? Why couldn't it have been a gypsy curse? Neither relationship has been established by Marge Bates's assertion.

*6. Argumentum ad populum.* A group of kindergartners are studying a frog, trying to determine its sex. "I wonder if it's a boy frog or a girl frog," says one student. "I know how we can tell!" pipes up another. "All right, how?" asks the teacher, resigned to the worst. Beams the child: "We can *vote*."[9]

This is *argumentum ad populum,* the belief that truth can be determined by more or less putting it to a vote. Democracy is a very nice thing, but it doesn't determine truth. Polls are good for telling you what people think, not whether those thoughts are correct. We are constantly bombarded with *ad populum* arguments. Often they simply reflect careful wording. Ask people if they want cleaner air and they'll say sure, who doesn't? Ask if they want cleaner air that will be imperceptibly cleaner to all except the most accurate instruments and say that you'll have to raise their gasoline prices to do it and you're going to lose a lot of those yeses. But the worst thing about *ad populum* arguments is that they assume expertise where it simply *cannot* be assumed. You don't need expertise to show that cleaner air is in general a good idea. You do need expertise to determine that making the air cleaner than it has already been made is good public policy in light of numerous conflicting considerations and that certain ways of getting the air cleaner are better than others.

Were *argumentum ad populum* applied to issues discussed in this book, the "truth" would probably be that Alar is a terrible carcinogen, that dioxin is horribly dangerous, that Agent Orange has caused many cancers and birth defects, and that America is in general becoming a more dangerous place in which to live. These beliefs simply reflect what nonexperts have been told.

*7. Genetic fallacy.* In this fallacy, you bypass the argument in favor of going after its origin.

*Example:* CBS's Ed Bradley *began* the second *60 Minutes* Alar show by attacking the credibility of Elizabeth Whelan, president of the ACSH, whom it invited onto the show to dispute the NRDC's Alar claims. Said Bradley: "Dr. Whelan readily admits her organization is subsidized by food processing companies and pesticide manufacturers, including Uniroyal, which makes Alar." Then he says to Whelan on camera: "It just seems to some people that you are supporting a chemical, Alar, and you're taking money from the people who make it; that therefore, that might influence your judgment." Yes, that's possible, but it does not address the issue at hand, which was the danger—or lack thereof—posed by Alar.

The genetic fallacy often, but not always, involves assigning motives to the opposition.

*Example:* Paul Brodeur regularly impugns the motives of those on the other side of his arguments. If they're expert witnesses in a court trial, they're only saying what they say because they're being paid. Here, as with most of the cases where one sees motives imputed, the reason may be to mask Brodeur's inability to put forth a scientific argument stronger than that of those whose credibility he's trying to impugn. Remember, also, that those who assign others' motives are usually fabricating those motives. Brodeur didn't ask those people, be they the expert witnesses or the newspaper editors, why they did what they did; he simply gave a motive to them.

*8. Either-or thinking.* This is also called the black-or-white fallacy. Essentially, it says, "Either you believe what I'm saying or you must believe exactly the opposite."

*Example:* One often hears environmentalists to claim, in so many words, "Since you don't believe that the earth is teetering on the edge of destruction, you must believe that pollution and other adverse effects that man has on the environment are of no concern whatsoever."

9. *Shifting the burden of proof.* Also known as argument from ignorance, this fallacy consists of demanding that others disprove our assertions. It is the job of one asserting a proposition to support it, not of someone else to refute it. Anything *can* be a problem; only some things are. Giving alarmists, including environmental alarmists, access to this fallacy means that the alarmists' assertions are simply presumed to be true.

*Example:* "Erring on the side of caution," an expression used by the besiegers of science throughout this book. Remember that this means *ipso facto* that the proponent is unable to prove his point. When you hear "Shouldn't we err on the side of caution?" you should interpret that to mean "I am unable to make a convincing argument; I just want you to do what I say anyway."

*Example:* In Chapter 7 (EMF fields) Gary Null is quoted asking: "Is it not time to shift the burden of proof and err on the side of caution until industry can prove to us beyond a reasonable doubt that it doesn't?"[10] It is a safe bet that utilities would never be able to prove, to Null's satisfaction, that power lines do not cause cancer.

10. *Irrational appeals.* These urge us to accept ideas at face value or on some basis other than their reasonableness. In effect, they say, "You don't have to think about this, there is no danger of error here." Included in false appeals are appeals to common sense, appeals to emotion, and appeals to authority. All such appeals are not *necessarily* irrational. They may, indeed, encourage critical thinking. But if used in the sense that they should be considered in a vacuum, then they are fallacious.

A. Appeal to common sense. This is really a bullying maneuver, designed to drag people along by shaming them into thinking you must be right because you're so confident. "Common sense" doesn't really mean a lot. At one time, it was common sense that couples having sex in the fields on Midsummer's Eve would make crops fertile, that an excess of blood—which could be alleviated through leeching—caused disease, and that exposure to a full moon could cause lunacy. "Common knowledge" has more meaning in that it simply implies something known by most people. "Sense" is a more amorphous term than "knowledge." Thus, when someone tells you to apply common sense, they're probably just saying, "Take my word for it."

*Example:* In Chapter 4 (dioxin) Lois Gibbs declared: "You don't have to be a scientist. You don't have to do a survey to find out—common sense'll tell you, there's something wrong in Love Canal." Thus, we are invited to reject the studies of learned professionals in favor of this concept of "common sense."

A close relative of the commonsense fallacy is the sneer or the smug statement. Instead of the words "common sense," you will see terms like "of course" or "everybody knows" or "it's obvious." In fact, there are whole books written about things that "everybody knows" that just aren't so. Americans all know that Marie Antoinette said of the starving French peasants, "Let them eat cake." In fact, the cake remark appeared in Jean-Jacques Rousseau's writings a few years before Marie Antoinette even arrived in France,[11] and the French are by and large unfamiliar with the story that says she said it.

*Example:* In *Time,* reporter Strobe Talbott wrote: "No respectable scientist denies" the theory of global warming.[12] All Talbott is really saying is that if you are a scientist who disagrees with him on global warming, he doesn't respect you. But the statement is couched in such a way as to simply smear that whole category of scientists whose beliefs don't match up to that of the polemicist.

B. Appeal to authority. This is a situation in which the arguer throws a big name around and expects that to be the end of the matter. There are several problems with this strategy. First, the authority may really not be one, as in the case of actors and actresses. Second, as we have seen repeatedly with the EPA, being commissioned to do a job doesn't mean one is doing that job well. Third, bona fide authorities in one area of science may not be that in another. Astronomer Carl Sagan speaking as a climatology expert is one example of this. Entomologist (a studier of insects) Paul Ehrlich speaking as an expert on human population patterns is another. Fourth, there may be authorities on both sides of an issue. All Supreme Court justices are legal authorities, but how often do all nine agree on any given case? Finally, a person may cease to become an authority over time. Peter Huber, in his book *Galileo's Revenge,* observes that Sir Isaac Newton ended up in alchemy; that Johannes Baptiste van Helmont, the seventeenth-century scientist who invented both the term and the concept of a "gas," later extolled the curative powers of magnetic forces; and that David Starr Jordan, onetime president of Stanford University and a staunch opponent of pseudoscience, nonetheless was himself a eugenicist.[13]

C. Appeal to emotion. An appeal to emotion is where the message is aimed at the gut rather than the brain.

*Example:* In Chapter 5, we saw how Lewis Regenstein tried to counter the assertion that Agent Orange does not cause birth defects by describing in horrid detail the birth defects of a little girl whose father claimed they were the result of Agent Orange. The horrible defects simply have no bearing on the assertion that Agent Orange was responsible.

Regenstein, in a nutshell, tried to do what people with weak arguments are always trying to do—pull you away from the real issues. Proper use of logic, along with knowing some of the facts, will always be your best defense.

# CHAPTER 10

# Terminal Illness: Are VDTs Killing You or Your Unborn Child?

[Clusters of disease from video display terminals] were investigated—and dismissed, in what was probably a combination of incompetence, stubborn ignorance, and deliberate denial—by nearly every U.S. government health agency.[1]

—Ellen Bilofsky, *Health/PAC Bulletin*

MISCARRIAGES AT "USA TODAY" CAUSE CONCERN, ran the headline on page one of the December 9, 1988, *Washington Post.* Fourteen women working in the newsrooms at the *USA Today* building in Arlington, Virginia, had suffered miscarriages since September 1987, the story reported.[2] It was a bit ironic, considering *USA Today*'s reputation for sensationalism and alarmism. Now the fear gun was turned on its own employees, one of whom told the *Post,* "Everyone is real frightened. You don't know what's going on. You don't know if it's over now. It's really an ordeal."[3]

As with extremely low-frequency electric and magnetic fields, the loudest ringer of the bells with VDTs is Paul Brodeur. In his book, *Currents of Death,* and in an article for the unofficial magazine of Apple Macintosh users, *MacWorld,* Brodeur has struck terror into the hearts of VDT users, especially those who are or may become pregnant.

Certainly health problems can be attributed to VDT use, and with perhaps forty million VDTs in this country, that can add up to a lot of health problems. Users have complained of eye strain,

288

irritation, blurred vision, and headaches, as well as musculoskel-etal strain and stress.[4] These ill effects can be reduced by con-cerned employers and employees through use of appropriate desks and chairs and by taking enough breaks. What Brodeur, and others, have claimed, however, is that *energy fields* emitted from the VDT are causing health problems. And that is quite another matter.

The controversy surrounds the lower bands of the energy spec-trum: very low frequency and, the subject of Chapter 7, extremely low frequency. Brodeur and others warning of VDT exposure do not attempt to implicate the higher bands emitted from VDTs, X-ray and low frequency, about which much more is known.[5] Chief among the alleged types of harm caused by the lower bands are cancer, miscarriages, birth defects, and cataracts.

## SO MUCH APPLESAUCE

In July 1990, *MacWorld* gave Brodeur ten pages of space for an article, "The Magnetic-Field Menace," along with his greatest claim to legitimacy in the area of VDTs. Indeed, the magazine went so far as to depict on its cover a computer monitor marked with the symbol of ionizing radiation,[6] prompting one radiologist to write in and point out that using the ionizing radiation symbol when there is no ionizing radiation—as indeed there is none emit-ted by a VDT—is illegal.[7] A sidebar accompanying the article gave field measurements at various distances from a variety of monochrome terminals, while an accompanying article looked at color ones.[8] Of the ten signatories to letters later printed by *MacWorld* concerning the article, the three who were health professionals all expressed disgust at the piece.[9] One who wrote in favor of it identified himself as the computer director/legislative assistant for the U.S. House of Representatives. He advised read-ers to "write your congressional representative with pen and paper," saying "It's too dangerous to use your word pro-cessor."[10]

*Time* magazine reported on Brodeur's story and said of the measurements reported in the sidebar: "The results are disturb-ing. At a distance of 10 cm (four inches) from the screen, *MacWorld* measured emissions that were, in some cases, ten times as high as those linked with cancer in children."[11] If you didn't know that this "link" was the tenuous one discussed in Chapter 7, that might sound a bit scary—at least until you think about how many people sit four inches away from their video terminal. You can barely even read a screen four inches away. That's like saying that electric lamps are extremely dangerous because if you unscrew the bulb, insert your tongue in the socket, and stand in a bucket of water, you could kill yourself or that going to the zoo is extremely dangerous because you might steal the keys to the tiger cage and throw yourself in. The point is made all the stronger when one considers that there is a dramatic drop-off in emission strength after that four-inch distance. As the accompanying *Time* diagram itself showed, the terminal used as an illustration had a field strength of 70.9 milligauss four inches to the right side but thirty-six inches to the right side it was but 1.1 milligauss.

Herbert Kohl, in a piece in *The Nation* praising Brodeur's *MacWorld* article, stated: "Three friends in the computer industry told me that Brodeur's information had been common knowledge in the field for several years and that they do keep their monitors at arm's length. All knew of people who, they suspected, had contracted cancer from spending too many hours close to the screen."[12] Kohl didn't say how his friends could tell a VDT-related tumor from another tumor. Certainly there is no doctor on the face of the earth who could do that.

The editor of the quarterly, *Health/PAC Bulletin*, told her readers in an article drawing on the *MacWorld* piece that the VDT clusters "were investigated—and dismissed," meaning there was a conspiracy of silence. She added as a nice accompanying touch two illustrations, one of a skeleton typing away at a VDT and another of four skeletons dancing around a terminal.[13] Meanwhile, the chairwoman of Citizens for Safer Electromagnetic Fields, Shirley D. Linde, suggested in the *Electricity Journal:* "Perhaps there should be a national moratorium on placing VDTs in elementary schools until further knowledge is gained."[14]

Such fears have had some businessmen licking their chops, just as was the case with pesticides, power lines, and many of the other fears discussed in this book. A variety of companies have offered monitors with lower-than-average EMF emissions, but you'll pay through the nose for them. A regular monochrome monitor can be purchased for less than $100, but one company sells thirteen different low-EMF monochrome monitors for prices ranging from $1,500 to $3,700.[15] Who would pay more for their monitor than for the rest of their computer system? Terrified people, that's who. One company selling such monitors sent out press kits to computer reporters hawking its product. "Since computer operators have an 80 percent increased rate of miscarriage," screamed its ad copy, "Safe Computing Company presents The Safe Monitor."[16] (The origin of this 80 percent figure will be discussed shortly.)

## SUPPRESSED BY THE PRESS?

Once more, Brodeur had found "a conspiracy so immense." To Brodeur, the "fact" that VDTs are so terribly dangerous, combined with a lack of the kind of newspaper coverage that such a danger would normally prompt, can mean only one thing. This time "they" is the press and the reason "they" don't want the truth to get out is because "they" have newsrooms packed with VDTs.[17] To be sure, *Time, MacWorld, USA Today,* and *The Washington Post* managed to run their scary VDT pieces without their newsrooms emptying out like rats abandoning a sinking ship, but it's also true that some major newspapers did not carry such stories. Again, the idea that maybe there is no cover-up because there is nothing *to* cover up is something Brodeur never considers.

Brodeur has two main allies in this effort to break the conspiracy of silence. First is the *Columbia Journalism Review (CJR)*, which continues to tell readers what it told them in early 1981: "If you want to learn about a health and safety controversy affecting thousands of journalists—and millions of other U.S. workers—don't rush out and buy a major daily."[18] Second is Louis Slesin, editor of the "Microwave News" and "VDT News" newsletters.

Each of these three—Brodeur, Slesin, and the *CJR*—provides the others with much of their material. It's one happy little circle. For example, in its July–August 1990 issue, the *CJR* turned its pages over to Slesin, who wrote a commentary leaving virtually no doubt in the reader's mind that VDTs are dangerous.[19] And while Slesin says it was Brodeur's earlier book, the alarming *The Zapping of America,* that got Slesin interested in EMF health effects in the first place,[20] Brodeur gives Slesin first place in the acknowledgments section of *Currents.*[21] None of this backscratch-ing would be that important except that there are so very few "expert" advocates of VDT dangers that it must be noted that these three are essentially one.

Part of the evidence that Brodeur and the rest of a handful of alarmists cite to support their case is animal studies. But here, even compared with the studies looking at EMF fields in general, there is a paucity of evidence. VDT alarmists, including Bro-deur,[22] Slesin, and *CJR,*[23] continually refer to the experiments of José M. Delgado and others in which incubating chicken eggs exposed to ELF radiation of various levels, depending on the level, "had a powerful effect on chicken embryogenesis, delaying or arresting it at a very early stage and limiting development."[24] Delgado, Alejandro Ubeda, and a third researcher published a follow-up paper which they believed supported a hypothesis that the shape of the magnetic-field pulse and the duration of the time it takes to reach peak intensity could have a harmful impact on embryos.[25] But as the American Medical Association Council on Scientific Affairs has pointed out: "Neither of these studies has been successfully replicated, and extrapolation of results to hu-mans remains doubtful."[26]

Brodeur's main weapon is the cluster study, which, as has been noted previously, is virtually always useless because clusters can be found anywhere if one is willing to segregate the data in enough imaginative ways.

Brodeur and his allies report on clusters of birth defects and miscarriages appearing all over North America, which they link to VDT use, yet which are ignored by the medical establishment and the press. According to Brodeur: "During the next two years, seven unusual clusters of birth defects and miscarriages involving women who operated VDTs were reported in Canada and the United States," after which he gives the details of some, including that seven out of thirteen pregnant women working at one airport miscarried. He then laments: "None of this, however, im-pressed . . . CDC [the federal Centers for Disease Control] of-ficials as significant."[27]

He could have included in that category the Council on Sci-entific Affairs of the AMA, which reported in the *Journal of the American Medical Association* in 1987: "No association has been found thus far between radiation emissions from VDTs and reported spontaneous abortions, birth defects, cataracts, or other injuries." It took full note of some of the same clusters reported by Brodeur, and others as well, and concluded: "Investigations in the United States, Canada, Japan, and Scandinavian countries have failed to establish a causal link between these disorders and radiation or other factors in the offices." Instead, it said, "authorities have indicated that the clusters are more apt to be chance occurrences," and that seemingly large numbers of these clusters will appear simply by chance.[28] In fact, looking at the clusters pointed out by Brodeur and others, the American College of Obstetricians and Gynecologists has noted that fifty such clusters could be expected to occur by chance over a three-year period.[29] That's far more than the VDT alarmists have been able to dig up.

Together, Brodeur-Slesin-*CJR* have brought America the story of the contracting of cataracts by five newspaper employees—two *New York Times* copy editors, two *Baltimore Sun* journalists, and a writer for the weekly *Chicago Reader*—from radiation and the attempted "cover-up."[30] Although they mention animal studies in which the development of cataracts may, by extrapolating from this to that, and assuming this and pinching that, lend some scientific color to their argument, their main evidence is that these men all used VDTs and developed cataracts at an unusually young age. The tale is told of a chance meeting of the two *New York Times* editors, of which one recalled of the other: "He looked up and said, '*You* have cataracts? I just found out that *I* have cataracts'—and we both knew something was going on." (Note the victim-as-epidemiologist fallacy.) One of these men was twenty-eight years old, the other thirty-five. To provide further buttressing of the argument a doctor, Milton M. Zaret, who has been an advocate of radiation as a cause of cataracts since 1959, is reported as diagnosing the cataracts as caused by "radiant energy."[31]

Consider the *New York Times* incident. What we are talking about here is a "cluster" of a grand total of two cases. How two sets of premature cataracts reported at one large newspaper at a time when at least twenty-three thousand VDTs were in use by newspapers[32] constitutes evidence of anything other than desperate groping for data is hard to fathom. Getting a fringe doctor to say that these cataracts fit his fringe theory is also not the best evidence in the world. And Zaret is definitely fringe. The Panel on Impact of Video Viewing on Vision of Workers discounted a report of his concerning ten cases of VDT-induced cataracts on two grounds: (1) his reports on these cases had not been published in a peer-reviewed scientific journal, suggesting that his work may not have been measured against accepted scientific criteria; and (2) only four of the ten claimed cases had significant visual impairment due to cataracts (many people have lens opacities that do not interfere with vision), and those four individuals were known to have had other exposure or predispositions that were more likely to have caused their cataracts than VDT exposure.[33] The International Commission on Illumination also rejected Zaret's claims on similar grounds and concluded that "reports of cataracts being caused by electromagnetic radiation emitted from VDUs [visual display units, in their terminology] should be considered as dubious."[34]

Neither was the AMA Council so easily convinced. It noted some of the same cataract clusters mentioned by Brodeur-Slesin-*CJR*, such as among reporters at the *New York Times* and the *Baltimore Sun*. But it noted many other things, as well. It mentioned, for example, the results of a 1982 study by the National Institute for Occupational Safety and Health (NIOSH) that found no greater incidence of cataracts among VDT users than among nonusers.[35] It mentioned testimony before the U.S. House of Representatives to the effect that while energy fields are considered to be a cause of cataracts, they were also considered to require ten thousand times the exposure one receives from a VDT. Finally, it noted that 25 percent of the population has opacities of the lens without impaired vision, and that about 4 percent of the population between the ages of thirty-five and forty-five years has naturally occurring cataracts.[36] In other words, if *The New York Times* had just two hundred workers using VDTs who were between the ages of thirty-five and forty-five, we would expect eight of them to have cataracts. Not two, *eight*. And even if there were several more than eight it would still be within the realm of statistical probability. In the above case, one of the men was below the age of thirty-five, and so that lowers the probability of his getting cataracts, but people of all ages can have the problem.

The Brodeur-Slesin-*CJR* revelation showed no more than that if you flip a coin several times you will sometimes get several heads in a row and sometimes several tails. This also applies to their observations of miscarriage clusters. When you have only thirteen people using a VDT in an office, you would expect about two noticed miscarriages, but with such low numbers you will find large swings in statistics ranging from zero miscarriages (where no one would think to claim that something in the office is *preventing* miscarriages) to several miscarriages where someone may come along and decide that something had to be responsible for that excess. It may be someone blaming the formaldehyde in the air from the insulation, the fluoride in the drinking water, the dioxin in the dirt around the building; or it could be Brodeur-Slesin-*CJR* blaming the emissions from VDTs.

Slesin, writing in the *CJR*, says of such clusters: "Basic statistics dictate that if these clusters are indeed random occurrences, they should also show up among office workers without VDTs. . . . No such clusters have been reported. Should we conclude that it takes the fear of VDTs to induce secretaries and clerks to discuss their reproductive problems?"[37] Yes, that is one very possible conclusion, that women who have heard that VDTs may cause birth defects and miscarriages who work at VDTs are reporting their miscarriages while the women who work at typewriters and *know* there's no connection to that device do not report theirs. The other possible conclusion is that outsiders such as Slesin are looking for a connection between VDTs and fetal health and not looking for them between typewriters and fetal health. Just as it is true that one can find a cluster absolutely anywhere if one looks enough, one can never find a cluster where one *doesn't* look.

## A NON-SMOKING GUN

The linchpin of Brodeur's indictment of VDTs as presented in *Currents of Death* and the *MacWorld* article was a study conducted by doctors at the Northern California Kaiser Permanente Medical Care Program. The Kaiser study, which appeared in the *American Journal of Industrial Medicine* in 1988, looked at a total of 9,564 pregnancies,[38] which it compared with matched controls. It found no significant association between birth defects and any level of VDT exposure and no significant association between low levels of VDT usage and miscarriages. Nevertheless, it did find an association between birth defects and use of VDTs more than twenty hours a week, indeed almost twice the number expected. (This is where the Safe Computing Company got its claim that "computer operators have an 80 percent increased rate of miscarriage.") On the other hand, the Kaiser researchers also noted that administrative support/clerical workers had more miscarriages than professional women.[39] Indeed, of the four categories of women observed who had less than or equal to twenty hours of VDT exposure weekly—managers/professional, technical/sales, service/blue-collar, and administrative support/clerical—all of the categories besides administrative support/clerical had risk ratios indicating *fewer* miscarriages than expected. Among managers/professionals, the number was 70 percent *less* than expected.[40] Does this mean that some VDT usage protects managers/professionals from miscarriage? Almost certainly not. What it means is that the type of job performed may be more important than whether that job happens to involve a VDT. Said one of the Kaiser authors, Robert A. Hiatt, to *Science News*: "This difference indicates that very likely something besides the VDT—physical environment, attitude toward the job, or stress—is causing the miscarriages."[41] That's a hefty disclaimer, and one that Brodeur somehow missed, even though a similar quote appeared in *Newsweek*.[42] But then, he also neglected to mention the connection between clerical workers and miscarriages. And, while Brodeur noted that *The New York Times* carried a front-page article on the Kaiser study, he did not relate that *The Times* reported that chief author of the study Marilyn Goldhaber said her "best guess" was that the miscarriages were not caused by any radiation from VDTs, largely because the amounts of radiation emitted are "so tiny," but that the more likely connection was discomfort in seating or work arrangement at the VDT or to stress related to the monotony or pressure of VDT work.[43]

Supporting the "other causes" theory, Rosalind Bramwell, speaking at an international conference on VDT safety in 1989, reported that her survey of 3,711 women who worked in the British public service found that women who worked with VDTs smoked more cigarettes, drank more coffee, and consumed more alcohol than women who did not. They also reported more menstrual distress, including cessation of menses, cramps, or irritability.[44]

To Brodeur's credit, he did mention that the Kaiser study was the very first such that had shown any adverse effects, that indeed one major study published the year before was completely at odds with his interpretation of the Kaiser research. This was an extremely large study of over 56,000 then-current and over 48,000 previous pregnancies among 56,012 women in the Montreal area, which appeared in the December 1986 *Journal of Occupational Medicine*. A current pregnancy was that which took place during the course of the study. The researchers found: "In current pregnancies, the proportion of [spontaneous] abortions in women interviewed in the first year of the study was 8.4 percent among VDU [video display units—the term preferred in Canada and Great Britain] users and 5.1 percent in nonusers." In the second year the rate among VDT users was still higher, but it was not statistically significant: "Overall, the proportion of abortions [miscarriages] was *lower* in pregnancies in which a VDU was used for 30 or more hours a week," noted the researchers (emphasis added). As to birth defects, the researchers found no statistically significant differences in defect rates between VDT users and nonusers.[45] They concluded that their data provided no evidence of adverse health effects on fetuses from VDTs. The slight elevation in spontaneous abortions in the first year of the study, they felt, was explained by bias on the part of both the women and the interviewers who knew of the allegations that VDT use could lead to such abortions.[46] The authors of the study suggested that while "the basis for [VDT] anxieties is obscure, deep-rooted fears of ionizing radiation with reports on the effects of atomic bomb exposure may be partly responsible."[47] As noted previously, VDTs emit no ionizing radiation, though many users have been convinced otherwise.

Brodeur's line of attack on the Montreal study was to blast the explanation of bias. He quoted Agent Orange researcher Jeanne Stellman saying the recall bias assertion was "specious" and that such reasoning "calls into question the validity of all census and socio-economic data, which are based on the assumption that people can be relied upon to remember and report recent events."[48] Actually, good epidemiologists *do* point out that recall bias is always a problem in retrospective studies. (And yes, it may say something about Stellman's Agent Orange studies, which were all retrospective, that she doesn't seem to know this and in fact took great offense when the CDC asserted this as a potential problem in her work.[49]) Indeed, the Kaiser researchers cited this same problem, noting in their article that "self-reporting of VDT exposure is inevitably inexact," and "recall [is] a problem."[50] Marilyn Goldhaber, in the same *New York Times* piece that related her opinion that terminals were not causing miscarriages, also said that the Kaiser results "could be entirely due" to a tendency by women who suffered miscarriages to overestimate the time they spent at VDTs as a possible explanation of their misfortune.[51] And no, Brodeur made no mention of that, either.

Nevertheless, at least Brodeur mentioned the existence of the Montreal study. By and large, other reporters have acted as if not only was the Kaiser study not an anomaly, but in fact it was the only game in town, making no mention of the Canadian or other negative studies[52]—even though it was published in at least as prestigious a publication and had ten times as many participants. This probably reflects less crusading or dishonesty than sheer ignorance that other studies were conducted, plus the old adage that good news is not news (although one writer for *Glamour* did falsely tell her readers that "a number of epidemiological studies show the same results as the Kaiser one"[53]). When the Montreal study and other studies came out showing no connection between pregnancy problems and VDTs, reporters didn't even hear about them. Suddenly a single positive study came out and all hell broke loose.

But the medical authorities have not been nearly as impressed as the popular media. A 1989 review in the *British Journal of Industrial Medicine* of all the VDT studies, including the Kaiser one, stated: "The main conclusion to be made is that there is no evidence for an effect of VDU work on pregnancy outcome, implying that either there is in reality no such effect or that if there is a risk increase it is so minor as to avoid 'detection' by the studies so far performed."[54]

Since then, the evidence has continued to come in indicating that emissions from VDTs are harmless. A large post-Kaiser study in Canada also found no association between miscarriage and VDT usage. The study was something of an improvement on earlier ones in that it broke the women down into groups depending on at which gestational period they were exposed. For no category did it find any elevated risk. The study, incidentally, spent a whole page discussing the subject of recall bias.[55]

But in March 1991 the National Institute for Occupational Safety and Health (NIOSH) released what is at this writing the definitive study on VDTs and adverse reproductive outcome. While the study did look at a large number of pregnancies, its chief advantage was its perspective. That is, it was organized before the women got pregnant and monitored them during their pregnancies. So doing, it eliminated the problem of recall bias. The NIOSH researchers enrolled and interviewed 2,430 women in the study, all of whom were employed at two different telephone companies as either directory assistance operators or general telephone operators (reached by dialing zero). The directory assistance operators used VDTs while the others did not; thus general telephone operators served as controls. The results, reported in the March 14, 1991, *New England Journal of Medicine,* were that for overall pregnancies the rate of spontaneous abortion for all VDT-exposed pregnancies was 14.8 while the rate for women with no exposure was a slightly higher but statistically insignificant 15.9. The researchers then looked at specific categories, for example women with twenty-five hours or more of VDT exposure a week versus those with none, and still found no difference.[56]

Concluded the authors:

In this study we found no increase in the risk of spontaneous abortion associated with the occupational use of VDTs. We did not observe an increased risk associated with three different measures of VDT use or with the VDT model used. . . . Separate analyses of early spontaneous abortion, late spontaneous abortion, all fetal loss, and spontaneous abortions reported to a physician also failed to identify an increased risk of spontaneous abortion associated with VDT use.[57]

But there were some factors that *were* associated with miscarriages. No, nothing spectacular like prescription drugs or a chemical in maternity clothes or something pumped into the air by a heartless factory owner. Indeed, nothing that could, directly at least, be blamed on any industry or business or employer. Both the moderately heavy to heavy drinking of alcohol and moderately heavy to heavy smoking of cigarettes categories showed an unmistakable relationship to miscarriage. Women in both categories tripled their chance of spontaneous abortion. The only other factor found to be of import was a thyroid disorder diagnosed before or during the first three months of pregnancy.[58] Other studies have found that illegal drug use has a strong relation both to miscarriage and other adverse pregnancy results.[59] By terrifying women over something that will not harm them, Brodeur and the VDT alarmists have almost certainly steered some of those women away from real risk factors. The danger to which these women was subjected wasn't VDTs, it was false information.

The world can always use another good muckraker, another thoughtful iconoclast, another man or woman who is brave enough to challenge authority. But no one is exempt from the responsibility of buttressing arguments with scientific facts. Antiscience crusaders prey on the desire of many of us to blame somebody big and faceless for our problems, on our fear of technology, on our desire to attribute to each negative effect a cause, and on our unwillingness to take the blame for our problems when we are in fact blameworthy.

So doing, they obfuscate two major problems. One is that we don't know what causes most cancers and most pregnancy problems. The other is that to the extent that we do know the causes of these, the causes are almost entirely self-inflicted. They aren't from chemical companies, petroleum companies, or power companies. They are from the cigarettes we put between our lips, the types and amounts of foods we put in our stomachs, and the alcohol we pour down our throats. No amount of government regulation and no amount of government spending can possibly counter the damage we inflict on ourselves. We may not be complete masters of our fate or that of our offspring, but we certainly exercise far more control over these than does anyone else. Many of us derive a great amount of security from the feeling that there is always someone else to blame for our problems and our ills. We eagerly bend our ears toward those who cater to this comfort. But that is a bad habit that is killing us just as surely as are the cigarettes, the alcohol, and the poor diets.

# CHAPTER 11

## Gasohol Pains

I think we could make between $20 million and $50 million [a year] from now on.[1]

—ethanol magnate Dwayne Andreas

In October 1990, the U.S. Congress sent to the President, who promptly signed, the most sweeping pollution-control bill in American history, the Clean Air Act of 1990. Parts of it will indeed help to clean the air; other parts will only clean out pockets. But few parts will do less to clean the air and more to clean out pockets than the transfer of wealth that Congress has arranged between the American motorist and one industry headed up by one man. The motorist is you, the industry is ethanol, and the one man is ethanol magnate Dwayne Andreas and his company, Archer Daniels Midland (ADM). Herein, a tale of dirty politics, dirty air, and a modern robber baron. It is the story of gasohol.

Ethanol alcohol is distilled from corn, sugarcane, or other grains, and is mixed with nine parts gasoline to create what is popularly called gasohol. Gasohol in 1990 was used primarily in the Midwest, and accounts for about 8 percent of the 110 billion gallons of gasoline sold annually in this country,[2] meaning that ethanol itself contributes less than 1 percent of what goes into American gas tanks. This, however, will soon change dramatically.

While alcohol as a motor fuel was introduced over one hundred years ago in Leipzig, Germany,[3] in recent years ethanol has acquired the reputation of a miracle fuel. Like the Greek sea god Proteus, it is able to change its form at will—in gasohol's case, to match the current national "crisis," whatever that crisis may be. During the so-called oil crisis of the late 1970s, it was supposed to dramatically reduce the nation's dependence on foreign oil. During the "farm crisis" of the 1980s, it was supposed to dramatically bolster sagging corn prices and save family farmers from bankruptcy. In the 1990s, in the earth-is-on-the-edge-of-destruction crisis, it has become a "clean fuel," capable of reducing the pollution in our major cities *and* of reducing carbon dioxide emissions, which some believe are contributing to global warming. Alas, like Proteus himself, ethanol the wonder fuel has more basis in myth than reality.

A fundamental drawback of ethanol is cost: about $1.25 to $1.45 per gallon, with gasoline wholesaling at less than half that,[4] though one would never know that gasoline was that cheap because it comes to us wrapped in taxes. (During the Gulf War crisis the American media was fond of pointing out that gasoline was cheaper than water in Saudi Arabia. They didn't seem to realize that, before being taxed, a gallon of gasoline is also cheaper than the average-priced gallon of water purchased from American grocery stores.) Considering that a gallon of ethanol produces only about two thirds the energy of gasoline,[5] (meaning it will only take your car two thirds as far), the economics are that much worse. In fact, most energy experts agree that the energy input in terms of cultivation and conversion of ethanol feedstock is about the same as or greater than the energy contained in the resultant product.[6] To make ethanol competitive, the federal and state governments have given tax exemptions of between $0.60 and $0.80 per gallon to gasohol producers, over $4.6 billion since 1980[7]—most of which would otherwise have gone into the Federal Highway Trust Fund to rebuild and maintain roads.[8] Ethanol also takes advantage of corn subsidies, over $1.2 billion since 1980, with about $1 billion of that since 1985.[9]

Moreover, the tax subsidies, by driving up the demand for and the price of corn, raise food prices. Yet the increase in the price of corn is so little that the U.S. Department of Agriculture (USDA) concluded in a study that as a farm program, ethanol is a waste.[10] The federal General Accounting Office (GAO), on the other hand, released a report in which it calculated that ethanol saved more by reducing farm subsidies than it costs in highway subsidies, but this assumed that farm subsidies would remain at their then high levels.[11] Further, tucked away in the next-to-last sentence of the report was, "However, expanded ethanol production could mean higher ethanol costs, which could increase the level of government subsidies and therefore offset, or more than offset, these budget savings."[12] Finally, the farm support program has shown an amazing ability to swallow all its allotted subsidies and keep going back to the trough for more. But even assuming the best-case scenario that ethanol could lower United States payments to farmers, it is hardly reassuring that one needless subsidy can be used to slightly reduce another subsidy, thereby allowing the supporters of either subsidy to point to the other as justification for its existence. As Congressman Sam Gibbons (D-Fla.) put it to ethanol lobbyists who apparently informed him of the GAO conclusion: "Why do we have to subsidize you to grow corn and then subsidize it further to make it into ethanol? It's got to be one of the stupidest things this country has ever done."[13]

Until recently, the glory days for ethanol producers were in 1986 when the United States Department of Agriculture (USDA) announced that it would be providing free of charge some $70 million in corn to gasohol producers from federal government stockpiles, over half of which went to ADM.[14] Taking the USDA estimate of an average of two and one-half gallons of ethanol per bushel of corn, and an average sale price of $2.40 per bushel (market price as of quotes in the *Wall Street Journal* on May 15, 1986) the value of this subsidy was $0.96 a gallon for each gallon of ethanol produced with the government corn. Since the corn is allotted on the basis of one bushel for each two and one-half bushels the alcohol producers were already going to use, the effect on producers' total supply would be diluted to a subsidy of $0.27 per gallon. This brought the total quantifiable subsidies (there are numerous important but unmeasurable subsidies, such as the import restrictions) for gasohol to $3.38 on a per-bushel basis or $1.35 on a per-gallon basis—even while corn was wholesaling at $2.40 a bushel and gasoline was wholesaling at $0.55 per gallon!

It may be something of a relief to observe that we Norté Americanos are not the only ones to have engaged in such folly. Consider the Brazilian experience. A decade ago that nation, with a $250 million loan from the World Bank, began to convert its automobiles to vehicles running on pure ethanol.[15] The use of cropland to grow sugarcane for distillation, along with heavy government subsidies to make ethanol competitive with gasoline, has contributed to making Brazil the third world's largest debtor and to its 1,000-percent inflation rate.[16] Last year, the World Bank released a study that called for the end of the alcohol program because it is inefficient and costly compared with world oil prices. Unfortunately, Brazilian manufacturers continue to turn out ethanol-powered vehicles, forcing the country to make huge purchases of over 100 million gallons of the fuel from United States companies.[17] All of which is a bitterly ironic ending to a program begun to reduce Brazil's dependence on imported fuel.[18] But they should have known better, since ethanol also had done nothing to reduce American petroleum imports in the 1970s, despite the claims of its backers.

Indeed, ethanol is such an inefficient product, it is doubtful that it would even exist as a fuel today in the United States without the massive lobbying effort of ADM, a Decatur, Illinois-based corporation, and its chairman and chief executive officer Dwayne O. Andreas. ADM, with gross annual revenues of about $7 billion, is the largest grain-processing company in the world. It also has a 60-percent share of the American ethanol market on a per-gallon basis, according to industry analyst George Dahlman of the Minneapolis firm Piper, Jaffray and Hopwood.[19]

ADM doesn't break out its earnings by specific products, but according to Dahlman, about 27 percent of its revenue, approximately $1.9 billion, comes from corn processing. About one third of that, or $633 million, comes from ethanol, while the rest comes from the sale of high-fructose corn syrup (HFCS), a sugar substitute.[20]

Like ethanol, HFCS has been around for some time but only since the late 1970s has it surpassed cornstarch, glucose, and dextrose as the primary sweetener product of corn refiners. In 1975, corn refiners produced only half a million tons of HFCS. By 1980 this had jumped to 2.2 million, and by 1985 5.2 million tons of HFCS was produced in this country. The U.S. Department of Agriculture estimated that 63 million tons would be produced in 1991.[21]

It is no coincidence that the increase in HFCS production has paralleled to a great extent the increase in gasohol production. Wet-milling ethanol plants, in which water is added during the milling process (including all of ADM's), can produce ethanol at lower cost than dry-milling ones (where water is added downstream of the milling process), in part because their facilities are shared with HFCS production. Ethanol can be produced using excess HFCS capacity during the winter when demand for HFCS is low owing to lower soft drink consumption. To this end, every subsidy, every food giveaway, every government support for ethanol is also a support for HFCS. Similarly, sugar price supports and sugar import restrictions, both of which ADM has worked for through its representatives, also support ethanol.[22] It is because of these tax breaks and import restrictions that the nondiet soda you drink is almost certainly sweetened with HFCS and not sugar, which, but for the government's interference, would be much cheaper and hence would be the ingredient of choice of the carbonated beverage producers. In other words, the government has, without ever directly having said so, told the soda bottlers that they are to put HFCS in their products. And, as will be seen shortly, they are now proceeding to tell you, without ever directly saying so, that you will put ethanol in your gas tank.

*Fortune* magazine has called ADM chairman Andreas a "fascinating executive type, a shrewd, tough-minded trader with the attitudes of a questing intellectual, the persuasive talents of a master salesman, and the zeal of a missionary."[23] Andreas has been blessed with friends in high places, indeed the highest of places. Three months before the last Soviet premier, Mikhail Gorbachev, took office, Andreas held a personal audience with him. When then-House Speaker Tip O'Neill later met Gorbachev, the Russian reportedly greeted him with "I hear you know my friend Dwayne Andreas."[24]

And like the robber barons of yore, Andreas and ADM couldn't have made it to the top without a little help from his friends in the government.

The so-called Age of the Robber Barons, from 1861 until early in the twentieth century, was a period of unparalleled economic expansion. In their efforts to build financial empires, the robber barons knew no limits, legal or ethical. Popular belief has it that those barons have become as extinct as the passenger pigeons that also thrived after the Civil War, that the Sherman and Clayton antitrust acts have put an end to such nefarious activity. But grain-refining magnate Andreas belies the belief. He has brought new meaning to the term "corporate welfare" and written a new chapter in the book of robber barons.

Like the robber barons of yore, most of Andreas's biggest power plays are committed in collusion with government officials. Back then, you'd hand money to a legislator and he'd give you a railroad monopoly. Today, attempts to influence legislators are usually far more subtle, taking the form of campaign contributions. ADM's political action committee, Dwayne Andreas personally, and members of Andreas's family have pumped more than $450,000 into the campaign coffers of various individual Republican and Democratic lawmakers since 1979. Key gasohol supporters who have received those funds include House Minority Leader Robert Michel (R-Ill.), recently retired Senator David Durenburger (R-Minn.), Senator James Exon (D-Neb.), and Congressman Richard Durbin (D-Ill.). Former Senator Charles Percy (R-Ill.) received at least $20,000 from the ADM PAC and an additional $5,000 from various Andreases. Often Andreas will fund opposing candidates in a race.

Andreas's bet-hedging also extends to the Executive Office. In 1974 he was tried and eventually acquitted on charges stemming from an unorthodox $100,000 contribution to Hubert Humphrey's 1968 presidential campaign,[25] while a $25,000 check to Humphrey's opponent, Richard Nixon, was to prove highly embarrassing to Andreas. It ended up as a cashier's check in the bank account of Watergate burglar Bernard Barker, providing investigators with one of the first links between the break-in and the Nixon campaign committee.[26]

## THE FARMER AND THE DOLE

The point man for Andreas's assault on the federal treasury has been Senate Minority Leader Robert Dole (R-Kan.). Dole sponsored the original 1978 amendment that provided a federal fuel tax break for gasohol and at least twenty-four other bills designed to promote the product.[27] For its part, ADM's political action committee and Andreas and his relatives have kicked in at least $87,000 to Dole's Senate and presidential campaign committees, more than it has given to any politician other than Hubert Humphrey.[28] The ADM Foundation also has contributed $160,000 to the Dole Foundation, a charitable organization established by the senator.[29] ADM has also provided the use of its planes for Dole's speaking, political, and vacation trips.[30] But by far the most lucrative contribution to Dole was ADM's cosponsorship (with Mobil Oil) of *Face-Off,* a daily three-minute radio debate between Dole and Senator Edward M. Kennedy (D-Mass.), in which Dole took part until he announced his candidacy for President in November of 1987. Broadcast daily since April of 1984, on over 160 stations of the Mutual Broadcasting System during prime time, the show provided Dole with a sounding board for his views that, had he paid for it, would surely have busted his campaign bank account. While Mutual Broadcasting would not give an exact figure on the cost of sponsoring the show for trade reasons, according to spokesman John Gudelanis, "a thousand dollars a day would not be too far out of the range." In addition, Gudelanis thought that the sponsors of *Face-Off* paid some of the production costs. At $1,000 a day, this unofficial in-kind contribution to undeclared presidential contender Dole over a three-year period was worth a whopping $840,000.[31]

Whatever his motivations, Dole always stands ready and willing to do ADM's bidding, no matter the interests of the nation or his state. In 1985, Dole explained to a reporter his reasoning for introducing and pushing legislation to slap an import tariff on Brazilian ethanol, saying, "I'm a farm-state senator."[32] But while it's true that ethanol production does prop up corn prices somewhat, Kansas is much more of a soybean-producing state and ethanol hurts soybean farmers since livestock feed, a by-product of ethanol production, competes with soybean meal. Such products as wet gluten feed entering the market reduce the demand for soybean meal. One USDA study found that large increases in ethanol production might cause as much as a 20 percent reduction in soybean prices.[33]

Dole's support for corn farmers via ethanol, then, comes only at the expense of his state's soybean farmers. Often, of course, farmers grow both these crops, rotating them every year, not realizing that the extra money they're making on their corn because of ethanol is depressing the price they're getting on their soybeans. Not incidentally, ADM, as a major processor of soybeans, must gain from this decline in soybean prices.

Yet the major crop of Kansas is wheat. Kansas is the nation's foremost wheat producer, and the grain accounts for three to four times the cash value of the state's corn crop.[34] And it is wheat farmers who have stood to lose the most from the Dole-Andreas ethanol protection. In 1980, Dole pursued alcohol tariff legislation against Brazil, even though, as *The Washington Post* reported, "the Justice Department, the Special Trade Representative's Office, and the Treasury Department all objected to a tariff on the grounds that it would raise costs to consumers, provoke a trade war with Brazil and grant too much market power to ADM."[35] Had the legislation been enacted, wheat would have been perhaps the first trade war target, since in the early 1980s Brazil was the world's fourth greatest importer of the grain.[36]

Despite their senior senator's best efforts, Kansas wheat farmers suffered no such retaliation. But they didn't fare so well in late 1985, when Brazilian Minister of Industry and Commerce Roberto Gusmao, with the aid of United States ambassador to Brazil Diego Asencio, made numerous suggestions whereby the United States would relax import restrictions against Brazilian alcohol in exchange for any number of possible concessions on the part of Brazil. One of those suggestions was that Brazil might buy the corn for Brazil's increased ethanol production from American farmers. Another was that it might increase its wheat allocation from the United States. Between a sudden drop in oil prices which therefore decreased the attractiveness of gasohol, and intense lobbying, the proposed deals fell through. Says Asencio: "My understanding was that this ran afoul of the objectives of Archer Daniels Midland. The minister came back crestfallen, convinced he had been torpedoed by Archer Daniels."[37]

Was Dole involved in the bargaining? Royal Daniel, a Washington, D.C., attorney who lobbied for the Brazilian government, believes he was. "How directly I just can't tell you. Dole followed very closely. ADM is one of his great benefactors, what with that 'Face-Off' show and all."[38]

Furthermore, even many corn farmers, in Kansas and elsewhere, are far from happy with the gasohol program. "The piggishness of ADM has caused a major political problem for the whole corn industry," says John Ford of the American Corn Growers Association. "The corn industry, the politics of it, is controlled by one man [Andreas], and Bob Dole is his gofer on the Hill," Ford told the *Kansas City Star*.[39]

In one of his more recent acts on behalf of ethanol and ADM, Dole, in November 1989, during a Senate floor debate on a steel import bill, blocked further action on the measure. With a recess looming, Dole offered to lift his hold on the steel bill *if* the excise tax credit for ethanol, mandated to expire in 1992, were extended to the year 2000. "Without hearings or publicity, and on just about the last day of a session," said one lobbyist, "Dole was trying to push through a seven-year multi-billion dollar tax expenditure. It was shameless."[40]

## RAKING IN THE (CORN) BREAD

For a while, ethanol proponents maintained that eventually the fuel would become competitive with gasoline. As late as 1987, commentator Paul Harvey declared that "the alcohol blends will very soon be cheaper."[41] Today, no one pretends that ethanol will ever be a viable fuel without either subsidies or mandates. But *with* subsidies and mandates it is not just viable but highly profitable.

Andreas said in 1990 he will not lose any sleep if ADM's ethanol plants simply shut down, insisting that after twelve years in the business ADM had had less than a 6 percent return on its investment—"less than all our other divisions." If they cancel ethanol, he said, "do you think I'm worrying?"[42] According to analyst George Dahlman, however, that figure doesn't have much meaning since it's all a matter of how one decides to calculate. Paramount Pictures, having been found liable to humorist Art Buchwald for taking his idea for the movie *Coming to America*, calculated that while their gross was around $300 million, they didn't actually net any money and therefore owed Buchwald a percentage of nothing.[43] Says Dahlman: "My sense is that corn sweeteners is [*sic*] more profitable than the rest of the company combined. I would put ethanol second, but not with a great deal of confidence." Further, noting the synergism between the two products, he adds that HFCS "wouldn't be nearly as profitable without ethanol."[44]

The man once known as the soybean king[45] now makes little of his money from beans. He's the corn king now, sitting atop a throne built with two commodities that wouldn't even exist but for government intervention.

With economics against him but a majority of Congress on his side, talk of the inherent inefficiency of gasohol bothers Andreas not in the least. In late 1985, even as oil prices were plummeting, ADM announced plans to increase the capacity of its four large ethanol plants from 350 million to 550 million gallons over the next two years. Estimated Andreas: "I think we could make between $20 million and $50 million [a year] from now on."[46]

Such optimism! What did Dwayne Andreas know?

## THE THIRD TIME'S THE CHARM

Crises are the godsend of scoundrels. That which they couldn't do in better times, they thrust onto an unwitting population during times of turmoil or perceived turmoil. The Bolsheviks waited for the dark days of World War I, the National Socialists for the hyperinflation of Weimar Germany. A clear-thinking, informed public would never consent to the kind of subsidies and mandates that would allow ethanol to compete, and ADM and the ethanol industry have always known this. Thus, they have always tied their product to a crisis, to times when people essentially haven't been thinking clearly.

In the late 1980s, ADM saw the future and the future was ecology. It began marketing a cornstarch additive used in allegedly biodegradable products such as trash bags. Yet, it has been pointed out that the bags are useless because they only degrade in the presence of oxygen and sunlight, neither of which exists at the bottom of a landfill. In fact, they may be worse than useless in that the cornstarch may weaken the plastic so much that manufacturers sometimes add more plastic.[47] These bags may fall apart on your curb, but if they get to the landfill they'll last forever. But "useless" is relative. The bags mean bucks for ADM and are good for their corporate image. Yes, ADM saw there was green in being green. And it set its lobbyists in motion.

ADM is generally thought to be the primary funder of two different progasohol lobbying organizations located on Capitol

Hill, the Renewable Fuels Association and the Corn Growers Association, although the groups will not release information concerning this. In the mid-1980s, these lobbying groups and others turned their guns on Colorado. The Renewable Fuels Association declared that a mandatory ethanol program in Colorado could increase national gasohol sales by 5 percent. Industry analysts noted that this alone would be a significant increase, but that Colorado could, by adapting such a program, lead to other states doing likewise and produce a tremendous boost in ethanol sales, perhaps even a tripling of total sales.[48] In 1987 a group called Women Involved in Farm Economics (WIFE) trucked to Denver from Nashua, Montana, nine hundred miles away, to hold a conference in support of initiating the oxy-fuels program. The women distributed cookies and cakes made from ethanol distillers' grain and they wore red coats as a reminder that "agriculture operates in the red," according to the WIFE president. Obviously, on the whole it doesn't, otherwise there would be no farming. Federal representation at the conference included David Lindahl, director of the Office of Alcohol Fuels for the Department of Energy, who responded to the criticism of ethanol that it could not operate without government subsidies by saying that the government also spent $10 billion on a synthetic fuels program that resulted in "not a drop of oil."[49] Compelling logic, indeed.

But on the subject of oil, where were the oil companies while ethanol was making its inroads? Surely with their massive assets, they could have countered the work of the ethanol lobby, couldn't they? Part of the explanation is that for the most part gasohol and its subsidies hasn't really bothered them that much. One oil company lobbyist I had contacted complained that while she personally was very concerned over ethanol, the companies who paid her were lackadaisical toward it. Publicly, only two of the oil companies have taken positions against the product, Amoco and to a lesser extent Marathon, although the industry-funded American Petroleum Institute has, as well. The oil companies' bottom line is every corporation's bottom line: How will this affect my profits? Even if ethanol were used in every gallon of automobile fuel pumped in this country, it would still only acquire a 10-percent share of the gasoline market, which in turn is just a portion of the petrochemical industry. At any rate, even the most drastic proposal has only called for half the gasoline in the country to contain ethanol—which would mean 5 percent of the market—and it *was* defeated. In great part, it appears that the oil companies have decided that if our elected representatives wanted to tax the public to pump money into ADM's account, that wasn't their concern.

One oil company spokesman, who wished to remain anonymous, and who did in fact make an active effort to oppose the ADM juggernaut, expresses the situation differently. Speaking of the industry in general, he says, "We don't have credibility. Very few people want to be seen as supporting the oil industry."

Indeed, through ADM's advertising and lobbying efforts, the public has been trained to think of ethanol in terms of stalks of corn waving in the breeze. Mention the oil companies and people think of the Exxon *Valdez*.

"The auto industry has visible supporters such as John Dingell [D-Mich.] and Don Riegle [D-Mich.], the gasohol industry has Dole and Durbin," the oil company spokesman said. But, he notes, there is no member of Congress who is so closely identified with the oil industry.

Moreover, he says, oil company lobbyists always look, smell, and act like oil company lobbyists. But, "ADM never shows up as the chief lobbyist. What you find instead may be the National Corn Growers. They'll lobby congressmen from farm communities. I'll talk to congressmen and they'll say they know it [ethanol] doesn't help the farmers, but that the farmers don't know that. Other groups like Coloradoans for Clean Air and Arizonans for Clean Air, which are pseudoenvironmental groups, will appeal to different interests. We know the money comes from ADM, but they *sound* like consumer groups."

"They're really good," he says of ADM. They're really inventive. They seize opportunities."

Until the 1990 Clean Air Act, the greatest success of the ADM lobbyists was when Colorado instituted an oxygenated fuel program in 1988 that lasted for two months during the winter. An oxygenated fuel, usually contracted to "oxy-fuel," is simply that, gasoline that has had something added to it to give it a slight oxygen content. Often that something is ethanol. Since then, the Colorado oxy-fuels program has been expanded to four months out of the year.

From the beginning, the oxy-fuels program has been heralded

as a great success—at least by those responsible for the program. Said then-Denver Mayor Federico Peña, under whose auspices the program began: "Something very positive is happening."[50] But it's the strangest thing, because aside from the folks running the program, authorities in air pollution who have studied the oxy-fuels program are almost unanimously critical.

To understand their concerns, it is first important to understand the theory of oxy-fuels. Most automobile air pollution happens when gasoline is incompletely burned in a car's cylinders, although some may be emitted when cars are fueled at the pump or from the gas tank. Nitrogen oxide and carbon monoxide, along with various trace substances (aldehydes, olefins, hydrocarbons collectively called "volatile organic compounds" or VOCs) spew out of tailpipes. Some of these substances, like carbon monoxide, directly cause pollution, while others, such as nitrogen oxide, hydrocarbons, and aldehydes, when cooked by sunlight, form ozone. When these non-carbon-monoxide pollutants come together and hang above a city, they form a sometimes unhealthy soup called smog.[51]

Some cities, like Los Angeles, have problems with both smog and ozone. Some, like Washington, D.C., only have to worry about ozone. Others still, like Denver, have little to worry about from ozone but instead have a problem with carbon monoxide, a colorless, odorless gas.* Denver's carbon monoxide problem, like Los Angeles's air pollution problem, results from its being beside a mountain range that can temporarily trap bad air and keep it from drifting away. In Denver and some other cities, these so-called "inversions" happen only in the winter although they are a year-round phenomenon in Los Angeles.

Denver is also unusual in that, as its nickname the Mile High City indicates, it lies at an extremely high altitude. At such altitudes the air contains about 18 percent less oxygen than at sea level, and Coloradans have lots of fun reading about the latest

---

*Carbon monoxide quickly causes death if inhaled in a massive dose because it replaces oxygen in the blood stream. For the same reason it can cause headaches at lower concentrations, just as one can get a headache from suddenly going to a higher altitude. It can also cause people to have temporary neuromotor deficiencies, but the evidence of any harm at the EPA 9.5 parts per million (ppm) eight-hour standard is questionable.

celebrity who came to the area for a weekend of skiing and ended up in the hospital instead with altitude sickness. But that which makes celebrities even more light-headed than they usually are can also make car engines run rich, with a mixture of fuel that has too little oxygen in it. That is all the worse in winter because cold engines require a heavier mixture to run properly. It is on this principle that the oxy-fuels program is based. By pumping an oxygen-containing additive into gasoline, a leaner burn is produced in the engine. That leaves less unexpended fuel to drift out the tailpipe and—voilà!—less carbon monoxide pollution. Maybe.

Two different additives have been used in Colorado and other states that followed up with oxy-fuels programs in the wake of Colorado's alleged success. One is MTBE, which is a combination of methanol (also called wood alcohol) and t-butanol, which is related to butane (the stuff they put in cigarette lighters). The other is ethanol. Like ethanol, MTBE is an octane booster. From November through February, Coloradans can only buy one of these two oxy-fuels.

And how does this theory about leaner-burning cars play out in the real world? According to promoters of the Colorado oxy-fuels program, the answer, my friend, is blowing in the wind. Or not blowing, as it were. Wrote then-Denver Metropolitan Air Quality Council Executive Director Steven Howard in an opinion piece: "Metro Denver's markedly cleaner air is the result of those very programs that are the common target of critics' ire."[52]

By "cleaner," what is meant is that Colorado is registering far fewer days in which its level of pollution exceeded the EPA's carbon monoxide limits. The problem is, the number of such days was steadily dropping long before the oxy-fuel program began. The number of carbon monoxide violations dropped from 136 in 1970 to only 19 in 1987, yet the oxy-fuels program didn't begin until 1988. In 1988 there were 11 such days and in 1989, 6.[53] (See chart below.) So, yes, the number of violations did continue to drop after the program began, but to attribute any of that to oxy-fuels is like saying, "Yes, the sun did come up for millions of years until I came on the scene but now that I'm here I'm responsible for its appearance each day."

Such is the bureaucratic mind-set. The primary job of a bureaucrat is to justify the existence of that job. His secondary job is to expand his domain, and that the Colorado bureaucrats have

# Air Quality

Measurements from Denver's air monitoring
program site at 21st and Broadway

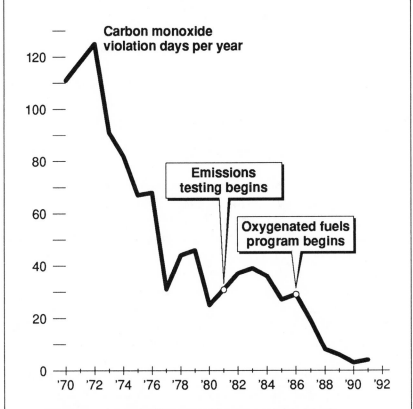

Despite the Colorado Dept. of Health's claim that the
decrease in carbon monoxide violation days in Denver can be
attributed to its emissions testing and oxygenated fuels
programs, its own data show that such violation days had been
steadily declining long before those programs began.

done as well, progressively expanding both the number of months of the oxy-fuel program (originally two and now four) and the amount of oxygen in the fuel. People who see a program being expanded often assume that the pilot program was a success. A Denver opinion phone-in poll sponsored by a local radio station and a local newspaper found that of 209 people calling in, 200 thought the state's clean air program had failed, but tellingly one of the supporters said, "I would say it passed . . . the air is a little cleaner. We have more warnings when not to light up the fireplace and when not to drive."[54] What impressed that man was that the state had decided to impose more restrictions than it had the year before.

The scientists, however, are not so easily impressed. While improvement in Denver's air is obvious enough, experts like Larry Anderson, a professor of atmospheric chemistry at the University of Colorado at Denver, seriously question whether there has been any real improvement in Denver's air quality as a result of *oxy-fuels*. "The oxy-fuels program may not have been necessary at all," he says. "I haven't seen anything that says it is effective."[55] Anderson was one of nine authors of an independent analysis of Colorado's clean air program conducted by the Milliken Research Group, sponsored by gasoline refiners and marketers. The study noted that carbon monoxide levels in Denver's air began dropping in the early 1970s, had declined an average of 29.1 percent each year since 1982,[56] and were expected to continue to decline until Denver complied with the federal ambient carbon monoxide standard, which could be achieved as early as 1992. It found that little if any deviation from this trend could be attributed to the oxy-fuels program, and that for the purpose of bringing Denver in compliance with federal standards, oxy-fuels would be worthless by 1993.[57]

The reason for the drop in carbon monoxide in the Denver area is the same as that for the drop in all major metropolitan areas, the technology-forcing Clean Air Act of 1970—perhaps the most effective pollution legislation ever passed by Congress—which mandated dramatically reduced auto emissions, resulting in catalytic converters and other exhaust system improvements.[58] How strange that oxy-fuels were responsible for the drop in Denver air pollution when cities across the country with no such fuels experienced the same drop. According to University of Denver

Director of Atmospheric Sciences Clay Smith, who worked on the study, oxy-fuels have probably done nothing to help bring Denver into compliance. "At best, oxy-fuels will put us into compliance one year earlier [than it already would have been]." Says Smith, "Oxy-fuels are of marginal benefit in improving air quality. It's too expensive."[59]

Yet the experiences in other states, whose officials enacted oxy-fuels programs in response to the lofty pronouncements of success streaming out of Colorado, may prove far worse. Gary Woodard, a researcher at the University of Arizona in Tucson, conducted a study for that state's legislature of the Arizona oxy-fuels program and other programs in other states. "The costs were a lot higher than most people expected," says Woodard. He found that the upper cost figure the Colorado Department of Health had been using for its program, about $8 million to $9 million, "is probably a low-end figure and the actual range is about nine to 15 million." (Researchers at the University of Denver, meanwhile, have estimated the cost of the Colorado program at about $25 million.)[60] Woodard found, too, that Colorado's program, far from being a good indicator of costs in other areas, represents the best-case scenario because of a more competitive fuel market, a shorter program (four months versus six in Phoenix and other cities), higher elevation, and other reasons.[61] Woodard reported that per pound of carbon monoxide removed from emissions, the oxy-fuels program in Phoenix cost four times that of Colorado's program.[62] Despite all this, it was the Colorado figures and claims of success that prompted other parts of the country to adopt oxy-fuels, which in turn led to its adoption by the nation as a whole in the Clean Air Act of 1990. And the figures put forth by the Colorado Department of Health are the ones that Congress looked at to estimate the cost of mandating oxy-fuels for much of the country.

Woodard also found that the oxy-fuels program in Arizona was considerably less cost-effective than the emissions inspection and maintenance program already in place and that it even appeared to hamper that program by allowing some cars to pass inspection that wouldn't have, leaving them to pollute excessively during the warm months when oxy-fuels are not used.[63]

Further, ethanol has been shown to corrode and to cause build-up on engine and fuel system parts, sometimes prompting expensive repairs in older cars. John Lesko, now a research specialist at the University of Denver, saw many such problems in his former job as a Denver mechanic after the oxy-fuels program began. Says Lesko, "Older vehicles often do not have parts compatible with ethanol and may suffer degradation." He notes that further mechanical trouble can result from the high volatility of ethanol, which means that it evaporates considerably faster than gasoline, especially on warm days, of which Denver and other western cities have several during the winter. "The volatility of ethanol can create vapor lock," he says, and this can result in the car stalling in stop-and-go traffic or simply not starting."[64] Lesko has presented large amounts of documentation to this effect to the Colorado Air Quality Control Commission and has testified in person before that commission, but has been completely ignored. Ralph Nader's Center for Auto Safety in Washington, D.C., has also been a vociferous opponent of oxy-fuels, in part because of the reports it has received from car owners of mechanical difficulties caused by ethanol use.[65]

## NO POLLUTION SOLUTION

Ethanol *can* reduce carbon monoxide emissions in some cars by adding oxygen to fuel, but at the same time it causes more of other types of emissions. One study done by Sierra Research concluded that ethanol would cut carbon monoxide by 25 percent, but that nitrogen oxides, which cause smog and acid rain, would rise by 8 to 15 percent, and hydrocarbons would rise by 50 percent. That works out to a 6-percent-higher level of ozone than would be produced by gasoline without ethanol.[66]

Said one of the authors of the study, Tom Austin, who is also the former head of the state of California's Air Resource Board (CARB) Mobile Sources Division: "Motorists will end up paying more for dirtier air."[67] Because the study was financed by the oil industry, alcohol producers cried foul. But CARB and the Northeast States for Coordinated Air Use Management, two entities with the toughest air standards in the world, have agreed with the findings.[68] One of the CARB officials who evaluated the report said: "If alcohol is used the way it is used today, the only conclusion you can have is that it hurts air quality."[69] The study also should have been of no surprise to the EPA, which found that the use of ethanol so increased evaporative emissions (that which evaporates out of the gas tank) that it could not qualify for use under the 1977 Clean Air Act. A loophole in the regulations allowed ethanol to be used without EPA permission.[70]

In 1992, the EPA said that under the 1990 Clean Air Act it could no longer turn a blind eye to ethanol's smog-producing tendencies and that therefore gasohol could not be certified as a pollution-fighting fuel for use in the nation's smoggiest cities. The gasohol/corn grower forces instantly went into action. Noted *The Wall Street Journal,* "Senate Republican Leader Robert Dole has lobbied the administration from President Bush on down. Within the Bush camp, the ethanol cause is pushed by former White House Chief of Staff Samuel Skinner, Agriculture Secretary Edward Madigan, and former domestic policy chief Clayton Yeutter."[71] One month before election day, with an apparent eye on the farm vote, former President Bush capitulated. While environmental groups had opposed the administration move, they were not especially nonplussed. "There is no good air quality reason for this initiative but we are thankful that, at least on the initial analysis, it does not have a major adverse effect," said Blakeman Early, a Washington representative of the Sierra Club. Likewise, a Natural Resources Defense Council attorney, David Doniger, was quoted as saying that the worst aspect of the move was that it "assures that a few agribusiness giants like Archer Daniels Midland will reap tens of millions of dollars in windfall profits."[72]

The biggest problem with the wonderful theory about leaner-burning engines producing cleaner-burning cars is that all cars built since the mid- to late 1980s have oxygen sensors that automatically adjust the burn mixture. For such cars with operating sensors, the oxy-fuels are simply a redundancy. The fuel-air mixture is already at optimum and a leaner mixture introduced into the fuel injector accomplishes nothing. One test of 249 cars of model years 1988 and 1989, conducted in 1989, found that only 1 of these was a gross polluter that could show a significant benefit from oxy-fuel.[73] Thus, the drivers of 248 such cars had to pay, in lowered mileage and higher costs, for the sins of the 1.

In older cars, and cars with broken oxygen sensors, oxy-fuels have been shown to reduce carbon monoxide emissions, but to mandate that everyone in an area use such fuels for the sake of those cars is rather like making everyone take aspirin each day because some people will develop headaches.

The oxy-fuels program wasn't the only pollution control scheme that began in Colorado and was adapted by other western states. Another was Denver's Better Air Campaign, including voluntary no-drive days that, like the oxy-fuels program, the Colorado Department of Health claimed was having a marked effect in reducing air pollution (even though, like the oxy-fuels program, it wasn't instituted until years after pollution levels in Denver had started to decline). But in 1989, it came to light that a statistical glitch was responsible for an alleged decrease in miles driven. There was no less driving than there had been; therefore less driving could not have played a role in reducing pollution levels. Faced with such a stark and indisputable figure, the Department of Health conceded it had goofed. The wonderful claims it had made for the program were fiction.[74]

But there is no such simple statistical glitch to prove beyond a shadow of a doubt that the oxy-fuels program, too, is a fraud. And so there will be no admission. Far from it, acting on the proud claims of the Colorado Department of Health, President Bush in 1989 said he wanted the entire nation to follow the Colorado model. A proud Colorado Governor Roy Romer clucked: "Nationally, they're looking at the place where it started. Our program has continued into the alternative fuels debate going on in Congress and the White House."[75] And so, Colorado's folly became the nation's, part of the Clean Air Act of 1990.

Of all the fuels being discussed these days as alternatives to gasoline, ethanol, bastard of science and creation of politics, gained the most from the act. In negotiations the week before the House approved its version of the Clean Air Act, proethanol Energy and Commerce Committee members met with environmental groups and members from farm states that produce ethanol and pushed through a compromise that would effectively mandate the use of MTBE or ethanol for the nation's nine ozone nonattainment areas year-round and for the forty-four carbon monoxide nonattainment areas for at least four months beginning in 1992.* If the five most serious carbon monoxide areas don't

---

*To determine whether a city is a nonattainment area, the carbon monoxide or ozone is measured hourly at stations spread strategically through the city. Eight consecutive hours are then averaged, and that average recorded. If the maximum percentage of particles allowed is violated (9 per million of carbon monoxide, 12 per billion of ozone), this is considered an exceedance day. EPA allows one such day as a "freebie," but two or more days puts the city in noncompliance.

achieve attainment by 1994 they will effectively be required to use ethanol only, since only ethanol, and not MTBE, can reach the oxygen level required.[76] Cosponsor of the legislation Bill Richardson (D-N.M.) said the amendment would "give credibility to the growing ethanol industry,"[77] as if a congressional edict could substitute for scientific evidence.

Meanwhile, Tom Daschle (D-S.D.) pushed through an amendment to the Senate bill that would effectively mandate MTBE or ethanol for high-ozone areas in the six coldest months of the year.[78] Cosponsor of the bill was Robert Dole. Originally the White House was opposed to the amendment, but the vote was scheduled for the same day as a major confrontation between the administration and Senator Robert C. Byrd (D-W.Va.) over his proposed aid to coal miners displaced by acid rain controls. But after the Byrd amendment was defeated, with the help of Dole, by one vote, the White House dropped its opposition to the ethanol amendment. "Dole delivered key votes against Byrd," one administration official explained to *Washington Post* reporters. "He was obviously carrying a lot of water for the administration. It was hard for us to cut down something he was partially sponsoring."[79] And so the amendment passed.

It seems to have mattered little to Richardson or Daschle or Dole, to the House or the Senate, or to the White House, that the evidence shows that ethanol actually aggravates the ozone problem. Nor will this increased smog come cheaply. The Congressional Research Service estimates the extra $0.10 to $0.15 per-gallon cost of the fuel in the nine ozone nonattainment areas alone would cost consumers in those cities $25 million to $50 billion annually. Under certain circumstances, however, it said the cost could be as high as $100 billion.[80] But while consumers are paying, you can bet somebody is going to be raking in the green. As Senator Don Nickles (R-Okla.) put it: "I do not have anything against ADM, but that is where most of the benefits are going to go."[81]

Unfortunately, the myth of environmentally benign "clean"

---

Among other reasons, the standard is controversial because often, as in the case with Denver, only one monitor in the city, located at the very worst traffic spot, will be triggered for one part of a day. Thus, a couple of hours of noncompliance at one monitor can brand a city as a high-pollution area.

ethanol lives on. It is even being touted as a partial solution to the alleged problem of global warming, or the "greenhouse effect." In advising her readers to buy ethanol-blended fuels, Marjorie Lamb writes in *Two Minutes a Day for a Greener Planet:*

> The beauty of ethanol is that the carbon it gives off as it burns is no more than the amount of carbon the grain absorbs as it grows, thus making the process a "closed loop." Theoretically, the burning of ethanol does not add to the greenhouse effect, and may even reduce atmospheric carbon dioxide levels in certain circumstances.[82]

Likewise, the *Denver Post,* as part of a drive to legitimize oxyfuels, flatly stated of ethanol that, "burning it doesn't contribute to the greenhouse effect."[83]

In fact, there is simply no scientific contention that ethanol burning produces carbon dioxide. The only issue is whether, by the time you factor in the amount of carbon dioxide absorbed by growing corn, ethanol produces less than does its equivalent in gasoline. Dr. Shih-Ping Ho, a researcher for Amoco Oil, released a study in 1989 which he claims shows that ethanol, when all things are considered, produces more carbon dioxide than gasoline.[84] The paper was in response to one released earlier that year by the Congressional Research Service (CRS). At that point, gasohol supporter Congressman Richard Durbin asked the CRS to investigate this matter. They gave him back the answer he wanted, that ethanol on the whole produces less carbon dioxide than gasoline.[85] Whereupon Ho and another researcher produced another paper indicating that the CRS was wrong,[86] and whereupon the CRS produced yet another paper admitting that they were wrong with their figures but claiming that the basic conclusion was still correct.[87] The argument really revolves around a single question: namely, how much energy does it require to produce a gallon of ethanol? That is the amount that must then be weighed against the amount of energy that burning that gallon of ethanol produces. The CRS originally used a figure for ethanol production, 40,000 British thermal units per gallon (BTU/gal), that simply took the low end of a range of estimates of from 38,000 to 67,000.[88] In the face of Ho's challenge, it chose a "compromise" figure of 48,000 BTU/gal that just happened to have been picked by the Renewable Fuels Association, the gasohol lobbyist (even though the Renewable Fuels Association declined to release data from a survey measuring BTU expenditures of its own members).[89]

Using the 57,000 figure, ethanol is a worse contributor to global warming than gasoline. Further, Information Resources, which is an ethanol industry organization, published a multiclient study in 1989 that showed that state-of-the-art ethanol plants using high-sulfur coal require 64,000 BTU/gallon of process energy while those using natural gas use 73,000 BTU/gallon.[90] This would mean that even Ho's figure showing ethanol to be a worse carbon monoxide contributor than gasoline is too low. At any rate, motor fuels are only estimated to contribute about 7 percent of the gases that go into the alleged greenhouse effect.[91] Even the slight improvement alleged by CRS would have about the same effect on global warming as sticking a pea under the mattress of a non-princess.

## DONALD STEDMAN AND HIS AMAZING FEAT

Gasoline, along with ethanol, will eventually go the way of whale oil. But that time will probably be decades hence. Until then, that which fuels our vehicles must be chosen on the basis of what will provide the optimum in terms of performance, price, and pollution. Sentimentalism and blind prejudice against gasoline should not be factors.

But okay, so ethanol is worse than nothing. Are we then condemned to eventually again have the air pollution levels from which so many of our major cities once suffered as the number of cars in the cities continues to grow? Dr. Donald Stedman thinks the answer is no.

Stedman is a transplant from the United Kingdom who formerly worked for the Ford Motor Company in Michigan. He is now a professor of chemistry at the University of Denver, to which he rides his one-speed bicycle every day. He says it's his little contribution, or noncontribution as it were, to reducing Denver's air pollution, though when pressed he admits he also needs the exercise.

Stedman is a man with a better mousetrap. His device, called FEAT (for "Fuel Emissions Automobile Test") could make a major contribution to further cleaning up the air above America's cities, and it might do so at a fraction of the cost of other proposals seeking to do the same.

Before discussing the FEAT system, however, and why it is so promising, one must understand the limitations of current systems.

First, most pollution comes from a small percentage of cars. One 1989 EPA study showed eighty vehicles emitting a total of 397 pounds of carbon monoxide: 338 pounds of that came from the four dirtiest. When the entire fleet was put on oxygenated fuel, the total emissions reduction was 203 pounds, with the dirty four contributing 107 pounds of that improvement. If the dirty four were tuned to emit the average of the rest of the fleet, they would emit *a total* of 20 pounds, a reduction in emissions of 318 pounds from the tune-up of only four vehicles. Stedman's tests of vehicle fleets and Denver automobiles have resulted in similar findings.[92]

Any system that makes all cars or car owners actively do something is putting an onus on the majority for the sins of the minority. Oxy-fuels is one example of this, but another is the emissions tests now mandated in many states and localities around the country. Under those programs drivers must, generally on an annual basis, take their cars to specially equipped service stations where the exhaust system is hooked up to a device that measures emissions. Granted, putting the burden on the majority might still be worthwhile in some cases—but not in this one.

The problem with the annual idle emissions tests is just that. They are indeed at most only once a year (in the nation's smoggiest city, Los Angeles, they are only every other year), and they are conducted with the car idled, which is not how cars burn most of their fuel.

Although the EPA in 1992 announced it would be ordering cities with the greatest pollution problems to begin switching to a new treadmill system that would greatly eliminate the idle problem, it also said that the test would be only every two years and thus would certainly do nothing to take care of the annual problem. That problem is that because the testing is infrequent and the driver knows when it will take place, it is a simple matter for him to buy a gasoline additive at an auto supply store to clean up car emissions for the duration of a test (guaranteed, or your

# Automotive Emissions

Emission test results from 56,000 U.S. vehicles

**% of total**
**Carbon Monoxide emissions**

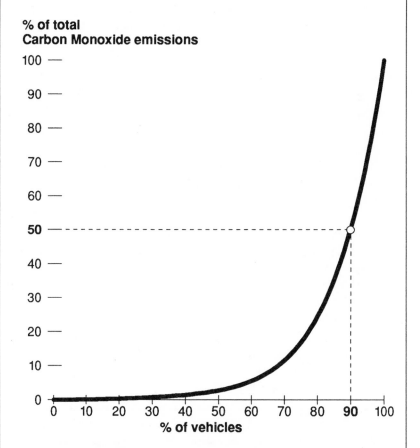

% of vehicles

Tests conducted by the University of Denver on automobiles at various locations in the country show that most cars barely pollute. The dirtiest 10 percent of vehicles caused close to 50 percent of all emissions.

money back), then rumble off and spew carbon monoxide and other gases into the atmosphere. Temporarily disconnecting a hose here or there can have the same result. Since only a small percentage of cars are responsible for most of the pollution, and presumably most of their drivers suspect they may have dirty-running cars (especially after the emissions tester informs them in no uncertain terms), it doesn't take many people who decide they'd rather spend $4.50 on a gasoline additive than perhaps more than $100 on emissions system repairs to wipe out the entire purpose of the emissions testing program. Such testing costs drivers in Stedman's home state of Colorado, for the administration of the program and the cost of the tests, about $17 million a year.[93] In Arizona annual emissions testing costs about $35 million to $37 million,[94] while in California it is about $400 million.[95] But in California they don't allow drivers to see exactly what the tests are costing them; instead the tests are subsidized through tax money—a cool $250 million annually.[96]

FEAT, however, avoids the problems of "idle" and "annual" (or biennial), and it doesn't penalize all cars for the sins of the few. The unit comprises two parts, which are set up on either side of a freeway ramp or anywhere with just one direction of traffic. One part shoots an infrared beam over to the other part. When a car or truck cuts through the beam, the device "reads" the beam to detect the amount of polluting emissions that the vehicle has put out. Currently the device reads for carbon monoxide, carbon dioxide, and hydrocarbons and will soon be able to detect nitrogen oxide as well.[97] FEAT can test up to fifteen hundred cars an hour, depending on traffic density. Stedman estimates that six of the units, each of which costs about $50,000, along with a couple of vans, could effectively monitor all the cars in a city of five hundred thousand.[98]

Then what? Well, it so happens that FEAT can also be hooked up to a video camera that can take a picture of the vehicle, license plate and all. Thus, emissions readings can be matched up to each vehicle. From there on out it's a matter of policy what should be done. One idea is to notify offenders that they are in violation and that if tagged again after, say, thirty days, they will be ticketed. A variation on this theme is that one could take all of the money that is currently spent on idle emissions tests, averaging nine dollars every year in Denver, and twenty-seven dollars every other year in Los Angeles, and instead add that to drivers' registration fees. Then the city could pool that money, use part of it to pay for the FEAT devices, and the bulk it could offer as vouchers for emissions repairs to vehicles found in violation.

To some, the idea of having a camera snapping your vehicle's license plate number and getting a warning or ticket based thereon seems Orwellian. In fact, radar detectors have been used for years for a similar purpose, the difference being that there is a human being behind the device and whether you get a ticket or not may well depend on what kind of a mood he's in. Elsewhere cameras are used to detect border crossings and for parking lot enforcement. Finally, if the camera idea is found to be just too unpalatable, the city could just put a policeman behind the device and then it would operate exactly like a radar detector. The police would pull over violators on the spot.

## TWO MYTHS UP IN SMOKE

Stedman's device, or more properly the results of its tests on more than 250,000 moving automobiles by University of Denver researchers, put to the lie two common beliefs about automobiles. One is that there is a steady correlation for every vehicle between its age and the amount of emissions it creates. Certainly there is a rough correlation; indeed, the main reason air pollution in cities has been declining is simply because older cars are being replaced by newer and cleaner-running ones.[99] But Stedman's data show that three fourths of all cars built before 1975, the first year American cars were equipped with catalytic converters, run cleanly. That is, their exhaust is less than 1 percent carbon monoxide.[100] Cars do become cleaner as the fleet becomes newer. Gross polluters represent 17 percent of 1975–80 model-year cars, 10 percent of 1981 and 1982, and only 0.3 percent of the 1988s, according to University of Denver tests.[101] Still, it is telling that three fourths of the cars without pollution controls run cleanly. Moreover, newer cars, if poorly tuned or if the oxygen sensor breaks, can become gross polluters. Three percent of Stedman's gross polluters fell into the 1983–89 category.[102]

Second, FEAT has demonstrated empirically the above theoretical argument that annual or biennial idle emissions tests are

fairly ineffective. For example, when Stedman's team put his remote sensing device on a road between El Paso and Teller counties
in Colorado, it showed very little difference in the tailpipe emissions of cars registered in El Paso, where vehicle emissions testing
is required and in Teller, where it is not. Thus, while the state
claims the emissions inspection and maintenance program reduces
emissions by 30 percent, Stedman puts the improvement figure
at less than 7 percent.[103]

Cynics would point out that Stedman and his department at
the university stand to make a small bundle if FEAT gains national
acceptance, the fact of which he cheerfully admits. But then,
Thomas Edison made a bundle off the electric light and nobody
insisted that therefore the lightbulb must not work. FEAT has
now been successfully tested in Colorado, California, Illinois,
Toronto, Mexico City, and London.[104]

Says Marc Pitchford, a research scientist with the EPA's environmental monitoring systems lab in Las Vegas, Nevada, "I
don't think there's any question that the device works. It makes
an accurate measurement of carbon monoxide [and is now being
improved to measure gases that lead to smog]. We've seen that
from our study and evidence from other researchers."[105] Bill Denham, a research economist for the Illinois Department of Energy
and Natural Resources worked with FEAT during its testing in
that state. "I certainly think it can be an effective tool," he says.
Noting that the state is still waiting for the results of FEAT testing
for hydrocarbons, he says, "If all we had to focus on were carbon
monoxide, we know it's an extraordinarily effective device. I
would recommend doing it as an enforcement mechanism."[106]

## BUREAUCRATIC BARRIERS

The Bible says: "A prophet is not without honor save in his
own country." To this Stedman says "Amen" although he would
change "country" to "state." Stedman has been working since
1988 to publicize his device, and although the Colorado media
has lately started to swing to his side, opposition from Colorado's
regulators has been nothing short of fierce. His efforts to obtain
funding from the Colorado Department of Health (CDH) have
been repeatedly rebuffed.[107] The reasons given don't hold up very

well. For example, Jerry Gallagher, program manager of the Air Pollution Control Division of the Mobile Sources Program of Colorado, one of the prime advocates of the oxy-fuels program, says that while FEAT may have some uses, it will never replace any programs already in place. One reason he gives is that a CDH review of the engineering literature has "shown that the accuracy of this device can be off by as much as 100 percent."[108] Stedman says that's absolutely right, but also irrelevant. At low enough measurements, such as 0.2 percent carbon monoxide, it might be off by 100 percent, he says, but since both readings are well within the "clean" zone, there's no more practical difference between 0.2 and 0.4 percent than there is between an oven thermometer that registers 355 when the oven is actually only 350. For all practical purposes the food will turn out just the same.[109]

Stedman, Gallagher says, "has never confirmed the data he collects with the standards of the industry." So, says Gallagher, "you only have one side of the equation," namely Stedman's. Gallagher says that 20 percent of the time, when compared with the EPA certified test procedure, he's misidentifying a clean car as dirty.[110] Stedman says that's true but the present CDH has an even worse correlation. "If you're going to apply that to Stedman, apply that to yourself," he says. More important, he says, "there's extremely good evidence that [FEAT] is measuring what the car is doing at the time it's being measured." It is the EPA test that is suspect, because it is taken under artificial conditions.[111]

But if the reasons given by Colorado officials to oppose FEAT don't make sense, here's one that does. Under the Clean Air Act Amendments of 1990 the EPA requires areas that do not attain certain levels of clean air to show that they are taking steps to reach attainment. Failure to do so may result in denial of federal highway funds.[112] What's key here is that the EPA does not require cleaner air. It merely requires states to show that they've implemented plans designed to achieve cleaner air. A state could theoretically have progressively dirtier air but still stave off sanctions by simply showing that it has implemented a plan that the EPA considers valid. In other words, instead of showing the EPA cleaner air, all the bureaucrats have to do is to display an impressive computer model.

Such computer models invariably assume that annual emissions testing and oxy-fuels programs are reducing air pollution. Stedman's device makes him unpopular with the bureaucrats because, first of all, testing done with it, such as the El Paso and Teller County comparison, reveals that annual emissions programs have been largely a failure. Rick Barrett, an air pollution control specialist with the CDH, told the Denver *Rocky Mountain News* that FEAT was of little value compared with the standard emissions tests, averring: "We've seen a pretty steep downturn in the number of violation days in recent years and we feel these programs are what's pulled us in that direction."[113] In fact, Denver carbon monoxide violation days had already dropped to twenty-five in 1980, the year *before* Colorado began its emissions testing program. The first year the program was in effect, there were six *more* violation days than the year before. These days continued to increase over the next few years until 1984 when they began to drop again.[114] (See chart, page 315).This is not to blame the increase on the emissions testing, merely to point out that as with the oxy-fuels program, the bureaucrats are trying to give credit to one of their program's pollution decreases that took place long before the program began, and refusing to take any blame for pollution increases that took place after the program was in place. With both oxy-fuels and the emissions testing, what the CDH is saying is that their programs were *so* effective that their impact actually reverberated back through time, thus cleaning the air long before the programs were in place. That sounds like an idea worthy of H. G. Wells.

Second, Stedman's device shows that the oxy-fuels program is a way of forcing all to pay for the dirty cars of a few, and that therefore whatever the computer models show, places relying on this measure to clean up the air really aren't doing so. Speaking for himself and the other air pollution researchers at the University of Colorado at Denver, Larry Anderson said: "Our concern is what is really happening, not what the model said should be happening."[115] The Colorado Department of Health simply doesn't share that concern. Apparently clean air is not the goal of these bureaucrats; their goal is to satisfy the EPA with impressive projections and claims of success.

As with Colorado's bureaucrats, some members of the CARB have no interest in a new device that would muscle in on their biennial smog tests. CARB spokesman Bill Sessa has asserted: "Our programs are accepted nationally. Mobile testing isn't a substitute for what we do now. There is no controversy about these issues."[116] Of course, saying there's no controversy about something is a common tactic of those who simply want to avoid controversy, as is clearly the case here. But since Sessa made that statement, a report on the testing of FEAT in the Los Angeles area, the chief author of which was Douglas R. Lawson of the Research Division of CARB, gave thumbs up to the remote sensing device, finding it "an effective surveillance tool to identify high CO-emitting vehicles."[117] But it found more than that. It also stated:

> High CO [carbon monoxide]-emitting cars identified by the FEAT are significantly higher emitters of CO and HC [hydrocarbons] when measured on the road than when measured during the previously scheduled Smog Check [the name of the state's biennial emissions testing program]. Possible reasons include mechanical adjustments, illegal or improper Smog Checks, tampering with emissions control equipment and deterioration of the vehicles after the regularly scheduled Smog Check.[118]

Indeed, said the study, "the presence of so many cars that had been tampered with in our set of 60 vehicles suggests that either the required [Smog Check] is not identifying tampering properly or that an appreciable fraction of the high-CO-emitting cars have been tampered with after passing the Smog Check." In other words, thumbs down for the idle emissions test.[119] Stedman's device was vindicated not only in its own ability to perform but in the inability of the system that it would replace.

The FEAT unit also threatens Colorado bureaucrats because it is clearly superior to the oxy-fuels program that, like the annual emissions testing, has as its prime purpose the impressing of EPA bureaucrats and not the cleaning of air. The CDH conducted an actual tune-up study of ten vehicles in 1978, in which it found that they emitted a total of 434 pounds of carbon monoxide using normal gasoline. When 10-percent ethanol fuels (gasohol) were used, the fleet emission dropped to 335 pounds, a reduction of 99 pounds of carbon monoxide. But when only the two dirtiest cars were tuned up, and the normal fuel retained, the fleet emissions dropped to 294 pounds, a reduction of 140 pounds.[120] This is the kind of targeting that FEAT would allow. Researchers working for the EPA have estimated that a mandated oxygenated fuel program in Colorado probably cost about $331 per ton of carbon monoxide removed but may actually cost more than three times that.[121] The estimates do not include realistic gas mileage loss, or any estimate of vehicle parts damage. These researchers have pegged annual exhaust pipe inspection and maintenance programs cost at about $780 per ton of carbon monoxide removed, and trip reduction ordinances at $1,000 to $5,000 per ton.[122] Trip reduction comprises mandatory van-pooling, car-pooling, busing and the like, which companies with a certain number of employees or higher must employ during the higher-pollution season. Stedman says his own estimate is $100 to $248 per ton for a program based on remote sensing and tune-up of the gross polluters.[123] He adds, however, that by combining this use of FEAT with a system of fines for violators, he believes the costs can be brought down much lower still.[124]

Just as Stedman's device throws a wrench into the regular idle emissions test programs and oxy-fuels programs, so too does it stultify a major aspect of the 1990 Clean Air Act, that which further decreases tailpipe emissions. The EPA says 1990-model cars run 96 percent cleaner than their 1970 counterparts as a result of tailpipe emissions restrictions demanded by Congress in the 1970 Clean Air Act and the 1977 amendments to that act. By all accounts the regulation, despite wailing and the gnashing of teeth from Detroit, was a success since it resulted in substantially reduced emissions at a relatively low cost. But then Congress got the idea that if a little medicine helped the patient, more medicine might help the patient even more. So, the Clean Air Act of 1990 has mandated that tailpipe emissions be reduced by another 50 to 75 percent.[125] That sounds impressive, but consider again: The 1970–71-model cars averaged about 23 grams per mile of carbon monoxide. Reducing that level by 75 percent would have meant a reduction of 17.5 grams per mile. And, in fact, a much greater reduction than that was achieved. But since 1983, emissions have averaged 4 grams for new cars. Reducing this amount by 75 percent would result in a reduction of only 2.55 grams. The result is that the new tailpipe emissions will take clean cars and make them run only a tiny bit cleaner. Thus, the chief of the EPA's Motor Vehicle Emissions Laboratory in Ann Arbor, Michigan, Charles L. Gray, Jr., has stated: "Just tightening the tailpipe standards doesn't give you significant additional emission reductions," adding that what counts is to keep the already efficient fuel systems working as they age.[126] This time, the automakers aren't claiming that the restrictions are too onerous, just that it's going to cost the consumer a bundle for practically nothing. And when a car company announces it's going to raise its prices, there's no reason to doubt its word.

Even considering that we're discussing the exhaust of tens of millions of cars, the small amount of emissions reduced will not be that important. What is important is a car that goes out of tune. Then it suddenly becomes a gross polluter and it does so regardless of what tailpipe emission regulation it complied with when it rolled off the assembly line. Says Stedman: "Tightening up tight tailpipe emissions standards even more is about like sharpening pencils a bit sharper. What really counts is *keeping* the tool sharp."[127] Stedman's data make it clear that brand-new cars aren't the problem and that increasingly expensive new regulations on tailpipe emissions aren't going to solve anything. And some of the regulators don't like that a bit.

In fact FEAT, though a regulatory tool itself, is in many senses the bane of the bureaucrat. Observed one writer in a story about FEAT: "Mobile on-road pollution checks . . . are a nightmare for regulators: They work, they're cheap, and they don't require an enormous bureaucracy to administer. New technologies offer a chance to solve once-insurmountable problems, a scary prospect for regulatory agencies that want to expand their fiefdoms."[128]

Stedman adds his belief that the EPA is worried about ceding power to the states. "Allowing mobile on-road testing would give state authorities more accurate information. It would also make them think about how they can clean up dirty cars. There's nothing in the enabling legislation of the EPA that requires [it] to think. Regulate, yes; think, no."[129]

For a brief shining moment, it appeared the FEAT story would have a happy ending. An amendment that Congressman Joe Barton (R-Tex.) tagged onto the House version of the 1990 Clean Air Act called for the use of on-road testing devices as part of the states' implementation plans. It made it through the House uncontested and the Senate-House joint committee and is now part of the 1990 Clean Air Act.[130] But don't think you can breathe any easier, for the EPA has decided to thwart the will of Congress and to discourage the use of FEAT by not giving credit to states who employ it as part of their clean air implementation plans. In other words, says the EPA, you can spend your money on the device if you wish, but it counts for nothing with us. Says an aide to Barton: "They are trying to emasculate [FEAT] by neglect . . . it appears they are trying to kill it."[131] The reason the EPA gives is that they haven't done enough testing with FEAT yet to justify its use and don't have enough money to do so. Instead, the EPA is pushing something called "in-flight testing," which is an on-board computer that monitors a car's emissions. This system is even more experimental than FEAT, but that bothers EPA not a whit. Somehow the EPA *has* found money in its budget for that device. The on-board system could also be tremendously expensive, on the order of $500 per car. Perhaps the single most important aspect of FEAT is that it is impossible to cheat because no tampering with anything on the car can avoid it. But since the "in-flight" system will be on the car, making it tamper-proof will prove difficult indeed.

Stedman says the EPA's action was "absolutely to be expected. It was déjà vu. Anytime you've been at cross purposes with an agency that seems to be more interested in permits and the letter of the law than in cleaning of the air, you shouldn't be surprised if they go on behaving that way."[132]

Donald Stedman and his device show that it is possible to get the cleaner air we want without giving up the freedom of privately owned gasoline vehicles. That while electric vehicles may be the hope of the future, there is much we can do here and now with what is available to us today. Regulators have the potential to do good things, as was the case with the Clean Air Act of 1970. Technology-forcing regulation and legislation *can* work. But regulators do not create. Regulators do not innovate. Regulators simply prevent things from happening or sometimes force them to happen and those things may have nothing in common with what those regulators are tasked with trying to reduce or eliminate. The real hope for preserving and improving the environment lies in the intelligent use of what so many alleged environmentalists consider the enemy—technology—technology that grows out of a free market, which in turn grows out of a free marketplace of ideas.

# CHAPTER 12

# A Closer Look at the Besiegers

We have wished, we ecofreaks, for a disaster or for a social change to come and bomb us into the Stone Age, where we might live like Indians in our valley, with our localism, our appropriate technology, our gardens, our homemade religion—guilt-free at last![1]

—Stewart Brand, writing in *The Whole Earth Catalogue*

Until now, we have essentially focused on the actions of those who have put science under siege. But it is also worth taking a closer look at the motivations of the various groups involved.

## THE BUREAUCRACY

Although professor Donald Stedman, who was discussed in the last chapter, might resist being compared with Galileo, since Galileo was imprisoned and Stedman has merely been severely hindered in marketing his device, there is a nice analogy. Galileo ended up behind bars not simply because his teachings were considered heretical, but because the Aristotelian professors, seeing their own reputations endangered, united against him and cast suspicion upon him in the eyes of the ecclesiastical authorities. Today an iconoclast's worst enemy is the bureaucracy—federal, state, local, or institutional.

The bureaucrat's first imperative is always to justify the existence of his job, since it is commonly believed that many bureaucratic jobs should not exist. That may sound rather cynical, but to take the scientific approach, we must remember that an organism's first priority is survival. The bureaucrat wishes to survive. The bureaucrat's second priority is to expand his job. That brings him more prestige, a better office, and a bigger paycheck. This is because, as that font of wisdom Citicorp informs us in its commercials, "Americans want to succeed, not just survive."

Understand these basic principles about bureaucrats and you will understand in good part why billions of dollars spent for the enactment of health regulations may bring about few health benefits, or for that matter why billions of dollars spent on safety regulations may bring about few safety benefits.

You will also understand why the bureaucrat is extremely conscious of media attention. Basically, he doesn't like it. Movie stars like media attention, but bureaucrats like to surround themselves with desks and good carpeting. That is because when they get media attention, it is almost always bad. You will never see a headline reading: FDA DELAYS APPROVAL FOR DRUG, THOUSANDS TO DIE. (Although AIDS activists have had success in driving this point home, albeit only with AIDS.) These deaths are invisible and hence the media has no interest in them. But God forbid if the FDA should approve something that ends up killing somebody or causing birth defects.

What the various consumer groups and environmental organizations have discovered is that bureaucracies always err on the side of caution, which in the case of a product means erring on the side of restrictions or an outright ban. This is simply because of the rule of visibility of off-site effects. That is, if a ban or restriction is imposed and someone suffers for it, it is quite likely that the suffering will be difficult to detect and not make it onto the evening news.

Conservatism is the name of the game with bureaucrats. This does not mean political conservatism; rather it means that anything as huge and layered as the EPA is afflicted by what may be called bureaucratic inertia. Bureaucratic inertia is like a supertanker. It takes bureaucracies almost forever to get the thing going and even longer to stop it or turn it around. It takes the EPA years to begin regulating something that the environmental groups demand that it regulate, and it will take years for the EPA to first admit it was wrong to listen to those groups and then to actually cut back on its regulations.

## THE POLITICIANS

The politician has much in common with the bureaucrat in that his primary job is to preserve his position and his secondary job is to enlarge it. The way a politician does this is to declare that a problem exists and that someone must take bold action to allay it. That someone, naturally, is he. Further, other than scandals, nothing hurts a politician more than being labeled a "do-nothing." And so, even when there is no crisis, or there is a crisis that is best resolved without government interference, we inevitably find the government interfering anyway. In this way, the politician is the opposite of the bureaucrat. He *wants* to make waves, and he does so through speeches—often demagogic—and through introducing and working for legislation.

No nationally known politician is more identified with environmental issues than Vice President Al Gore, who began an essay in *Scientific American:* "The world is in the midst of an environmental crisis beyond anything yet experienced; unless radical steps are taken to safeguard the planet, our future on it cannot be secured." Gore utters the usual cliché indicators of crisis, including "Species are dying at an unprecedented rate: 1,000 times faster than at any time in the past 65 million years,"[2] a statement that is wholly without substantiation but never fails to get the attention of a crowd.[3]

In late twentieth-century America and elsewhere, the politician has developed two special tools to stay in office and expand his power base. The first is the crusade. The second is the taking of resources from other representatives' constituencies and funneling them back into one's own, an approach commonly known by the expression "pork barrel." Many politicians are not beyond using false science to further either of these.

The crusade, often marked by the use of war metaphors, necessitates a crisis. The original crusade was necessitated by the fall of Jerusalem into Muslim hands. Today it is the "revelation" that a chemical causes cancer, that a device is unsafe, that a species is threatened. It may be that the chemical does cause cancer, that the device is unsafe, that the species is indeed threatened. But that is often beside the point. The point is to be seen as the hero poised to take back the Holy City.

Whatever motivates our Congress, it is clear that this body is not only grossly ignorant scientifically but almost proud of it. What else to explain their treating Meryl Streep as a scientific expert? Granted, this is no worse than when a congressional committee invited Jessica Lange, Sissy Spacek, and Jane Fonda to testify on farm problems because, yes, all had starred in movies concerning farms.[4] That which they can't get respectable scientists and economists to say, they get respectable actresses to say.

It's one thing for Joe Average to act upon celebrity product endorsements, but we should expect more from those who run the government.

## THE MEDIA

In some ways, too, the reporting method and the scientific method are simply at odds with each other. Jeff Greenfield, reporting for ABC News's *Nightline* on the dioxin issue, stated:

> It's a basic rule in journalism to get the human angle, to tell the story so the average viewer can relate to it. That's fine. But with a complicated technical story like dioxin, the concerns, the worries, the fears of people like us will always carry more weight than the disputes and the cautions of the experts. Human drama, human emotion is what works well on television. Maybe sometimes too well.[5]

Researchers have confirmed Greenfield's suspicion. Michael Greenberg of Rutgers University, along with colleagues David B. Sachsman, Peter M. Sandman, and Kandice L. Salomone, conducted a study on "Network Evening News Coverage of Environmental Risk." Examining the evening news broadcasts of the major networks from January 1984 to February 1986, they looked at news stories on man-made environmental risks and found little relationship between the amount of coverage in the news and the corresponding health risk. Instead, the report found that such determinants as timeliness, proximity to the viewer, consequences, and human interest were the major reasons for focusing on an issue as news. Coverage of a potential killer was essentially inverse to probability. Thus, smoking/tobacco health risks, known to cause several hundred thousand deaths per year, got 57 stories; while airplane safety and accidents, which claim a few hundred lives per year in the United States, got 482 stories; and environmental risks, to which we can solidly attribute virtually no deaths, got 564 stories. Greenberg concluded that the "visual impact" criterion was perhaps the most significant factor in determining the degree of coverage.[6] Is it any wonder that such happenings as Love Canal, with its oozing gunk and its residents screaming about how they're being murdered, makes national news repeatedly, even if there is nothing to the allegations?

This lack of correlation between the real world and the world of the news no doubt represents a degree of ideological crusading on the part of the media, but clearly we are also witnessing the man-bites-dog phenomenon. Hundreds of thousands of deaths a year from smoking is old hat, but possible death by toxic waste, now *that's* exciting. The problem is, such presentations distort the ability of viewers to engage in accurate risk assessment. The average viewer who watches story after story on the latest alleged environmental terror can hardly be blamed for coming to the conclusion that cigarettes are a small problem compared with the hazards of parts per quadrillion of dioxin in the air, or for concluding that the drinking of alcohol, a known cause of low birth weight and cancer, is a small problem compared with the possibility of eating quantities of Alar almost too small to measure. This in turn results in pressure on the bureaucrats and politicians to wage war against tiny or nonexistent threats. The "war" gets more coverage as these politicians and bureaucrats thunder that the planet could not possibly survive without their intervention, and the vicious cycle goes on.

Of course, it could well be argued that the media is just giving the public what it wants. Columnist Linda Ellerbee, while her politics are on the opposite side of former Vice President (and media basher extraordinaire) Spiro Agnew, nevertheless agreed with him that the media are "nattering nabobs of negativism" and "hopeless, hysterical hypochondriacs of history," noting that pollsters had found that what the news people seemed to like best was the bad news. She observed that two thirds of the nation closely watched the buildup to war in the Persian Gulf in 1990, but at no point did more than 30 percent of all Americans closely follow the historic fall of communism in all of Eastern Europe.

The single story that year that captured the attention of most of the American people, according to the Times Mirror Center for the People and the Press, was President Bush's distaste for broccoli.[7] So, add silly news to bad news.

Later in the same show on which Greenfield made his remark, host Ted Koppel identified yet another problem with media coverage of scientific scares in response to criticisms of then-American Medical Association Chairman Dr. John Coury. Said Koppel:

> The fact of the matter is, you are scientists and we are journalists. We deal in daily news. Now, sometimes we hold it up for a week or two, or if you folks tell us you're on the verge of making a discovery and could we please hold up for a month or two, we'll do that, too. But if I understand you correctly, you're saying hold up indefinitely until we give you something definite, even though there's all kinds of evidence around that there may be a danger.[8]

The point is well-taken, as it was by Dr. Coury, but it was overstated as well. As soon as someone shouts the alarm on any important scientific issue, the media run with it. They don't hold it up a week or two; they turn it out by the five o'clock deadline. And they don't necessarily wait to get a response from the true scientific community.

At best, reporting is often merely a battle of press releases. Writes Dorothy Nelkin in her book *Selling Science:* "Applying naive standards of objectivity, reporters deal with scientific disagreement by simply balancing opposing views, an approach that does little to enhance public understanding of the role of science."[9]

Dartmouth President John Kemeny, when he was chairman of President Carter's commission inquiring into the accident at Three Mile Island, commented after dealing with the media about his report:

> I left Washington fully expecting to read the following story in one of our morning newspapers: "Three scientists, named Galileo, Newton, and Einstein, have concluded on the basis of their research that the earth is round. However, the *New York Times* has learned authoritatively that Professor John Doe of Podunk College has conclusive evidence that the earth is flat.[10]

One reason for such reporting, in which both sides are given equal time regardless of a major degree of silliness on one side, is that both science writers and the public often suffer from the absurd belief that scientists can have no politics, and that even if they did this would never spill over into their work.

Sheer sloppiness and the crunch of deadlines also cannot be ruled out as factors in media misinformation. Often, for example, journalists will eschew reading a science or medical magazine article in favor of simply reading the abstract. Thus, after the *New England Journal of Medicine* (*NEJM*) published a study on AIDS virus infections on college campuses, some reporters, including those working for Cable News Network[11] and the Associated Press,[12] declared that it was a new study that showed an "alarming increase" in infections over those reported in an old one. In fact, this *was* the old study, which *NEJM* had simply decided to take eighteen months to publish.[13] The date of the study was made clear in the article but was absent from the abstract; hence these important news outlets missed it. The assertion that a study could show an "alarming increase" over what turned out to be the same study merely illustrates the ability of the media to find something new and alarming in absolutely anything.

The average reporter works toward two things because the average newspaper cares about two things. The first is making deadlines; the second is being interesting. Accuracy is not high up in the hierarchy. Indeed, accuracy is detrimental to both of these goals. Accuracy slows you down tremendously. It means doing extra background work. It means getting confirmations. It means doing research, as opposed to the "he said, she said" game of calling up a few experts and quoting their opinions.

The only kind of inaccuracy many newspapers care about—and ultimately many newspaper reporters, because their job is to satisfy the boss—is the kind that appears in the corrections section the next day. Misquote somebody and it will end up in the corrections box. Get the names wrong of the ladies who attended the community bake sale and it will end up in the corrections box. Write a fallacious series of articles about a toxic waste site and it will never be acknowledged.

There are a variety of factors at play in the media's distortion of the news: sensationalism, the crunch of deadlines, sheer ignorance and laziness, and, yes, a tendency to adopt a cause. All of those were evident in the Alar incident. A public relations firm launched a massive, brilliantly planned campaign intended to tell the media exactly what to think about the issue. Bombarded with one viewpoint, the media then ran with it. It certainly helped that it was a terribly exciting story, involving as it did the specter of tens of thousands of little children being slowly poisoned to death by greedy producers and a major chemical company.

The system inherently favors those who sound alarms, as opposed to those who seek to counter them, for two reasons. For one, the shout of "Fire!" is always more exciting than that of "No fire!" Don't ever expect to see a bold headline in a newspaper reading, EARTH NOT DESTROYED; BILLIONS DON'T DIE, even if that paper had regularly carried articles indicating that such a fate was imminent. For another, to sound an alarm is to strike first, while to seek to negate is to be heard second. As then-FDA Commissioner Frank Young stated after the Alar scare: "In retrospect, I would have loved to jump into it earlier. . . . If you can't get in within the first 24 hours, the story is lost."[14]

Political bias also plays a role. Professors S. Robert Lichter, Stanley Rothman, and Linda Richter found in their surveys of the "media elite" that 54 percent of leading journalists describe themselves as liberals, while only 17 percent place themselves as conservatives[15]—compared with 25 percent liberal and 35 percent conservative in the general population at the time.[16] Looking at the presidential elections from 1964 to 1976, Lichter and Rothman found that media elite support for the Democratic candidate ranged from 81 percent to 94 percent, even though the popular vote went to the Republican in two of those elections.[17]

But do politics affect reporting? The Alexandria, Virginia-based Media Research Center, in its book *And That's the Way It Isn't,* and in its newsletter, "MediaWatch," makes a very impressive case using quotes and statistics that ideology is very important in determining what is reported and how.

For example, one graph in *That's the Way It Isn't* has the years 1981 to 1986 running along the bottom. Two graph lines are shown. The first charts the unemployment rate and the second the media's use of the term "Reaganomics." The higher the unemployment rate went during the recession in 1982, the more often the term "Reaganomics" was used. But as conditions improved, the use of the term declined accordingly. When the economy hit full stride, the use of "Reaganomics" practically disappeared.[18]

The authors also found that ideological tagging occurs much

more often with conservative candidates and groups than with liberal ones. A think tank that dispenses liberal ideas is just a think tank. One that dispenses conservative ones, however, is invariably identified as "conservative" or "right wing." In a study of six media organs over a two-year period of time, the Media Research Center found that conservative groups were labeled as such 58 percent of the time, liberal ones as such only 2 percent of the time. Reporters labeled the conservative Heritage Foundation more than thirty-five times as often as the liberal Brookings Institution. The conservative Concerned Women for America got tagged almost twenty times more often than the liberal National Organization for Women.[19] It's easy to see how that happens. To a liberal reporter, a liberal group is "normal" while a conservative one is extraordinary. There's no reason to identify the normal, only the exceptional.

As to how this ideological slant affects the bad-news syndrome, American Enterprise Institute scholar Ben Wattenberg says: "Liberals tend to believe that . . . accentuating the negative will let . . . others see . . . problems and this, in a free society, will engender further progress." Wattenberg believes that this may have validity in the political process but that in the media it is a different matter. People don't want, and certainly don't expect, reporters to be policymakers. They expect them to relate reality. That is why reporters are called reporters and not interpreters. That is why newscasters are called newscasters and not newsmakers. Wattenberg also argues that the decision to exaggerate the negative is probably not a conscious one. But we all tend to see reality through some sort of filter (though certainly some people's filters are a lot thicker than others'). "The liberal bias is not conspiratorial," opines Wattenberg. "They're only telling the truth as they see it."[20]

The European media seems to suffer less from a political bias, surprisingly, perhaps, because in Europe there is no pretense to being nonpartisan. There are papers that are openly identified as being conservative or liberal, or favoring another political party. In Great Britain, for example, the *Times* is identified with the Conservative party, while the *Guardian* is identified with the Labor party, which is politically liberal. The result is that the reader knows ahead of time where the reporter is coming from politically and knows that for a balanced view she may have to read two different newspapers. In the United States, however, we have developed a tradition for nonpartisanship that is often merely cosmetic.[21] We haven't eliminated bias, and we never will. All we have eliminated is easy identification of that bias.

Former *Washington Post* editor Ben Bradlee readily admitted that his paper, one of the most important in the country, adopted advocacy positions. As was recorded in Chapter 1, Charles Alexander declared: "As the science editor of *Time* I would freely admit that on this issue we have crossed the boundary from news reporting to advocacy." That makes one of the most important newspapers and one of the three most important newsmagazines. How about television? According to Teya Ryan, senior producer of Turner Broadcasting's CNN-produced *Network Earth* series: "The 'balanced' report, in some cases, may no longer be the most effective, or even the most informative. Indeed, it can be debilitating. Can we afford to wait for our audience to come to its own conclusions? I think not."[22]

The two remaining major factors in the bad-news syndrome, according to Wattenberg, are adversarial tilt and self-righteousness. Since Vietnam, he explains, many journalists—typically younger ones—have come to believe that only their vigilant eyes can keep the nation from international adventurism, political skullduggery, and corporate corruption.[23] This surely is a category that comprises but a small portion of journalists. It can hardly apply to sports or life-style reporters or those people who insert the recipes in the Sunday edition. But it only takes a few. A single journalist in the right place can do a tremendous amount of good or an equal amount of damage. It is self-righteousness combined with arrogance that allows all too many journalists to become part of the problem instead of the solution. Gadflies and muckrakers are all to the good. We need more of them, not fewer. "Question authority" should be the motto of every investigative reporter. But muckrakers and gadflies have no less obligation than anyone else to be honest with their readers and with themselves. The nobility of the crusade cannot excuse the sloppiness of the reporting.

## BUSINESS

This book has portrayed two sides of business. There have been the businesses that went honestly about their jobs of providing services and products for a price, and the businesses that to some extent or other dishonestly went about capitalizing on fears and anxieties they helped create.

There is a double standard that says that an employee is entitled, even expected, to pull in as much as he can from his employer, but that if that employer tries to make a good profit, it is engaging in immoral activities. Making money, indeed making lots of money, is not inherently wrong. But sometimes when you find a company making truly tremendous profits, it's because the government has made it possible for them to do so by granting them protection from competitors or by giving people no choice but to use their products or services. Such is the case with gasohol and ADM. Elsewhere, I have written of asbestos abatement firms as another example of questionable government regulations leading to tremendous profits. The cost of abatement is so tremendous that even those wrongly convinced that it is better to remove asbestos would generally nonetheless keep it in place save for various national, state, and local regulations forcing it to be removed. The government has guaranteed the abaters a huge market.

Businesses comprise people and act accordingly. Some people steal and kill. Some businesses will steal and kill. But to characterize businesses as thieves and killers—which is exactly the characterization given to them by so many of their detractors in the media and the environmentalist movement—is wrong.

Still, even the freest of free-marketers realize that certain restrictions on business activity are necessary. Since very few people will concern themselves with (or even know, for that matter) how much pollution resulted from making a product, there is no inherent free-market restriction on pollution. Somebody has to step in and force manufacturers to reduce their pollution.

Garrett Hardin, in his famous 1968 essay "The Tragedy of the Commons,"* defines the problem as such:

---

*Simply put, the tragedy of the commons means that when something is owned in common, individuals may, in an effort to improve their own positions, despoil

> The tragedy of the commons . . . is averted by private property, or something formally like it. But the air and waters surrounding us cannot readily be fenced, and so the tragedy of the commons as a cesspool must be prevented by different means, by coercive laws or taxing devices that make it cheaper for the polluter to treat his pollutants than to discharge them untreated.[24]

Indeed, if this is done correctly then none of the manufacturers will even complain, since all their competitors are being forced to do what they are doing and hence their ability to compete is unharmed. Until recently, very few people concerned themselves with the safety of products. Again, somebody from the outside had to step in and impose safety regulations. (There are some who will argue that tort liability laws will perform this service, but others have argued that the application of such law is so haphazard as to be useless for anything but lining lawyers' pockets.[25]) Thus, some regulations are quite necessary. But those regulations must be applied in the sense that also makes clear: "We realize that you are trying to make a living and that if you altruistically engage in an activity that increases your bills and your competitors don't follow suit, then you will be out of business and nobody will gain."

The problem is that we have become so fixated with regulating industry that often we seem to be regulating for regulation's sake, promulgating rules and laws that in perspective simply make no sense. The regulators regulate, but who's regulating them? Those who should, namely our elected representatives, always seem to have better things to do.

What is needed when it comes to environmental issues is a more realistic approach to business and to its adversaries. All of them need to be seen as human beings acting according to principles of self-interest.

---

the land (or the air or the water). The classic example is the farmer who puts a new cow onto land that is held in common and is already being overgrazed. The result is that he will get a bit more meat or milk than he otherwise would, but that overall the farmers will be worse off. Ultimately, this will result in starvation of the entire herd. By fencing the land off to individual farmers, this is prevented. Where fences are impossible, such as with the atmosphere, Hardin points out, other methods are needed.

## THE SCIENTISTS

Writes Professor Leonard A. Cole in his book *Politics and the Restraint of Science:* "If one expects that people who have bright minds, specialty training, and international eminence will, on the strength of these characteristics, reject politically condoned quackery, the Lysenko affair stands in contradiction."[26] Trofim Lysenko was a Soviet biologist and agronomist whom Joseph Stalin appointed to a high position because Lysenko advocated a theory of genetics that was devoid of scientific basis but nonetheless supported the Marxist theory of dialectical materialism. While some Soviet scientists defied Lysenko and Lysenkoism, Cole notes, many others went along with it even in the face of its absurdity. Says Cole: "When encouraged by the political system, quackery prevailed and 'good' scientists deferred to politically imposed scientific truth."[27]

He makes his point even starker with a discussion of the willingness of German scientists to sell out to National Socialism long before the Nazi party was capable of inflicting any harm on anyone. For example, Philipp Lenard and Johannes Stark, both winners of the Nobel Prize in physics, made a joint statement in 1924 that read:

As recognized natural scientists we should like herewith to announce in conformity with our innermost feeling that in Hitler and his comrades we discern the same spirit which we always looked for, strove upward, developed out of ourselves in our work that it might be deep going and successful. . . . This, however, is exactly the spirit which we earlier recognized and advanced in the great scholars of the past, in Galileo, Kepler, Newton, Faraday. We admire and adore it likewise in Hitler, Ludendor, Pohner and their comrades; we recognize in them our nearest relatives in spirit.[28]

Years later, when words such as these were translated into programs of genocide and involuntary euthanasia, many such scientists continued to acquiesce or even take an active role. Cole notes that after the war broke out in 1939, mentally deficient persons were ordered exterminated by Hitler. Popular disapproval mounted when word of the program spread, but the dissent was led not by scientists or doctors but by a few Protestant and Catholic clergy. This disapproval climaxed, in August 1941, when the bishop of Munster publicly denounced the executions. Immediately afterward, writes Cole, "fearing public unrest, the government halted the program and the leading opponents of the euthanasia program went unmolested. While scientists remained silent about the regime's corruption of their disciplines, others demonstrated that opposition to Nazi policies could be effective."[29]

All of which is to say that scientists are, yes, human beings. They are corruptible. On the whole, Americans have much greater respect for them than they do for other key players in the book—lobbyists, politicians, journalists, and lawyers—though when one thinks about it, that's not saying a whole lot. In fact, scientists are held in very high regard. And that can be dangerous because we can make the mistake of taking a rule that applies generally and insisting on applying it specifically.

## Sins of Commission

The scientists who slam you over the head with ridiculous conclusions supported by false data are the easiest to spot. The astronomer who reports that the image of Elvis's face has been carved into the Martian landscape will find himself appearing in the *Weekly World News* but nowhere else. Some of the scientists who more subtly offend science are ironically those who are the best known to the public. They are the sensationalists who are staples on such shows as *Nightline, Good Morning America,* and *The Today Show.* They appear occasionally on the news and even on afternoon shows like Oprah Winfrey's. They are the jack-of-all-trades scientists, experts in, well, just about everything. And it is this willingness to speak on everything that ensures that they are usually wrong because they will usually be speaking outside of their areas of expertise. Rarely, for example, will you find epidemiologists making sensational comments about an epidemiological study. Orthopedic surgeons, yes; general practitioners, yes; virologists, yes.

One specific name that comes to mind among the sensational scientists is Carl Sagan, who presents himself as an expert on a wide variety of scientific subjects from evolution to global warming to the so-called nuclear-winter effect to the effect of the Kuwaiti oil fires on global temperatures. Only with the last could his assertions ever be put to the test, and there he was completely wrong.[30] Sagan's training is as an astronomer. Another such prognosticator is population control advocate Paul Ehrlich, whose 1968 best-seller *The Population Bomb* predicted "hundreds of millions" of deaths owing to famine in the 1970s regardless of any crash programs,[31] a figure that happened to be off by hundreds of millions.[32] Ehrlich's training is in entomology; his specialty is butterflies.

What would it sound like if the sports reporter on the evening news kept referring to his interview subject as "an athlete"? Yet, time and again scientists and doctors are introduced simply as "a scientist" or "a doctor." If journalists would bother to identify what kind of a scientist or what kind of a doctor, they might think twice about using those people to speak about subjects outside of their knowledge.

Why do the media go to these people? To some extent, it is out of sheer ignorance. To many reporters, a scientist *is* an expert in all the natural sciences and a doctor *is* an expert in all areas of medicine, at least if he claims to be. But the other reason may be that sometimes it is "necessary" to go to someone outside of the field in question in order to obtain a comment that is scientifically incorrect but politically correct or sensational.

Funding for many scientists is a continual problem, and funding can lead to corruption. Many funders—be they foundations, independent organizations, or government agencies—are more concerned with what may be hazardous than what may not be. Thus, even a scientist who has every intention of doing a responsible study is pressured to play up the potential hazards in whatever area he is exploring. One such scientist, Edwin Carstensen, who studies electric and magnetic fields [EMF] and their health effects, relates how he has felt such pressure:

> I would conclude there is no basis for concern [over EMF]. But from a second point of view you could say there are interesting clues that ought to be followed up. The problem is, there are a number of people with that point of view, and unfortunately in today's world they cannot do this without money so they have to convince others to support them. If you speak to the national media in inflammatory ways, I don't think that's responsible, but it can get you your funding.[33]

Publicity can be a route to funding, and may have value to some in and of itself. Most of us do have an inside longing to claim that fifteen minutes of fame that Andy Warhol promised we'd have. And if it's publicity you want, the shortest route is alarmism. Dr. Ralph E. Lapp zeroes in on environmental stories when he writes in his book *The Radiation Controversy:* "The scientist with the deepest voice of gloom and the direst prophecy wins the precious air seconds of prime time."[34]

## Sins of Omission

But for every scientist who intentionally leads the public astray, there are vast numbers who simply don't make an effort to redirect the flock. Drs. George Claus and Karen Bolander, in their book *Ecological Sanity,* observe:

> One of the most obvious questions that may come to the reader's mind is: If the authors alleged that a considerable number of the scientific claims of the environmentalists are false and some of the papers which support these claims are worthless or filled with errors, how does it happen that out of more than 200,000 scientists in the United States so few have spoken up . . . ?"[35]

That is a darned good question. One reason that the alarmist scientists grab attention is that to some extent it has become their stock in trade, they have become expert showmen, masters of both the ten-second sound bite and the press release. Thus, while the responsible scientists are sweating away in their laboratories, doing what responsible scientists do, the irresponsible ones are calling press conferences. When journalists find a scientist who claims to have expertise in an area and is very accessible (returns phone calls promptly) and friendly, they like to go back to him over and over. It is simply easier, especially in the face of a deadline. As for me, my early-warning alarm goes off when I hear a doctor or scientist speak in sound bites and repeating certain phrases over and over again, on the assumption that these are what will be put in my story. A good science journalist has the ability to translate scientific jargon into the king's English; he doesn't need a sound bite emitter.

Another problem is that scientists are sick and tired of being quoted out of context by a journalist trying to make a point. Less responsible ones will be so happy to see their names in print that they don't care so much; and anyway they are more likely to be quoted accurately by a reporter crusading on the same side of an issue. Others, however, must feel as Dr. Merril Eisenbud does when he explains:

> Many of us complain that we are expected to take the time to be taped for TV or radio interviews, but have no control over what finally appears. All too often, the most useful things we say end up on the cutting-room floor. Over the years, I have grown camera-shy because all too often a single brief sentence, totally out of context, is all that is aired after an interview that involved many minutes of taping. I believe that unless the interview is going to be published in its entirety, it is proper that the scientist be given an opportunity to approve the edited version.[36]

All of these, however, are explanations not excuses. As the late president of the National Academy of Sciences, Dr. Philip Handler once said: "Scientists best serve public policy by living within the ethics of science, not those of politics. If the scientific community will not unfrock the charlatans, the public will not discern the differences—science and the nation will suffer."[37]

## THE ENVIRONMENTALISTS

Our final besiegers are the environmentalists, the ones who are going to save the earth for us. We have found upon closer inspection that they have a number of goals that they wish to achieve along the way. To better understand those goals, it is necessary to better understand how they think and who they are.

### The Cult of the Natural

The French philosopher Jean-Jacques Rousseau may be the father of the cult of the natural. His book *Émile,* written in 1762, states: "God makes all things good; man meddles with them and they become evil."[38] To quote a more modern philosopher of sorts, Dave Foreman, author of *Ecodefense: A Field Guide to*

*Monkey Wrenching* and founder of the radical Earth First! environmental group: "We must . . . reclaim the roads and the plowed land, halt dam construction, tear down existing dams, free shackled rivers, and return to wilderness millions and tens of millions of [acres of] presently settled land."[39] (Practicing what he preached, he pleaded guilty in 1991 after he was charged with conspiracy to sabotage power lines to nuclear power plants.[40]) And finally consider this insight into the antipesticide, antiirradiation mind-set provided by Jim Hightower's book, *Eat Your Heart Out:* "Food is one of the few real things left in our lives. To industrialize food, to make it conform to technologies and systems, is to industrialize ourselves and finally to surrender the quality of our lives to the mass-produced standard of big business."[41]

And you thought a carrot was just a carrot. Of course, in any real sense, food was "industrialized" long ago. It is grown on huge farms with chemical fertilizers using tractors shipped in from Michigan or elsewhere, transported in trucks or by rail to the cities, and then laid out in huge supermarkets.

These nature revelers are all romantics, but hardly in the sense of the noble Don Quixote, who dedicates his life to helping his fellow man. Instead, whether it's Earth First!'s nasty habit of putting nails in trees to injure loggers or the efforts of the antiirradiation and antipesticide activists to force all of us to go without these modern conveniences, the name of the game is to get us to change our lives to suit their vision of communing with nature. And their vision is a very narrow one.

Declaiming against the cult of the natural, one letter writer to the *New England Journal of Medicine* stated:

> The underlying assumption of those who value things because they are natural is their belief that nature is a benign force whereas human power tends to be evil. They equate naturalness with goodness. One can quickly rebut this belief by cataloging the natural things that work against human interests. Wastage of potential human life is natural; spontaneous abortions are so common that only about a third of fertilized human eggs end up as babies. . . . Death in childbirth is natural, too, as are viruses, germs and cancer. Epidemics are natural; it is stemming them that is not. Earthquakes, volcanic eruptions, avalanches, floods, and droughts are all natural. Indeed, death itself is an unavoidable natural experience common to all living things.[42]

Likewise, Gregg Easterbrook, in a lengthy *New Republic* essay with the provocative title "Everything You Know About the Environment Is Wrong," subtitled "A Liberal Skeptic's Guide to Earth Day," writes: "Nature makes toxins, pollutants, and radioactive materials in far greater quantities than man does. Nature discards creatures with a pitilessness that makes humanity seem saintly: more than 99 percent of the species ever to come into existence have been rendered extinct." He suggests that the "conventional wisdom that natural arrangements are metaphysically superior to artificial ones" is probably explained by "our sitting at the pinnacle of the food chain."[43] An antelope that spends most of its life in a desperate search for food before having its neck cruelly broken by a lion probably doesn't have the benign view of nature that a plump environmental lobbyist sitting in an air-conditioned office does.

But none of this seems to be of import to those to whom Mecca is a tree. The same double standard that they apply between synthetic carcinogens and natural carcinogens is applied to nature itself. Nature is always good. And the best way of living with this good nature is an agrarian society where everyone coexists in peace and harmony with nature and with their fellow man—few though those fellow men may be under such a scheme. These are the agrarian utopians, those who long for and seek to emulate a time they think to have gone by, but which in fact never was.

## The Agrarian Utopia

Margaret Maxey, a professor of bioethics at the College of Engineering at the University of Texas at Austin, writes: "Network television programming fuels this nostalgia by dramatizing life with *The Waltons* or *Little House on the Prairie,* not to mention *Grizzly Adams.*" Such dramas, she says, "extol the simplicities of life in the wilderness or in an agrarian society, sustained by friendly neighborhood gatherings in rural communities and by a sense of belonging within small-town community life."[44]

Similarly, the new *Twilight Zone* series that ran in the 1980s, one of the more politically correct television shows of the time, when it sought to present an idyllic civilization in another dimension (it did so on at least two episodes) depicted an agrarian society with horse-drawn wagons. The highly popular television series *Star Trek: The Next Generation,* in its 1991 run, had a show about a planet that suffered from constant warfare until it decided, for ecological reasons, to become an agrarian society, at which time the warfare magically ceased as well. By the same token, TV and cinema science fiction usually depict the future as dark and horrifying, as with *Blade Runner, The Terminator,* or *Soylent Green,* the last of which portrays a grossly overcrowded planet, burning up as the result of global warming, which has become so unable to feed its population that it has state-sponsored euthanasia and turns dead bodies into food.

The bible of these utopians is the late Ernst Joseph Schumacher's *Small Is Beautiful: Economics as if People Mattered,* a 1973 cult book that spins out a version of "Buddhist economics" in which people do not use machines, there is no mass production, and essential economic tasks are handled in small production units such as were common at the time in communist countries.[45]

But the next time you think about how wonderful it would be to live in some bygone era, consider that you can't pick and choose. The bad has to come with the good. Former governor of the state of Washington Dixy Lee Ray, now in her seventies, grants in her book *Trashing the Planet* that in the "natural age" into which she was born carbon monoxide and ozone pollution weren't problems, but the streets were practically paved with pony pooh. Kerosene, coal, and wood pollution filled the air indoors and out. (London's famous fog, for example, exists no longer because in fact it was not fog but pollution from millions of coal and wood stoves, now replaced by natural gas, oil, or electric heaters.) It was, by today's standards, a cruel world of filth, discomfort, and disease. Heating was poor, air conditioning and refrigeration nonexistent. There were no washing machines, dishwashers, or microwave ovens.[46] Most people knew someone who had been horribly crippled or killed by a sexually transmitted disease. No, not AIDS—syphilis. Like Uganda, the turn of the century is a place many of us would like to visit but few of us would care to live in, least of all the environmental activists who live in air-conditioned ivory towers tapping out their prose on word processors, then transmitting it to their publishers on their modems or facsimile machines.

Somehow, the agrarian utopians seem to be unaware of the

hardships that existed in the time to which they long to flee. The one environmentalist who is probably most identified with being antitechnology is lobbyist and lecturer Jeremy Rifkin. In a review of his most recent book, *A New Consciousness for a New Century*,[47] Gina Maranto notes in *The New York Times Book Review* that Rifkin "romanticizes the lot of the feudal serf by presenting him as living in a state of 'communal self-sufficiency,' on a land that for hundreds of years provided him with 'spiritual as well as economic security.' " In fact, points out Maranto, "the life of the feudal servant was truly nasty, brutish, and short."[48] Indeed, the life of the modern peasant continues to fit that description.

There are serious, serious problems in the thinking of a man who believes it would be good if we all became serfs again. But Rifkin is in the mainstream of the environmentalists.

Easterbrook comments that "Enviros [environmentalists] commonly cite E. F. Schumacher's theory that people are better off spending their lives in small village economies living by their own resources, because this gives you mastery over your own fate." But, says Easterbrook, "I've observed some of the world's peasant population at the village level and can't image any way to have less mastery over your fate, but still, nothing's stopping enviros from living this way, today, in the United States. Except convenience."[49]

## FEAR AND LOATHING OF TECHNOLOGY

Just as agrarian utopianism is part and parcel of the cult of the natural, so too is technophobia. Newness has always brought with it fear. Declared one congressman on the floor of the House:

> This begins a new era in the history of civilization. Never before has society been confronted with a power so full of potential danger and at the same time so full of promise for the future of man and for the peace of the world. The menace to our people . . . would call for prompt legislative action, even if the military and economic implications were not so overwhelming.

The year was circa 1950 and the subject was nuclear energy, you say? Guess again. The year was 1857. The subject was the internal combustion engine.[50]

Michael Brown's articles for the *Niagara Falls Gazette* set off the Love Canal debacle, and clearly technophobia was a motivator for Brown. In his book on hazardous waste sites, *Laying Waste,* Brown concludes the section on Love Canal by quoting an Indian saying: "Now we see the results of technology gotten out of hand. And now, the earth is reacting very badly."[51]

To technophobes, progress is anything but progressive. "We continue to delude ourselves," says Jeremy Rifkin, "that this is the age of progress."[52] Thus, while some people oppose nuclear power because they feel it is too dangerous, or too impractical, others oppose it because they fear it would be too *practical.* "It would be little short of disastrous for us to discover a source of clean, cheap, abundant energy because of what we might do with it," wrote Amory Lovins in *Mother Earth.* "We . . . could do mischief to the earth and to each other."[53] Wrote Paul Ehrlich, in a statement that also betrays his elitist position: "Giving society cheap, abundant energy . . . would be the equivalent of giving an idiot child a machine gun."[54] In an article in *Quest* magazine, titled "The Case Against Abundant, Cheap Energy," Dartmouth professor Noel Perrin wrote: "I don't *want* nuclear technology (or solar, or any other kind) to work because the blessings of abundant energy are even more to be feared than its risks" (emphasis in original).[55] Two years later he would write in *The New York Times:* "What's needed from the nuclear industry is an actual catastrophe—such as it almost gave us at Three Mile Island. . . . We do need a nuclear accident—a nice big one. Soon! Three Mile Island would have done nicely . . . probably no more than a hundred people would have died from the initial contact with the radioactive steam."[56] There's no reason to accept the good professor's estimate on deaths, but that he apparently thought these people would be expendable is certainly revealing of his mind-set.

Similarly, after the news broke that researchers at Brigham Young University might have discovered a way of producing cold fusion, with its promise of cheap, safe energy, the technophobes were aghast. "The worst thing that could happen to our planet," commented Jeremy Rifkin.[57] And Easterbrook writes of the sad tale of John Todd, an environmental biologist who became concerned that modern sewage treatment systems were ecological failures because they produced toxic sludge. It occurred to him to mix the sludge with microbes that naturally metabolize toxics. A trial run in Providence, Rhode Island, worked beautifully. "So are environmentalists happy about this breakthrough?" asked Easterbrook. "No, they're furious. Todd says some of his old friends no longer speak to him: By discovering a solution to a man-made offense, he takes away an argument against growth."[58]

Such mindless fear of progress and technology eventually has to provoke reactions among the more thoughtful environmentalists. Such was the case in 1977, when environmentalists led by Rifkin were involved in a spirited fight against recombinant-DNA genetic engineering. Environmentalist literature began to bristle with stories about supergerms, environmental disasters, and breakdowns of world ecosystems. Groups including the NRDC and Friends of the Earth threatened to sue the Department of Health, Education, and Welfare (HEW) to block federally funded research,[59] and the Environmental Defense Fund (EDF) fought it as well.[60] Books appeared with names like *Biohazard, Playing God,* and *Genetic Politics.* Late in 1977, Lewis Thomas, president of the Memorial Sloan-Kettering Cancer Center of New York, resigned his long-standing position as a member of Friends of the Earth's advisory council, saying: "I am in flat disagreement on straightforward scientific grounds with the rigid position taken by their organization." Weeks later, René Dubos, a founder of the NRDC, stunned the organization by resigning the position of trustee he had held for ten years. Dubos, whose name was on the letterhead used in NRDC correspondence on the genetic engineering issue, informed HEW in an angry letter: "I had no idea that NRDC was involved in the recombinant-DNA problem, for which it has no competence. . . . Failure on the part of the NRDC to communicate with me . . . reveals either an irresponsible lack of familiarity with the literature in this field, or an intellectual dishonesty in using my name for a cause that I regard as ridiculous."[61]

The British novelist and physicist Charles P. (C. P.) Snow died in 1980, before most of the crises discussed in this book had arisen. But he well understood the nature worshipers, the technophobes, and the agrarian utopians. In this 1959 book *The Two Cultures and the Scientific Revolution,* he wrote of "literary intellectuals at one pole—at the other scientists . . . Between the two a gulf of mutual incomprehension."[62] Said Snow:

One truth is straightforward. Industrialization is the only hope of the poor. . . . It is all very well for us, sitting pretty, to think that material standards of living don't matter all that much. It is all very well for one . . . to reject industrialization—do a modern Walden, if you like, and if you go without much food, see most of your children die in infancy . . . then I respect you for the strength of your aesthetic revulsion. But I don't respect you in the slightest if, even passively, you try to impose the same choice on others who are not free to choose. In fact, we know what their choice would be. For, with singular unanimity, in any country where they have had the chance, the poor have walked off the land into factories as fast as the factories could take them.[63]

So much for Jeremy Rifkin's blissful serfs.

## ENVIRONMENTALISM AS RELIGION

This book has already discussed the fact that many of the values held by environmentalism are simply a matter of faith without science. Yet, sometimes that faith may go so far as to constitute something approximating religion. Noting that one (allegedly) scientific theory—the Gaia theory—actually claims that the earth is a living organism, essayist Charles Krauthammer writes that "contemporary environmentalism . . . indulges in earth worship to the point of idolatry."[64] Cathy Young, writing in the *Detroit News,* quoted one environmentalist saying his religion is "deep ecology," while a letter writer to the editor of *The New York Times* says she won't use a clothes dryer, conceding that this might have little impact on the environment but "like all religious rituals, the importance of these acts lies not so much in their effect on society as in their role in the life of the believers." The writer went on to say: "The environment is not a political cause. It is a religion. We earth lovers are not just another special-interest group. We are prophets, would-be transformers of the world. We are not seeking merely a new law or a new program, but a new vision to guide us."[65]

But are such worshipers of nature as these at the very extreme end of the environmental activist spectrum? Only, perhaps, in their choice of words. In early 1990, Carl Sagan and twenty-two other well-known scientists appealed to world religious leaders to join them in protecting the environment. At a Moscow conference

Sagan asserted that there was "a religious as well as scientific dimension" to the problems of global change. The scientists, who included physicist Hans Bethe, MIT President Jerome Weisner, and evolution theorist Stephen Jay Gould, signed an appeal stating that "efforts to safeguard and cherish the environment need to be infused with a vision of the sacred."[66]

Nature worshipers often approach environmental issues with the unreasoning zeal of crusaders in a holy war. That was clearly evident in the wording of the 1972 Clean Water Act, which called for a zero level of discharge into the nation's navigable waterways by 1985,[67] a declaration akin to that of a preacher urging his congregation to cleanse themselves of all sin. It is impossible to prevent all pollution. Pollution is a by-product of processes, both natural and man-made, that allow life to sustain itself. When a bear relieves itself in a stream, that's pollution. It can be harmful. Drink out of that stream without disinfecting the water and you may become intimately familiar with the inside of your toilet bowl. Man-made pollution can be minimized, but not completely eliminated. By assigning the goal of elimination, the pollution problem is turned into a crusade and into a moral one at that. Pollution is no longer seen as a part of life and part of the ecosystem, but as an enemy to be dealt with only on the basis of unconditional surrender. A quasi-religious moralistic approach makes very difficult or impossible the application of cost-benefit analysis and results in massive amounts of money being thrown at problems that have been identified as the enemy, leaving little money for problems that may be just as severe or even more so but haven't been made the subject of anyone's particular crusade.

## THE CRISIS INDUSTRY

To listen to the increased pitch of environmentalist warnings, the earth is on the very edge of destruction. On the first Earth Day in 1970, the talk was of improving things; on Earth Day 1990 the most often-used expression was "Save the planet." In fact, in almost all measurable ways, the environment in the United States has improved markedly in those two decades. EPA estimates of air emissions of the six prevalent air pollutants or their precursors—particulate matter, sulfur oxides, nitrogen oxides, volatile organic compounds, carbon monoxide, and lead—"indicate that, since 1970, there has been a substantial decrease in emissions of each of these pollutants except nitrogen oxides." This in turn has led to a marked decrease in ground-level ozone formation. Lead emissions, generally considered the worst of these, dropped 88 percent. Sulfur dioxide, which contributes to acid rain, has dropped by more than a third. Among major emissions, only nitrogen oxides and suspended particulates have not seen large reductions. Water quality has stayed the same or improved in most of the nation's streams and lakes. If synthetic pesticides worry you, you'll be glad to know that their use peaked in 1981 and has stabilized at a lower level.[68] The loss of wetlands has slowed dramatically.[69] Soil erosion is greatly reduced. Farmland in the United States is not decreasing, and the destruction of the world's forests has been grossly exaggerated.[70]

Indeed, by standards of previous generations, even the state of the environment in 1970 was a tremendous improvement in many ways over previous generations. As late as December 1952, air pollution suspended over London killed four thousand people.[71] It was the same smog that hid so well Jack the Ripper during his bloody forays in Whitechapel in the 1880s. But by 1970, because of pollution controls and a switch to cleaner fuels, "London fog" was beginning to mean little more than the name of a famous raincoat manufacturer, and fish again swam belly down in the Thames. Yet the year before that, Paul Ehrlich proclaimed: "If I were a gambler, I would take even money that England will not exist in the year 2000."[72] How many years would Ehrlich have given England in 1952? Five? Ten?

The point isn't that everything is wonderful now, or that we couldn't or shouldn't make more progress. It is that good progress has been made but that you'd never know it from the environmental activists. What they have done in these two decades since the first Earth Day is, first of all, to ignore that progress. The founder of EarthWorks Group, publisher of the *Fifty Simple Things You Can Do to Save the Earth* and other books with similar titles, John Javna, says: "The air is unbreathable in most cities."[73] Rhetorical exaggerations are common and acceptable, but "unbreathable"? Really? Second, environmentalists have replaced problems whose dimensions—and the chances for improvement—were measurable with those that are not. Now they warn us about the danger of global warming, a danger that remains unproven[74]—though you wouldn't know that to hear them. Indeed, despite this lack of evidence, there are those who assert this issue as strongly as Samuel Epstein did about dioxin in 1983, that there is no scientific dispute left, that the only holdouts are wishful thinkers and advocates of industry.

One estimated price to stop the alleged global warming effect is, at "present value," $800 billion to $3.6 trillion in cumulative costs over the next century for the United States alone, according to a study by economists Alan Manne of Stanford University and Richard Richels of the Electric Power Research Institute.[75] By contrast, according to EPA estimates the nation is now spending $115 billion a year on *all* environmental protections combined, which itself is almost four times (in 1990 dollars) what the country spent in 1972 for those protections.[76]

Is this really the sort of thing into which we should plunge "just in case" this time the Sam Epsteins of the world turn out to be correct? It should be disconcerting to hear that by and large the same groups that have pushed the alarms discussed in great detail in this book are the same ones advocating drastic action to curtail global warming. It should be disconcerting to hear that the author of *The Genesis Strategy: Climate and Global Survival,* Stephen Schneider—who is probably quoted more frequently about global warming than any other authority[77]—told *Discover* magazine in October 1989 that scientists should consider stretching the truth "to get some broad-based support, to capture the public's imagination." Said Schneider: "That, of course, entails getting loads of media coverage. So, we have to offer up scary scenarios, make simplified, dramatic statements, and make little mention of any doubts we may have. . . . Each of us has to decide what the right balance is between being effective and being honest."[78] It should be disconcerting to hear that the same National Academy of Sciences that has lent qualified credence to the global warming theory warned in 1977 that a new ice age "is upon us," citing "evidence as diverse as the duration of arctic snow cover, animal migration, sea surface temperatures and microfossils on the ocean floor, not to mention *declining* average global temperatures" (emphasis added).[79] It should be disconcerting to hear that Stephen Schneider wrote a book back in the 1970s warning that the world might be facing—and must take steps to prepare for—a "Little Ice Age,"[80] and that his acknowledgments page in that book reads like a who's who of anti-industrial environmental apocalyptics, with the first acknowledgment going to Paul Ehrlich.

In Vice President Gore's aforementioned essay in *Scientific American,* two conspicuous words popped up: "radical" and "crisis."[81] Those two words appear repeatedly in the environmentalist literature of the 1990s. Throughout history, men have waited in the wings for a crisis during which to strike. But if it is true that the confusion of a crisis allows small minorities to seize power they could not otherwise have gained during more stable times, so too can a manufactured crisis do the job as well. Long before the multitude of crises discussed in this book ever occurred, the nature worshipers, the technophobes, and the agrarian utopians sought to impose their values on society. Some worked through literature, such as Ernst Joseph Schumacher with his *Small Is Beautiful,* and others worked through outright violence, such as the machine-destroying British Luddites of the early nineteenth century.

It is not unreasonable to assume that the reason some environmentalists don't mind spending hundreds of billions of dollars on worthless and near-worthless industry restraints is that they happen to favor industry restraints for their own sake. If your name were Fred and somebody alleged a problem that could only be cured by giving each person named Fred a million dollars, you'd be awfully happy about that problem. Solving such a problem is not an end, merely a means to an end. As Senator Timothy Wirth (D-Colo.) put it: "We've got to ride the global warming issue. Even if the theory of global warming is wrong, we will be doing the right thing, in terms of economic policy and environmental policy."[82] Similarly, some environmentalists of today are thrilled that they seem to have discovered problems that, they are all too happy to inform us, require major life-style changes. And by grand coincidence, those happen to be exactly the major life-style changes that Schumacher, and his followers and predecessors, have been advocating all along. If they can't get people to adopt them by honest persuasion, they'll do so by scare tactics and coercion.

There are legitimate environmentalists who continue to do legitimate work, but they are not the ones you read about in the newspaper or see on TV, and they appear to be a dying breed. The new breed—represented by relatively new organizations such as the Natural Resources Defense Council and the EDF and even by some of the older organizations like the Audubon Society and the Sierra Club—do not share the goals of traditional environmentalists. Indeed, calling them environmentalists at all may be stretching the definition. Those people have a very tenuous lineage from the conservationists of not so long ago who were just as likely to be conservative as liberal, as likely to be Republican as Democratic or Marxist. Conservationists saw improving the state of nature as a way of improving conditions for humanity; they did not see humans as a cancer upon the land. To them, the damage that man had wrought could be undone. They had no philosophers like Bill McKibben who claimed that the damage done by man could never be repaired, no matter how pristine its final condition. These were the Sierra Clubs and Audubon Societies of old, now scorned by the new breed as a bunch of stodgy birdwatchers.

In 1991, the National Audubon Society, which had already for some time been sliding toward political activism, dumped its magazine's editor of twenty-five years and attempted to drop its ninety-year-old logo of the egret until negative publicity forced its reinstatement. "We want to be Greenpeace," said one of the magazine's editors.[83] The society began as an organization to protect birds that were being hunted to extinction, the most well-known case being that of the egret. The first game warden in the country to give his life for his cause was an Audubon member defending those egrets. The attempted dropping of that symbol from the logo was tremendously symbolic. Noted *The New York Times:* "Over a century later . . . its causes are multiplying from birds and wildlife habitats to toxic waste and population control. The old guard says the society is losing its focus. The new guard talks about redefining nature." According to the *Times,* the old editor, Les Line, "appears too much of a conservationist for [President Peter A. A.] Berle's vision." Said Line: "Berle told me that the primary reason I had to go was my interest in nature and natural resources and that was not where the action was."[84] To Berle, a former government bureaucrat and a Harvard-educated lawyer, "the action" appears to be litigation and lobbying. Not that Line was a stodgy old birdwatcher himself. His magazine led the way in exploring subjects like toxic waste, pesticides, and the destruction of the Everglades. A contributor to that magazine, John Mitchell, said of the new Audubon Society: "They have become so big, so top-heavy, that to keep the apparatus running they have in many ways become like the institutions they battle."[85] Line echoes that sentiment. "The Society has moved away from its historic mission," he says. "There's tremendous competition out there for money among all these environmental groups. And we've gotten top-heavy with bureaucrats and accountants and fund-raisers who are all good professionals, but I don't think you'd catch them sloshing through a marsh."[86]

Not incidentally perhaps, the editor chosen to replace Line came directly from a bastion of credibility and solid responsible reporting—the supermarket scandal sheet, the *Star*.

The old guard environmentalists were people who loved the woods and spent their time in them. They had virtually nothing in common with the young Turks in business suits who file lawsuits and send out press releases from suites in the concrete jungles of Manhattan, Washington, D.C., and San Francisco. These were people who saw the beautiful side of nature, but they saw the ugly side as well. They suffered no delusions that prompted them to turn nature into a godlike entity. They knew what roughing it was like and hence they appreciated more than anyone the wonderful amenities of modern living.

The worst kind of wolf is the one that wears the clothes of a lamb. Just so, the worst organizations for the environment are the ones that drain off the dollars and the good intentions of so many Americans who are concerned about the environment and turn around and use those dollars and that clout to pursue agendas that are at very best marginally related to the causes they claim to advance. Who will now do what the old Audubon Society and the old Sierra Club used to do?

Perhaps nobody. "The big groups make policy decisions based on their fund-raising campaign rather than the other way around," says Amos Enos of the National Fish and Wildlife Foundation, part of the Interior Department. "The big issue in Congress now is the Clean Water Act and wetlands preservation, and the big groups are just not there. It's not the stuff of fund-raising appeals."[87]  The insincerity of the environmental activist organizations does not necessarily hold for their members. In fact, it is by virtue of disinformation that they get, hold, and motivate their members. Whatever the motivation of the officers of the NRDC or the EDF, it is probably a good bet that the motivations of most of their members are the stated goals of those groups, not the surreptitious goals of the leaders. And this, too, is a tragedy.

Who are the people who run these groups? As the author of *Progress and Privilege,* William Tucker has noted:

> Environmentalists today are not saying anything different than what most aristocracies have been saying all along. Invariably, there's a strong conservatism, a strong cautiousness and a tendency to downgrade industrial society and industrial accomplishments. Environmentalism is a kind of elite expression of a group which is already well off, and doesn't welcome new upstarts or technologies. It's the old "we can do without it" sort of attitude that aristocracies have always had toward progress and innovation.[88]

Tucker believes that many of those calling themselves environmentalists are basically selfish people who have the means to make sacrifices by giving up "material production," which they personally don't need anyway, to make marginal gains in health and safety.[89] He says that there is nothing environmentalists hate more than being considered an elite special interest,[90] but that is an image that has a strong basis in reality. He notes that when Vernon Jordan of the Urban League was asked to attend a joint conference on urban and environmental affairs, he made reference to the snail darter fish, which environmental activists had declared an endangered species in order to hold up for years the building of a Tennessee dam. "Walk down Twelfth Street [in Washington, D.C.] and ask the proverbial man on the street what he thinks about the snail darter and you are likely to get the blankest look you ever experienced," said Jordan. "Ask him what he thinks the basic urban environmental problem is, and he'll tell you jobs. I don't intend to raise the simple-minded equation of snail darters and jobs, but that does symbolize an implicit divergence of interests between some segments of the environmental movement and the bulk of black and urban people."[91]

## THE NEW ENVIRONMENTALISM VERSUS SCIENCE

Joseph Paehlke, in his book *Environmentalism and the Future of Aggressive Politics,* writes: "Natural and social scientists have tended to view their role as scientists and citizens as separate.

Environmentalists, in contrast, have generally seen these roles as irretrievably linked. Not since the nineteenth century, when Marx, Engels, and many others sought (so wrongheadedly at times) to blend science and ideology, has there been so explicit an effort in this regard."[92]

Paehlke is not entirely unsympathetic to this effort, but he cannot fail to point out that "Marx and Engels erred in part because they made little attempt to distinguish between the historical outcomes they preferred and those predicted 'scientifically' using their methods." Likewise, he says, "environmentalists have tended to use science to extrapolate fearsome futures."[93]

Paehlke says that to achieve the environmentalists' ends, "environmentalism must blend the natural sciences, values, and social sciences in a distinctive way. No particular set of findings in the natural sciences can determine an ideological perspective. . . . The findings of the ecological, toxicological, and resource-related sciences must be integrated conceptually, generalized at a level with which many natural scientists are uncomfortable."[94]

That may be a nice prescription for success for environmentalist activists' goals, but what of the goal of scientific veracity? What if the goal is simply to allow humans to use the earth's resources while causing the minimum damage? That is why, as Paehlke later notes, "many scientists deeply resent the claims and style of environmentalists."[95] Those scientists resent the environmentalists for the same reason a good doctor resents a quack. Both make money, but the good doctor wants to heal, while the quack has no such motivation. When you've worked as an epidemiologist for decades and somebody comes along with a highly publicized book turning epidemiology on its head, you resent it. When you've worked in carcinogenesis for decades and somebody publishes a report on an alleged cancer-causing agent that gets tremendous media attention but has a kindergartener's understanding of what causes cancer, you resent it. Some of these scientists are very concerned with the earth's welfare, some perhaps not. Some vote liberal, some conservative. But they don't like to see their areas of science subjugated to someone else's political cause. They don't want to see a "blend[ing of] the natural sciences, values, and social sciences," because inevitably this leads to the subjugation of scientific truth.

# CHAPTER 13

# Ending the Reign of Terror

As a security measure, it was necessary to exterminate the bad citizens. The massacres lasted four days. There were more than 1400 victims in Paris. But in many other towns, there was the same expeditious process.[1]

—O. Garreau and D. Legrand, *La Révolution Française en 100 Questions*

We are clearly in the midst of an environmental revolution. This stage of the revolution, unfortunately, correlates with the Reign of Terror in the French Revolution. In the name of ideals perhaps as worthy as *"liberté, égalité, fraternité,"* we are expending amazing amounts of energy to accomplish amazingly little. True, there are some groups and individuals who have tremendously improved their own positions, as was the case during the Terror, but they have done little if anything to promote the causes for which they claim to be fighting and to help the world that they claim to be saving. With each fall of Madame Guillotine's sharp blade these days, the air does not become cleaner, the food and water supply does not become safer, and humans do not become healthier. All that can be said for sure is that more heads are ending up in the basket. Just as with the Terror, there was no correlation between lopped individual heads and true enemies of the people, neither has there been in recent years any significant correlation between the persecutions of chemicals, processes, devices, and the manufacturers thereof, and the prevention of illness. Organizations'

367

coffers have been filled, personal fortunes have been made, individual fame has been achieved, a variety of agendas have been or are in the process of being fulfilled, and over $100 billion a year is being spent, all in the name of making the country a safer, better place in which to live, or, to use the more recent expression, of "saving the earth." Yet there is little evidence that the country is much, if at all, safer as a result of the environmental crusades of the past decade and a half.

True, lop enough heads and you'll eventually remove a guilty one, but the cost is frightful in terms of squandered resources and human terror.

Environmentalists know the story well. At one time, American bison herds were so large that they were said to hold up trains for as much as three days at a time. Meanwhile, passenger pigeon flocks darkened the skies, so great were their numbers. But hunters, within a few decades' time, wiped out the pigeons to a single bird and almost did the same with the buffalo. Environmentalists would say the lesson in this is that man has the capability of destroying even that which is so large that it seems indestructible, and they are right. What they do not seem to realize is, first, that *all* resources are scarce, and second, that the definition of "resources" goes far beyond that with which they have concerned themselves—air, water, soil, the rain forests, animal and plant species, and so on. Money is a resource and fear and attention are also resources, and nobody more actively squanders those resources than those who do so in the name of the environment.

The United States economy is the largest and the most powerful in the world. It can take a heavy beating, as could the buffalo herds and passenger pigeon flocks. But ultimately, struck hard enough, the economy like the mighty buffalo can be brought to its knees. The fiscal year 1991–92 saw the nation endure a prolonged recession. While recessions are merely part of the normal business cycle, the length of this one was by no means necessary. The Democrats blamed the Republicans and the Republicans blamed the Democrats, but in truth economists warned that you don't raise taxes during a recession and that's just what the Republican President and the Democratic Congress agreed to do. Yet the bottom line is that anything that diverts money away from business into something on which business would not spend that money is a drag on the economy—something akin to shooting a buffalo or a passenger pigeon. Shoot a few and the effect is unnoticeable, but keep shooting at a higher and higher rate and the herds and the flocks begin to grow smaller.

Dale W. Jorgenson, a professor of economics at Harvard University, and Peter J. Wilcoxen, an economist at the University of Texas, have estimated that if not for environmental regulations enacted prior to 1990 (thus not counting the most expensive single piece of legislation—the Clean Air Act of 1990), the real gross national product would be about 2.6 percent higher than its current level.[2] "That may not sound like much," says Robert Crandall, a senior fellow at the liberal Brookings Institution, a think tank in Washington, D.C., "but this GNP gap translates into about $150 billion, or about half of the current defense budget." He adds, "It is also about half of combined federal, state, and local expenditures on education."[3] He also notes that given current trends, it will soon exceed defense spending.[4] Yet a study by Michael Hazilla, associate professor of economics at American University in Washington, D.C., and Raymond J. Kropp, of Resources for the Future, a Washington-based think tank, shows that real GNP was 5.8 percent lower in 1990 than it would have been without clean air and clean water regulations.[5] And Crandall thinks even that figure is actually low, "because the only thing they can include are actual expenditures on environmental controls" on old ventures, and not the cost to the economy of companies that decide against new ventures because the regulatory costs are too high.[6] Conservationists back in the nineteenth century might have told you, there's nothing wrong with culling some animals for useful purposes; just make sure your purposes *are* useful and proceed carefully. But so many of the environmental regulations slapped directly on businesses and indirectly on the consumer—the final payer of all costs—fulfill neither of these dictates. They are imposed in response to the agitation of special interest groups, to media scaremongering, to business lobbying, and to irrational fears of the American public.

How ironic it is that some of the same people who conclude that the earth is as fragile as a spider's web, that the human body is a sitting duck for anything synthesized by man, nevertheless see the American economy's capacity for absorbing ever-higher taxes and regulations as being as boundless as the universe. Even short of national bankruptcy, needless health and safety regulations can dramatically harm our capability to compete with other nations. That is because by and large other nations don't suffer from the fears we do. To be sure, they may have some of their own—fear of "mad cow" disease in Great Britain, for example. But this willingness to pump massive amounts of money down a hole because somebody somewhere claims to have found a cluster of disease is something very American. It's true that American firms will be able to compete against other American firms no matter how onerous regulations become, simply because those other firms will have to comply with those same regulations. (Although small firms may be driven out of business because they will usually have less capital available to meet new requirements.) But if those regulation-strapped American firms must then compete with overseas businesses that suffer fewer controls, they will find that they cannot compete.

Because pollution controls are expensive, the best guarantee of being able to deal with pollution is to have an economy that is strong and a nation that's wealthy. It may be that in a country with no industry there is the least amount of pollution and environmental harm in the normal sense of the word, but the United States will never deindustrialize. Nobody really wants that, including the agrarian romantics and technophobes who so desperately think they do. But among those nations that are industrial, it is the wealthy ones that have the least pollution.[7] The residents of many American cities know they have an air pollution problem only because they are told they do, based on pollution monitors located downtown where traffic is densest. But go to Poland and you may find yourself forced to go to one of their underground "clinics" in uranium mines just to breathe relatively clean air. For that matter, half of Poland's cities, including Warsaw, do not even treat their waste. In the heavily industrial countries of Germany and Austria, the Danube is a beautiful river. Inside Hungary it becomes a moving cesspool. Societies that can barely feed their people don't have time to worry about practices that may cause disease thirty years down the road. That is a luxury for the countries of the first world— and one that will be lost if those countries fall to Third World economic levels.

But tangible resources aren't the only ones with which we should concern ourselves. Interest and fear, too, are important and scarce resources. One cannot be interested in everything.

One cannot fear everything. Instead, we make lists in our minds of those things we fear the most, fear less, and fear not at all; those which interest us the most, interest us less, interest us not at all.

The two major causes of premature death in this country are heart disease and cancer. Smoking, drinking, and overeating are the most efficient ways to die of one of those illnesses, along with getting sundry other maladies. These are public health enemies one, two, and three. Yet those of us who smoke, drink, and eat to excess find ourselves terrified of parts per quadrillion of headline-grabbing chemicals. There may be other real culprits out there waiting to be discovered, but while the public remains mesmerized with the plunges of the guillotine blade, there is little incentive to look for them.

The chemical companies, big and faceless and run by CEOs who sometimes make obscene amounts of money, make wonderful whipping boys, but it is amazing how many of us gladly ingest toxins and pollutants far, far worse for health than anything those companies have dreamed of pouring into the atmosphere or water. Eating vegetables and fruits treated with pesticides made by Dow or Uniroyal is incomparably safer than downing the delicious ice cream produced by the environmentally and politically correct company Ben and Jerry's, chock-full of saturated fat. And by the way, Ben and Jerry's does not list nutrient information on its high-fat products, though its owners do use their packaging to talk about the causes they support such as helping the family farm. Probably more people die from cigarette smoking in a day than have ever died from every chemical the Natural Resources Defense Council has railed against, but that doesn't stop the NRDC from accepting money from foundations that made their money selling cancer and heart disease in little white tubes.[8] Paper companies must reduce their emissions of dioxin from parts per quadrillion to parts per quintillion we cry, but don't lay a finger on my Butterfinger!

We are a nation that desperately needs to reevaluate its priorities in terms of health risks. Industrial pollutants should be on the list, but the list's order must be determined by the scope and severity of the risk and the cost of alleviating it, not by the latest *60 Minutes* exposé or the latest direct mail drive of the Natural Resources Defense Council.

The democracy which eventually came after the French Revolution was good, and what prompted that revolution may have been necessity. Necessity has to some extent prompted the environmental revolution and what eventually comes out of it may be good. What is needed is to end our Reign of Terror, to restore sanity and sound principles to our revolution. It is time for the pendulum to start swinging back the other way, so that we may eventually end up somewhere in the middle of the two extremes of "I don't care" and "React to every scare." It is time to begin shaping policies on the basis of science, rather than shaping science to fit policies. It is time to go back to the good ideas of the early environmentalists and conservationists and to reject those of the fanatics and faddists who have since jumped aboard the bandwagon. Protection of human health and institutions and proper stewardship of the earth demand no less.

# Notes

If reference is to a specific fact or quote, the exact page number is given. References to an entire article will list the first page of the article only.

## Introduction

1. George Orwell, *1984* (New York: Harcourt Brace Jovanovich, 1983), p. 218.
2. Joan Claybrook, Public Citizen, undated membership and fundraising appeal, as cited in Elizabeth Whelan, *Toxic Terror* (Ottawa, Illinois: Jameson Books, 1985), p. 5.

## Chapter 1: The Alarm over Alar

1. "Overheard," *Newsweek,* March 27, 1989, p. 15.
2. CBS, *60 Minutes,* " 'A' Is for Apple," February 26, 1989, transcript p. 10.
3. Martha Groves, "Schools' Action Widens the Apple Controversy," *Los Angeles Times,* March 13, 1989, p. 1.
4. "Bitter Fruit," *The Economist,* August 12, 1989, p. 29.
5. Groves, op. cit. p. 1.

6. Timothy Egan, "Apple Growers Bruised and Bitter After Alar Scare," *New York Times,* July 9, 1991, p. A1.

7. Personal telephone communication with Desmond O'Rourke, professor of agriculture and economics and director of the Impact Center at Washington State University in Pullman, July 3, 1991.

8. Carole Sugarman, "Agencies Say Apples Safe, Chemical Not Imminent Risk," *Washington Post,* March 17, 1989, p. A57.

9. Tim Tesconi, "Apple Cooperative Goes Under: Sebastopol Group Blames Alar Scare," *Santa Rosa* (Calif.) *Press-Democrat,* December 8, 1989, pp. E1, E6.

10. "It's About Apples, and Growers' Attempt to Make Them Redder," *Los Angeles Times,* August 24, 1986, part I, p. 18.

11. Ibid. pp. 18, 20.

12. Ibid.

13. *60 Minutes,* op. cit. p. 13.

14. Quoted in Natural Resources Defense Council, "Chronology for Daminozide," typescript, undated, p. 4. (available from NRDC, 25 Kearny Street, San Francisco, Calif. 94108).

15. Ibid. pp. 1–3.

16. Federal Register, January 16, 1987, p. 1913.

17. Federal Register, July 29, 1987, p. 28,257.

18. Eliot Marshall, "Science Advisers Need Advice," *Science,* Vol. 245, No. 4913 (July 7, 1989), p. 21.

19. Comment made not for attribution.

20. Joseph D. Rosen, "The Death of Daminozide," in *Pesticides and Alternatives,* ed. J. E. Casida (New York: Elsevier, 1990), p. 59.

21. Ibid. p. 59.

22. Environmental Protection Agency, "EPA Accelerates Process to Cancel Daminozide Uses on Apples; Extends Tolerance," press release, February 1, 1989, p. 1.

23. Robert J. Bidinotto, "The Great Apple Scare," *Reader's Digest,* October 1990, pp. 55–56; and confirmed through personal communication with Chris Wilkenson.

24. Personal telephone communication with Stephen Schatzow, October 29, 1991.

25. Bidinotto, op. cit. p. 56.

26. Ibid.

27. *Donahue,* transcript no. 120387 (1987), p. 2.

28. Pharmakon Research Institute, "Ames/Salmonella Plate Incorporation Assay (UDMH)," Report No. PH301-UN-005-86 (Waverly, Penn.: December 9, 1986), unpublished report; Pharmakon Research Institute, "*In Vitro* Chromosome Abberation Analysis in Chinese Hamster Ovary (CHO) Cells (UDMH)," Report No. PH320-UN-002-86 (Waverly, Penn.: December 9, 1986), unpublished report; Pharmakon Research Institute, "Rat Hepatocyte Primary Culture/DNA Repair Test (UDMH)," Report No. PH311-UN-001-86 (Waverly, Penn.: December 6, 1986), unpublished report.

29. L. F. Stankowski, "Unsymmetrical Dimethylhydrazide (UDMH) CHO/HPRT Mammalian Cell Forward Gene Mutation Assay," Report No. PH314-UN-001-88 (Waverly, Penn.: Pharmakon Research International, September 12, 1988, unpublished report.)

30. Bidinotto, op. cit. p. 56.

31. Marshall, op. cit. p. 21.

32. Quoted in Marshall, p. 21.

33. *60 Minutes*, " 'A' Is for Apple," op. cit. p. 10.

34. Rosen, p. 60.

35. Christine F. Chaisson, "Overview of the Evaluation of Carcinogenic Risk of Daminozide and UDMH," typescript, p. 6 (Technical Assessment Systems, 1000 Potomac Street, N.W., Washington, D.C. 20007), undated, unpublished report.

36. Edwin I. Goldenthal, "Two Year Oncogenicity Study in Rats," typescript (Mattawan, Mich.: International Research and Development Corporation, 1989), p. 13.

37. Ibid. p. 16.

38. "EPA Accelerates Process," op. cit. p. 1; Michael Weisskopf, "EPA Targets Chemical Used on Apples," *Washington Post,* February 2, 1989, p. 4A.

39. Philip Shabecoff, "Hazard Reported in Apple Chemical," *New York Times,* February 2, 1989, pp. A1, A18.

40. "EPA Accelerates Process," op. cit. p. 2.

41. See Edith Efron, *The Apocalyptics* (New York: Simon and Schuster, 1984), pp. 191–93.

42. "EPA Accelerates Process," op. cit. p. 2.

43. Shabecoff, op. cit. pp. A1, A18.

44. Robert S. Taylor, "Group's Influence on U.S. Environmental Laws, Policies, Earns It a Reputation as a Shadow EPA," *Wall Street Journal,* January 13, 1986, p. 50.

45. Gregg Easterbrook, "Everything You Know About the Environment Is Wrong," *New Republic,* April 30, 1990, p. 18.

46. *Nader* v. *Environmental Protection Agency,* 859 F.2d 747 (9th Cir. 1988).

47. Bradford Sewell and Robin Whyatt, *Intolerable Risk: Pesticides in Our Children's Foods* (New York: Natural Resources Defense Council, February 1989).

48. Andrea Arnold, *Fear of Food* (Bellevue, Wash.: Free Enterprise Press, 1990), pp. 95–96, citing Annual Registration Statements, Office of Foreign Agent Registration, Internal Security Division, Department of Justice, Washington, D.C.

49. Fenton Communications, "Intolerable Risk: Transforming Public Awareness of the Hazards of Pesticides, Report on a Media Campaign Conducted by Fenton Communications for the Natural Resources Defense Council," May 22, 1989 (typescript), p. 2.

50. Ibid., pp. 2–3.

51. Malcolm Gladwell, "Some Fear Bad Precedent in Alar Alarm," *Washington Post,* April 19, 1989, p. A12.

52. Fenton, op. cit. pp. 3–4.

53. Arlene Fischer, "The Foods That Are Poisoning Your Child," *Redbook,* May 1, 1989, p. 116.

54. Fenton, op. cit. pp. 3–4.

55. Gladwell, op. cit. p. A1.

56. Fenton, op. cit. p. 4.

57. All comments from David Brooks, "Journalists and Others for Saving the Planet," *Wall Street Journal,* October 5, 1989, p. A28.

58. Transcript, U.S. Congress, Senate Committee on Labor and Human Resources, Subcommittee on Children, Family, Drugs and Alcoholism, "Health Effects of Pesticide Use on Children," 101st Cong., 1st Sess., March 16, 1989, oral statement of Meryl Streep, p. 53.

59. Ibid. p. 17.

60. *60 Minutes,* " 'A' Is for Apple," op. cit. p. 11.

61. Gladwell, op. cit. p. A12.

62. Maura Dolan, "Tests Show Alar Traces on Apples in Two County Stores," *Los Angeles Times,* March 30, 1989, p. 26.

63. Keith Schneider, "Safeway Accused of Breaking Promise on Apples," *New York Times,* February 3, 1988, p. B6.

64. Fenton, op. cit. p. 5.

65. Nanci Helmuth and Patrick O'Driscoll, "The Fight to Clean Up Our Food Hits TV," *USA Today,* March 8, 1989, p. 1A.

66. Anastasia Toufexis, "Watch Those Vegetables, Ma," *Time,* March 6, 1989, p. 57; Anastasia Toufexis, "Dining with Invisible Danger," *Time,* March 27, 1989, p. 28; Margaret Carlson, "Do You Dare to Eat a Peach?" *Time,* March 27, 1989, p. 24; Laura Shapiro et al., "Warning: Your Food, Nutritious and Delicious, May be Hazardous to Your Health," *Newsweek,* March 27, 1989, p. 16; Tim Friend and Nanci Hellmich, "Fear: Are We Poisoning Children?" *USA Today,* February 28, 1989, p. 1A; "Ms. Streep Goes to Washington to Stop a Bitter Harvest," *People,* March 20, 1989, p. 50; Claire Safran, "Are Pesticides Poisoning Our Children?" *Woman's Day,* April 18, 1989, p. 106.

67. Lawrie Mott quoted in Egan, op. cit. p. A16.

68. CBS News, *60 Minutes,* "What About Apples?" May 14, 1989, transcript p. 3.

69. Daniel E. Koshland, Jr., "Scare of the Week," *Science* editorial, April 7, 1989, p. 9.

70. See Center for Science in the Public Interest, *Voodoo Science, Twisted Consumerism: The Golden Assurances of the American Council on Science and Health* (Washington, D.C.: Center for Science in the Public Interest, March 1982), pp. 3–10.

71. For example, Gary Null, *Clearer, Cleaner, Safer, Greener* (New York: Villard, 1990), p. 125.

72. Elizabeth Whelan, *Toxic Terror* (Ottawa, Ill.: Jameson Books, 1985), p. 282.

73. Formally published in 1990 as Anne Witte Garland, *For Our Kids' Sake: How to Protect Your Child Against Pesticides in Food* (San Francisco, Sierra Club Books, 1990).

74. Anne Witte Garland, "The Newest Problem on the Food Front," *Ms.,* November 1985, p. 78.

75. Kenneth Smith, "Alar: One Year Later" (New York: American Council on Science and Health, March 1990), p. 7.

76. Smith, op. cit. p. 7.

77. David Kotelchuck, "The Third-Wave Asbestos Conference: High Drama in Science," *Health-PAC Bulletin,* Vol. 20, No. 4 (Winter 1990), p. 14, making reference to State of New York Asbestos Advisory Board, *Second Annual Report,* February 1990.

78. State of New York Asbestos Advisory Board, Second Annual Report, paper presented to Governor Mario M. Cuomo (February 1, 1990) (typed), p. 7.

79. Michael Fumento, "The Great Asbestos Rip-off," *The American Spectator,* Vol. 22, No. 10, October 1989, p. 172.

80. Transcript, U.S. Congress, Senate Committee on Labor and Human Resources, Subcommittee on Children, Family, Drugs and Alcoholism, op. cit., prepared statement of Janet S. Hathaway and Al Meyerhoff, pp. 71, 74.

81. Transcript, U.S. Congress, Senate Committee on Labor and Human Resources, Subcommittee on Children, Family, Drugs and Alcoholism, op. cit., oral statement of James A. Wylie, Jr., and response of Janet S. Hathaway, p. 85.

82. John A. Moore, "Speaking of Data: The Alar Controversy," *EPA Journal,* Vol. 15, No. 3 (May–June 1989), p. 8.

83. Moore, op. cit. p. 9.

84. Bidinotto, op. cit. p. 57.

85. Bidinotto, op. cit. p. 57.

86. Leslie Roberts, "Alar: The Numbers Game," *Science,* Vol. 243, No. 4897 (March 24, 1989) p. 1430.

87. Hathaway and Meyerhoff statement, op. cit. p. 71.

88. Fischer, op. cit. p. 116.

89. Transcript, U.S. Congress, Senate Committee on Labor and Human Resources, Subcommittee on Children, Family, Drugs and Alcoholism, op. cit., attachment to prepared statement of Charles J. Carey, pp. 89, 95.

90. U.S. Congress, Senate Committee on Labor and Human Resources, Subcommittee on Children, Family, Drugs and Alcoholism, op. cit. p. 8.

91. Transcript, U.S. Congress, Senate Committee on Labor and Human Resources, Subcommittee on Children, Family, Drugs and Alcoholism, op. cit., prepared statement of John A. Moore, p. 29.

92. F. Hoerger, "Some Current Views on Risk Assessment," presented

at a seminar entitled, "Understanding Environmental Risk," sponsored by the Public Research and Dissemination Program, University of California at Davis, Sacramento, Calif., 1985, as cited in Jay H. Lehr, "Toxicological Risk Assessment Distortions," (Dublin, Ohio: American Ground Water Trust, 1990), p. 10.

93. Philip Shabecoff, "Apple Industry Says It Will End Use of Chemical," *New York Times,* May 16, 1989, p. A1.

94. Malcolm Gladwell, "Uniroyal Halts Sale of Alar and Orders Recall," *Washington Post,* June 3, 1989, p. D12.

95. Personal telephone communication with Fred Hageman, Crops Division, Uniroyal Chemical Company, June 12, 1991.

96. Ibid.

97. Oral statement of James A. Wylie, Jr., op. cit. p. 65.

98. S1061, "A bill to prohibit the distribution, sale, or use of daminozide for food use, to cancel the registration for daminozide for food use, to revoke the tolerance for daminozide in or on food, and for other purposes," 101st Cong., 1st Sess., 1989.

99. Ministry of Agriculture, Fisheries and Food (United Kingdom), "Advisory Committee on Pesticides Review of Daminozide," press release, December 13, 1989.

100. Allan R. Gold, "Company Ends Use of Apple Chemical," *New York Times,* October 18, 1989, p. A18.

101. Personal communication with Hageman, June 12, 1991.

102. Christine Russell, "The Pesticide Scare Grows," *Washington Post* (Health Section), February 27, 1990, p. 12.

103. Gladwell, "Some Fear," op. cit. pp. A1, A12.

104. Gladwell, "Some Fear," op. cit. p. A12.

105. *60 Minutes,* "What About Apples?" op. cit. p. 5.

106. Marshall, op. cit. p. 21.

107. William K. Reilly, "EPA Scientific Advisory Panels," letter, *Science,* Vol. 250, No. 4977 (October 5, 1990), p. 15.

108. Marshall, op. cit. p. 22.

109. Quoted in "After Scare, Suit by Apple Farmers," *New York Times,* November 29, 1990, p. A22.

110. "The PR Wizard Who Stopped Alar: An Interview with David Fenton," *Propaganda Review,* Summer 1989, p. 17.

111. Maura Dolan, "The People Who Blew the Whistle on Alar," *Los Angeles Times,* March 29, 1989, p. 3.

112. "Absolutely Anathema," *Wall Street Journal,* November 14, 1989, p. A22; editorial.

113. Null, op. cit. p. 127.

114. See Kenneth W. Kizer, Thomas E. Warriner, and Steven A. Book, "Sound Science in the Implementation of Public Policy," *Journal of the American Medical Association,* Vol. 260, No. 7 (August 19, 1988), pp. 951–52.

115. Quoted in George Melloan, "Food Scaremongers Are Beginning to Push Their Luck," *Wall Street Journal,* October 10, 1989, p. A19.

116. Keith Schneider, "Five Supermarket Chains Open Effort Against Pesticide Use," *New York Times,* September 12, 1989, p. B9.

## Chapter 2: Of Mice (and Rats) and Men: The Politics of Cancer Testing

1. Alan Gregg, "A Medical Aspect of the Population Problem," *Science,* Vol. 121, No. 681 (May 13, 1950), p. 682; cited as an epigraph in Mihajlo Mesarovic and Eduard Pestel, *Mankind at the Turning Point: The Second Report to the Club of Rome* (London: Hutchinson, 1974), p. 1.

2. See Nicholas S. Martin, "Environmental Myths and Hoaxes," *Vital Speeches of the Day,* Vol. 54, No. 14 (May 1, 1990), p. 435.

3. Joseph D. Rosen, "The Death of Daminozide," (New Brunswick, N.J.: Department of Food Science, Cook College, Rutgers University, undated, unpublished report), pp. 9, 11.

4. Martin, op. cit. p. 435.

5. Bruce N. Ames and Lois S. Gold, "Carcinogens and Human Health: Part 2," letter, *Science,* Vol. 4989, No. 251 (January 4, 1991), p. 12.

6. *Donahue,* transcript no. 120387 (1987), p. 5.

7. *Cancer Research,* Vol. 47, No. 13 (July 1, 1987), cover.

8. John Higginson, "Overview," in *Environmental Cancer: Causes, Victims, Solutions,* summary of proceedings of a conference held March 21–22, 1977, sponsored by the Urban Environment Conference, and primarily funded by the National Cancer Institute, as well as the National Institute for Environmental Health Sciences and the Environmental Protection Agency (Washington, D.C.: Urban Environment Conference, 1978), p. 2; as cited in Edith Efron, *The Apocalyptics* (New York: Simon and Schuster, 1984), p. 310.

9. Lorenzo Tomatis et al., "Evaluation of the Carcinogenicity of Chemicals: A Review of the Monograph Program of the International Agency for Research on Cancer (1971 to 1977)," *Cancer Research,* Vol. 38, No. 4 (April 1978), p. 883.

10. Efron, op. cit. p. 316.

11. CBS, "The Politics of Cancer" (1967), transcript; as cited in Efron, op. cit., p. 75.

12. Ibid.

13. Lois S. Gold et al., "Target Organs in Chronic Bioassays of 533 Chemical Carcinogens," *Enviromental Health Perspectives,* Vol. 93 (1991), pp. 243–44.

14. Richard Peto, "Epidemiological Reservations About Risk Assessment," in *Assessment of Risk from Low-Level Exposure to Radiation and*

*Chemicals,* ed. Avril D. Woodhead et al. (New York: Plenum Press, 1985), p. 4.

15. International Agency for Research on Cancer, *IARC Monographs on the Evaluation of Carcinogenic Risks to Humans* (England: International Agency for Research on Cancer, 1986), p. 312.

16. Gold et al., "Target Organs," op. cit., p. 233.

17. Gold et al., "Target Organs," op. cit.

18. Lois S. Gold et al., "Carcinogenic Potency Database of the Standardized Results of Animal Bioassays," *Environmental Health Perspectives,* Vol. 58 (December 1984), p. 9; Lois S. Gold et al., "Chronological Supplement to the Carcinogenic Potency Database," *Environmental Health Perspectives,* Vol. 67 (August 1986), p. 161.

19. Lester B. Lave et al., "Information Value of the Rodent Bioassay," *Nature,* Vol. 336, No. 6200 (December 15, 1988), p. 632; citing J. E. Huff, E. E. McConnel, and J. K. Haseman, *Environmental Mutagenesis,* Vol. 7 (1985), p. 427, and Herbert S. Rosenkranz, *Environmental Mutagenesis,* Vol. 7 (1985), p. 428.

20. Lave et al., op. cit. p. 632; citing T. Matsushima, *Chemical Safety Evaluation in Japan* (1987), pp. 175–78.

21. Lave, et al., op. cit. p. 631; citing Fanny K. Ennever, T. J. Noonan, and H. S. Rosenkranz, *Mutagenesis,* Vol. 2 (March 2, 1987), p. 73.

22. Personal telephone communication with Ames, June 17, 1992.

23. Efron, op. cit. p. 180.

24. Ibid.

25. See Kris Newcomer, "Iron-Rich Vitamins Kill Baby," *Rocky Mountain News,* June 8, 1991, p. 8.

26. Quoted in Occupational Safety and Health Administration, U.S. Department of Labor, *Identification and Regulation of Potential Occupational Carcinogens,* Part VII, Book 2, in Federal Register (January 22, 1988), p. 5155.

27. Efron, op. cit. pp. 83–84.

28. Frederica P. Perera, "Carcinogens and Human Health: Part I," letter, *Science,* Vol. 250, No. 4988 (December 21, 1990), p. 1644.

29. Gerald M. Cohen et al., "Anticarcinogenic Effects of 2,3,7,8-Tetrachlorodibenzo-p-dioxin on Benzo(a)pyrene and 7,12-Dimethylbenz(a)anthracene Tumor Initiation and Its Relationship to DNA Binding," *Cancer Research,* Vol. 39, No. 10 (October 10, 1979), p. 4027.

30. Umberto Saffiotti, "Comments on the Scientific Basis for the 'Delaney Clause,' " *Preventive Medicine,* Vol. 2 (1973), pp. 127–28; cited in Efron, op. cit. p. 89.

31. Vincent James Cogliano et al., "Carcinogens and Human Health: Part III," letter, *Science,* Vol. 251, No. 4994 (February 8, 1991), p. 607.

32. Office of Science and Technology Policy, Executive Office of the President, *Identification, Characterization, and Control of Potential Human Carcinogens: A Framework for Federal Decision-Making* (Washington,

D.C.: Office of Science and Technology Policy, February 1, 1979), p. 14; cited in Efron, op. cit. p. 357.

33. For a lengthy discussion of the Delaney Clause, see *Regulatory Aspects of Carcinogenesis and Food Additives: The Delaney Clause,* ed. Frederick Coulston (New York: Academic Press, 1979).

34. *60 Minutes,* " 'A' Is for Apple," Vol. 21, No. 23 (February 26, 1989), transcript, p. 13.

35. "Test Methods: The Weak Link?" *Consumer Reports,* Vol. 54, No. 5, (May 1989), p. 289.

36. "Bad Apples, Alar: Not Gone, Not Forgotten," *Consumer Reports,* Vol. 54, No. 5 (May 1989), p. 289.

37. See Maura Dolan, "Tests Show Alar Traces on Apples in Two County Stores," *Los Angeles Times,* March 30, 1989, p. 26. According to the director of pesticide registration for the EPA, as paraphrased by the reporter: "Any residue above one ppm probably results from current use of Alar. Smaller amounts may be found on apples one or more years after the grower has stopped using the chemical because it persists in the soil and root system of the tree."

38. George B. Koelle, "The Zero-Tolerance Concept," *Perspectives in Biology and Medicine,* Vol. 20 (1977), p. 507; cited in Efron, op. cit. p. 350.

39. John Allen Paulos, *Innumeracy: Mathematical Illiteracy and Its Consequences* (New York: Hill and Wang, 1988), p. 24.

40. Quoted in Julian Simon, *Population Matters* (New Brunswick, N.J.: Transaction Publishers, 1990), p. 388.

41. National Academy of Sciences, *Regulating Pesticides in Food: The Delaney Paradox* (Washington, D.C.: Government Printing Office, 1987).

42. Colin Norman, "EPA Sets New Policy on Pesticide Cancer Risks," *Science,* Vol. 242, No. 4877 (October 21, 1988), p. 366.

43. Quoted in Simon, op. cit. p. 388.

44. See Keith Schneider, "Court Expands Pesticide Ban to Cover Many Used in Food," *New York Times,* July 9, 1992, p. A1.

45. Federal Register, Vol. 45, No. 15 (January 22, 1980), p. 5200; cited in Efron, op. cit. p. 368.

46. Henry L. Mencken, *Prejudices, First Series* (New York: Alfred A. Knopf, 1919), p. 46.

47. Natural Resources Defense Council, "Cancer: The Price of Technological Advancement," *NRDC Newsletter,* Vol. 5, No. 2 (Summer 1976); cited by Merril Eisenbud, *Environmental Technology, and Health: Human Ecology in Perspective* (New York: New York University Press, 1978), p. 187; cited in Efron, op. cit. p. 130.

48. Barry Commoner, "Hiroshima at Home," *Hospital Practice* (April 1978), p. 63; as cited in Efron, op. cit. p. 120.

49. Samuel S. Epstein, *The Politics of Cancer,* rev. ed. (Garden City, N.Y.: Anchor/Doubleday, 1979), p. 510.

50. Quoted in Bill Gilbert, "All in Favor of Cancer, Say 'Aye,' " *Audubon Magazine,* Vol. 81, No. 2 (March 1979), p. 59.

51. *Face the Nation,* 1976; cited in Efron, op. cit. p. 425.

52. "The Disease of the Century," *Time,* (October 20, 1975), p. 67.

53. Quoted in CBS News, "The American Way of Death" (1975); cited in Efron, op. cit. p. 425.

54. NRDC, "Cancer: The Price of Technological Advancement," op. cit. p. 130.

55. Richard Doll and Richard Peto, "The Causes of Cancer: Quantitative Estimates of Avoidable Risks of Cancer in the United States Today," *Journal of the National Cancer Institute,* Vol. 66, No. 6 (June 1981), p. 1256; see also Ernst L. Wynder and Gio B. Gori, "Contribution of the Environment to Cancer Incidence: An Epidemiological Exercise," Vol. 4, No. 58 (April 1977), p. 825.

56. Devra Lee Davis et al., "International Trends in Cancer Mortality in France, West Germany, Italy, Japan, England and Wales, and the USA," *Lancet,* Vol. 336, No. 8713 (August 25, 1990), p. 474.

57. Stan C. Freni and Catherine Hall, Ellen Benhamou, and Françoise Doyon, "Trends in Cancer Mortality," letters, *Lancet,* Vol. 336, No. 8725 (November 17, 1990), pp. 1262–64. See also response by Davis et al., op. cit. pp. 1264–65.

58. Natalie Angier, "Study Finds Mysterious Rise in Childhood Cancer Rate," *New York Times,* June 26, 1991, p. A12.

59. Angier, op. cit. p. A12.

60. Personal telephone communication with Edward J. Sondik, June 5, 1991.

61. John Tierney, "Not to Worry," *Hippocrates,* Vol. 2, No. 1 (January-February 1988), p. 29.

62. Efron, op. cit. p. 121.

63. For example, Robert C. Paehlke, *Environmentalism and the Future of Progressive Politics* (New Haven, Conn.: Yale University Press, 1989), p. 33.

64. Samuel S. Epstein, et al., "Cancer and Diet," letter, *Science,* Vol. 224, No. 4650 (May 18, 1984), p. 666.

65. Richard Peto, "Distorting the Epidemiology of Cancer: The Need for a More Balanced Overview," *Nature,* Vol. 284, No. 5754 (March 27, 1980), p. 297.

66. For example, Bruce N. Ames and Lois Swirsky Gold, "Too Many Rodent Carcinogens: Mitogenesis Increases Mutagenesis," *Science,* Vol. 249, No. 4972 (August 31, 1990), p. 970; Bruce N. Ames and Lois Swirsky Gold, "Chemical Carcinogenesis: Too Many Rodent Carcinogens," *Proceedings of the National Academy of Sciences,* Vol. 87, No. 19 (October 1990), p. 7772.

67. Rachel Carson, *Silent Spring* (Boston: Houghton Mifflin Co., 1962), p. 219.

68. Robert Bazell, "Cancer Warp," *The New Republic*, Vol. 201, No. 25 (December 18, 1989), p. 13.

69. Personal telephone communication with Al Meyerhoff.

70. See Bruce N. Ames, Renae Magaw, and Lois Swirsky Gold, "Ranking Possible Carcinogenic Hazards," *Science*, Vol. 236, No. 4799 (April 17, 1987), p. 277.

71. Doll and Peto, op. cit.; Sheldon W. Samuels and Richard H. Adamson, "Quantitative Risk Assessment: Report of the Committee on Environmental Carcinogens, National Cancer Advisory Board," *Journal of the National Cancer Institute* (April 1985), p. 945; E. J. Calabrese, "Suitability of Animal Models for Predictive Toxicology: Theoretical and Practical Considerations," *Drug Metabolism Review*, Vol. 15 (1984), p. 505; cited in Ames, Magaw, and Gold, op. cit. p. 273.

72. See Ames, Magaw, and Gold, op. cit. p. 277.

73. Bruce N. Ames, Margie Profet, and Lois Swirsky Gold, "Dietary Pesticides (99.99 Percent All Natural)," *Proceedings of the National Academy of Sciences*, Vol. 87, No. 19 (October 1990), p. 7778, table 4.

74. Ames and Gold, "Too Many Rodent Carcinogens," op. cit. p. 970.

75. Tierney, op. cit. p. 29.

76. H. Maarse, ed., *Volatile Compounds in Food, Quantitative Data*, Vol. 2 (Zeist, the Netherlands: Division for Nutrition and Food Research, TNO-CIVO Food Analysis Institute, 1983); cited in Bruce N. Ames and Lois S. Gold, "Pesticides, Risk, and Applesauce," letter, *Science*, Vol. 244, No. 4906 (May 19, 1989), p. 756.

77. Lois S. Gold et al., "Second Chronological Supplement to the Carcinogenic Database," *Environmental Health Perspectives*, Vol. 74 (1987), p. 237.

78. Ames and Gold, "Pesticides, Risk, and Applesauce," loc. cit.

79. Doll and Peto, op. cit. p. 1256, table 20.

80. Food and Drug Administration, Code of Federal Regulations, Title 21, Part 740 (Docket No. 77P-0353), FDA Cosmetic Product Warning Statements; Coal Tar Hair Dyes Containing 4-Methoxy-M-Pheny-4-Diaminoanisole Sulfate), Federal Register, Vol. 44, No. 201 (October 16, 1979), p. 59513; cited in Efron, op. cit. p. 413.

81. Richard A. Merrill, "Regulation of Toxic Chemicals," *Texas Law Review*, Vol. 58, No. 463 (1980), p. 479; cited in Efron, op. cit. p. 413.

82. Ames, Magaw, and Gold, op. cit. pp. 271–72.

83. All figures from ibid. p. 273, table 1.

84. Ames and Gold, "Pesticides, Risk, and Applesauce," op. cit. p. 756.

85. *Donahue,* transcript no. 120387 (1987), p. 1.

86. Bruce N. Ames and Lois S. Gold, "Carcinogens and Human Health: Part 1," letter, *Science*, Vol. 250, No. 4988 (December 21, 1990), p. 1645.

87. Ames and Gold, "Pesticides, Risk, and Applesauce," op. cit. p. 756, citing S. J. Jadhav, R. P. Sharma, and D. K. Salunkhe, *CRC Critical Reviews*

*in Toxicology,* Vol. 9 (1981), p. 21 and J. H. Renwick et al., *Teratology,* Vol. 30 (1984), p. 371.

88. Ames and Gold, "Pesticides, Risk, and Applesauce," op. cit. p. 756, citing S. F. Berkley et al., *Annals of Internal Medicine,* Vol. 105 (1986), p. 351 and P. J. Seligman et al., *Archives of Dermatology,* Vol. 123 (1987), p. 1478.

89. "Interview with Bruce Ames," *Omni,* Vol. 13, No. 5 (February 1991), p. 76.

90. Ibid. p. 77.

91. Ames and Gold, "Too Many Rodent Carcinogens," op. cit. p. 970.

92. Ibid.

93. *60 Minutes,* " 'A' Is for Apple," op. cit. pp. 10–11.

94. Andrea Arnold, *Fear of Food* (Bellevue, Wash.: Free Enterprise Press, 1990), pp. 69–74.

95. *60 Minutes,* "What About Apples?" Vol. 21, No. 34 (May 14, 1989), transcript, p. 4.

96. For example, Ames, Magaw, and Gold, op. cit. p. 277: "Our knowledge is also more certain about the enormous toll of tobacco—about 350,000 deaths per year."

97. Personal correspondence from David Gelber to Bruce Ames (facsimile), May 25, 1989.

98. *60 Minutes,* "What About Apples?" op. cit. p. 4.

99. National Toxicology Program, Division of Toxicology Research and Testing, *Chemical Status Report* (Research Triangle Park, N.C.: National Toxicological Program, April 7, 1989), pp. 17, 19.

100. See Ames, Profet, and Gold, "Dietary Pesticides (99.99 Percent All Natural)," p. 7779, table 2. This table details a wide variety of foods and their constituent chemicals that have proven either in and of themselves or as breakdown products to be rodent carcinogens.

101. Ames and Gold, "Pesticides, Risk, and Applesauce," op. cit. p. 756.

102. Personal correspondence from Bruce Ames to Don Hewitt, June 29, 1989, p. 3.

103. Personal correspondence from David Gelber to Bruce Ames, August 11, 1989, pp. 2–3.

104. Anastasia Toufexis, "Dining with Invisible Danger," *Time,* March 27, 1989, p. 28.

105. Robert J. Scheuplein, "Food-Borne Carcinogenic Risk," paper delivered at the Symposium on Current Issues in Food Safety and Food Labeling at the American Association for the Advancement of Science, 156th Annual Meeting, New Orleans, February 15–20, 1990, p. 368, table 10.

106. Personal telephone communication with Dr. Byron Butterworth, Chemical Industry Institute of Toxicology, 1990.

107. Ibid.

108. Ames and Gold, "Carcinogens and Human Health: Part I," op. cit. p. 1645.

109. Personal telephone communication with Butterworth.

110. Richard Peto, "Distorting the Epidemiology of Cancer: The Need for a More Balanced Overview," *Nature,* Vol. 284, No. 5754 (March 27, 1980), p. 300.

111. Personal telephone communication with Bruce Ames, June 20, 1991.

112. Personal telephone communication with Bruce Ames, July 9, 1991.

113. Edward Groth III, "Alar in Apples," letter, *Science,* Vol. 244, No. 4906 (May 19, 1989), p. 755.

114. Bill McKibben, *The End of Nature* (New York: Random House, 1989).

115. Personal telephone communication with Lois Gold, June 11, 1991.

116. Quoted in Arnold, op. cit. p. 71.

117. Scheuplein, op. cit. pp. 366 (table 9), 367, 369.

118. For a discussion of the link between fat and one type of cancer, that of the breast, see Geoffrey R. Howe et al., "A Cohort Study of Fat Intake and Risk of Breast Cancer," *Journal of the National Cancer Institute,* Vol. 83, No. 5 (March 6, 1991), p. 336.

119. F. J. C. Rose et al., "Risks of Premature Death and Cancer Predicted by Body Weight in Early Adult Life," *Human and Experimental Toxicology,* Vol. 10 (1991), p. 285.

120. Doll and Peto, op. cit. p. 1256, Table 20.

121. Michael Gough, "How Much Cancer Can EPA Regulate Away?" *Risk Analysis,* Vol. 10, No. 1 (March 1990), p. 1.

122. *Donahue,* transcript no. 02085 (1985), p. 13.

123. Personal correspondence from Bruce Ames to the Honorable Art Torres, November 11, 1985.

124. Ames and Gold, "Too Many Rodent Carcinogens," op. cit. p. 971.

125. Isaac Berenblum, "Chemical Carcinogenesis: Predictive Value of Carcinogenicity Studies," *British Journal of Cancer,* Vol. 41 (1980), p. 490; Isaac Berenblum, "Cancer Prevention as a Realizable Goal," in *Accomplishments in Cancer Research 1980,* ed. J. G. Fortner and J. E. Rhoads (Philadelphia: J. B. Lippincott Co., 1980), pp. 101–104, both cited in John Higginson, "Changing Concepts in Cancer Prevention: Limitations and Implications for Future Research in Environmental Carcinogenesis," *Cancer Research,* Vol. 48, No. 6 (March 15, 1988), p. 1381.

126. Higginson, op. cit. p. 1381.

127. Quoted in Ray Reece, *The Sun Betrayed: A Report on the Corporate Seizure of U.S. Solar Energy Development* (Boston: South End Press, 1979), p. 26, cited in Rael Jean Isaac and Erich Isaac, *The Coercive Utopians* (Washington, D.C.: Regnery Gateway, 1983), pp. 57–58.

128. Alix M. Freedman, "Furor over Rating of Store Produce," *Wall Street Journal,* June 23, 1988, p. 35 (graphic).

129. Higginson, op. cit. p. 1381.

130. CDC, National Institute of Child Health and Human Development,

"Combination Oral Contraceptive Use and the Risk of Endometrial Cancer," *Journal of the American Medical Association,* Vol. 257, No. 6 (February 13, 1987), p. 796.

131. For a discussion of tamoxifen as prophylaxis for breast cancer, see David T. Kiang, "Chemoprevention for Breast Cancer: Are We Ready?" *Journal of the National Cancer Institute,* Vol. 83, No. 7 (April 3, 1991), p. 462.

132. Higginson, op. cit. p. 1386.

133. Alan Carlin, *Environmental Investments: The Cost of a Clean Environment, A Summary* (Washington, D.C.: Environmental Protection Agency, December 1990), p. 2-1.

134. "An Interview with Bruce Ames," op. cit. p. 103.

## Chapter 3: A Fairly Brief, Nonboring Lesson in the Pitfalls of Amateur Epidemiology

1. *Bartlett's Book of Familiar Quotations,* ed. Emily Beck (Boston: Little, Brown & Co., 1980), p. 463.

2. Ibid. p. 464.

3. John Allen Paulos, *Innumeracy: Mathematical Illiteracy and Its Consequences* (New York: Hill and Wang, 1988), pp. 44–45.

4. For a discussion of this topic, see Bruce N. Ames and Lois Swirsky Gold, "Chemical Carcinogenesis: Too Many Rodent Carcinogens," *Proceedings of the National Academy of Sciences,* Vol. 87, No. 19 (October 1990), p. 7772.

5. Data from Rocky Mountain Cancer Service, Colorado Springs, Colorado.

6. See, E. Paci, "Malignant Mesothelioma in Non-Asbestos Textile Workers in Florence," *American Journal of Industrial Medicine,* Vol. 11, No. 3 (March 1987), p. 249.

7. Associated Press, "Alzado Says Steroids to Blame," *Denver Post,* June 28, 1991, p. D1. (Carried in various other newspapers with other titles.)

8. Lyle Alzado, "I'm Sick and I'm Scared," *Sports Illustrated,* July 8, 1991, p. 20.

9. Cable News Network, July 18, 1991.

10. Anna Quindlen, "Lyle Alzado: My Strength Is My Heart," *Denver Post,* July 12, 1991, p. 9B. (Carried in various other papers with various titles.)

11. Irva Hertz-Picciotta and Steven J. Samuels, "Incidence of Early Loss of Pregnancy," letter, *New England Journal of Medicine* (hereafter *NEJM*), Vol. 319, No. 22 (December 1, 1988), p. 1483.

12. Allen J. Wilcox et al., "Incidence of Early Loss of Pregnancy," *NEJM,* Vol. 319, No. 4 (July 28, 1988), p. 189.

13. One large survey (67,277 infants) found a 2.24-percent rate. Kathryn

Nelson and Lewis B. Holmes, "Malformations Due to Presumed Spontaneous Mutations in Newborn Infants," *NEJM,* Vol. 320, No. 1 (January 5,
1989), p. 19.

14.. Ibid. p. 20, table 1.

15. See generally, Nelson and Holmes, ibid.

16. Personal telephone communication with Dorothy Warburton, June
14, 1991.

17. Personal telephone communication with Lewis Holmes, June 14,
1991.

18. Elizabeth D. Stierman, "Emotional Aspects of Perinatal Death,"
*Clinical Obstetrics and Gynecology,* Vol. 30, No. 2 (June 1987), p. 353.

19. Fredrick J. Stare, Robert E. Olson, and Elizabeth M. Whelan, *Balanced Nutrition* (Holbrook, Mass.: Bob Adams, Inc., 1989), p. 94.

20. Carol Kreck, "Flats Report No Comfort to Parents," *Denver Post,*
December 15, 1988, p. 1C.

21. Chris Raymond, "Nagging Doubt, Public Opinion Offer Obstacles
to Ending 'Cluster' Studies," *Journal of the American Medical Association,*
Vol. 261, No. 16 (April 28, 1989), p. 2297.

22. Quoted in ibid. p. 2297.

23. Ibid.

24. Ibid.

25. Raymond Richard Neutra, "Counterpoint from a Cluster Buster,"
*American Journal of Epidemiology,* Vol. 132, No. 1 (July 1990), p. 3.

26. Neutra, op. cit. p. 4.

27. Ibid. p. 7.


## Chapter 4: Dioxin: "The Most Deadly Chemical
## Created by Man"

1. Quoted in Laura Shapiro, "The Lesson of Salem," *Newsweek,* August
31, 1992, p. 64.

2. "The Politics of Poison," KRON-TV, San Francisco, April 1979.

3. Lewis Regenstein, "Across America, Dioxin," *New York Times,*
March 8, 1983, p. A31.

4. *Los Angeles Times,* May 9, 1983; as cited in Dorothy Nelkin, *Selling
Science* (New York: W. H. Freeman, & Co., 1987), p. 66.

5. Michael Gough, *Dioxin, Agent Orange* (New York, Plenum Press,
1986), p. 234.

6. Dale Blumenthal, "Deciding About Dioxins," *FDA Consumer,* Vol.
24, No. 1 (February 1990), p. 11.

7. Christopher Hitchens, "Minority Report," *The Nation,* Vol. 238, No.
21 (June 2, 1984), p. 662.

8. See Fred H. Tschirley, "Dioxin," *Scientific American,* Vol. 254, No.
2 (February 1986), p. 29.

9. Quoted in Sharon Begley et al., "Dioxin: How Great a Threat?" *Newsweek,* July 11, 1983, p. 66.

10. Cited in "Odds and Ends," *Wall Street Journal,* October 25, 1989, p. B1.

11. Ralph Nader, Ronald Brownstein, and John Richard, *Who's Poisoning America?* (San Francisco: Sierra Club Books, 1981), p. 272; citing Thomas Whiteside, *The Pendulum and the Toxic Cloud* (Yale University Press, 1979), p. 14.

12. Pete Earley, "Dioxin Is Still a Mystery," *Washington Post,* February 27, 1983, p. B5.

13. "Dioxin Puts Dow on the Spot," *Time,* May 2, 1983, p. 62.

14. "How Dangerous Is Dioxin?" ABC News's *Nightline,* Vol. 482 (March 15, 1983), transcript p. 7.

15. Rebecca L. Rawls, "Dioxin's Human Toxicity Is Most Difficult Problem," *Chemical and Engineering News,* Vol. 61, No. 23 (June 6, 1983), p. 37.

16. Fred H. Tschirley, "Dioxin," *Scientific American,* Vol. 254, No. 2 (February 1986), p. 31.

17. Rawls, loc. cit.

18. Environmental Defense Fund, "Dioxins in Paper," Environmental Information Exchange Fact Sheet (available from EDF, 1616 P Street, N.W., Suite 150, Washington, D.C. 20036.

19. Gough, op. cit. p. 186.

20. Ibid. pp. 187–88.

21. Rawls, op. cit. p. 46.

22. L. Hardell and O. Axelson, "Phenoxyherbicides and Other Pesticides in the Etiology of Cancer: Some Comments on the Swedish Experience," paper presented at the University of California, San Francisco, December 7–8, 1984; cited in Gough, *Dioxin, Agent Orange,* op. cit. p. 196.

23. G. Eklund, "Does Occupational Exposure to Chemical Pesticides Increase the Cancer Risk?" *Weed and Plant Protection Conferences,* (Uppsala: Swedish University of Agricultural Sciences Research Information Center, 1983), pp. 6–12 (translated from Swedish); as cited in Gough, *Dioxin, Agent Orange,* op. cit. p. 196.

24. V. Riihimaki, S. Asp, and S. Hernberg, "Mortality of 2,4-dichlorophenoxyacetic Acid and 2,4,5-trichlorophenoxyacetic Acid Herbicide Applicators in Finland: First Report of an Ongoing Perspective Study," *Scandinavian Journal of Work, Environment, and Health,* Vol. 8 (1982), p. 37.

25. Gough, *Dioxin, Agent Orange,* op. cit. p. 196.

26. For example, E. Lynge, "A Follow-up Study of Cancer Incidence among Workers in Manufacture of Phenoxy Herbicides in Denmark," *British Journal of Cancer,* Vol. 52, No. 2 (August 1985), p. 259; James S. Wood et al., "Soft Tissue Sarcoma and Non-Hodgkin's Lymphoma in Relation to Phenoxyherbicide and Chlorinated Phenol Exposure in Western Washing-

ton," *Journal of the National Cancer Institute,* Vol. 78, No. 5 (May 1987), p. 899; Paolo Vineis et al., "Incidence Rates of Lymphomas and Soft-Tissue Sarcomas and Environmental Measurements of Phenoxy Herbicides," *Journal of the National Cancer Institute,* Vol. 83, No. 5 (March 6, 1991), p. 362.

27. For example, Allan H. Smith et al., "Soft Tissue Sarcoma and Exposure to Phenoxyherbicides and Chlorophenols in New Zealand," *Journal of the National Cancer Institute,* Vol. 73, No. 5 (November 1984), p. 1111; Neil E. Pearce, "Non-Hodgkin's Lymphoma and Farming: An Expanded Case-Control Study," *British Journal of Cancer,* Vol. 39, No. 2 (February 15, 1987), p. 155.

28. William H. Wolfe, "Health Status of Air Force Veterans Occupationally Exposed to Herbicides in Vietnam," *Journal of the American Medical Association* (hereafter *JAMA*), Vol. 264, No. 14 (October 10, 1990), p. 1829.

29. Karen B. Webb et al., "Medical Evaluation of Subjects with Known Body Levels of 2,3,7,8—Tetrachlorodibenzo-p-Dioxin," *Journal of Toxicology and Environmental Health,* Vol. 28, No. 2 (1989), pp. 187–90.

30. Webb et al., op. cit. p. 186.

31. Marilyn Fingerhut et al., "Cancer Mortality in Workers Exposed to 2,3,7,8-Tetrachlorodibenzo-p-dioxin" (hereafter "Cancer Mortality"), *New England Journal of Medicine* (hereafter *NEJM*), Vol. 324, No. 4 (January 24, 1991), pp. 212–13.

32. Marilyn A. Fingerhut et al., "Mortality Among U.S. Workers Employed in the Production of Chemicals Contaminated with 2,3,7,8-Tetrachlorodibenzo-p-dioxin (TCDD)," (Cincinnati, Ohio: U.S. Department of Health and Human Services, National Institute for Occupational Safety and Health, January 1991): 15. (This is the long version of the same report presented in the *NEJM.*)

33. Fingerhut et al., "Cancer Mortality," op. cit. pp. 215–16.

34. Fingerhut et al., "Cancer Mortality," op. cit. p. 214, table 2.

35. Personal telephone communication with Michael Gough, February 27, 1991.

36. Fingerhut et al., "Cancer Mortality," op. cit. p. 215.

37. Fingerhut et al., "Cancer Mortality," op. cit. p. 216. For the assertion as to the general United States population, the authors cite Constance Percy, Edward Stanek III, and Lynn Gloekler, "Accuracy of Cancer Death Certificates and Its Effect on Cancer Mortality Statistics," *American Journal of Public Health* (hereafter *AJPH*), Vol. 7 (1981), p. 242.

38. Fingerhut et al., "Cancer Mortality," op. cit. p. 215.

39. Personal telephone communication with Edward J. Sondik, June 5, 1991.

40. Fingerhut et al., "Cancer Mortality," op. cit. p. 214, table 2.

41. John C. Bailar III, "How Dangerous Is Dioxin?" *NEJM,* Vol. 324, No. 4 (January 24, 1991), p. 261.

42. Fingerhut et al., "Cancer Mortality," op. cit. p. 214, table 2.

43. A. Manz et al., "Cancer Mortality in Chemical Plant Contaminated with Dioxin," *Lancet,* Vol. 338, No. 8773 (October 19, 1991), p. 659.

44. Michael Gough explains that studies that rely on people's memories, instead of company records, to make lists of deaths insert a strong element of bias. "When you have a friend who died of cancer, are you more likely to remember him when somebody asks about health risks, or are you more likely to remember the friend who died in a traffic accident? Yet, if we don't remember the accident death, that changes the denominator." Personal communication with Gough, January 28, 1992.

45. Bailar, op. cit. p. 261.

46. Quoted in Fingerhut et al., "Cancer Mortality," op. cit. pp. 214, 217.

47. Council on Scientific Affairs, "The Health Effects of 'Agent Orange' and Polychlorinated Dioxin Contaminants: An Update, 1984," typescript (Chicago: American Medical Association, 1984), p. 41.

48. CDC, "Preliminary Report: 2,3,7,8-Tetrachlorodibenzo-p-Dioxin Exposure to Humans—Seveso, Italy," *Morbidity and Mortality Weekly Report*  (hereafter *MMWR*), Vol. 37, No. 48 (December 9, 1988), p. 733, table 1.

49. For a lengthy description of the events surrounding the Seveso incident, see Thomas Whiteside, "A Reporter at Large: Contaminated," *The New Yorker,* Vol. 54, No. 29 (September 4, 1978), p. 34.

50. "The Deadly Cloud," *Time,* August 16, 1976, p. 39.

51. "Poisoned Suburb," *Time,* August 14, 1978, p. 36.

52. Raymond Carroll and Loren Jenkins, " 'Our Own Hiroshima,' " *Newsweek,* August 16, 1976, p. 49.

53. Eileen Keerdoja, "Persistent Poison," *Newsweek,* June 13, 1977, p. 10.

54. John G. Fuller, *The Poison That Fell from the Sky* (New York: Random House, 1977), jacket flaps.

55. CDC, op. cit. pp. 734–35.

56. Quoted in Eileen Keerdoja, Rick Ruiz, and Carolyn Friday, "Fears Still Cloud Italy's Toxic Town," *Newsweek,* May 10, 1982, pp. 14–15.

57. Thomas Whiteside, "A Reporter at Large: The Pendulum and the Toxic Cloud," *The New Yorker,* July 25, 1977, p. 48.

58. Pierpaolo Mastroiacovo et al., "Birth Defects in the Seveso Area After TCDD Contamination," *JAMA,* Vol. 259, No. 11 (March 18, 1988), p. 1668; citing H. Reheder et al., "Pathologischembryologische Untersuchungen an Abortusfallen im Zusammenhang mit dem Seveso-Unglück," *Schweiz Medizinisch Wochenschrift,* Vol. 108 (1978), p. 1617.

59. Mastroiacovo et al., op. cit. p. 1668; citing M. L. Tenchini et al., "Approaches to the Evaluation of Genetic Damage After a Major Hazard in the Chemical Industry: Preliminary Cytogenetic Findings in TCDD-Exposed Subjects After the Seveso Accident," in Berg, K., ed., *Genetic Damage in Man Caused by Environmental Agents* (Orlando, Fla.: Academic Press, 1979), p. 301.

60. Mastroiacovo et al., op. cit. p. 1670.

61. Ibid.

62. Keerdoja, Ruiz, and Friday, op. cit. pp. 14–15.

63. G. Reggiani, Interpharco, Inc., formerly medical director of Roche, Switzerland, personal communication to Michael Gough, July 1985; cited in Gough, *Dioxin, Agent Orange,* op. cit. p. 154.

64. Paolo Mocarelli et al., "Clinical Laboratory Manifestations of Exposure to Dioxin in Children," *JAMA,* Vol. 256, No. 19 (November 21, 1986), p. 2687. The alterations were in y-glutamyltransferase and alanine aminotransferase, detected in urine tests.

65. Pier Alberto Bertazzi et al., "Ten-Year Mortality Study of the Population Involved in the Seveso Incident in 1976," *American Journal of Epidemiology,* Vol. 129, No. 6 (June 1989), p. 1196.

66. Bertazzi et al., op. cit. pp. 1191–94, 1196.

67. See CDC, "Comments on the Paper: Ten-year Mortality Study of the Population Involved in the Seveso Incident in 1976, Pier Alberto Bertazzi, et al.," as appears in U.S. Congress, Committee on Government Operations, transcript, p. 31.

68. Will Steger and Jon Bowermaster, *Saving the Earth: A Citizen's Guide to Environmental Action* (New York: Alfred A. Knopf, 1990), p. 159.

69. Michael Brown, *The Toxic Cloud* (New York: Harper and Row, 1987), p. 21.

70. KRON-TV, "The Politics of Poison," op. cit. 1979.

71. Joseph N. Bell, "What Happened to My Baby?" *McCall's,* January 1980, p. 12.

72. Alfred F. Naylor and Dorothy Warburton, "Sequential Analysis of Spontaneous Abortion, II. Collaborative Study," *Fertility and Sterility,* Vol. 31, No. 3 (March 1979), p. 282.

73. Irva Hertz-Picciotta and Steven J. Samuels, "Incidence of Early Loss of Pregnancy," letter, *NEJM,* Vol. 319, No. 22 (December 1, 1988), p. 1484.

74. Gough, *Dioxin, Agent Orange,* op. cit. p. 139.

75. Ibid. p. 140.

76. Ibid. pp. 140–41.

77. "Report of Assessment of a Field Investigation of Six Year Spontaneous Abortion Rates in Three Oregon Areas in Relation to Forest 2,4,5-T Spray Practices," Environmental Protection Agency, February 28, 1979; cited in Gough, *Dioxin, Agent Orange,* op. cit. p. 140.

78. Federal Register, Vol. 44, No. 52 (March 15, 1979), pp. 15,874–920.

79. S. L. Wagner et al., "A Scientific Critique of the EPA Alsea II Study and Report with the November 16, 1979 Supplement" (Cornwallis, Ore.: Oregon State University Environmental Health Sciences Center, October 25, 1979); cited in Gough, *Dioxin, Agent Orange,* op. cit. p. 144.

80. Gough, *Dioxin, Agent Orange,* op. cit. p. 144.

81. Ibid. pp. 144–45.

82. Ibid. p. 237.

83. Ibid. pp. 145–46.

84. "A Plague on Our Children," WGBH Educational Foundation, October 2, 1987.

85. Donald G. McNeil, Jr., "Upstate Waste Site May Endanger Lives," *New York Times,* August 2, 1978, p. B9.

86. Donald G. McNeil, Jr., "Health Chief Calls Waste Site a 'Peril': Asks Pregnant Women and Infants to Leave Niagara Falls Sector," *New York Times,* August 3, 1978, p. A1.

87. Samuel Epstein, Lester Brown, and Carl Pope, *Hazardous Wastes in America* (San Francisco: Sierra Club Books, 1981), p. 89.

88. See Eric Zuesse, "Love Canal: The Truth Seeps Out," *Reason,* Vol. 12, No. 10 (February 1981), p. 20.

89. Elizabeth Whelan, *Toxic Terror* (Chicago: Jameson Books, 1985), p. 95.

90. Dorothy Gallagher, "The Tragedy of Love Canal," *Redbook,* April 1979, p. 67.

91. "The Neighborhood of Fear," *Time* (June 2, 1980), p. 62.

92. New York State Department of Health, "Love Canal: A Special Report to the Governor and Legislature," April 1981, p. 8. See also illustration, p. 11.

93. See ibid. p. 43.

94. Lewis Regenstein, *America the Poisoned* (Washington, D.C.: Acropolis Books, 1982), p. 138; citing *Environmental Quality 1979: The 10th Annual Report of the Council on Environmental Quality* (Washington, D.C.: December 1979), p. 176.

95. McNeil, op. cit. p. A1.

96. Whelan, op. cit. p. 96.

97. Regenstein, op. cit. pp. 138–39.

98. Ibid.

99. Quoted in "Chromosome Changes in Love Canal Victims," *Science News,* Vol. 117, No. 21 (May 24, 1980), p. 325.

100. Nader, Brownstein, and Richard, op. cit. p. 305.

101. Personal telephone communication with Dorothy Warburton, May 14, 1991. See also Gina Bari Kolata, "Chromosome Damage: What It Is, What it Means," *Science,* Vol. 208, No. 4449 (June 13, 1980), p. 1240.

102. Office of Technology Assessment, *Technologies for Detecting Heritable Mutations in Human Beings* (Washington, D.C.: U.S. Government Printing Office, 1986).

103. Irvin Molotsky, "Damage to Chromosomes Found in Love Canal Tests," *New York Times,* May 17, 1980, p. A1.

104. Gina Bari Kolata, "Love Canal: False Alarm Caused by Botched Study," *Science,* Vol. 208, No. 4449 (June 13, 1980), p. 1239.

105. Kolata, "Love Canal," op. cit. p. 1239.

106. Richard J. Meislin, "Carey Panel Discounts Two Studies on Love Canal Problem," *New York Times,* October 11, 1980, p. 26.

107. "Carter Signs Cleanup Bill on Upstate Toxic Wastes," *New York Times,* October 2, 1980, p. B12.

108. Regenstein, op. cit. p. 140.

109. Georgette Jason, "Major Risks Are Posed by Years of Dumping Industrial Wastes," *Wall Street Journal,* May 22, 1979, p. 1.

110. Deed of Love Canal property land transfer, April 28, 1953.

111. Zuesse, op. cit. p. 19.

112. Ibid. p. 29.

113. Michael Brown, *Laying Waste: The Poisoning of America by Toxic Chemicals* (New York: Pantheon, 1979).

114. Zuesse, op. cit. pp. 28, 30, 31.

115. Ron Nordland and Josh Friedman, "Poison at Our Doorsteps," *Philadelphia Inquirer,* September 23–28, 1979 (reprint of series); cited in Regenstein, op. cit. p. 143.

116. Alison Mitchell, "Carey Assails Love Canal Study," *Newsday,* May 31, 1980, p. 1; see also, Robin Herman, "Carey Criticizes Aspects of Study at Love Canal," *New York Times,* May 19, 1980, p. B3.

117. Lois Gibbs, *Love Canal: My Story* (Albany, N.Y.: State University of New York Press, 1982), p. ix.

118. "Report of the Governor's Panel to Review Scientific Studies and the Development of Public Policy on the Problems Resulting from Hazardous Waste," Lewis Thomas, chairman, October 1980 (typescript), p. 20.

119. Josh Barbanel, "Love Canal Skeptic Favors Relocations," *New York Times,* October 12, 1980, p. 39.

120. See Gibbs, op. cit. pp. 68, 81, 98, 132.

121. David Axelrod, "Address on Love Canal Delivered at New York University Medical School," *Northeastern Environmental Science,* Vol. 1, No. 2 (1982), p. 85.

122. Michael H. Brown, "Love Canal, U.S.A.," *New York Times Magazine,* January 21, 1979, p. 23.

123. Dwight T. Janerich et al., "Cancer Incidence in the Love Canal Area," *Science,* Vol. 212, No. 4501 (June 19, 1981), p. 1404.

124. Transcript, joint hearing, U.S. House of Representatives, Committee on Interstate and Foreign Commerce, Subcommittee on Oversight and Investigations; Committee on Government Operations, Subcommittee on Environment, Energy, and Natural Resources, "Love Canal: Health Studies and Relocation," 96th Cong., 2nd Sess., May 22, 1980, oral statement of Steven Barron, pp. 49–50.

125. Kolata, "Love Canal," op. cit. p. 1239.

126. Stephen Gage, "Love Canal Chromosome Study," letter, *Science,* Vol. 209, No. 4458 (August 15, 1980), pp. 752, 754.

127. Kolata, "Love Canal," op. cit. p. 1241.

128. Ibid.

129. Quoted in ibid.

130. Quoted in ibid. p. 1242.

131. Quoted in Robin Herman, "Cancer at Love Canal Found Near Rates for Rest of State," *New York Times,* June 12, 1981, p. B1.

132. Personal telephone communication with Warburton, June 14, 1991.

133. CDC, "Cytogenetic Patterns in Persons Living near Love Canal, New York," *MMWR,* Vol. 32, No. 20 (May 27, 1983), p. 261.

134. Clark W. Heath, Jr., et al., "Cytogenetic Findings in Persons Living near the Love Canal," *JAMA,* Vol. 251, No. 11 (March 16, 1984), p. 1437.

135. "A Second Look at Love Canal," editorial, *New York Times,* June 20, 1981, p. 22.

136. Kolata, "Love Canal," op. cit. p. 1243.

137. Gibbs, op. cit. pp. 9–12.

138. See Gibbs generally.

139. Michael J. Weiss, "Lois Gibbs, the Love Canal Heroine, Is Making Hazardous Wastes an Industry of Her Own," *People,* February 22, 1982, p. 42.

140. CBS, *Lois Gibbs and the Love Canal,* Glenn Jordan, director, 1982.

141. Quoted in Gallagher, op. cit. p. 69.

142. Weiss, op. cit. p. 45.

143. Quoted in *Donahue,* transcript no. 06200, p. 6.

144. For example, *The Oprah Winfrey Show,* "Remote from Louisiana: The Massive Human Experiment," May 22, 1989.

145. "Awards for Global Environment Crusaders," *Science,* Vol. 248, No. 4954 (April 27, 1990), p. 447.

146. Quoted in Weiss, op. cit. p. 45.

147. Quoted in *Donahue,* transcript no. 06200, p. 21.

148. Samuel Epstein, "The Dioxin Debate: What *You* Should Know," *Good Housekeeping,* September 1983, p. 272.

149. See Gibbs, op. cit. pp. 9–11; see also Zuesse, op. cit. p. 30.

150. Michael Brown, *Laying Waste,* op. cit, cover; Michael Brown, *The Toxic Cloud,* cover.

151. Quoted in Robert A. Kittle, "Living with Uncertainty: Saga of Love Canal Families," *U.S. News & World Report,* June 2, 1980, p. 32.

152. "The Neighborhood of Fear," *Time,* June 2, 1980, p. 62.

153. *Donahue,* transcript no. 06200 (June 20, 1980).

154. Michael Clugston, "A Deadly Love Story," *Maclean's,* June 2, 1980, p. 25.

155. Fern Marja Eckman, "Our Fear Never Ends," *McCall's,* June 1980, p. 134.

156. *Donahue,* transcript no. 06200, pp. 1, 5, 8, 15, 20, 21.

157. James N. Brewster, "Love Canal: Redefining Disaster," *Christian Century,* August 4–11, 1982, p. 829.

158. *Donahue,* transcript no. 06200, p. 15.

159. Herman E. Hilleboe, "History of the Newburgh-Kingston Caries-fluorine Study," *Journal of the American Dental Association,* Vol. 52, No. 3 (March 1956), p. 293.

160. Rosanne M. Philen, "Mass Sociogenic Illness by Proxy: Parentally Reported Epidemic in an Elementary School," *Lancet,* Vol. II, No. 8676 (December 9, 1989), p. 1372.

161. Philen et al., op. cit. p. 1375.

162. Ibid. pp. 1372, 1374.

163. For cancer, see, Maureen Hatch et al., "Cancer Rates After the Three Mile Island Nuclear Accident and Proximity of Residence to the Plant," *AJPH,* Vol. 81, No. 6 (June 1991), p. 719, and accompanying editorial; Dwight T. Janerich, "Can Stress Cause Cancer?" *AJPH,* ibid. p. 687. As to fetal problems, Dr. Hatch says there appears to be a relationship between the occurrence of the Three Mile Island scare and fetal development, depending on the trimester in which the scare started. "There seems to be quite a nice dose-response relationship," she says. The biological explanation is that stress may cause an extraordinary release of hormones that affects cardiovascular activity and in turn affects the amount of oxygen sent across the placental barrier. This can slow fetal development and also trigger early contractions, both of which would lead to low-birthweight babies. Low birthweight is the single most important cause of neonatal death. (Personal telephone communication with Maureen Hatch, July 12, 1991.)

164. Leslie Roberts, "Counting on Science at EPA," *Science,* Vol. 249, No. 10 (August 1990), p. 616.

165. Howard Kunreuther and Ruth Patrick, "Managing the Risks of Hazardous Waste," *Environment,* Vol. 33, No. 3 (April 1991), p. 14.

166. Kunreuther and Patrick, p. 14.

167. U.S. Congress, Office of Technology Assessment, *Coming Clean: Superfund Problems Can Be Solved* (Washington, D.C.: U.S. Office of Technology Assessment, October 1989), p. 6.

168. Frank Viviano, "Superfund Costs May Top S&L Bailout," *San Francisco Chronicle,* May 29, 1991, p. A1.

169. Kunreuther and Patrick, op. cit. pp. 14–15.

170. Begley et al., op. cit. p. 66.

171. Quoted in Leslie Roberts, "Dioxin Risks Revisited," *Science,* Vol. 251, No. 4994 (February 8, 1991), p. 624.

172. Quoted in ibid. p. 624.

173. Quoted in ibid. pp. 624–25.

174. Ibid. p. 625.

175. Ibid. p. 626.

176. Jeffrey L. Fox, "Agent Orange: Guarded Reassurance," *Science,* Vol. 225, No. 4665 (August 31, 1984), p. 909.

177. Nora Zamichow, "Vietnam Workers Stonewalled on Agent Orange Studies," *Ms.,* August 1986, p. 26.

178. Ivars Peterson, "Doubts Surface on Love Canal," *Science News,* Vol. 122, No. 7 (August 14, 1982), p. 102.

179. Joan C. Amatniek, "Dioxin Strategy Announced by EPA," *Science News,* Vol. 124, Nos. 26–27 (December 24–31, 1983), p. 406; Linda Garmon, "Dioxin in Missouri," op. cit. p. 61.

180. Malcolm Gray, William Lowther, and David Todd, "Alarm over Paper Goods," *Maclean's,* October 26, 1987, p. 58.

181. For a general, essentially contemporaneous history of the Times

Beach incident, see Linda Garmon, "Dioxin in Missouri: Troubled Times," *Science News,* Vol. 123, No. 4 (April 22, 1983), p. 60.

182. Quoted in Tom Uhlenbrock, "Official: Times Beach Evacuation Order an Overreaction," *St. Louis Post-Dispatch,* May 23, 1991, p. A1.

183. Quoted in ibid. p. A8.

184. Quoted in ibid.

185. Quoted in ibid.

186. "Hazardous Substances, Dioxin Risk May Be Greater Than What EPA Last Publicized, Scientists Say," *Bureau of National Affairs Daily Report for Executives,* June 12, 1992.

187. Ibid.

188. *World News Tonight,* June 10, 1992.

189. Karen F. Schmidt, "Dioxin's Other Face," *Science News,* Vol. 141, No. 2, January 11, 1992, p. 24.

190. Karen F. Schmidt, "Puzzling over a Poison," *U.S. News & World Report,* April 6, 1992, p. 60.

191. Personal telephone communication with James P. Whitlock, May 1992.

192. Personal telephone communication with Gough, January 28, 1992.

193. Cinema 5/Columbia (U.S.) and EMI (U.K.), *Monty Python and the Holy Grail,* Terry Jones and Terry Gilliam, codirectors, 1975.

194. *Nightline,* "How Dangerous Is Dioxin?" Vol. 482 (March 15, 1983), transcript p. 9.

195. Ibid.

196. *Nightline,* "Electromagnetic Field Hazards," Vol. 2295 (March 9, 1990), transcript p. 5.

197. Brown, *The Toxic Cloud,* op. cit. p. 251.

198. Dale Blumenthal, "Deciding About Dioxins," *FDA Consumer,* Vol. 24, No. 1 (February 1990), p. 11.

199. "Dioxin-in-Paper Update," *Science News,* Vol. 136, No. 6 (August 5, 1989), p. 94.

200. Quoted in Erik Calonius, "What Is a Nondetectable Level of Dioxin?" *Fortune,* Vol. 121, No. 7 (March 26, 1990), p. 88.

201. Tom Charlier, "Paper Mill's Pollution of Leaf River Led to Suits in Four States," Scripps Howard News Service, January 31, 1991.

202. This information is from a copy of a contract that the author received.

203. Personal written communication from Lee Davis Thames of Butler, Snow, O'Mara, Stevens and Cannada, Attorneys at Law, June 3, 1991.

204. Charlier, op. cit.

205. Betsy Kauffman, "Pigeon River Fight May Set National Precedent," *Knoxville* (Tenn.) *News-Sentinel,* April 15, 1991, p. A1.

206. Betsy Kauffman, " 'Widowville' Bears Scars of Pollution: Dioxin-Damaged River Still Haunts Hartford Residents," *Knoxville* (Tenn.) *News-Sentinel,* November 30, 1990, p. A3.

207. Ibid.

208. Personal telephone communication with Tom Kraner, May 14, 1991.


## Chapter 5: The (Agent) Orange and the Green

1. Karl Grossman, *The Poison Conspiracy* (Sag Harbor, N.Y.: The Permanent Press, 1983), p. 55.

2. Janet Raloff, "Agent Orange: What Isn't Settled," *Science News,* Vol. 125, No. 20 (May 19, 1984), p. 314.

3. Clarke Watson, "How Conveniently Americans Forget," *Rocky Mountain News* (Denver), January 23, 1991, p. 51.

4. Rae Tyson and Sam Vincent Meddis, "Kuwait Blazes Compared to Agent Orange," *USA Today,* March 15–17, 1991, p. 1D.

5. Ibid. p. 2D.

6. Monica Collins, "Unnatural Causes: An Inspiring Battle," *USA Today,* November 10, 1986, p. D1.

7. See Raloff, op. cit. p. 319 (table).

8. Michael Gough, *Dioxin, Agent Orange* (New York: Plenum Press, 1986), pp. 60–61.

9. Young et al., p. I-19; as cited in Gough, op. cit. p. 52.

10. Gough, op. cit. pp. 52, 53.

11. Ibid. p. 56–58.

12. Han K. Kang, "Dioxin and Dibenzofurans in Adipose Tissue of U.S. Vietnam Veterans and Controls," *American Journal of Public Health* (hereafter *AJPH*), Vol. 8, No. 3. (March 1991), p. 344.

13. Claire Safran, "Did Agent Orange Kill My Babies?" *Woman's Day,* June 20, 1989, p. 60.

14. Ibid. p. 58.

15. Gough, op. cit. p. 259.

16. For calculations of how much dioxin might fall on a man standing under an Operation Ranch Hand spray mission, see ibid. pp. 259–62.

17. Ibid. p. 51.

18. Ibid. p. 262.

19. Ibid. and personal telephone communication with Michael Gough, July 1, 1991.

20. William H. Wolfe et al., "Health Status of Air Force Veterans Occupationally Exposed to Herbicides in Vietnam," *Journal of the American Medical Association* (hereafter *JAMA*), Vol. 264, No. 14 (October 10, 1990), p. 1829, table 10.

21. Epidemiology Research Division, Armstrong Laboratory, *Air Force Health Study,* Vol. 1 (Brooks Air Force Base, Texas, March 1991), p. vi.

22. Wolfe et al., loc. cit.

23. Epidemiological Research Division, op. cit. p. ix.

24. For a brief discussion, see ibid. pp. vi, ix.

25. Han K. Kang et al., "Soft Tissue Sarcomas and Military Service in Vietnam: A Case Comparison Group Analysis of Hospital Patients," *Journal of Occupational Medicine,* Vol. 28, No. 12 (December 1986), p. 1215.

26. Epidemiology Research Division, op. cit. p. 3-3.

27. Quoted in Warren E. Leary, "High Dioxin Levels Linked to Cancer," *New York Times,* January 24, 1991, p. A12.

28. Marilyn A. Fingerhut et al., *Mortality Among U.S. Workers Employed in the Production of Chemicals Contaminated with 2,3,7,8-Tetrachlorodibenzo-p-dioxin (TCDD)* (Cincinnati, Ohio: U.S. Department of Health and Human Services, National Institute for Occupational Safety and Health, January 1991), p. 15. (This is the unabridged version of the same report presented in the *New England Journal of Medicine* [hereafter *NEJM*]).

29. The average level found in Vietnam veterans is 13.4 ppt, according to Kang, "Dioxin and Dibenzofurans in Adipose tissue of U.S. Vietnam Veterans and Controls," p. 346, table one. These figures are extrapolated therefrom.

30. Marilyn Fingerhut et al., "Cancer Mortality in Workers Exposed to 2,3,7,8-Tetrachlorodibenzo-p-dioxin," (hereafter "Cancer Mortality") *NEJM,* Vol. 324, No. 4 (January 24, 1991), p. 216.

31. Steven D. Stellman, Jeanne Mager Stellman, and John F. Sommer, Jr., "Combat and Herbicide Exposures in Vietnam Among a Sample of American Legionnaires," *Environmental Research,* Vol. 47, No. 2 (December 1988), p. 112.

32. Steven D. Stellman, Jeanne Mager Stellman, and John F. Sommer, Jr., "Health and Reproductive Outcomes Among American Legionnaires in Relation to Combat and Herbicide Exposure in Vietnam," *Environmental Research,* Vol. 47, No. 2 (December 1988), p. 150. See also Janet Raloff, "Agent Orange Linked to Some Veterans' Ills," *Science News,* Vol. 134, No. 21 (November 19, 1988), p. 325.

33. Quoted in Wayne Beissert, "Agent Orange Study: Exposure Widespread," *USA Today,* November 11, 1988, p. 3A.

34. Transcript, U.S. Congress, Committee on Government Operations, Subcommittee on Human Resources and Intergovernmental Relations, "Oversight Review of CDC's Agent Orange Study," July 11, 1989, prepared statement of Vernon N. Houk, p. 21.

35. U.S. Congress, Committee on Government Operations, prepared statement of Vernon N. Houk, transcript, p. 22.

36. Epidemiology Research Division, Vol. 1. op. cit. p. 6-2.

37. Hellen Gelband, "OTA Review of The Columbia University-American Legion Vietnam Veterans Study," typescript (Washington, D.C.: Office of Technology Assessment, January 1989), pp. 1–2.

38. "Agent Orange in the Docket," *Newsweek,* May 14, 1984, p. 79.

39. J. M. Friedman, "Does Agent Orange Cause Birth Defects?" *Teratology,* Vol. 29 (1984), p. 193; cited in Gough, op. cit. p. 106.

40. Gough, op. cit. p. 106.

41. Ralph Nader, Ronald Brownstein, and John Richard, *Who's Poisoning America?* (San Francisco: Sierra Club Books, 1981), p. 242.

42. J. E. Aldred et al., "Report of the Consultative Council on Congenital Abnormalities in the Yarram District," presented to the Australian Parliament, typescript, vii + 55 pp., 1978; cited in Gough, op. cit. p. 215.

43. W. P. McNulty, "Feticidal and Teratogenic Actions of TCDD," in *Public Health Risks of the Dioxins,* ed. W. W. Lawrence (Los Altos, Calif.: William Kaufman, 1984), pp. 245–53.; cited in Gough, op. cit. p. 216.

44. Gough, op. cit. p. 106.

45. J. David Erickson et al., "Vietnam Veterans' Risks for Fathering Babies with Birth Defects," *JAMA,* Vol. 252, No. 7 (August 17, 1984), pp. 904–05.

46. Ibid. pp. 907, 910.

47. Ibid. p. 911; citing J. W. Donovan, *Case-Control Study of Congenital Anomalies and Vietnam Service* (Sydney, Australia: University of Sydney, 1983).

48. Erickson et al., loc. cit.; citing P. Kunstadter, *A Study of Herbicides and Birth Defects in the Republic of Vietnam: An Analysis of Hospital Records* (Washington, D.C.: National Academy Press, 1982).

49. Erickson et al., loc. cit.; citing Ton That Tung et al., "Clinical Effects of Massive and Continuous Utilization of Defoliants on Civilians: Preliminary Survey," *Vietnamese Studies,* Vol. 29 (1971), p. 53.

50. Donald E. Davis, "Dioxin and the Vietnam Veteran," letter, *Bulletin of the Atomic Scientists,* Vol. 35, No. 8 (October 1979), p. 58.

51. Edward Kohn, "The Poison Harvest," *Rolling Stone,* August 24, 1978, p. 31.

52. Eileen Kerdoja, "Persistent Poison," *Newsweek,* June 13, 1977, p. 10; Raymond Carroll and Loren Jenkins, " 'Our Own Hiroshima,' " *Newsweek,* August 16, 1976, p. 49.

53. W. A. Thomasson, "Deadly Legacy: Dioxin and the Vietnam Veteran," *Bulletin of the Atomic Scientists,* Vol. 35, No. 5 (May 1979), p. 16.

54. Edith Schloss, "The Poisoning of Italy," *The Nation,* October 16, 1976, p. 363.

55. Fred A. Wilcox, *Waiting for an Army to Die* (Cabin John, Md.: Seven Locks Press, 1989), pp. 51–54, 130–31, 171. (Originally published in 1983.)

56. Ibid. p. 171.

57. Erickson et al., op. cit. p. 910.

58. Lewis Regenstein, *America the Poisoned* (Washington, D.C.: Acropolis Books, 1982), p. 33; citing Eric Jansson, "Background Paper to Petition for an Imminent Hazard for 2,4,5,T . . ." and attachments (Washington D.C.: Friends of the Earth, May 26, 1978).

59. Elmo Zumwalt III and John Grossmann, "A War with Hope," *Health,* Vol. 19, No. 6 (June 1987), p. 86.

60. Mary A. Fergus, "Vets Slow to Respond to Testing," *Northwest Herald* (Ill.), September 24, 1990, p. 1.

61. Margaret Hornblower, "A Sinister Drama of Agent Orange Opens in Congress," *Washington Post*, June 27, 1979; as cited in Regenstein, op. cit. p. 60.

62. Regenstein, op. cit. p. 60.

63. Jane Sims Podesta, "Some Vietnam Vets Get Compensation for Agent Orange Exposure, But Others Claim It's Still Not Justice," *People*, February 25, 1985, p. 37.

64. Clifford L. Linedecker, *Kerry: Agent Orange, and an American Family* (New York: St. Martin's Press, 1982).

65. Wilcox, cover and first unnumbered page.

66. C. D. B. Bryan, "The Veteran's Ordeal," *New Republic*, June 27, 1983, p. 27.

67. Wilcox, op. cit. p. xi.

68. U.S. Department of Commerce, *Statistical Abstract of the United States* (Washington, D.C.: Department of Commerce, 1989), p. 82, table 121.

69. Figures calculated from Linda Williams Pickle et al., *Atlas of U.S. Cancer Mortality Among Whites, 1950–1980* (Washington, D.C.: U.S. Department of Health and Human Services, 1987), p. 151, and U.S. Census Bureau Figures.

70. Personal telephone communication, National Center for Health Statistics, Division of Vital Statistics.

71. Wilcox, op. cit. pp. 17, 24.

72. Gough, op. cit. p. 67, fn. 4.

73. National Cancer Institute, *Testicular Cancer Research Report* (Bethesda, Md.: National Cancer Institute, March 1990), p. 3.

74. Personal telephone communication with Michael Gough, May 24, 1991.

75. Carolyn Pesce, "Vets Put Agent Orange on Trial," *USA Today*, May 7, 1984, p. 3A.

76. Dow Chemical, Diamond Shamrock, Monsanto, T. H. Agriculture and Nutrition, Hercules Inc., Uniroyal, Thompson Chemical Corporation.

77. Paula Dwyer, "The Agent Orange Settlement is Still Unsettled," *Business Week*, September 15, 1986, p. 47.

78. John McGowan and Timothy Kenny, "Victims Torn About $250 Million Fund," *USA Today*, May 8, 1984, p. 3A.

79. John P. Dwyer, "Claims of Injury," *Science*, Vol. 235, No. 4788 (January 30, 1987), p. 598.

80. "Orangemail: Why It Got Paid," editorial, *New York Times*, March 8, 1985, p. A34; see also "Agent Orange—Let it Lie," editorial, *New York Times*, September 4, 1986, p. A26.

81. Steve Marshall, "Agent Orange Payments Started," *USA Today*, March 10, 1989, p. 3A.

82. Timothy Kenny, "Two Firms to Sue over Defoliant," *USA Today,* May 9, 1984, p. 3A.

83. Peter C. Kahn et al., "Dioxins and Dibenzofurans in Blood and Adipose Tissue of Agent Orange-Exposed Vietnam Veterans and Matched Controls," *JAMA,* Vol. 259, No. 11 (March 18, 1988), p. 1661.

84. See William Booth, "Agent Orange Study Hits Brick Wall," *Science,* Vol. 237, No. 4820 (September 11, 1987), p. 1285.

85. Transcript, U.S. Congress, Committee on Government Operations, op. cit., prepared statement of Vernon N. Houk, pp. 12–13.

86. Gary Taubes, "Unmasking Agent Orange," *Discover,* April 1988, p. 46.

87. Centers for Disease Control Vietnam Experience Study, "Health Status of Vietnam Veterans," three articles, *JAMA,* Vol. 259, No. 18 (May 13, 1988), p. 2701.

88. Selected Cancers Cooperative Study Group, *Association of Selected Cancers with Service in the U.S. Military in Vietnam* (Atlanta, Ga.: U.S. Department of Health, Public Health Service, Centers for Disease Control, September 1990).

89. Ibid. p. 34.

90. See Mitchell H. Gail et al., "Projections of the Incidence of Non-Hodgkins Lymphoma Related to Acquired Immunodeficiency Syndrome," *Journal of the National Cancer Institute,* Vol. 83, No. 10 (May 15, 1991), p. 695.

91. Selected Cancers Cooperative Study Group, op. cit. p. 3.

92. Transcript, U.S. Congress, Committee on Government Operations, op. cit., prepared statement of Vernon N. Houk, p. 17.

93. Selected Cancers Cooperative Study Group, op. cit. pp. 36, 88.

94. Ibid, p. 44.

95. Taubes, op. cit. p. 43.

96. Quoted in Taubes, p. 46.

97. Janet Gardner, "Answers at Last?" *The Nation,* April 11, 1987, p. 461.

98. Kahn et al., op. cit. p. 1661.

99. Associated Press, "Reagan Officials Accused in Agent Orange Project: House Panel Charges Obstruction of Study," August 10, 1990; Keith Schneider, "American Legion to Sue U.S. Over Agent Orange," *New York Times,* August 2, 1990, p. A16.

100. Quoted in Taubes, op. cit. p. 46.

101. Quoted in Marcia Barinaga, "Agent Orange: Congress Impatient for Answers," *Science,* Vol. 245, No. 4915 (July 21, 1989), p. 249.

102. Quoted in ibid. p. 249.

103. Quoted in ibid.

104. Quoted in ibid.

105. Ibid. p. 249.

106. Ibid.

107. Transcript, U.S. Congress, Committee on Government Operations, op. cit., prepared statement of Vernon N. Houk, p. 22.

108. Transcript, U.S. Congress, Committee on Veterans' Affairs, "Centers for Disease Control Selected Cancers Study and Scientific Reviews of the Study," 100th Cong., 2nd Sess., April 4, 1990, oral statement of Hellen Gelband, p. 6.

109. "Study Clears Agent Orange, Vietnam Vets Groups Say Report Inadequate to Weigh Cancer Risk," Associated Press, March 30, 1990; Warren E. Leary, "Higher Risk of Rare Cancer Found for Vietnam Veterans," *New York Times,* March 30, 1990, p. A10.

110. Transcript, U.S. Congress, Committee on Veterans' Affairs, op. cit., oral statement of Hellen Gelband, p. 7.

111. See David Brock, "Politicizing the Government's Watchdog," *Wall Street Journal,* July 16, 1986, p. 22.

112. Associated Press, "GAO Says $6.6 Million Misspent," October 21, 1990. (Title may vary in individual newspapers.)

113. See generally, U.S. General Accounting Office, "Agent Orange Studies: Poor Contracting Practices at Centers for Disease Control, Increased Costs," Washington, D.C.: GAO/GGD-90-122BR Agent Orange Studies, September 1990.

114. Ibid. pp. 2, 19–28.

115. U.S. Congress, House of Representatives, Committee on Government Operations, 101st Cong., 2nd Sess., August 9, 1990, "The Agent Orange Coverup: A Case of Flawed Science and Political Manipulation," p. 28.

116. Transcript, U.S. Congress, House of Representatives, Committee on Government Operations, dissenting members, p. 41.

117. Ibid. p. 42.

118. Ed Magnuson and Jay Peterzell, "A Cover-Up on Agent Orange?" *Time,* July 23, 1990, pp. 27–28.

119. Samuel O. Thier and Paul D. Stolley, "Fallout from Agent Orange," letter, *Time,* August 20, 1990, p. 8.

120. Ed Magnuson, Peter Stoler, and J. Madeleine, "The Poisoning of America," *Time,* September 22, 1980, p. 63.

121. Magnuson and Peterzell, op. cit. p. 28.

122. Transcript, U.S. Congress, House of Representatives, Committee on Veterans' Affairs, 101st Cong., 2nd Sess., April 4, 1990, oral statement of Dr. M. Donald Whorton, pp. 9–10.

123. David Brooks, "Journalists and Others for Saving the Planet," *Wall Street Journal,* October 5, 1989, p. A 28.

124. Magnuson and Peterzell, op. cit. p. 27.

125. Transcript, U.S. Congress, House of Representatives, Committee on Government Operations, Subcommittee on Human Resources and Intergovernmental Relations, "Links Between Agent Orange, Herbicides, and

Rare Disease," June 26, 1990, oral statement of Admiral Elmo R. Zumwalt, Jr., pp. 4–5.

126. Ibid. p. 3.

127. Ibid. pp. 3–4.

128. Transcript, U.S. Congress, House of Representatives, Committee on Government Operations, p. 4.

129. Elmo Zumwalt, Jr., and Elmo Zumwalt III with John Pekkanen, *My Father, My Son* (New York: Macmillan, 1986), p. 163.

130. Quoted in Marshall, op. cit. p. 3A.

131. Transcript, U.S. Congress, House of Representatives, Committee on Government Operations, op. cit., prepared statement of Admiral Elmo R. Zumwalt, Jr., p. 22.

132. Ibid. pp. 57–58.

133. Ibid. p. 64; citing Ross C. Brownson et al., "Cancer Risks Among Missouri Farmers," *Cancer,* Vol. 64, No. 11 (December 1, 1989), p. 2381.

134. Brownson et al., op. cit. p. 2383.

135. Ibid. pp. 2383–84.

136. Ibid. p. 2384.

137. Transcript, U.S. Congress, House of Representatives, Committee on Government Operations, Subcommittee on Human Resources and Intergovernmental Relations, oral statement of Ted Weiss, p. 173.

138. Prepared statement of Admiral Elmo R. Zumwalt, Jr., op. cit., transcript, p. 81.

139. Transcript, U.S. Congress, Committee on Veterans' Affairs, op. cit., oral statement of Ellen Silbergeld, p. 330.

140. Transcript, U.S. Congress, Committee on Veterans' Affairs, op. cit., oral statement of Mary R. Stout, p. 334.

141. Adam Clymer, "Bill Passed to Aid Veterans Affected by Agent Orange," *New York Times,* January 31, 1991, p. C19.

142. Han K. Kang et al., "Dioxin and Dibenzofurans in Adipose Tissue of U.S. Vietnam Veterans and Controls," *AJPH,* Vol. 81, No. 3 (March 1991), pp. 346–47.

143. Ibid. pp. 346 (Table 1), 347.

144. For all the separate breakdowns, see ibid. p. 347, Table 2.

145. Ibid. pp. 347–48.

146. Personal telephone communication with Gough, May 24, 1991.

147. Kang et al., op. cit. p. 348.

148. Michael Gough, "Agent Orange: Exposure and Policy," *AJPH,* Vol. 81, No. 3 (March 1991), p. 290.

149. Quoted in Richard Harwood, "Victims of Agent Orange?" *Washington Post,* September 30, 1990, p. D6.

150. Quoted in ibid.

151. Ibid.

152. Gough, "Agent Orange: Exposure and Policy," op. cit. p. 290.

## Chapter 6: Food Irradiation: Drumsticks and Double Standards

1. Quoted in Anastasia Toufaxis, Janice M. Horowitz, and Dick Thompson, "Food Fight over Gamma Rays," *Time,* September 22, 1986, p. 65.

2. Warner Brothers, *The Beast from 20,000 Fathoms,* Eugene Lourie, director, 1953.

3. Toho (Japan), *Godzilla,* Inshiro Honda, director, date given by various sources as 1954, 1955, and 1956.

4. Warner Brothers, *Them,* Gordon Douglas, director, 1954. The pronoun refers to giant ants—man-eating, naturally.

5. Allied Artists, *The Giant Behemoth,* Eugene Lourie, director, 1958.

6. Allied Artists, *Attack of the Crab Monsters,* Roger Corman, director, 1956.

7. Cecil Adams, *More of the Straight Dope* (New York: Ballantine, 1988), p. 414. The devices were called fluoroscopes, and approximately ten thousand shoe stores had them. They were notoriously poorly regulated and while they usually put off just 7 to 14 roentgens per dose, one study found that some machines emitted as much as 116 roentgens. By comparison, a person standing within fifteen hundred meters of ground zero at Hiroshima received 300 roentgens or more. Shoe store fluoroscopes were outlawed by most states in the late 1950s.

8. See generally, Howard L. Rosenberg, *The Atomic Soldiers* (Boston: Beacon Press, 1980).

9. Beverly Merz, "Studies Illuminate Hazards of Ingested Radiation," *Journal of the American Medical Association* (hereafter *JAMA*), Vol. 258, No. 5 (August 7, 1987), p. 584.

10. Both quotes from William F. Allman, "Irradiated Food," *Science 81,* October 1981, p. 14.

11. The countries are listed in the *Food Irradiation Newsletter,* Vol. 14, No. 1 (May 1990), supplement (Vienna, Austria: Food and Agricultural Organization/International Atomic Energy Agency).

12. Paisan Loaharanu, "Food Irradiation: Facts or Fiction?" *International Atomic Energy Bulletin,* Vol. 32, No. 2 (1990), p. 48.

13. *Food Irradiation Newsletter,* Vol. 12, No. 2 (June 1988).

14. Barry Rosenberg, *Science Digest,* Vol. 94, No. 9 (September 1986), p. 30.

15. *Donahue,* transcript no. 06246 (1986), p. 10.

16. Personal correspondence with George G. Giddings, Food Preservation Section, Joint United Nations Food and Agricultural Organization/International Atomic Energy Division, Vienna, Austria, April 30, 1991.

17. Chris W. Lecos, "The Growing Use of Irradiation to Preserve Food," *FDA Consumer,* Vol. 20, No. 6 (July–August 1986), p. 13.

18. Quoted in Darcy Meeker, "Atomic Edibles?" *Health,* Vol. 20, No. 1 (January 1988), pp. 65–66.

19. See Walter M. Urbain, *Food Irradiation* (Orlando, Fla.: Academic Press, 1986), pp. 121–23.

20. Personal correspondence from Edward S. Josephson, June 24, 1991; see also, Urbain, op. cit. pp. 121–26, 205–12.

21. Quoted in Toufaxis, Horowitz, and Thompson, op. cit. p. 65.

22. Quoted in Dick Yost, "Now: Food That Lasts (Almost) Forever," *Popular Science,* Vol. 224, No. 4 (April 1984), p. 44.

23. Irradiation—It Cuts the Gas," *Science News,* Vol. 125, No. 5 (February 4, 1985), p. 72.

24. Quoted in David Kennedy and Sharon Moran, "Bringing Irradiated Food to Market," *Technology Review,* Vol. 87, No. 5 (July 1984), pp. 72–73.

25. Douglas H. Bosco, "Food Irradiation: Dangerous to Your Health?" *USA Today* (magazine), Vol. 116, No. 2512 (January 1988), p. 17.

26. H.R. 956, "Food Irradiation Safety and Labeling Requirement Act of 1987," 100th Cong., 1st Sess., 1987.

27. Personal telephone communication with Irv Rothstein, April 22, 1991.

28. Transcript, U.S. Congress, House of Representatives, Committee on Energy and Commerce, Subcommittee on Health and the Environment, June 19, 1987, prepared statement of Edward S. Josephson, p. 162; personal telephone communication with Dr. Tanya Roberts, U.S. Department of Agriculture Economic Research Service, April 23, 1991.

29. Tanya Roberts, "Microbial Pathogens in Raw Pork, Chicken and Beef: Benefit Estimates for Control Using Irradiation," *American Journal of Agricultural Economics,* Vol. 26, No. 5 (December 1985), p. 957.

30. Transcript, U.S. Congress, House of Representatives, Committee on Energy and Commerce, op. cit., prepared statement of Josephson, p. 162; personal telephone communication with Roberts, April 23, 1991.

31. Kathryn Simmons Raithel, "Concerns, Challenges of Keeping Nation's Food Supply Safe in 21st Century Being Studied Now," *JAMA,* Vol. 260, No. 1 (July 1, 1988), p. 15.

32. *American Family Physician,* Vol. 35 (1987), p. 353; cited in Raithel, op. cit. p. 15.

33. *Annual Review of Nutrition,* Vol. 5 (1970), p. 25; cited in Raithel, op. cit. p. 15.

34. Raithel, op. cit. pp. 15–16.

35. Transcript, U.S. Congress, House of Representatives, Committee on Energy and Commerce, op. cit., prepared statement of Josephson, p. 162.

36. Laura Tangley, "Uncertainty Surrounds Promising Pesticide Alternative," *Bioscience,* Vol. 5, No. 34 (May 1984), p. 287.

37. For more information on the pros and cons of irradiation for insect control, see A. A. Kader et al., "Irradiation of Plant Products," and E. W. Tilton and S. O. Nelson, "Irradiation of Grain and Grain Products for Insect Control," (Ames, Iowa: Council for Agricultural Science and Technology (CAST), 1984). (Available from CAST, P.O. Box 1550, Iowa State University Station, Ames, IA 50010-1550.)

38. Bosco, op. cit. p. 17.

39. Quoted in Yost, op. cit. p. 44.

40. Figures and quote from Mr. Mahaman Balla, World Food Program of the U.N., personal telephone communication, May 7, 1991.

41. Linda Pim, as quoted in Anne Witte Garland, "The Newest Problem on the Food Front," *Ms.*, November 1985, p. 79.

42. Gary Null, *Clearer, Cleaner, Safer, Greener* (New York: Villard, 1990), p. 166.

43. Willard F. Libby and Edwin F. Black, "Food Irradiation: An Unused Weapon Against Hunger," *Bulletin of the Atomic Scientists*, Vol. 34, No. 2 (February 1978), p. 55.

44. "Maine Zaps Irradiated Food," *Wall Street Journal*, July 7, 1987, p. 31; U.S. Congress, House of Representatives, Committee on Energy and Commerce, prepared statement of Giddings, p. 153.

45. Colleen Shannon, "Hot Potatoes from the U.S.," *New Statesman and Society*, Vol. 2, No. 56 (June 30, 1989), p. 23.

46. Samuel S. Epstein, *The Politics of Cancer* (San Francisco: Sierra Club Books, 1978), p. 27.

47. Lois Gibbs, *Love Canal: My Story* (Albany, N.Y.: State University of New York Press, 1982), p. 22.

48. Transcript, U.S. Congress, House of Representatives, Committee on Energy and Commerce, 100th Cong., 1st Sess., June 19, 1987 oral statement of Donald Louria, p. 89.

49. Ibid. p. 146.

50. Jacques Leslie, "Food Irradiation," *Atlantic*, September 1990, p. 28.

51. Western Minute Men, U.S.A., "Red Scheme for Mass Control," *American Mercury*, Vol. 89, No. 430 (November 1959), p. 135.

52. Tangley, op. cit. p. 288.

53. Edwin F. Black and Leona M. Libby, "Commercial Food Irradiation," *Bulletin of the Atomic Scientists*, Vol. 39, No. 6 (June–July 1983), p. 48.

54. Quoted in Maura Moynihan, "Food Wars: Diet and Irradiation," *Vogue*, October 1987, p. 487.

55. Tangley, op. cit. p. 286.

56. Report of Joint FAO/IAEA/WHO Expert Committee, "Wholesomeness of Irradiated Food," WHO Technical Report Series 659 (Geneva, Switzerland: 1981).

57. Tangley, op. cit. p. 288.

58. Federal Register, Vol. 50 (July 22, 1985), p. 29,658.

59. Transcript, U.S. Congress, House of Representatives, Committee on Energy and Commerce, op. cit., prepared statement of Josephson, p. 162.

60. Federal Register, Vol. 51 (April 18, 1986), p. 13399.

61. Lecos, op. cit. p. 12.

62. Federal Register, Vol. 55 (May 2, 1990), p. 18538.

63. William M. Wardell, "A Close Inspection of the 'Calm Look,' " *JAMA*, Vol. 239, No. 19 (May 12, 1978), p. 2010.

64. See Sam Kazman, "Deadly Overcaution: FDA's Drug Approval Process," *Journal of Regulation and Social Costs,* Vol. 1, No. 1 (September 1990), p. 47.

65. Ibid.

66. Quoted in Yost, op. cit. p. 44.

67. Daniel P. Puzo, "Consumers More Wary About Food," *Los Angeles Times,* May 14, 1987, Sec. VIII, p. 2.

68. Quoted in Schmitz, p. 29.

69. See Moynihan, op. cit. p. 405; for a technical discussion of this, see Urbain, op. cit. p. 22.

70. *Donahue,* transcript no. 06246, p. 19.

71. For example, see testimony of Ellen Hass, Donald B. Louria, and Richard Piccioni, in transcript, U.S. Congress, House of Representatives, Committee on Energy and Commerce. All are opponents of food irradiation; none mentioned birth defects.

72. Transcript, U.S. Congress, House of Representatives, Committee on Energy and Commerce, op. cit., oral statement of Young, p. 24.

73. U.S. Congress, House of Representatives, Committee on Energy and Commerce, prepared statement of Dr. Frank E. Young, p. 37.

74. Transcript, U.S. Congress, House of Representatives, Committee on Energy and Commerce, op. cit., pp. 37–38.

75. Ibid.

76. Quoted in Toufaxis, Horowitz, and Thompson, op. cit. p. 65.

77. Transcript, U.S. Congress, House of Representatives, Committee on Energy and Commerce, op. cit., prepared statement of Josephson, pp. 166–67.

78. Personal telephone communication with George H. Pauli, April 23, 1991.

79. Ibid.

80. Garland, op. cit., p. 78.

81. See George H. Pauli and Clyde A. Takeguchi, "Irradiation of Foods—and FDA Perspective," *Food Reviews International,* Vol. 2, No. 1 (1986), p. 96.

82. Marjorie Sun, "Renewed Interest in Food Irradiation," *Science,* Vol. 223, No. 4637 (February 17, 1984), p. 668.

83. Pauli and Takeguchi, op. cit. p. 99.

84. Transcript, U.S. Congress, House of Representatives, Committee on Energy and Commerce, op. cit., prepared statement of Morrison, p. 13.

85. For example, Gary Gibbs, "Zap, Irradiated Foods Aren't Coming, They're Here," *Progressive,* September 1987, p. 23.

86. Quoted in Pauli and Takeguchi, op. cit. p. 99.

87. Ibid.

88. C. Bhaskaram and G. Sadasivan, "Effects of Feeding Irradiated Wheat to Malnourished Children," *American Journal of Clinical Nutrition,* Vol. 28, No. 2 (1975), p. 130.

89. Transcript, U.S. Congress, House of Representatives, Committee on Energy and Commerce, op. cit., prepared statement of Srikantia, pp. 132–39.

90. Transcript, U.S. Congress, House of Representatives, Committee on Energy and Commerce, op. cit., prepared statement of Josephson, pp. 173–74.

91. Ari Brynjolfsson, "Comments on Studies on Polyploidy in Humans and Animals Fed Freshly Irradiated Wheat"; as reprinted in U.S. Congress, House of Representatives, Committee on Energy and Commerce, prepared statement of Josephson, pp. 180–87.

92. "Food and Radiation," *Harvard Medical School Health Letter,* December 1987, p. 4.

93. Leslie, op. cit., p. 28; P. C. Kesavan, "Indirect Effects of Radiation in Relation to Food: Facts and Fallacies," *Journal of Nuclear and Agricultural Biology* (1985), p. 107.

94. Personal correspondence from Dr. J. S. Rao, science counselor, Embassy of India, to a Mr. Prichard of the Atomic Industrial Forum, December 22, 1986, as reprinted in transcript, U.S. Congress, House of Representatives, Committee on Energy and Commerce, prepared statement of George G. Giddings, p. 159.

95. Personal telephone communication with George Pauli, April 23, 1991.

96. Moynihan, op. cit. p. 405.

97. Darcy Meeker, "Atomic Edibles?" *Health,* Vol. 20, No. 1 (January 1988), p. 65.

98. Gibbs, op. cit. p. 22.

99. Seth Rolbein, "Atomic Food," *Boston,* November 1987, p. 137.

100. Richard G. Piccioni, Food and Water, Inc., "Comments to the Food and Drug Administration in Regards to Irradiation in the Production, Processing, and Handling of Food," final rule; Part 179 [docket nos. 86E-0507, 865–0509], a final rule to permit the irradiation of poultry, June 1, 1990, table 1.

101. For example, Null, op. cit., pp. 161, 163–64. 166–67, 170; Rolbein, op. cit. p. 138.

102. Richard G. Piccioni, Food and Water, Inc., op. cit. p. 8.

103. Ibid. table II.

104. Edith Efron, *The Apocalyptics* (New York: Simon and Schuster, 1984), pp. 162–64.

105. Sonia L. Nazario, "Cooking Process May Increase Risk of Cancer," *Wall Street Journal,* October 22, 1991, p. A9.

106. For an at-length discussion of the possible carcinogenicity of nitrites and the politics surrounding this issue, see Efron, op. cit. pp. 270–77.

107. Quoted in Rick Weiss, "The Gamma-Ray Gourmet," *Science News,* Vol. 132, Nos. 25–26 (December 19, 1987), p. 398.

108. Transcript, U.S. Congress, House of Representatives, Committee on Energy and Commerce, op. cit., oral statement of Louria, p. 90.

109. *Donahue,* transcript no. 06246, p. 1.

110. Personal correspondence with Josephson, June 14, 1991.

111. Linda Gasparello, "Food Irradiation Re-heats in U.S.," *World Food and Drink Report,* Vol. 340 (April 27, 1989), p. 2.

112. Quoted in Daniel P. Puzo, "Irradiation Approval Pending," *Los Angeles Times,* August 8, 1985, Sec. II, p. 8.

113. "Ionizing Energy in Food Processing and Pest Control, Section I, Wholesomeness of Food Treated with Ionizing Energy," Report #109 (Council for Agricultural Science and Technology, Ames, Iowa: July 1986).

114. Bosco, op. cit. p. 17; U.S. Congress, House of Representatives, Committee on Energy and Commerce, prepared statement of Hon. Douglas H. Bosco, p. 5.

115. *Accident Facts* (Chicago: National Safety Council, 1989), p. 2.

116. Transcript, U.S. Congress, House of Representatives, Committee on Energy and Commerce, prepared statement of McCormick and Company, op. cit., transcript p. 194.

117. See, for example, Toufaxis, Horowitz, and Thompson, op. cit. p. 65; Bosco, op. cit. p. 17; Gibbs, op. cit. p. 24; Ken Terry, "No Fried Food in New Jersey," *Progressive,* September 1987, p. 25.

118. Peter Dworkin, "Irradiated Food: Is It Safe?" *U.S. News & World Report,* August 11, 1986, p. 58.

119. Shannon, op. cit.,p. 23.

120. Personal telephone communication with Irv Rothstein, editor of NCSFI newsletter, May 22, 1991.

121. Leslie, op. cit. p. 29.

122. Written communication with T. Donna Coates, Nordion International, May 3, 1991; Leslie, op. cit. p. 29.

123. Meeker, op. cit. p. 67.

124. Garland, op. cit. p. 79.

125. Personal written communication with Josephson, April 12, 1991.

126. Nordion International, "Cobalt 60" (promotional literature), p. 5. Available from Nordion International, 447 March Road, P.O. Box 135000, Kanata, Ontario, Canada K2K 1X8.

127. Personal correspondence from Josephson, June 14, 1991.

128. George Cheney and Craig Nagoshi, "Rocky Flats a Cancer on Denver and the World," (Denver) *Rocky Mountain News,* October 2, 1987, p. 97.

129. Quoted in Leslie, op. cit. p. 29.

130. U.S. Congress, House of Representatives, Committee on Energy and Commerce, op. cit., prepared statement of Giddings, p. 151.

131. Leslie, op. cit. p. 30.

132. Ibid.

133. Personal telephone communication with Dr. Richard B. Chitwood,

U.S. Department of Energy, Office of Isotopes Production and Distribution, April 22, 1990; Leslie, op. cit. p. 30.

134. Transcript, U.S. Congress, Committee on Energy and Commerce, op. cit., prepared statement of Giddings, p. 152.

135. Personal telephone communication with Chitwood, April 22, 1991.

136. Leslie, op. cit. p. 30.

137. U.S. Congress, House of Representatives, Committee on Energy and Commerce, op. cit., prepared statement of Giddings, p. 152.

138. Null, op. cit. p. 174.

139. Ken Terry, "Why Is DOE for Food Irradiation?" *The Nation,* February 7, 1987, p. 142.

140. Ibid. p. 144.

141. Beatrice Trum Hunter, "Food Irradiation Update," *Consumers' Research,* Vol. 68, No. 8 (August 1985), p. 21.

142. "Food and Radiation," op. cit. p. 4.

143. Schmitz, op. cit. p. 28.

144. Puzo, "Irradiation Approval Pending," op. cit. p. 8.

145. For a more lengthy discussion, see A. Steward Truswell, "Food Irradiation," *British Medical Journal,* Vol. 294, No. 6585 (June 6, 1987), p. 1438.

146. U.S. Congress, House of Representatives, Committee on Energy and Commerce, op. cit., prepared statement of Josephson, p. 169.

147. Hunter, "Food Irradiation Update," op. cit. p. 21.

148. Personal telephone communication with Edward Josephson, May 17, 1991.

149. Punya Temcharden and William G. Thilly, "Removal of Aflatoxin B, Toxicity but Not Mutagenicity by One Megarad Gamma Radiation of Peanut Meal," *Journal of Food Safety,* Vol. 4, No. 4 (1982), p. 199.

150. Personal telephone communication with Josephson, May 17, 1991.

151. Linda Mason Hunter, *The Healthy Home* (Emmaus, Pa.: Rodale Press, 1989), p. 138.

152. Toufaxis, Horowitz, and Thompson, op. cit. p. 65.

153. *Donahue,* transcript no. 120387 (1987), p. 5.

154. "FIN Link" newsletter, Vol. 2 (May 1990), p. 1.

155. Edwin F. Black and Leona M. Libby, "Commercial Food Irradiation," *Bulletin of the Atomic Scientists,* Vol. 39, No. 6 (June–July 1983), p. 48.

156. Transcript, U.S. Congress, House of Representatives, Committee on Energy and Commerce, op. cit., p. 9.

157. Robert Rodell, "Irradiated Food," *Prevention,* Vol. 34, No. 1 (January 1982), p. 10.

158. Petr Beckmann, "Echoes and Updates," *Access to Energy,* Vol. 45, No. 9 (May 1988), p. 4; citing the *Co-op News* (Berkeley, Calif.), March 19, 1988.

159. Seth Rolbein, "Atomic Food," *Boston,* November 1987, p. 138.

160. Transcript, U.S. Congress, House of Representatives, Committee on Energy and Commerce, Subcommittee on Health and the Environment, op. cit., prepared statement of Josephson, pp. 175–76.

161. For example, Hunter, "Food Irradiation Update," op. cit. p. 23.

162. Schmitz, op. cit. p. 28.

163. Nodal R. McNeil, "The Polemics of Fluoridation," *The Nation* (February 4, 1961), p. 98.

164. Transcript, U.S. Congress, House of Representatives, Committee on Energy and Commerce, op. cit., oral testimony of Hon. Sid Morrison, p. 15.

165. Loaharanu, op. cit. p. 46.

166. Daniel P. Puzo, "First Irradiated Fruit on Market Sells Quickly," *Los Angeles Times,* October 9, 1986, Sec. VIII, p. 22.

167. Daniel P. Puzo, "FDA Extends Irradiation Labeling," *Los Angeles Times,* May 26, 1988, Sec. VIII, p. 12.

168. Trish Ratto, "Consumers Zap Back," *American Health,* Vol. 7, No. 5 (June 1988), p. 106.

169. Transcript, U.S. Congress, House of Representatives, Committee on Energy and Commerce, op. cit., oral statement of Andrew Levin, p. 142.

170. Gordon Graff, "Food Irradiation Gets a Go-ahead," *New York Times,* September 8, 1985, p. 4F.

171. Quoted in Trish Hall, "Food Industry Eyes Irradiation Warily," *New York Times,* April 1, 1987, p. C1.

172. Quoted in ibid.

173. Federal Register, Vol. 55, No. 75 (April 18, 1990), pp. 144, 413.

174. Sun, op. cit. p. 668.

175. Rael Jean Isaac and Erich Isaac, *The Coercive Utopians* (Washington, D.C.: Regnery Gateway, 1983), p. 2.

176. Quoted in Yost, op. cit. p. 45.

177. Quoted in Alston Chase, Universal Press Syndicate, November 29, 1989; cited in Andrea Arnold, *Fear of Food* (Bellevue, Wash.: Free Enterprise Press, 1990), p. 7.

178. Susan Watts, "Have We the Stomach for Engineered Food?" *New Scientist,* Vol. 128, No. 1741 (November 3, 1990), p. 24.

## Chapter 7: Currents of Misinformation: The Shocking Facts About Electric and Magnetic Fields

1. Paul Brodeur, *Currents of Death* (New York: Simon and Schuster, 1989), front jacket flap.

2. Bernard Dixon, "Scientifically Speaking," *British Medical Journal,* Vol. 296, No. 6622 (March 26, 1988), p. 940.

3. Quoted in Peter Huber, "Electrophobia," *Forbes*, September 4, 1989, p. 313.

4. Paul Brodeur, *Outrageous Misconduct* (New York: Pantheon Books, 1985), back flap.

5. M. Granger Morgan, "Exposé Treatment Confounds Understanding of a Serious Public-Health Issue," *Scientific American*, Vol. 262, No. 4 (April 1990), p. 118.

6. Philip Elmer-DeWitt, "Hidden Hazards of the Airwaves," *Time*, July 30, 1990, p. 53.

7. Mary-Lou Weisman, "Should You Be Worried About Electricity?" *Woman's Day*, May 22, 1990, p. 126.

8. Pam Black, "Rising Tension over High-Tension Lines," *Business Week*, October 30, 1989, p. 160.

9. *Nightline*, "Electromagnetic Field Hazards," Show No. 2295 (March 9, 1990).

10. Kevin McCullen, "Boulder Refuses Plea to Bury Power Line," (Denver) *Rocky Mountain News*, May 23, 1991, p. 31.

11. Anastasia Toufaxis and Bruce van Voorst, "Panic over Power Lines," *Time*, July 17, 1989, p. 71.

12. "Woman Camps in Backyard to Protest Power Line," *Ottawa Citizen*, August 16, 1989, p. A5.

13. Bill Paul, "Recent Ruling Blocking Children from Playing near Power Lines May Fuel Growing Controversy," *Wall Street Journal*, June 21, 1989, p. B3.

14. Alan Gottlieb, "PSC Picks Speer-Leetsdale Route for Power Line," *Denver Post*, August 11, 1989, p. 1A.

15. George Lane, "Power Line May Hold Up Airport," *Denver Post*, August 20, 1990, pp. 1A, 9A.

16. "The Airport's Electric Fence," editorial, *Denver Post*, August 21, 1990, p. 6B.

17. Lee Siegel (Associated Press), "Invisible Forces and Cancer Fears," *Asbury Park Press*, May 5, 1991, p. A11.

18. Quoted in Black, op. cit. p. 158.

19. "What's New?" *Popular Science*, April 4, 1990, p. 16.

20. Healthwaves brochure, undated. Available from P.O. Box 149, T.C.B., West Orange, NJ, 07052.

21. Quoted in Siegel, "Invisible Forces and Cancer Fears," loc. cit.

22. Quoted in Lee Siegel (Associated Press), "The Cost of Changes Could Run in Billions," *Asbury Park Press*, May 6, 1991, p. A1.

23. U.S. Environmental Protection Agency, *Evaluation of the Potential Carcinogenicity of Electromagnetic Fields* (Washington, D.C.: Environmental Protection Agency, October 1990), pp. 1–5.

24. *Microwaves and Thermal Regulation*, ed. Eleanor R. Adair (New York, Academic Press, 1983).

25. Eleanor R. Adair, "Nurturing Electrophobia," *IEEE Spectrum*, Vol. 27, No. 8 (August 1990), p. 11.

26. Edwin L. Carstensen, *Biological Effects of Transmission Line Fields* (New York: Elsevier, 1987).

27. Personal telephone communication with Edwin L. Carstensen, January 11, 1991.

28. Nancy Wertheimer and Ed Leeper, "Electrical Wiring Configurations and Childhood Cancer," *American Journal of Epidemiology* (hereafter *AJE*), Vol. 109, No. 3 (March 1979), p. 273 (abstract).

29. David A. Savitz et al., "Case-Control Study of Childhood Cancer and Exposure to 60-Hz Magnetic Fields," *AJE,* Vol. 128, No. 1 (July 1988), p. 23.

30. Taylor Moore, "Pursuing the Science of EMF," *EPRI Journal,* Vol. 15, No. 1 (January-February 1990).

31. M. Granger Morgan et al., "Power-Line Fields and Human Health," *IEEE Spectrum,* Vol. 22, No. 2 (February 1985), p. 66.

32. Much of this section is adapted from M. Granger Morgan, "Electric and Magnetic Fields from 60 Hz Electric Power: Possible Health Risks?" *Chance: New Directions for Statistics and Computing,* Vol. 2, No. 4 (October 1989), pp. 12–15.

33. Paul Brodeur, "Radiation Alert," *Family Circle,* November 7, 1989, p. 85.

34. Brodeur, "Annals of Radiation: The Hazards of Electromagnetic Fields," part 1, Vol. 65, No. 17 (June 12, 1989), p. 51; part 2, Vol. 65, No. 18 (June 19, 1989), p. 47; part 3, Vol. 65, No. 19 (June 26, 1989), p. 39.

35. U.S. Congress, Office of Technology Assessment, *Biological Effects of Power Frequency Electric & Magnetic Fields—Background Paper,* OTA-BP-53 (Washington, D.C.: U.S. Government Printing Office, May 1989), p. 6.

36. Indira Nair and M. Granger Morgan, "Electromagnetic Fields: The Jury's Still Out, Part III: Managing the Risks," *IEEE Spectrum,* Vol. 27, No. 8 (August 1990), p. 32.

37. Moore, op. cit. p. 11.

38. Ibid. pp. 11, 12.

39. Quoted in ibid.

40. Ibid.

41. The first reference is Brodeur, *Currents,* op. cit. p. 35.

42. See Carstensen, Chapter 4 generally.

43. Quoted in Karen Fitzgerald, "Electromagnetic Fields: The Jury's Still Out, Part II: Societal Reverberations," *IEEE Spectrum,* Vol. 27, No. 8 (August 1990), p. 29.

44. Morgan et al., "Power-line Fields and Human Health," op. cit. p. 62.

45. See, for example, John Donovan, "High-Tech Healing, Reimers Charges Toward Recovery with Electronic Device," *Cincinnati Post,* September 13, 1990, p. 1B.

46. See Moore, op. cit. p. 8.

47. Nair and Morgan, "Part I: Biological Effects," op. cit. p. 24.

48. Ibid.

49. OTA, *"Biological Effects of Power Frequency,"* paper, OTA-BP-53 (Washington, D.C.: U.S. Government Printing Office, May 1989), p. 3.

50. Ibid. pp. 3, 63, 65.

51. Michael Shepard, "EMF: The Debate on Health Effects," *EPRI Journal,* Vol. 12, No. 7 (October-November 1987), p. 10.

52. U.S. Congress, Office of Technology Assessment, op. cit. p. 63.

53. Shepard, op. cit. p. 10.

54. U.S. Congress, Office of Technology Assessment, op. cit. pp. 62, 63.

55. Adair, "Nurturing Electrophobia," op. cit. p. 11.

56. Quoted in Shepard, op. cit. p. 7.

57. Morgan, "Exposé," op. cit. p. 119.

58. Morgan et al., op. cit. p. 64.

59. R.A.F. Cox, "Health Effects of Electromagnetic Fields," editorial, *Journal of the Royal Society of Medicine,* Vol. 83, No. 2 (February 1990), p. 63.

60. Tar-Ching Aw, "Living Under Pylons," *British Medical Journal,* Vol. 297, No. 6551 (October 1, 1988), pp. 804–5.

61. Brodeur, *Currents,* op. cit. p. 157.

62. Savitz et al., op. cit. pp. 25–26, 36.

63. Ibid. pp. 29, 33–34.

64. Ibid. p. 30, table 3.

65. Ibid. p. 34, table 7.

66. Ibid. p. 32, table 5.

67. David A. Savitz and Lisa Feingold, "Association of Childhood Cancer with Residential Traffic Density," *Scandinavian Journal of Work, Environment, and Health,* Vol. 15, No. 5 (October 1989), p. 362.

68. Robert A. Rinsky et al., "Benzene and Leukemia: An Epidemiological Risk Assessment," *New England Journal of Medicine,* Vol. 316, No. 17 (April 13, 1987), p. 1044.

69. Savitz and Feingold, op. cit. p. 360.

70. Quoted in Fitzgerald, op. cit. p. 30.

71. Stephanie J. London et al., "Exposure to Residential Electric and Magnetic Fields and Risk of Childhood Leukemia," *AJE,* Vol. 134, No. 9 (November 1, 1991), pp. 925–26.

72. Ibid. pp. 935, 937.

73. Brodeur, *Currents,* op. cit. p. 313.

74. Ibid., pp. 185–86.

75. David A. Savitz, "Persons Concerned About Reports of Electromagnetic Fields and Childhood Cancer," undated, p. 1 (Available from School of Public Health, Department of Epidemiology, University of North Carolina at Chapel Hill, Chapel Hill, N.C. 27514).

76. Brodeur, *Currents,* op. cit. pp. 73–78, 83–84, 86, 124, 167.

77. Quoted in Chris Sinacola, "EMF Cancer Risk Unclear," *Worcester* (Mass.) *Sunday Telegram,* October 15, 1989, p. A16.

78. Robert Pool, "Flying Blind: The Making of EMF Policy," *Science,* Vol. 250, No. 4977 (October 5, 1990), p. 1098.

79. Quoted in Michael E. Newman, "The Search for the Missing Link— Electromagnetic Fields and Cancer," *Journal of the National Cancer Institute,* Vol. 81, No. 22 (November 15, 1989), p. 1687.

80. Pool, op. cit. p. 1098.

81. Quoted in Paul Brodeur, "Danger in the Schoolyard," *Family Circle,* Vol. 103, No. 13 (September 25, 1990), p. 65.

82. Paul Brodeur, "Radiation Alert," *Family Circle,* Vol. 102, No. 13 (November 7, 1989), p. 90.

83. Fitzgerald, op. cit. p. 28.

84. Quoted in "Power Frequency Magnetic Fields in the Home," *IEEE Transactions on Power Delivery,* January 4, 1989, p. 469, table 3.

85. For example, with Savitz, the median "very high" level was 2.01 and the mean was 2.92. Savitz et al., op. cit. p. 33, table 6.

86. Fitzgerald, op. cit. p. 32.

87. London et al., op. cit. p. 935.

88. Brodeur, *Currents,* op. cit. p. 229–30.

89. Nancy Wertheimer and Ed Leeper, "Possible Effects of Electric Blankets and Heated Waterbeds on Fetal Developments," *Bioelectromagnetics,* Vol. 7, No. 1 (1986), pp. 18–21.

90. David A. Savitz, Esther M. John, and Robert C. Kleckner, "Magnetic Field Exposure from Electric Appliances and Childhood Cancer," *AJE,* Vol. 131, No. 5 (May 1990), pp. 766, 767 (table 1).

91. Ibid. pp. 763 (abstract), 769 (table 3).

92. Brodeur, *Currents,* op. cit. p. 158.

93. For example, René Vereault et al., "Use of Electric Blankets and Risk of Testicular Cancer," *AJE,* Vol. 131, No. 5 (May 1990), p. 759.

94. Nair and Morgan, "Part III: Managing the Risks," op. cit. p. 33.

95. Black, op. cit. p. 160.

96. Sinacola, op. cit. pp. A16 and B17.

97. David Zinman, "Seeking a Link: LIers Ask U.S. to Study Breast Cancer and the Environment," *Newsday* (Nassau and Suffolk ed.), May 12, 1992, p. 3.

98. Quoted in Susan E. Kinsman, "Utilities Facing Fear of an Invisible Force," *The Hartford Courant,* December 24, 1990, p. 1.

99. Nair and Morgan, "Part III: Managing the Risks," op. cit. p. 35.

100. Gene Shrouf, "Beware Danger of Radiation," letter, *Albuquerque Tribune,* August 4, 1989, p. A7.

101. Paul Brodeur, *The Zapping of America* (New York: W. W. Norton & Co., 1977).

102. Alix M. Freedman, "The Microwave Cooks Up a New Way of Life," *Wall Street Journal,* September 19, 1989, p. B1.

103. Brodeur, *Zapping,* op. cit. pp. 226–27, 231, 240, 241, 243–47, 324; Brodeur, *Currents,* op. cit. pp. 100–32 and elsewhere.

104. See generally Brodeur, *Zapping,* op. cit.

105. "Moscow Signal Is No Death Ray but Still Cryptic," *Science,* Vol. 204, No. 4400 (June 29, 1979), p. 1388.

106. Transcript, U.S. Congress, Senate, Committee on Commerce, Science, and Transportation, "Microwave Irradiation of the U.S. Embassy in Moscow," 96th Cong., 1st Sess. (Washington, D.C.: U.S. Government Printing Office, 1979), p. 23.

107. Brodeur, *Currents,* op. cit. p. 115.

108. Transcript, U.S. Congress, Senate, Committee on Commerce, Science, and Transportation, op. cit. p. 16.

109. Ibid. p. 19 (adult dependents), 20 (child dependents), 23.

110. "Currents of Death: Power Lines, Computer Terminals, and the Attempt to Cover Up Their Threat to Your Health," book review, *Publishers Weekly,* August 18, 1989, p. 43.

111. Judith Eannarion, "Currents of Death: Power Lines, Computer Terminals, and the Attempt to Cover Up Their Threat to Your Health," book review, *Library Journal,* October 1, 1989, p. 112.

112. Robert W. Casey, "Beware Your Electric Blanket," *USA Today,* December 19, 1989, p. 7B.

113. Morgan, "Exposé," op. cit. p. 120.

114. Brodeur, *Currents,* op. cit. pp. 188, 196–97.

115. Ibid. p. 185.

116. Ibid. p. 316 (index).

117. Ibid. p. 25.

118. Ibid. pp. 332–33 (index).

119. Ibid. p. 16.

120. Brodeur, "Annals," op. cit. p. 57.

121. David A. Savitz, "Electric Current and Health," *JAMA,* Vol. 264, No. 5 (August 1, 1990), p. 636.

122. Paul Brodeur, "Annals of Radiation: Calamity on Meadow Street," *New Yorker,* July 9, 1990, pp. 57–58.

123. Ibid. p. 59.

124. Paul Brodeur, "Department of Amplification," *New Yorker,* November 19, 1991, pp. 149–50.

125. Brodeur, "Annals," op. cit. p. 48.

126. "Trial Lawyers for Public Justice Sues Connecticut Utilities for Brain Tumor Caused by Electromagnetic Radiation," *Business Wire,* January 6, 1992.

127. Lorne Manly, "The Best of Magazines: Nominations for American Society of Magazine Editors National Magazine Awards," *Media Week,* Vol. 1, No. 15, April 22, 1992.

128. "Panel in Connecticut Finds No Cancer–Power Line Link," *New York Times,* June 6, 1992, p. 9.

129. Brodeur, "Annals," op. cit. pp. 57–58.

130. Stanley N. Wellborn, "An Electrifying New Hazard," *U.S. News & World Report*, March 30, 1987, p. 72.

131. Reinhard Metz, "Build This Magnetic Field Meter," *Radio Electronics*, Vol. 62, No. 4 (April 1991), p. 34.

132. Lee Siegel (Associated Press), "Some Perceive Risks and Act to Avoid Them," *Asbury Park Press*, May 7, 1991, p. C10.

133. Personal telephone communication with Nair, June 19, 1991.

134. Personal telephone communication with George Koodray, June 19, 1991.

135. Personal telephone communication with Koodray, June 28, 1991.

136. Personal telephone communication with Nair, June 19, 1991.

137. Quoted in Rae Tyson, "Safety of Power Lines is Debated," *USA Today*, April 15, 1986, p. 3A.

138. Brodeur, *Currents,* op. cit. p. 314.

139. Gary Null, *Clearer, Cleaner, Safer, Greener* (New York: Villard, 1990), p. 210.

140. Brodeur, *Currents,* op. cit. p. 311.

141. Morgan et al., p. 68; citing William C. Clark, "Witches, Floods and Wonder Drugs: Historical Perspectives on Risk Management," in *Societal Risk Assessment: How Safe Is Safe Enough?,* ed. Richard C. Schwing and Walter A. Albers, Jr. (New York: Plenum Publishing, 1980), pp. 287–318.

142. Null, op. cit. p. 213.

143. Ibid. p. 214.

144. Nair and Morgan, "Part III: Managing the Risks," op. cit. p. 33.

145. Ibid. p. 35.

146. David A. Savitz, "Persons Concerned about Reports of Electromagnetic Fields and Childhood Cancer," undated, p. 1. (Available from School of Public Health, Department of Epidemiology, University of North Carolina at Chapel Hill, Chapel Hill, N.C. 27514).

147. Quoted in McCullen, op. cit. p. 31.

## Chapter 8: A Fairly Brief, Truly Nonboring Lesson in Risk Taking

1. Aaron Wildavsky and Mary Douglas, *Risk and Culture* (Berkeley, Calif.: University of California Press, 1982), p. 10.

2. Ibid. p. 9.

3. David Wallechinsky, Irving Wallace, and Amy Wallace, *The Book of Lists* (New York: Bantam Books, 1978), p. 457.

4. David M. Bee et al., "Delayed Death from Ingestion of a Toothpick," letter, *New England Journal of Medicine,* Vol. 320, No. 10 (March 9, 1989), p. 673.

5. Wallechinsky, Wallace, and Wallace, op. cit. p. 455.

6. "Ice Cream Rack Falls, Killing Delivery Man," *Denver Post,* April 11, 1991, p. 7A.

7. National Safety Council, *Accident Facts* (Chicago: National Safety Council, 1989), p. 11.

8. Ibid. p. 11.

9. Gregg Easterbrook, "Everything You Know About the Environment Is Wrong," *The New Republic,* Vol. 202, No. 18 (April 30, 1990), p. 21. Calculations by Dr. James Enstrom, UCLA School of Public Health.

10. National Safety Council, op. cit. p. 53.

11. George James, "Perrier Recalls Its Water in U.S. after Benzene is Found in Bottles," *New York Times,* February 10, 1990, p. 10.

12. Warren Brookes, "The Wasteful Pursuit of Zero Risk," *Forbes,* April 30, 1990, p. 163.

13. *Donahue,* transcript. no. 02085, p. 19.

14. Nicholas S. Martin, "Salad Days Are Scaring Us to Death," *Dayton* (Ohio) *Daily News,* January 6, 1990, cited in Andrea Arnold, *Fear of Food* (Bellevue, Wash.: Free Enterprise Press, 1990), p. 6.

15. Quoted in Jay H. Lehr, "Toxicological Risk Assessment Distortions," (Dublin, Ohio: American Ground Water Trust, 1990), p. 13.

16. Douglas and Wildavsky, op. cit. p. 2.

17. Henry Fairlie, "Fear of Living," *The New Republic,* January 23, 1989, p. 14.

18. WGBH-TV, "What Are My Chances?" transcript no. 12, April 3, 1991, p. 4.

19. Quoted in John Tierney, "Straight Talk," *Rolling Stone,* November 17, 1988, p. 132.

20. John Allen Paulos, *Innumeracy: Mathematical Illiteracy and Its Consequences* (New York: Hill and Wang, 1988), p. 8.

21. Leslie Roberts, "Counting on Science at EPA," *Science,* Vol. 249 (August 10, 1990), p. 616.

## Chapter 9: Prejudice and Logic:
## How to Spot a Smelly Argument

1. From *The Crime of Sylvestre Bonnard* (1881); quoted in *Bartlett's Familiar Quotations,* ed. Emily Morrison Beck (Boston: Little, Brown, 1980), p. 655.

2. Environmental Defense Fund, "EDF Condemns EPA Approval of Virginia Dioxin Standard," press release, February 25, 1991.

3. Jon Naar, *Design for a Livable Planet* (New York: Harper and Row, 1990), p. 114.

4. For a refutation of Naar's assertion and an accompanying one about

the loss of species, see Julian Simon, *Population Matters* (New Brunswick, New Jersey: 1990), pp. 149–158.

5. Quoted in Karen Fitzgerald, "Part II: Societal Reverberations," *IEEE Spectrum,* Vol. 27, No. 8 (August 1990), p. 29.

6. Paul R. Ehrlich and Anne H. Ehrlich, *The Population Bomb* (New York: Simon and Schuster, 1990). Redford says he hopes the book "will be read by anyone who wants to understand why our planet is threatened and what we can do about it" (citation from back cover).

7. Holly G. Miller, "Elizabeth Taylor's Crusade Against AIDS," *Saturday Evening Post,* September 1987, p. 102; Associated Press, "Children Should Be Told about Sex, Madonna Says," (Denver) *Rocky Mountain News,* July 20, 1991, p. 98. (Appears in different newspapers under different names.)

8. *Donahue,* transcript no. 120387 (1987), p. 5.

9. Thanks for this enlightening story to Peter Huber in *Galileo's Revenge* (New York: Basic Books, 1991), p. 65.

10. Gary Null, *Clearer, Cleaner, Safer, Greener* (New York: Villard, 1990), p. 213.

11. *Bartlett's Book of Familiar Quotations,* ed. Emily Morrison Beck (Boston: Little, Brown, 1980), p. 359, fn. 2.

12. Quoted in David Brooks, "Saving the Earth from Its Friends," *National Review,* April 1, 1990, p. 29.

13. Huber, op. cit. pp. 198–99.

## Chapter 10: Terminal Illness:
## Are VDTs Killing You or Your Unborn Child?

1. Ellen Bilofsky, "Terminal Illness?" *Health/PAC Bulletin,* Vol. 20, No. 4 (Winter 1990), p. 18.

2. Dana Priest, "Miscarriages at 'USA Today' Cause Concern," *Washington Post,* December 9, 1988, p. A1.

3. Quoted in ibid.

4. Council on Scientific Affairs, American Medical Association, "Health Effects of Video Display Terminals," *Journal of the American Medical Association* (hereafter *JAMA*), Vol. 257, No. 11 (March 20, 1990), p. 1510.

5. Ulva O. V. Berqvist, "Video Display Terminals and Health: A Technical and Medical Appraisal of the State of the Art," *Scandinavian Journal of Work, Environment, and Health,* supp. Vol. 2, No. 1 (1984), p. 68.

6. Paul Brodeur, "The Magnetic-Field Menace," *MacWorld,* July 1990, p. 136.

7. David E. Drum, "Alarmist Views," letter, *MacWorld,* July 1990, p. 146.

8. Robert Eckhardt, "Color Monitors Put to the Test," *MacWorld,* July 1990, p. 146.

9. Drum, op. cit. p. 37; and David R. Arday and Susan L. Arday, "The Evidence is Lacking," letter, *MacWorld*, July 1990, pp. 47–48.

10. John C. Towler, Jr., "Write Your Representative," letter, *MacWorld*, July 1990, pp. 43–44.

11. "Danger from a Glowing Screen," *Time*, July 18, 1990, p. 76.

12. Herbert Kohl, "Screen Test," *The Nation*, August 27–September 3, 1990, p. 205.

13. Bilofsky, op. cit. pp. 18, 20.

14. Shirley D. Linde, "A Citizen-Activist Looks at EMF," *Electricity Journal*, April 1991, p. 25.

15. Marjory Roberts, "Computer Waves," *U.S. News & World Report*, September 10, p. 86.

16. John Helliwell, "There Are Other Answers to the Hazards of VDTs," *PC Week*, May 6, 1989, p. 17.

17. Paul Brodeur, *Currents of Death* (New York: Simon & Schuster, 1989), pp. 260–65.

18. Jeff Sorensen and Jon Swan, "VDTs: The Overlooked Story Right in the Newsroom," *Columbia Journalism Review*, Vol. 19, No. 5 (January–February 1981), p. 32.

19. Louis Slesin, "Uncovering Radiation," *Columbia Journalism Review*, Vol. 29, No. 2 (July–August 1990), p. 4.

20. Peter Blumberg, "Paul Brodeur's War on Electromagnetic Fields," *Washington Journalism Review*, Vol. 13, No. 1 (January– February 1991), p. 43.

21. Brodeur, *Currents*, op. cit. p. 7 (unnumbered).

22. Ibid. pp. 266–68, 270, 273–75, 279–80, 282, 302–3, 305 (Delgado); 268, 275, 280 (Ubeda).

23. Louis Slesin, "VDT Radiation: What's Known, What Isn't," *Columbia Journalism Review*, Vol. 23, No. 4 (November–December 1984), p. 40.

24. José M. R. Delgado et al., "Embryological Changes by Weak, Extremely Low Frequency Electromagnetic Fields," *Journal of Anatomy*, Vol. 134 (1982), p. 533; cited in American Medical Association Council on Scientific Affairs, "Health Effects of Video Display Terminals," *JAMA*, Vol. 257, No. 11 (March 20, 1987), p. 1509.

25. Alejandro Ubeda et al., "Pulse Shape of Magnetic Fields Influences Chick Embryogenesis," *Journal of Anatomy*, Vol. 137 (1983), p. 513; cited in AMA Council on Scientific Affairs, op. cit. p. 1509.

26. Ibid.

27. Brodeur, "Currents," pp. 240–41.

28. Council on Scientific Affairs, op. cit., pp. 1509, 1511.

29. U.S. House of Representatives, Committee on Health and Safety, Subcommittee on Education and Labor, 99th Cong., 1st Sess., 1984, prepared statement of M. B. Bond, American College of Obstetricians and Gynecologists; cited in AMA Council on Scientific Affairs, op. cit. p. 1509.

30. Sorensen and Swan, op. cit. p. 32; Brodeur, *Currents*, op. cit. p. 261 (only *New York Times* mentioned).

31. Sorenson and Swan, op. cit. p. 34.

32. Ibid. p. 32.

33. National Research Council, Committee on Vision, *Video Displays, Work, and Vision* (Washington, D.C.: National Academy Press, 1983), pp. 58–60.

34. International Commission on Illumination, *Vision and the Visual Display Unit Workstation* (Paris: Comité d'Électricité International, 1984), p. 8.

35. AMA Council on Scientific Affairs, op. cit. p. 1509; citing Smith et al., "Report of a Cross-Sectional Survey of Video Display Terminal (VDT) Users at the *Baltimore Sun* (Cincinnati, Ohio: National Institute for Occupational Safety and Health, 1982).

36. AMA Council on Scientific Affairs, op. cit. p. 1509; citing U.S. House of Representatives, Committee on Education and Labor, Subcommittee on Health and Safety, 1985, "A Staff Report on the Oversight of OSHA with Respect to Video Display Terminals in the Workplace."

37. Slesin, op. cit. p. 41.

38. Marilyn Goldhaber, Michael R. Polen, and Robert A. Hiatt, "The Risk of Miscarriage and Birth Defects Among Women Who Use Visual Display Terminals During Pregnancy," *American Journal of Industrial Medicine*, Vol. 13, No. 6 (June 1988), p. 697.

39. Ibid. p. 703.

40. Ibid. p. 701, Table 5.

41. Quoted in Melissa Hendricks, "VDTs on Trial," *Science News*, September 10, 1988, p. 174.

42. Jean Seligmann, Pamela Abramson, and Mary Hager, "Are Computer Screens Safe?" *Newsweek*, June 20, 1988, p. 53.

43. Quoted in Philip M. Boffey, "Video Terminals and Health: A Reawakening of Concern," *New York Times*, June 15, 1988, p. B10.

44. Fran Lowry, "VDTs and Health: Many Studies, Few Answers," *Canadian Medical Association Journal*, Vol. 141 (November 1, 1989), p. 977.

45. Alison D. McDonald, et al., "Visual Display Units and Pregnancy: Evidence from the Montreal Survey," *Journal of Occupational Medicine*, Vol. 28, No. 12 (December 1986), p. 1228.

46. Ibid. pp. 1230–31.

47. Ibid. p. 1226; citing R. L. Brent, "The Effects of Embryonic and Fetal Exposures to X rays, Microwaves and Ultrasound," *Clinical Obstetric Gynecology*, Vol. 26 (1983), p. 484.

48. Brodeur, *Currents*, op. cit. p. 287.

49. Transcript, U.S. House of Representatives, Committee on Government Operations, Subcommittee on Human Resources and Intergovernmental Relations, "Oversight Review of CDC's Agent Orange Study," "Response to CDC Criticisms of the American Legion–Columbia University Study of Vietnam Era Veterans," by Jeanne M. Stellman and Steven D. Stellman, July 11, 1989, pp. 211, 217.

50. Goldhaber, Polen, and Hiatt, op. cit. p. 704. See also Harry Rob-

inson, "The Risk of Miscarriage and Birth Defects Among Women Who Use Visual Display Terminals During Pregnancy," letter, *American Journal of Industrial Medicine,* Vol. 15, No. 3 (March 1989), p. 357; and authors' response, Marilyn K. Goldhaber, Michael R. Polen, and Robert A. Hiatt, "VDTs and Miscarriage," letter, *American Journal of Industrial Medicine,* Vol. 15, No. 3 (March 1989), pp. 359–60.

51. Quoted in Boffey, p. B10.

52. For example, Christine Gorman, Elaine Lafferty, and Janice Simpson, "All Eyes on the VDT," *Time,* June 27, 1988, p. 51; Linda Weber, "How Safe Are VDTs?" *Good Housekeeping,* November 1988, p. 267.

53. Cindi Leive, "Why I Can't Stop Thinking About My Computer," *Glamour,* October 1990, p. 162.

54. U. Bergqvist, "Possible Health Effects of Working with VDUs," *British Journal of Industrial Medicine,* Vol. 46, No. 4 (April 1989), pp. 218–19.

55. Heather E. Bryant and Edgar J. Love, "Video Display Terminal Use and Spontaneous Abortion Risk," *International Journal of Epidemiology,* Vol. 18, No. 1 (March 1989), pp. 132, 137–38.

56. Teresa M. Schnorr et al., "Video Display Terminals and the Risk of Spontaneous Abortion," *New England Journal of Medicine,* Vol. 324, No. 11 (March 14, 1991), pp. 728–29.

57. Ibid. p. 730.

58. Ibid. p. 731.

59. For a general look at the costs of maternal drug usage, see generally Joel W. Hay, "The Harm They Do to Others," paper presented at the Hoover Institution Conference on Drug Policy, November 15, 1990 (typescript).

## Chapter 11: Gasohol Pains

1. Quoted in Michael Isikoff, "Andreas: College Drop-out to Global Trader," *Washington Post,* December 8, 1985, p. H6.

2. Michael J. Weiss, "The High-Octane Ethanol Lobby," *New York Times Magazine,* April 1, 1990, p. 19.

3. Leonard W. Schruben, "Economic Evaluation of Industrial Use of Cereals: The Alcohol Fuel Case," paper presented at the International Symposium on Industrial Utilization of Cereals, Carlsberg Institute, Copenhagen, Denmark, August 13, 1981, p. 685.

4. U.S. Department of Energy, *Assessment of Costs and Benefits of Flexible and Alternative Fuel Use in the U.S. Transportation Sector,* Progress Report One (Washington, D.C.: U.S. Department of Energy, January 1988); cited in California Council for Environmental and Economic Balance, *Alternative Motor Vehicle Fuels to Improve Air Quality* (San Francisco: California Council for Environmental and Economic Balance, January 1990), p. 46.

5. California Council for Environmental and Economic Balance, op. cit. p. 45.

6. Ibid. p. 46; citing California Air Resources Board, "Role of Alternative Fuels in Reducing Air Pollution," staff presentation, January 1988.

7. Weiss, op. cit. p. 20 (chart), using figures from Information Resources, Inc. and the U.S. Department of Agriculture.

8. "Soiled Clean Air Bill," editorial, *Wall Street Journal,* April 30, 1990, p. A16.

9. Personal telephone communication with representative of U.S. Department of Agriculture, 1990.

10. U.S. Department of Agriculture, "Fuel Ethanol and Agriculture: An Economic Assessment," August 1986.

11. U.S. General Accounting Office, "Alcohol Fuels: Impacts from Increased Use of Ethanol Blended Fuels," RCED-90-156, July 1990, p. 28.

12. Ibid. pp. 23–33.

13. Quoted in Holman Jenkins, Jr., "Grain King's Business Is a Daily Grind for Profit," *Insight,* February 19, 1990, p. 15.

14. Michael Isikoff, "Ethanol Producer Reaps 54 Percent of U.S. Subsidy," *Washington Post,* January 29, 1987, p. A14.

15. "Tables Turned as Brazil Imports Ethanol from the United States," *Clean Fuels Report,* Vol. 1 (February 1990), p. 91.

16. Jonathan Kandell, "Brazil's Costly Mix: Autos and Alcohol," *Wall Street Journal,* September 29, 1989, p. A18.

17. "Tables Turned," op. cit. p. 91.

18. Lane Palmer, "Should We Mandate Ethanol?" *Farm Journal,* mid-January 1988, p. 32.

19. Personal telephone communication with George Dahlman, Minnesota office of Piper, Jaffray and Hopwood, July 27, 1990.

20. Ibid.

21. All data from Dr. Fred Gray, Economic Research Service, U.S. Department of Agriculture.

22. See Michael Fumento, "Some Dare Call Them Robber Barons," *National Review,* March 13, 1987, p. 33.

23. Irwin Ross, "Dwayne Andreas's Bean Has a Heart of Gold," *Fortune,* October 1973, p. 137.

24. Quoted in Mark D. Anastasio, "Dwayne Andreas Gains an Apparent Position as Kremlin Favorite," *Wall Street Journal,* December 26, 1986, p. 14.

25. Jenkins, op. cit. p. 12.

26. Ross, op. cit. p. 137.

27. Information on House and Senate bills from the Library of Congress LOCIS system.

28. Data from Federal Election Commission, Washington, D.C.

29. John E. Yang, "Legislation Would Assist Corn Farms, Ethanol Firm," *Wall Street Journal,* April 4, 1990, p. A14.

30. Edward T. Pound, "Minority Leader's Backer Gains on Gasohol Issue," *Wall Street Journal,* September 25, 1987, p. 50.

31. Personal telephone communication with John Gudelanis, 1987.

32. Quoted in Weiss, op. cit. p. 20.

33. USDA Economic Research Service, *Ethanol: Economic and Policy Trade-offs,* Agricultural Economic Report No. 585 (Washington, D.C.: USDA, April 1988), p. 34.

34. According to U.S. Department of Agriculture figures, for 1984, the cash value of production for Kansas corn was $270,000,000, for soybeans $198,000,000 and for wheat, $1,469,000,000.

35. "Cash, Connections Fuel Cause," *Washington Post,* December 8, 1985, p. H7.

36. Source: U.S. Export Sales, Food and Agricultural Service, U.S. Department of Agriculture.

37. Personal telephone communication with Diego Asencio, 1987.

38. Personal telephone communication with Royal Daniel, 1987.

39. Quoted in "Soiled Clean Air Bill," *Wall Street Journal,* editorial, May 2, 1990, p. A16.

40. Quoted in Weiss, op. cit. p. 20.

41. Paul Harvey, "Use of Ethanol Would Be a Help," (Nampa-Caldwell) *Idaho Press Tribune,* June 5, 1987.

42. Quoted in Weiss, op. cit. p. 40.

43. Larry Rohter, "Buchwald Gets Damages in Film Suit," *New York Times,* December 22, 1990, p. 17.

44. Personal telephone communication with Dahlman, May 3, 1991.

45. Jenkins, op. cit. p. 9.

46. Quoted in Michael Isikoff, loc. cit.

47. Michelle P. Fulcher, "Degradable Plastic a Myth, Critics Say," *Denver Post,* January 4, 1990, pp. 1A, 7A.

48. James Coates, "Smog Fight Fuels Farmers Hopes," *Chicago Tribune,* June 29, 1987, p. 8.

49. Quoted in Barry Noreen, "Women's Convoy Fueled by a Cause," *Colorado Springs Gazette Telegraph,* November 12, 1987, p. B1.

50. Quoted in C. Edwin Baker, "Oxyfuels May Be Part of Problem, Not Solution," (Denver) *Rocky Mountain News,* April 12, 1989, p. 39.

51. For further reading, see Kenneth W. Chilton and Anne M. Sholtz, "Battling Smog: No Easy Victory in Sight" (St. Louis: Washington University Center for the Study of American Business, July 1989), pp. 13–14.

52. Steven Howard, "Critics Clouding Facts About Clean Air Campaign," (Denver) *Rocky Mountain News,* April 28, 1989, p. 57.

53. Joseph B. Verrengia, "Air Cleaner, but Reasons Murky," (Denver) *Rocky Mountain News,* January 15, 1990, p. 8 (graphic).

54. "Question of the Week," (Denver) *Rocky Mountain News,* March 5, 1991, p. 134.

55. Quoted in Mary George, "Professors Challenge Use of Trailblazing Oxyfuel," *Denver Post,* January 14, 1991, p. 1B.

56. Milliken Research Group, "Benefits and Costs of Oxygenated Fuels in Colorado" (Denver: Rocky Mountain Oil and Gas Association, June 1990), p. ES-8.

57. Ibid. 75, 86.

58. Eliot Marshall, "Gasoline: The Unclean Fuel?" *Science*, Vol. 246, No. 4927, October 13, 1989, p. 199.

59. Personal telephone communication with Clayton Smith, July 27, 1990.

60. James E. Peterson and Donald H. Stedman, "Oxygenated Fuels Versus Targeted Sensing and Repair," typescript, undated, p. 6.

61. Personal telephone communication with Gary Woodard, May 31, 1990.

62. Gary Woodard et al., *Arizona Carbon Monoxide Emissions Reduction Study* (Phoenix, Ariz.: Arizona Department of Environmental Quality, May 1990), p. 6-63, table 6-19.

63. Ibid. p. 18-1 and personal telephone communication with Woodard.

64. Personal telephone communication with John Lesko, May 1, 1991.

65. Clarence M. Ditlow III and Robert L. Dewey of the Center for Auto Safety, untitled 18-page report on oxygenated fuels, pp. 3–4, (available from Center for Auto Safety, 2001 S Street, N.W., Suite 410, Washington, D.C. 20009); Barry Noreen, "Consumer Group Opposes Fuel Plan," *Colorado Springs Gazette Telegraph*, June 19, 1987.

66. Sierra Research, Inc., *The Air Pollution Consequences of Using Ethanol-Gasoline Blends in Ozone Non-Attainment Areas*, Report No. SR90-05-01, prepared for the American Petroleum Institute, May 8, 1990, pp. 1–2, table 2; p. 17, table 6; Matthew L. Wald, " 'Gasohol' May Cut Monoxide but Raise Smog, Study Asserts," *New York Times*, May 9, 1990, p. A1.

67. Quoted in Wald, op. cit. p. D2.

68. Ibid. p. A1.

69. Quoted in ibid. p. D2.

70. Sierra Research, op. cit. pp. 5–6.

71. Barbara Rosewicz, "Big Ethanol Problem for Bush Prompts White House to Mull Special Concessions," *Wall Street Journal*, September 8, 1992, p. A3.

72. Rudy Abramson, "Bush Permits 'Gasohol' in Nation's Nine Smoggiest Cities," *Los Angeles Times*, October 2, 1992, p. 16.

73. Gary A. Bishop and Donald H. Stedman, "On-Road Carbon Monoxide Emission Measurement Comparisons for the 1988–1989 Colorado Oxy-Fuels Program—Final Report," produced for the Chemistry Department, University of Denver, October 17, 1989 (unpublished report), p. i.

74. Leroy Williams, Jr., "Air Campaign Facing Revision," (Denver) *Rocky Mountain News*, March 3, 1989, p. 6.

75. Quoted in Janet Day, "Battle for Better Air," (Denver) *Rocky Mountain News*, October 8, 1989, p. 30.

76. Clean Air Act of 1990, Sec. 214.

NOTES

77. Quoted in Charles R. Babcock and Michael Weisskopf, " 'Clean Gasoline' Pact Unveiled," *Washington Post,* May 22, 1990, pp. A1, A10.

78. 101 P.L. 549; 1990 S. 1630; 104 Stat. 239 (Clean Air Act of 1990), Sec. 219.

79. Babcock and Weisskopf, op. cit. p. A10.

80. Yang, op. cit. p. A14.

81. Quoted in ibid.

82. Marjorie Lamb, *Two Minutes a Day for a Greener Planet* (New York: Harper and Row, 1990), p. 60.

83. "Picking a Fuel for the Future," editorial, *Denver Post,* September 5, 1989, p. 6B.

84. S. P. Ho, "Global Warming Impact of Ethanol Versus Gasoline," paper presented at the 1989 National Conference on "Clean Air Issues and America's Motor Fuel Business," Washington, D.C., October 3–5, 1989.

85. Migdon Segal, *Ethanol Fuel and Global Warming* (Washington, D.C.: Congressional Research Service of the Library of Congress, March 6, 1989).

86. S. P. Ho and T. A. Renner, "The Global Warming Impact of Attainment Strategies Using Alternative Fuels," paper presented at Air and Waste Management Conference on Tropospheric Ozone and Environment, Los Angeles, March 19–22, 1990.

87. Migdon Segal, "Ethanol Fuel and Global Warming: Response to Amoco Critique," memorandum to Congressman Richard J. Durbin (Washington, D.C.: Congressional Research Service of the Library of Congress, April 10, 1990).

88. Studies listed in Segal, "Ethanol Fuel and Global Warming," op. cit. p. 16.

89. Ibid. p. 3.

90. Carroll R. Keim, "Ethanol," in "U.S. Gasoline Outlook 1989–1994," (Washington, D.C.: Information Resources, 1989), p. XV-33, table XV-11; calculated by Shi-Ping Ho of Amoco Oil, Naperville, Ill., in correspondence to Migdon Segal, Congressional Research Service, October 16, 1989 (attachment).

91. Ho and Renner, op. cit. p. 18, figure one.

92. Donald H. Stedman, "Dirty-Car Tuneups Beat Oxy-Fuels by a Mile," *Wall Street Journal,* February 6, 1990, p. A22.

93. Personal telephone communication with Jerry Gallagher, June 10, 1991.

94. Gary C. Woodard and Craig M. Horn, "Oxygenated Fuels in Arizona: The Cost of Cleaner Air," *Arizona's Economy,* June 1990, p. 7.

95. Estimate from California Bureau of Auto Repair.

96. Henderson, op. cit. p. 34.

97. Personal written correspondence with Donald Stedman, p. 1.

98. Henderson, op. cit., p. 32.

99. University of Denver, "An Analysis of On-Road Remote Sensing as

a Tool for Automobile Emissions Control," prepared for Illinois Department of Energy and Natural Resources (Denver: University of Denver, March 1990), undated, unpublished report, pp. xi-xii.

100. Bishop and Stedman, op. cit. p. i, table.

101. Ibid. p. 6, table.

102. Ibid. p. i.

103. University of Denver press release, untitled, January 26, 1989; Dick Foster, "State Pooh-poohs Auto Emissions Study," (Denver) *Rocky Mountain News,* January 27, 1989, p. 32; Donald H. Stedman and Gary A. Bishop, "On-Road Remote Sensing and Motor Vehicle Inspection and Maintenance Programs," typescript, undated, table 1.

104. Personal correspondence with Stedman, May 10, 1991, p. 2.

105. Personal telephone communication with Marc Pitchford, June 21, 1990.

106. Personal telephone communication with Bill Denham, May 17, 1991.

107. Bryan Abas, "Take a Deep Breath," *Westword* (Denver), March 23–29, 1988, pp. 16–20.

108. Written communication from Jerry Gallagher to Vernon P. Dorweiler, Associate Professor of Management and Law, Michigan Technological University, August 30, 1989, p. 1.

109. Personal written correspondence with Stedman, May 10, 1991, p. 2.

110. Personal telephone communication with Jerry Gallagher, June 10, 1991.

111. Personal telephone communication with Stedman, June 26, 1991.

112. Clean Air Act of 1990, op. cit., Sec. 179.

113. Quoted in Foster, op. cit. p. 32.

114. Verrengia, op. cit. p. 8 (graphic).

115. Quoted in Mary George, "Front Range Eligible for Ozone Honors," *Denver Post,* October 17, 1990, p. 3B.

116. Henderson, op. cit. p. 36.

117. Douglas R. Lawson, "Emissions from In-Use Motor Vehicles in Los Angeles: A Pilot Study of Remote Sensing and the Inspection and Maintenance Program," *Journal of the Air and Waste Management Association,* Vol. 40, No. 8 (August 1990), p. 1101.

118. Ibid.

119. Ibid.

120. Donald Stedman, "Dirty-Car Tuneups Beat Oxy-Fuels by a Mile," op. cit. p. A22.

121. Ari M. Michelsen, Joshua B. Epel, and Robert D. Rowe, "Economic Evaluation of Colorado's 1988–1989 Oxygenated Fuels Program," (draft), prepared for U.S. Environmental Protection Agency (Washington, D.C., May 10, 1989), p. 4-3, as modified by Joshua B. Epel, Marina Skumanich, and Robert Rowe, "Draft Report, The Colorado Oxygenated Fuels

Program: Evaluation of Program Costs for 1989–1990 and for Alternative Program Designs," prepared for U.S. Environmental Protection Agency, Denver, May 17, 1990, p. 2-25. The second report notes that the first report only took into account four months of the program when in fact a four-month program really equates to five months because of lead-in and lead-out times. Thus the figures in the first report were understated by 25 percent.

122. Michelsen, Epel, and Rowe, op. cit. p. 4-3.

123. University of Denver, "An Analysis of On-Road Remote Sensing as a Tool for Automobile Emissions Control," op. cit. p. xii.

124. Personal telephone communication with Stedman, June 10, 1991.

125. Clean Air Act of 1990, Sec. 203.

126. Quoted in Eliot Marshall, "Gasoline: The Unclean Fuel?" *Science,* October 13, 1989, p. 199.

127. Personal correspondence with Stedman, June 10, 1991, p. 3.

128. Henderson, op. cit. p. 36.

129. Quoted in ibid.

130. P.L. 101-549, 104 Stat. 2433, Subpart 2, Section 182, B and C (1990).

131. Personal telephone communication with Steve Sayle, aide to Congressman Joe Barton, 1991.

132. Personal telephone communication with Stedman, June 10, 1991.

## Chapter 12: A Closer Look at the Besiegers

1. Stewart Brand, *The Whole Earth Catalogue;* cited in Dixy Lee Ray and Lou Guzzo, *Trashing the Planet* (Washington, D.C.: Regnery Gateway), p. 166.

2. Al Gore, "A New Initiative to Save the Planet," *Scientific American,* Vol. 262, No. 4 (April 1990), p. 124.

3. See Julian Simon, "Truth Almost Extinct in Tales of Imperiled Species," *Washington Times,* September 19, 1984; and Julian Simon, "Disappearing Species, Deforestation and Data," *New Scientist,* Vol. 110, No. 1508 (May 15, 1986), p. 60, both reprinted in Julian Simon, *Population Matters* (New Brunswick, N.J.: Transaction, 1990), pp. 145–58.

4. See Associated Press, "Actresses Appeal for Farm Aid," *New York Times,* May 7, 1985, p. A18.

5. ABC News's *Nightline,* "A 'Media Witch Hunt'?" June 24, 1983, transcript p. 3.

6. Michael Greenberg et al., "Network Evening News Coverage of Environmental Risk," *Risk Analysis,* Vol. 9, No. 1 (March 1989),p. 125.

7. Linda Ellerbee, "The Bad News Is All About Bad News," (Denver) *Rocky Mountain News,* January 17, 1991, p. 55 (carried by various newspapers under various titles).

8. ABC News's *Nightline,* "A 'Media Witch Hunt'?" transcript p. 7.

9. Dorothy Nelkin, *Selling Science* (New York: W. H. Freeman, 1987), p. 68.

10. John G. Kemeny, "Saving American Democracy: The Lesson of Three Mile Island," *Technology Review,* Vol. 83, No. 7 (June–July 1980), p. 64.

11. "A New report from the Centers for Disease Control indicates that AIDS infections are on the rise on college campuses." CNN Broadcast of November 29, 1990.

12. Associated Press, "One in 500 College Students Has AIDS Virus," *Denver Post* (carried by various newspapers under various titles), November 29, 1990, p. 3A.

13. Helene D. Gayle et al., "Prevalence of the Human Immunodeficiency Virus Among University Students," *New England Journal of Medicine* (hereafter *NEJM*), Vol. 323, No. 22 (November 29, 1990), p. 1538.

14. Quoted in Malcolm Gladwell, "Some Fear Bad Precedent in Alar Alarm," *Washington Post,* April 19, 1989, p. A12.

15. S. Robert Lichter, Stanley Rothman, and Linda Richter, *The Media Elite* (Washington, D.C.: Adler and Adler, 1986), p. 21, table 1; p. 28.

16. Ben Wattenberg, *The Good News Is the Bad News Is Wrong* (New York: Simon and Schuster, 1984), p. 375.

17. Lichter, Rothman, and Lichter, op. cit. p. 30, table 2.

18. L. Brent Bozell III and Brent H. Baker, eds., *And That's the Way It Isn't* (Alexandria, Va.: Media Research Center), p. 176.

19. Ibid. p. 101.

20. Wattenberg, loc. cit.

21. For a discussion of why the different American system came about, see Nelkin, p. 92; summarizing material in Dan Schiller, *Objectivity and News* (Philadelphia: University of Pennsylvania Press, 1981).

22. Notable Quotables from "MediaWatch," November 26, 1990, p. 2, citing the Summer 1990 *Gannett Center Journal.*

23. Wattenberg, op. cit. p. 376.

24. Garrett Hardin, "The Tragedy of the Commons," in Garrett De Bell, ed., *The Environmental Handbook* (New York: Ballantine Books/ Friends of the Earth, 1970), p. 39.

25. See generally Peter Huber, *Liability: The Legal Revolution and Its Consequences* (New York: Basic Books), 1988.

26. Leonard A. Cole, *Politics and the Restraint of Science* (Totowa, N.J.: Rowman and Allanheld, 1983), p. 32.

27. Quoted in Max Weinrich, *Hitler's Professors: The Part of Scholarship in Germany's Crimes Against the Jewish People* (New York: Yiddish Scientific Institute—YIVO, 1946), p. 12.

28. Cole, op. cit. p. 45. For his source, Cole cites Gunter Lewy, *The Catholic Church and Nazi Germany* (New York: McGraw-Hill Book Co., 1964), pp. 264–66.

29. Ibid.

30. For a discussion on why Sagan was wrong, see Eliot Marshall, " 'Nuclear Winter' from Gulf War Discounted," *Science,* Vol. 251, No. 4992, (January 25, 1991), p. 372.

31. Paul R. Ehrlich, *The Population Bomb* (New York: Ballantine Books/ Sierra Club, 1968), p. 11.

32. See William Tucker, *Progress and Privilege* (New York: Doubleday, 1982), pp. 100–111.

33. Personal communication with Edwin Carstensen, January 11, 1991.

34. Ralph E. Lapp, *The Radiation Controversy* (Greenwich, Conn.: Reddy Communications, 1979), p. 140.

35. George Claus and Karen Bolander, *Ecological Sanity* (New York: David McKay, 1977), p. 49.

36. Merril Eisenbud, statement before the Public Information and Public Relations Panel, New York Academy of Medicine Symposium on the Health Aspects of Nuclear Power Plant Incidents, April 7–8, 1983; quoted in Elizabeth Whelan, *Toxic Terror* (Ottawa, Ill.: Jameson Books, 1988), p. 292.

37. Philip Handler, "Science and the American Future," speech at Duke University, March 6, 1980; quoted in Whelan, op. cit. p. 293.

38. Jean-Jacques Rousseau, *Émile* (New York: Dutton, 1966), p. 5.

39. Dave Foreman, *Ecodefense: A Field Guide to Monkey Wrenching* (Tucson, Ariz.: Ned Ludd Books, 1987); cited in Dixy Lee Ray and Lou Guzzo, *Trashing the Planet* (Washington, D.C.: Regnery Gateway, 1990), p. 166.

40. Rae Tyson, "For Activist, Earth Still First," *USA Today,* August 15, 1991, p. 3A.

41. Quoted in "Irradiated Feast," *The Progressive,* June 1982, p. 12.

42. Helen B. Hiscoe, "Does Being Natural Make It Good?" *NEJM,* Vol. 308, No. 24 (June 16, 1983), p. 1475.

43. Gregg Easterbrook, "Everything You Know About the Environment Is Wrong," *New Republic,* April 30, 1990, p. 22.

44. Margaret Maxey, *Managing Environmental Risks: What Difference Does Ethics Make?,* publication no. 90 (St. Louis: Center for the Study of American Business, Washington University, May 1990), p. 3.

45. See Ernst Joseph Schumacher, *Small Is Beautiful: Economics as if People Mattered* (New York: Harper and Row, 1973).

46. Ray and Guzzo, op. cit. pp. 14–17.

47. Jeremy Rifkin, *A New Consciousness for a New Century* (New York: Crown Publishers, 1991).

48. Gina Maranto, "Biosphere Politics," *New York Times Book Review,* June 16, 1991, p. 13.

49. Easterbrook, op. cit. pp. 18–19.

50. Quoted in Ray and Guzzo, op. cit. p. 22.

51. Michael Brown, *Laying Waste* (New York: Pantheon, 1979), pp. 58–59.

52. Quoted in Paul Ciotti, "Fear of Fusion: What If It Works?" *Los Angeles Times,* April 19, 1990, p. 1.

53. Amory Lovins, "The Plowboy Interview," *Mother Earth,* 48 (November–December 1977), p. 16.

54. Paul Ehrlich, "An Ecologist's Perspective on Nuclear Power," *FAS Public Issues Report,* May–June 1978; quoted in *Access to Energy,* Vol. 16, No. 9 (May 1989), p. 4.

55. Quoted in Petr Beckmann, "Echoes and Updates," *Access to Energy,* Vol. 11, No. 3 (November 1983), p. 4.

56. Noel Perrin, "What This Country Needs Is a Good Meltdown," letter, *New York Times,* August 20, 1983, p. 21.

57. Quoted in Ciotti, op. cit. p. 1.

58. Easterbrook, op. cit. p. 26.

59. Tucker, op. cit. pp. 271–72, 277.

60. Michael Rogers, *Biohazard* (New York: Alfred A. Knopf, 1977); June Goodfield, *Playing God: Genetic Engineering and the Manipulation of Life* (New York: Random House, 1977); Marc Lappé, *Genetic Politics: The Limits of Biological Control* (New York: Simon and Schuster, 1979); also Laurence E. Karp, *Genetic Engineering: Threat or Promise?* (Chicago: Nelson-Hall Publishers, 1976).

61. Quoted in Eliot Marshall, "Environmental Groups Lose Friends in Effort to Control DNA Research," *Science,* Vol. 202, No. 4375 (December 22, 1978), pp. 1266–67.

62. Charles P. (C. P.) Snow, *The Two Cultures: And a Second Look* (London: Cambridge University Press, 1964), p. 4. First published in 1959 as *The Two Cultures.*

63. Ibid. pp. 25–26.

64. Charles Krauthammer, "Saving Nature, But Only for Man," *Time,* June 17, 1991, p. 82.

65. Quoted in Cathy Young, "Worshipping at the Altar of Environmentalism," *Detroit News,* January 6, 1991, p. B3.

66. Seth Shulman, "Sagan Appeals to World Religious Leaders," *Nature,* 343, February 1, 1990, p. 398.

67. P.L. 9250, Federal Water Pollution Control Act, 33 U.S.C. 1251(a) (1972).

68. Alan Carlin, *Environmental Investments: The Cost of a Clean Environment, A Summary* (Washington, D.C.: Environmental Protection Agency, December 1990), pp. 5-2–5-6.

69. According to the U.S. Department of the Interior, Fish and Wildlife Service, an average of 458,000 acres a year of wetlands were lost from 1955 to 1974, and 290,000 a year from 1975 to 1985. Personal telephone communication with Mike Smith, Fish and Wildlife Service, October 22, 1991.

70. Julian Simon, *Population Matters* (New Brunswick, N.J.: Transaction, 1990), pp. 118–144, 149–58.

71. Robert C. Paehlke, Environmentalism and the Future of Progressive Politics (New Haven: Yale University Press, 1989), p. 29.

72. Quoted in Bernard Dixon, *What Is Science For?* (New York: Harper

and Row, 1973), p. 198; citing Ehrlich speech to Britain's Institute of Biology, held in London, September 1969.

73. Quoted in Michael W. Miller, " 'Greens' Add to Junk Mail Mountain," *Wall Street Journal,* May 13, 1991, p. B1.

74. See generally, Robert C. Balling, *The Heated Debate: Greenhouse Predictions Versus Climate Reality* (San Francisco: Pacific Research Institute for Public Policy, 1992); for a more technical discussion concentrating on carbon dioxide, see generally, Sherwood Idso, *Carbon Dioxide and Global Change: Earth In Transition* (Tempe, Ariz.: IBR Press, 1989); for the author's own writings on the subject, see Michael Fumento, "Global Warming or Hot Air?" *Investor's Business Daily,* June 2, 1992, p. 1; and Michael Fumento, "Is $CO_2$ Buildup Really A Crisis?" *Investor's Business Daily,* June 3, 1992, p. 1.

75. Carolyn Lochhead, "The Alarming Price Tag on Greenhouse Legislation," *Insight,* April 16, 1990, p. 10.

76. Carlin, op. cit. p. 2-1.

77. Carolyn Lochhead, "Global Warming's Heated Debate" *Insight,* April 16, 1990, p. 9.

78. Quoted in Jonathan Schell, "Our Fragile Earth," *Discover,* October 1989, p. 47.

79. See Lochhead, "Global Warming Forecasts," op. cit. p. 18.

80. Stephen H. Schneider, *The Genesis Strategy* (New York: Plenum Press, 1976), pp. 84–92.

81. Al Gore, "A New Initiative to Save the Planet," *Scientific American,* April 1990, p. 124.

82. Dwight Lee, "The Perpetual Assault on Progress," Contemporary Issue Series 42 (St. Louis: Center for the Study of American Business, Washington University, May 1991), p. 14; citing Robert James Bidinotto, "Environmentalism: Freedom's Foe for the 90's," *The Freeman,* November 1990, p. 418.

83. Quoted in Anne Raver, "Old Environmental Group Seeks Tough New Image," *New York Times,* June 9, 1991, p. A1.

84. Quoted in Sharon Begley, "Audubon's Empty Nest," *Newsweek,* June 24, 1991, p. 57.

85. Quoted in Raver, op. cit. p. 22.

86. Quoted in Begley, op. cit. p. 57.

87. William Tucker interview in *ACSH* (American Council on Science and Health) *News and Views* (September–October 1983), pp. 4–5.

88. Tucker interview, op. cit. p. 5.

89. Tucker, *Progress and Privilege,* op. cit. p. 5.

90. Vernon E. Jordan, Jr., speech delivered to the National Conference on the Urban Environment, April 9, 1979; reprinted as "Forging New Alliances," *New York Times,* May 27, 1979, p. E19.

91. Paehlke, op. cit. p. 114, referring the reader to Friedrich Engels, *The Dialectics of Nature* (New York: International Publishers, 1940) and

Friedrich Engels, *Herr Eugen Duhring's Revolution in Science* (New York: International Publishers, 1939).

92. Paehlke, op. cit. pp. 114–15.

93. Ibid. p. 115.

94. Ibid.

### Chapter 13: Ending the Reign of Terror

1. O. Garreau and D. Legrand, *La Révolution Française en 100 Questions* (Paris: Clé International, 1988), p. 44.

2. Dale W. Jorgenson and Peter J. Wilcoxen, "Impact of Environmental Legislation on U.S. Economic Growth, Investment and Capital Costs," typescript, prepared for the American Council on Capital Formation, Center for Policy Research, Washington, D.C., September 12, 1991, p. 3.

3. Robert Crandall, *Why Is the Cost of Environmental Regulation So High?* (St. Louis: Center for the Study of American Business, Washington University, February 1992), p. 3.

4. Crandall, op. cit. p. 20, note 9.

5. Michael Hazilla and Raymond J. Kropp, "Social Cost of Environmental Quality Regulations: A General Equilibrium Analysis," *Journal of Political Economy,* Vol. 98, No. 4 (August 1990), p. 867.

6. See Michael Fumento, "The Hidden Cost of Regulation," *Investor's Business Daily,* March 9, 1992, p. 2.

7. See William K. Reilly, "The Green Thumb of Capitalism," *Policy Review,* Fall 1990, p. 16.

8. In its most recent report of foundation contributors, April 1990–September 1991, the NRDC lists the Mary Reynolds Babcock Foundation. For a lengthy profile of the NRDC and its donors, see Stuart Nolan, *Natural Resources Defense Council* (Washington, D.C.: Capital Research Center, 1992).

# Index